The
Old Outboard

BUSINESS/SCIENCE/TECHNOLOGY DIVISION

BAKER & TAYLOR BOOKS

Greetings of the Season To You
1919 is going to be a great year for
the "Out-o'-doors". The "Boys" coming back
from "Over there" and camp life "over here"
are going to be strong for going, hiking,
woods and water trails. Here's hopin' you
get your share, and then some, of this new
business.

Yours,
Dixie Carroll

The Old Outboard Book

Peter Hunn

International Marine
Publishing
Camden, Maine

Published by International Marine Publishing

10 9 8 7 6 5 4 3 2

Library of Congress Cataloging-in-Publication Data.

Hunn, Peter.
　　The old outboard book / Peter Hunn.
　　　　p.　　cm.
　　Includes index.
　　ISBN 0-87742-265-6
　　1. Outboard motors—Collectors and collecting. 2. Outboard motors—Conservation and restoration. I. Title.
　　VM771.H86　　1990
　　623.8′7234′075—dc20　　　　　　　　　　　　　　90-43452
　　　　　　　　　　　　　　　　　　　　　　　　　　　　CIP

TAB BOOKS offers software for sale. For information and a catalog, please contact TAB Software Department, Blue Ridge Summit, PA 17294-0850.

Questions regarding the content of this book should be addressed to:

International Marine Publishing
P.O. Box 220
Camden, ME 04843

Typeset by Foam House Composition, Chichester, NH
Printed by Fairfield Arcata, Fairfield, PA
Design by Edith Allard
Edited by J.R. Babb, Heidi V.N. Brugger, and Eivind Boe

Contents

Dedication

For my dad, John E. Hunn, who impressed my (future) mother by running an air-cooled outboard in a dented trash can full of bubbling water.

Acknowledgments

This book was written at a 1,000-watt radio station in upstate New York. Between tunes, local news, and lost dog announcements, my gummy portable typed out text on the backs of expired press releases. I sent off these uneven pages, painted with editing notations, to Susan Gower, who transferred them from paper to computer discs. Suzie's ability, patience, and dedication to detail were much help. My thanks also goes to fellow antique outboarders Arthur DeKalb, John Millen, and Douglas Penn, whose ideas for photos and stories moved things along. Many of the best pictures in this book were provided by Outboard Marine Corporation, Mercury Marine, Champion Spark Plugs, Clinton Engines, and the Shipyard Museum. The kindness of these organizations is greatly appreciated. Finally, I'd like to thank my lovely wife Carol for coping with my mercurial writing personality, and for appearing interested in witnessing old motors being tested in a barrel.

The summer of 1958 saw my family's Rambler station wagon bouncing along the lengthy dirt driveway of an Adirondack resort. Near the end of that dusty thoroughfare, a woman motioned us to stop and apologized to all arrivals that the camp chef had just run off with Wanda, the waitress.

Rather than get a refund and point the Rambler back to New Jersey, or go broke eating in restaurants for a fortnight, my folks looked up some old friends who, coincidentally, had a vacation home a few miles away.

After dinner, our hosts treated us to a boat ride, and I got to sit right in front of the craft's bright blue, 35-horse Evinrude outboard. The big motor's throaty purr so impressed my five-year-old mind that it triggered an obsession with engines present, past, and future.

Since then, I've had the opportunity to amass lots of outboard literature and more than 100 vintage motors. This book is about some of those rigs and many other makes, one of which may be yours. It is written in a nontechnical style for anyone who has ever had an interest in outboard motors. Its pages should help you identify the year and history of your favorite motor, help you discover what kind of spark plugs and oil mixture it wants, and provide you with a look at dozens of classic outboards from the 1890s through the 1950s, both the recognizable and the unusual.

But be warned: Because old outboarding is relatively inexpensive and quite contagious, this book could lead you to enjoy "vintage iron" more than others feel is necessary. Even my immediate family can't help wondering what I could have written about if Wanda hadn't run off with the cook.

Introduction

Sue Miller's husband, Jack, had retired recently, and his strange behavior had her worried. Jack's new conduct either kept him in the cellar or combing through back rooms of seedy outbuildings. And, he kept dragging home all kinds of weird items. . . . Sue just didn't understand. It all began when the couple was enjoying a leisurely drive to the grocery store. Suddenly, Jack hit the brakes, and, leaving the car door wide open, ran for a foul-smelling greasy thing leaning against a pine tree.

"I don't believe my eyes," Jack beamed. "This is a 1928 Elto Speedster outboard motor! When I was a kid, the guy next door had one. It was the hottest rig on the lake!"

Seconds later, the surprised yard-sale cashier folded away a pair of 10-dollar bills and watched as the joyful husband and his skeptical spouse loaded the vintage outboard into their car.

"What in the world are you going to do with that old thing?" Sue asked when they arrived at the grocery store. "You already have a nice new fishing motor the kids gave you."

"I'm gonna fix it up," Jack retorted happily while pushing the shopping cart a bit faster than normal.

"And revitalize that old Elto, he did," Sue later recounted to her friends. "Trouble is, then Jack found another obsolete outboard to fix up . . . and another . . . and another!"

The Girls cautiously looked down the basement stairs and consoled Sue. "What does he do with all of those?" they wondered aloud.

"Well, he works on them during the week and then putt-putts around the lake all weekend. Now other old motor people are calling here asking for Jack . . . wanting to buy or sell, or to stop over to see his outboard collection. And Jack, he's always happy—especially when his trunk is full of junk. However, I never expected retirement to be quite like this."

Dave Wyler was years from retirement and regretted not having enough free time to spend with his youngster. He was searching for some hobby or common interest around which father and son could relate. The solution came rather unexpectedly at a local sporting goods shop, where he and his boy had gone to see about picking up an economical aluminum rowboat and a little fishing gear. Without adequate funds for a current model motor, Dave asked about used outboards.

"Take a look on the racks in back," the proprietor said.

"We'll have to find something affordable," cautioned Dave as he and his son went to have a look-see. Near the end of the top row, Dave's son noticed a small red kicker with its starter cord dangling toward a pile of related parts. Nuts and screws in a grimy plastic bag were secured to the rubber steering handle via sticky electrical tape.

"Dad, how much do you think that one would be?"

"Don't know, but it looks really shot, son."

"Well, maybe we could fix it up together this winter."

"Yes, maybe we could do just that!"

"The old Sea King horse and a half?" queried the shop owner. "Kinda hate to see it go . . . been around so long. Oh, let's see. . . . How about five bucks? I'll even throw in the original parts booklet!"

Throughout the next six months, the Wylers took their little Sea King down to the last bolt, cleaned it up, and reassembled it. A new paint job highlighted the duo's endeavor. Everyone involved agreed that the motor looked and ran great. All for $5 plus a few parts.

Unlike retiree-turned-antique-outboard-collector Jack Miller, Dave Wyler and his boy never amassed a cellarful of vintage egg beaters, but they did receive a lot of pleasure running their Sea King. Every once in a while, however, they do talk about getting another, forgotten old outboard—maybe a bigger one—and enjoying another father-son collaboration.

Wally Jenkins never projected any historical value onto his 1956 Buccaneer outboard. As a commercial fisherman, he relied on the 25-horse twin as a partner; it was not an "antique motor" to him. When fellow saltwater anglers suggested he should upgrade, however, prices of the new kickers sent Walt into sticker shock. Soon, a deeper level of appreciation bonded him to his colorful "25." He became interested in locating replacement parts, and even curious about the Buccaneer's lineage. Spruced-up, the engine delighted Wally by prompting positive comments from peer and vacationer alike. Pride in ownership paced Mr. Jenkins' fishing rig a step ahead of more ordinarily powered outboard craft.

Throughout the years, millions of outboard motors have been manufactured in the United States. Although many no longer exist, scores of them reside everywhere from formal collections to rickety backyard sheds. It is difficult to imagine any area without a good share of still undiscovered motors. Contrasting with the numbers of available old iron, are the relatively few people wanting them. As a result, vintage outboard prices have not aproached (and probably never will match) those of classic cars or other antiques.

Anyone liking old outboard motors, especially if interested in garden variety (Evinrude, Johnson, Merc, Sears-Elgin, etc.) fishing rigs, is assured an adequate supply of inexpensive engines and parts. Sometimes they may have to search a little, but that's typically part of the fun.

Best of all, an old kicker collection, be it 2 or 200, can be put to use. Few folks have ever turned down a rowboat ride powered by some ancient putt-putt. The conversations, interest, and local newspaper articles these rigs generate are legendary.

Those using "space limitations" as an excuse not to enter antique outboarding have never seen a 1940, 9-pound, ½-hp Evinrude. One New York City motor buff stores his four-member Mercury collection in a hall closet. Lack of funds seldom stop old outboard nuts either. While some very rare racing models or pre-

World War I rigs bring big ($500-plus) bucks, Antique Outboard Motor Club swap meets, boat shops, and garage sales often feature common kickers with price tags between $5 and $50. By the way, unusual is the collector who hasn't been the beneficiary of at least one *free* motor, and sometimes 10!

Vintage outboard motors are simply the hot dogs and hamburgers of our technological world. People from all walks of life enjoy them. And just like a good summer cookout, there are many ways to savor such machines. While it's perfectly acceptable to cruise your favorite waterway with a vintage outboard, some folks use theirs to water-ski, troll, or race in sanctioned as well as informal events.

Whether you plan to take just a few hours per year working on a kicker alone, involve your family in the collecting and/or restoring of an old outboard, or join an Antique Outboard Motor Club chapter and really get involved, you will be surprised at how much satisfaction and discovery is waiting within that little motor. It's true; others will see just a bunch of dented aluminum, but you will recognize that old outboard as the key to a real adventure.

Keep your starter rope dry and enjoy *The Old Outboard Book!*

The
Old **Outboard**
Book

1

Outboard Motor Pioneers

Sometime in 1960, the Johnson Outboard Company ran a small advertisement picturing a pistol-toting, bikini-clad woman in bare feet and cowboy hat. A surrealistic "marshal's star" frivolously pinned to the top of her swimsuit centered attention on the fact that Johnson was seriously looking for old outboard motors. That ad, promoting "The Great Sea Horse Trackdown," has been an old outboard collector's nightmare ever since.

Although Johnson was indeed searching for some of its vintage products, many of the engines sought were extremely rare. Should one possess such a rig, one was supposed to cart the motor to the nearest Johnson Sea Horse dealer for model and serial number verification. A 25-or-fewer-word statement why Johnsons were the most dependable brand also had to be composed. Only then could the owner be registered for a chance to win a new Johnson outboard.

That exclusive contest quickly took its place in portable marine propulsion history as the "Free Outboard" story and spread through the country faster than a rumor of a bathroom tissue shortage.

Of course, that contest is long gone, and today many might consider those 1960 prize motors to be antiques. Nevertheless a few folks remain completely convinced that they can trade their "old," salt-scored, early-seventies fishin' engine for a new boat-motor-trailer-tackle-box combo if they simply "write the factory" to come pick up their classic outboard.

While these incidents prove aggravating for old outboard enthusiasts trying reasonably to pry a rusty kicker from some guy's damp basement, they do serve to raise a question pertinent to the beginning of this book: Specifically, just how old is an old outboard motor?

Many custom laws define *antique* as 100 years old or older. Since outboards were first invented a little over a century ago, few are truly antique, in that sense of the word. However, all the outboards in this book qualify as "objects of a period earlier than the present," and in this sense are antiques. Some kicker collectors make a distinction between *antique* and *old*, drawing the line at 1950, after which post-World War II technology rapidly

The granddaddy of U.S.-built outboard motors is the 1896 American, with reversible prop and mesh-gear lower unit steering. A single ancient picture is all that's left of the American Motor Company, a Long Island firm said to have produced some 25 of these vintage kickers.

made itself evident in the outboard industry. No collector questions the antique status of the very first outboards.

The 1887 Harthan

In 1887 S. Emerson Harthan of Worcester, Massachusetts received a patent for "his self-contained steam motor (with 4-bladed propeller) that could be completely detached from the stern" of a small boat.[1]

Reportedly, though the plans looked interesting, the inventor eventually decided his steam outboard would fall into a category no more glorious than that of "confounded contraption" and elected to leave it on the drawing board. While this book focuses primarily on gasoline-powered outboards produced in the United States, Mr. Harthan's patent is mentioned because it "prevent[ed] anyone else from getting full protection" for any subsequent outboard motor.[2]

The 1896 American

The earliest documentation of an American gasoline-powered outboard motor describes a small 1896 line of detachable rowboat engines from the American Motor Company of Long Island City, New York.

A late-nineteenth-century book, *Gas, Gasoline and Oil Vapor Engines for Stationary, Marine, and Vehicle Motive Power*,[3] devoted four pages to the novel 4-cycle, air-cooled engines. The single-cylinder model featured a 3¼-inch bore, a 4-inch stroke, battery ignition, and 1 to 2 hp at 400 to 600 rpm.

Also mentioned was a twin-cylinder version of the American. This may have been a pair of single-cylinder power plants mated to a common flywheel and drive shaft. The twin boasted exactly twice the smaller unit's power. On both models a remote fuel tank was standard. A simple carburetor was attached to the gas tank, and fuel vapor reached the crankcase via a flexible tube. Although primitive, the 1896 American outboard's basic layout would not be unrecognizable to present-day boaters.

The 1898 Miller

Folks in antique outboard circles often quote 25 as a production figure for the American outboard motor. I am not certain where such a number originated and really wonder if any at all were ever produced. Respected outboard historian W.J. "Jim" Webb, once a top executive with the Evinrude Company, tried to track down additional information on the American. He discovered that the firm's building had passed into the hands of a movie company. No traces of the motors, or anyone with firsthand knowledge of the early outboard venture, have ever been located.

It is possible the American Motor Company's outboards (if produced) were not labeled American. In the same fashion that no General Motors car is called a General, the American outboard may have sported some other model name. To add to the mystery, a Detroit company produced an early (1913 to 1918) detachable rowboat motor. It, too, was known as the American.

The name Harry Armenius Miller is inseparably linked to the glory days of the American race car scene. His cars, his unique carburetors, and, most notably, his 91-cubic-inch engines claimed many prestigious victories. In addition to automotive speed records, the Miller 91- and 151-cubic-inch power plants, when mounted in a speedboat, "were nearly invincible on water."[4]

A Wisconsin native with a keen interest in machinery, Harry Miller traveled west, where he worked in a Los Angeles bicycle shop. A few years later he married and quickly took his wife to his hometown of Menomonie.

Shortly after his 1897 return to the Midwest, Harry built a special bicycle equipped with a single-cylinder motor. Some say this was America's first motorcycle. In any event no patents were ever requested.

Harry Miller usually stayed interested in a project only until a new one could be dreamed up.[5] He mentioned to a few close friends that his ideas came from someone (in another world) telling him what to do.[6]

In the summer of 1898 the spirit moved him and "he worked out a peculiar 4-cylinder [outboard] engine, clamped it to a rowboat, and showed his cronies how to enjoy their afternoons off."[7] Although the motor apparently did what it was designed to do, Miller lost interest in the outboard and sought no patents. It is not known what became of the pioneer rig.

Miller's wife longed to return west, so shortly after the outboard incident, they headed to California. The Golden State became home to other Miller projects including the manufacture of carbs, race engines, and cars, as well as what may have been the first aluminum pistons in the United States.[8]

While it's evident that Harry Miller's circa 1898 outboard never went into any kind of mass production, the possibility that the previously mentioned 1896 American may not have, in fact, gotten off the drawing board, places Miller's as the first U.S. gasoline-powered outboard with a written record of actual operation. Interestingly, one eyewitness to the Miller outboard excursion could have been another young Wisconsin native who worked with Harry in the Menomonie shop. That fellow's name was Ole Evinrude.[9]

In the early 1930s a California company produced a very strange looking four-cylinder outboard motor. The firm belonged to Harry Miller.

The 1898 Savage

Nineteenth-century rowboats, no doubt, started Rochester, New York, resident Edward Savage thinking about a power source more swanky than oars. The inventor put together an aft-pointing, single-cylinder, 2-cycle outboard sporting an enclosed lower-unit gear case, a sight oiler, and variable-pitch prop. (This contraption's power head looked a bit like the 1896 American.) The rudder-steered Savage outboard made its debut on Lake Ontario in 1898. Although one neat-looking prototype was built, Ed Savage's other interests (in the toy design field) kept the motor from further production.

The 1900 Imperial

A family-owned Minneapolis machine shop advertised its detachable boat engine in 1900. This early outboard, called the Imperial, weighed 75 pounds and produced 2 hp. Its creators, Fred and Robert Valentine, claimed the water-cooled, rudder-steered outboard could be hooked to any boat within 15 minutes and provide speeds of 6 to 8 mph.[10]

As is the case with many long-expired firms, no one is certain what happened to the Valentine brothers' company. None of its vintage outboards has been discovered. In fact, had an Antique Outboard Motor Club member in 1982 not seen an old ad in a dusty city directory, the Imperial wouldn't have received its rightful place in this book.

The 1906 Submerged

Some six years after the introduction of its 1900 electric outboard, the Submerged Electric Motor Company added a "new portable gasoline submerged propeller" to the small-boat propulsion line. The one-cylinder engine on the Submerged appeared to be, indeed, under water (like the 1930s Clarke Troller), while its cylindrical fuel tank made up the unit's top. The tube joining top and bottom sections rode on an adjustable collar so the Submerged could be "raised and lowered to run in shallow water."

Although few competitors made up the day's outboard field, the Menomonie, Wisconsin, firm claimed the Submerged (being the "lightest, most practical, most powerful, and easiest applied") was the genre's front-runner. The early outboard company also promised its gas-powered rowboat motor was "sure to go." Unfortunately, the whole outfit went the way of the wind a few years later.

Waterman's "Coughing Sarahs"

A 1903 autumn evening in New Haven, Connecticut, set the stage for Yale law student Cameron B. Waterman to consider servicing his Regal motorcycle. The little power plant on that two-wheeler

"Vertical cylinder" Waterman outboard, circa 1907. After the motor starts, you have to quickly pull the starting crank from its fitting on top of the crankshaft, then gingerly adjust the carb, making sure water is exiting the cylinder water jacket pipe and that lubrication from the glass-sight oiler is dripping properly. Note the exposed lower unit gears (which require waterproof grease!) and the cylindrical fuel tank, which is mounted on a wooden steering handle. Ignition is via battery, spark coil, and timer. The Waterman was America's first commercially successful outboard motor, in the days when a "good" kicker was one that ran at least half the times you tried it! (Mercury Marine)

made in Chicopee, Massachusetts, needed cleaning, and since the motor looked light, young Waterman carried the one-cylinder device up to his room.

After the revitalization, Waterman scanned the room for a place to brace the engine during a test run. Minutes later the Regal motor was sputtering away clamped to the back of a wooden chair. The future lawyer, an avid fisherman who judged rowing to be an activity that "stinks,"[11] suddenly pictured the rear of that chair as the stern of a small boat. The idea floated along with him through graduation.

Upon returning to his native Detroit, Cameron Waterman briefed his friend George Thrall (owner of a local boiler factory) on the outboard concept. The pair secured a Curtiss motorcycle engine, fastened it to the stern of a rowboat, and via a drive chain, rigged the motor to turn a propeller. That experiment occurred in the winter of 1905. The crude outboard motor was started by twirling its prop. Actually, everything worked OK until pieces of ice in the cold Detroit River knocked the chain off the propeller sprocket.[12]

Waterman and Thrall discarded the chain in favor of an open drive shaft and bevel gears. A revised "coughing Sarah,"[13] as skeptics called it, was exhibited at the 1906 New York Boat Show.

A couple of easygoing fishing buddies let their pre-1910 Waterman outboard take them to their favorite angling spot. Note that the battery to fire the sparkplug is on the stern seat. This early kicker publicity still was shot from a boat in tow. ("Ah, that's when a smoke was a smoke and cruisin' was cruisin'!") (Mercury Marine)

Apparently, a few of these air-cooled asthmatic motors were, in fact, assembled in late 1905. A 1950 newspaper article quotes Mr. Waterman:

> We began commercial production in 1905. Here's a catalog showing the motor. You see we had a drive shaft instead of a chain. However, we had this flywheel hung so low that every time the boat dipped, it hit the water and gave us a shower bath. The next year we put the flywheel back inside the casing.[14]

The fellow who probably helped with the flywheel redesign was Oliver Barthel, a production engineer hired by Waterman in early 1906. Barthel refined the workings of the air-cooled single.[15] Twenty-five of these 1906 model year Waterman outboards were made. Twenty-four were sold.[16] The new engineer believed water was the best way to cool a boat motor and convinced Waterman to institute such a design in 1907. Sportsmen bought up 3,000 of the vertical-cylinder, water-cooled rigs that year, a sales figure duplicated the following year and doubled in 1909.[17]

As a young motor nut, with very little grasp on accurate chronology, I sent a postcard to outboard pioneer Cameron Waterman. The note simply asked if he had any old owner's manuals that could be sent my way. Unfortunately, Mr. Waterman had passed away years before that postcard arrived. But, his son and namesake graciously answered with a manila envelope containing interesting articles and recollections. As part of the parcel, Mr. Waterman Jr. wanted his young correspondent to know that in the early days there was no convenient flywheel magneto for spark:

> We used a battery ignition (on the first Waterman motors). We would carry a black wooden box on the boat's rear seat. This box contained four dry cells and a spark coil.

The June, 1969 letter revealed an example of informal research, which caused production changes back at the Waterman

Late-teens Waterman clip art.

factory. Cameron Waterman Jr. noted his dad's outboards had a spark plug mounted close to the operator on the end of the tantalizing cylinder assembly. "I well remember hitting the spark plug with my hand and being rewarded for my clumsiness by a sharp poke!" Complaints to his father resulted in "later models having a rubber (spark plug) cover."

By 1912 the Waterman outboards, long since dubbed Porto (as in *portable*) by the manufacturer, featured rudder steering and horizontally placed cylinders. The 1914 deluxe Porto outboards sported magneto instead of battery ignition.

Three years later intense competition caused the man who coined the term *outboard motor* to sell his Waterman Marine Motor Company, for $20,000, to the Arrow Motor and Machine Company of Newark, New Jersey. This firm, which marketed a twin-cylinder outboard of its own, floundered with the Waterman line and left business altogether in 1924.

Cameron Waterman devoted the rest of his life to the legal profession. A few years before his 1956 passing, the grandfather of the American outboarding industry was forwarded a letter dotted with foreign postage stamps. A man in Panama wanted a new cylinder for a Waterman Porto.[18]

Notes

1. Wm. Taylor McKeown, "The Old Kicker and How it Got Slicker," *True* (April 1964), p. 110.
2. Harry LeDuc, "Detroiter Honored in NY as Inventor of First Outboard Motor," *Detroit News* (28 January 1950).
3. Gardner D. Hiscox, M.E., *Gas, Gasoline and Oil Vapor Engines for Stationary, Marine, and Vehicle Motive Power* (New York: Norman W. Henley Company, 1897), pp. 203–206.
4. Griffith Borgeson, *The Golden Age of the American Racing Car* (New York: W.W. Norton & Co., 1966), p. 202.
5. Ibid., p. 69.
6. Ibid., p. 65.
7. Ibid., p. 64.
8. Ibid., p. 65.
9. Ibid., p. 64.
10. Robert Brautigam, "Outboard World Rocked by New Discovery," *Antique Outboarder* (January 1983), pp. 44–45.
11. Red Smith, "Views of Sport: The Outboard Heresy," *New York Herald Tribune* (11 January 1950).
12. LeDuc, op. cit.
13. Ibid.
14. Smith, op. cit.
15. Robert Whittier, *The Outboard Motor and Boat Book* (Concord, MA: Voyager Press, 1949).
16. Smith, op. cit.
17. Ibid.
18. LeDuc, op. cit.

2

Evinrude

A young Milwaukee woman really wanted some ice cream. Coming from a hard-working, proper-minded single girl, such a craving had nothing to do with maternity, but it did serve as the mother of invention to a brand new outboard motor.

The lady fair, Bess Carey, and her lack of dessert during a warm August island picnic, caused suitor Ole Evinrude to hop in their rented rowboat and man the oars. A few miles later the love-motivated fellow finally reached a lakeside ice cream shop and, panting, placed the order. Upon his return, that ice cream (which most versions of the tale place in a cone, while a few others put it in a dish) had become sun-scorched, sugary soup.

Ole might have briefly thought, "Oh, *women!*" That, however, would make for lousy legend. So, according to the famous Evinrude soggy ice cream saga, Ole simply began thinking about ways to build a detachable rowboat motor.

Over the years details have been added to the incident's recounting. One source went to the extreme of identifying the ice cream as "double-dip caramel pecan fudge with chocolate sauce."[1] If the accounts of Harry Miller's 1898 outboard (Chapter 1) are accurate, Ole Evinrude (who was said to have seen Miller's motor in action) may have skipped all of the story's "perhaps I could invent the outboard motor" theme and deduced "why not rig up a portable gasoline boat motor like Harry's weird contraption?" In any event, following the picnic, Mr. Evinrude started piecing together a crude outboard motor.

Ole's confidence in tackling the project was rooted in his past successes with machinery repair, design, and construction. Ole grew up on a Wisconsin farm. Although his formal schooling was through only the third grade, he possessed a natural aptitude that earned him a reputation as a mechanical genius. At 16, Ole left the bucolic life in favor of larger communities containing machine shops and factories.

After mastering a number of the trade's finer points (at firms in Pennsylvania, Illinois, and Wisconsin), he settled in Milwaukee and marketed a single-cylinder auto engine of his own design. While the car motor was fine, Ole's infrequent attention to office details caused the venture's demise. Because of his fine

Bess Evinrude, co-founder of two successful outboard motor companies (Evinrude and Elto), handled all the office responsibilities; husband Ole took care of product design and manufacturing. Bess often signed official correspondence "B. Evinrude" to keep those making materials bids from knowing they'd be dealing with a woman. She was always fair but never a pushover. Ole's motors were well received, but he cited his wife's expertise in business as the reason for the family's prosperity. (Outboard Marine Corp.)

Ole Evinrude put on his "corporate" suit for this 1920s publicity shot. He needed no extra promotion at the Milwaukee-based Elto plant; there wasn't an employee in the shop who didn't truly admire the soft-spoken outboard pioneer. (Outboard Marine Corp.)

mechanical record (especially as a pattern maker), the young man had little trouble gaining employment at someone else's shop.

Ole and Bess were married, and the new husband worked on a surprise in the basement. You can imagine a conversation something like this one:

> "Honey, come on down the cellar," said Ole to his bride. "Let me show you what I've done."
> "What's that unusual thing?" Bess asked. "It looks like a coffee grinder!" Alas, Bess was a practical woman and saw no purpose for such a gizmo.

Mr. Evinrude would undoubtedly have been distressed by his wife's lack of enthusiasm. Determined, Ole enlisted Bess's brother, Rob Carey, to help prove a point.

In April 1909 the pair toted Evinrude's kooky-looking kicker to the Kinnikinnic River and attached the contraption to a rented rowboat. Ole and Rob returned to Bess with reports of success.

Bess may have suggested that the little motor be improved, because a new prototype was concocted in 1909. This one (which was eventually retired to the Evinrude factory service department until getting accidentally discarded after World War II) ran better than the first.

Ole loaned the 2-cycle, water-cooled, forward-pointing, single-cylinder kicker to a friend embarking on a fishing trip. The angler came back wanting his own Evinrude motor and had orders for nine more. Soon patterns for the improved Evinrude went to the foundry, resulting in parts for 25 motors. Each was built by hand.

An old issue of *Fortune* magazine picks up the story:

> [Evinrude] never visualized any business possibilities in the outboard beyond occasional sales to Milwaukee sportsmen, and it was Bess who kept after him to perfect the "coffee grinder" as she called it, and who sat down at her kitchen table one evening and wrote their first advertisement. DON'T ROW! THROW THOSE OARS AWAY! USE AN EVINRUDE MOTOR! This went into a motor magazine and pulled so many inquiries that there could be no doubt that a market for outboards existed.[2]

To grow in the burgeoning marketplace, Ole and Bess accepted $5,000 for a half interest in their Milwaukee-based Evinrude Detachable Rowboat Motor Company. Chris Meyer (owner of a tugboat firm) was the guy with the five grand; his money was used to rent a modest factory, acquire needed parts, and hire a small staff to help Ole build outboards. Bess (by then the mother of a toddler) worked overtime running the office and kept handing her busy husband orders for even more motors.

This was in 1911. Within a couple of years, not only were numerous battery-fired, flywheel-knob-started, Evinrude singles churning up American waterways, but many were exported. A few thousand were purchased by Scandinavian fishing fleets for more versatile net access. Every time the mailman arrived, it became clearer that boaters the world over were literally beating a paper path to the Evinrudes' door.

All this activity, while exciting, affected Bess's health and strained Ole's business relationship with Chris Meyer. Mr. Evinrude suggested he'd sell his half of the firm for $150,000. Meyer quickly arranged delivery of such a check. And, upon Ole's pledge to stay out of the outboard business for at least five years, the deal was closed (in late 1913), pushing the Evinrudes from the field they had helped pioneer.

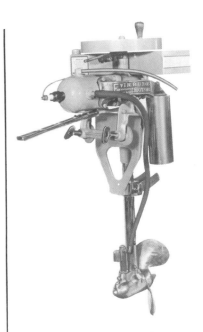

The famed Evinrude rowboat motor, circa 1912, with wooden "knuckle buster" starting knob on the flywheel. Note the rubber water tube. Earlier models had no name embossed into the exhaust assembly. Ole's first (1909) version, which someone at Evinrude accidentally threw away, reminded his wife of a coffee grinder. The lower unit on older rowboat motors had no skeg; the steering arm moved only the lower unit assembly, not the powerhead. (Outboard Marine Corp.)

Daylight illuminates the "motor assembly room" at Milwaukee's Evinrude factory. Once the rowboat motors were complete, each one was tested in the tank visible to the left of the facility's open door. A wooden mat prevented employees from slipping on a floor wet down by churning propellers. (Outboard Marine Corp.)

Make Any Rowboat
A Motor Boat

A 1912 Evinrude advertisement.

Ole and Bess departed on an extended vacation shortly prior to the establishment of a new outboard factory capable of turning out rowboat motors with much greater ease than before.

In 1912 Ole had started a guy called "Jump Spark" Miller (no relation to Harry Miller) working on what would become the flywheel magneto. The Evinrude company began outfitting its motors with flywheel mags for 1914. It also sold its invention to other outboard firms. A couple of these magneto-fired rigs went to Teddy Roosevelt. The former U.S. President reported great success with the Evinrudes, which were used on an expedition on uncharted South American rivers. TR did suggest that the motors would be more useful in primitive areas if they could be run on universally available kerosene.[3]

The Chris Meyer–controlled Evinrude company continued to enjoy the lion's share of the outboard market. It even sold boats, including a *sailing* dinghy!

However, a real classic junkster was introduced for the 1916 model line. Someone in the firm felt a nearly 100-pound, 4-horse opposed twin employing the 4-cycle principle would prove irresistible to buyers. This darn thing had a flywheel mag and "distributor" to fire the two cylinders alternately. Even though it was 4-cycle, you still had to mix oil with the gas.

While the ads said, "Starting is easy and the motor picks up quickly and runs with a smooth hum," the PR department could have sold more of these nearly impossible-to-operate monstrosi-ties by re-decaling them with EVINRUDE BOAT ANCHOR. The 4-cycle Big Twin was quickly discontinued in 1917, and the leading outboard maker returned to the promotion of its better running 2-cycle singles. All went well for the Evinrude company . . . for a while.

The real Evinrude family had been spending time touring the country by car and cabin cruiser. As Bess got healthier, Ole took more time toying with a new idea in portable boat motoring. New Orleans served as the Evinrudes' winter 1917 base.

"Ole spent most of his time locked up in a hotel room fooling around with plans for a new [lightweight] motor."[4] By 1919 the drawings led to a 47-pound opposed twin made mostly of World War I–proved aluminum. This revolutionary rig was presented to Chris Meyer at the outboard firm bearing the Evinrude name. Meyer was very skeptical and quickly shot down Ole's project motor.

Meyer's attitude seems to have been, Who'd ever want some wimpy lightweight thing like that when people can buy a hefty, iron and bronze, remarkably sturdy Evinrude Detachable Rowboat Motor?

Meyer's rejection turned out to be a tremendous blunder. The mistake soon caused his firm to lose a big share of the outboard pie to a newcomer. In 1921 this well-managed company began marketing Bess and Ole *Evinrude's* new *Light Twin Outboards*—Eltos. And, because the Elto was easier to carry, ran smoother, and started quicker than any other outboard to date, it sold like hotcakes.

An Elto Ruddertwin, circa 1924, being inspected by a trio of company models. Ole Evinrude had a hard time naming his aluminum kicker (he liked the description "silvery"), so wife Bess came up with the acronym Elto, from Evinrude's Light Twin Outboard. Note the water scoop in the rudder of this battery-ignition product. Exhaust exited through the propeller hub. A clothesline tied to the rudder control assembly allowed for steering from any position in the boat. (Outboard Marine Corp.)

Meanwhile, back at the original Evinrude outfit, Chris Meyer got a great idea—*for people who want lighter outboards, design an aluminum one!*

The result was the Evinrude model K Lightweight. This poor thing, simply an aluminum version of the old rowboat motor, was rushed into production shortly after Meyer witnessed the less-cumbersome Eltos being snapped up by boaters, fishermen, and hunters.

Forged with castings appropriate only for bronze and iron, the aluminum model K was indeed lighter than its predecessors. Unfortunately, however, this reduction was often due to the fact many of the silver kicker's pieces cracked and fell off the motor.

Ads said the rig had been in the planning stages for seven years. Outboard historian Jim Webb observed that it was more like seven weeks or less. The 1922 Evinrude model K Lightweight was such a disaster that note of its existence is absent from most Evinrude specification booklets.

Meyer knew only too well that every Elto nameplate carried the message DESIGNED AND BUILT BY OLE EVINRUDE. Consequently, his products' decals began boasting THE ORIGINAL EVINRUDE. In 1924 this "original" firm introduced a nice 2½-hp Sportwin. It was a much better aluminum model than the K and helped the old company perk up a little.

In any event, Meyer had had enough and in 1925 decided to sell Evinrude to a fellow named Walter Zinn. Within a year of the purchase, this gentleman had lost $150,000. He quickly chalked up outboard making to experience and let the Evinrude company go (in early 1926) to August Petrie.

Owner of the Milwaukee Stamping Company, Petrie knew he'd have to put some money into the Evinrude firm in order to get it back on track. Koban, a longtime producer of twin-cylinder outboards, was acquired and closed by the new Evinrude management. With one less competitor (albeit a weak one), Mr. Petrie began revitalizing Evinrude.

Fuel tank ID plate for a 1929 High Speed (note "H" after serial number) Elto Speedster.

Evinrude

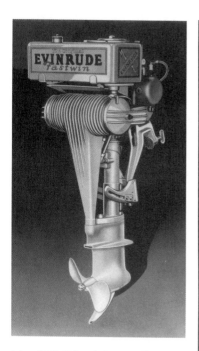

A late-1920s Evinrude Fastwin. The fuel tank decal says "The *Original* Evinrude," to distinguish it from Elto's "Designed and Built by Ole Evinrude" slogan. Mr. Evinrude had sold his "original" outboard company in 1914, but had reacquired it by 1930.

The venerable kicker firm's repair coincided nicely with an exciting increase of outboard speed. From 1926 to 1928 outboard motoring's clip improved from a putt-putt troll to a wave-jumping roar. The new president of Evinrude opened his 1928 catalog this way:

> The last few years have been especially important ones in the development of the Evinrude Motor. In a remarkably short span of years, speeds have increased unbelievably. This season [1928] will see unprecedented interest in speed contests. While this is going on, we shall be ever mindful of the majority of users of Evinrudes who do not engage in racing, giving them to the best of our ability, motors capable of maximum racing performance, yes, but giving besides, the utmost in instant starting, sturdiness, dependability, reliability, long life, up-to-date design—champions in every way. Our organization is dedicated to faithfully serve the users of our products, and these are built with the purpose of making them paramount in their field ever before us.
>
> Yours very truly,
> Aug. J. Petrie
> President, Evinrude Motor Co.

Certainly, by 1928 Petrie had placed Evinrude on surer footing. Although Ole's old rowboat motor (the 2¼-hp Utility Single) was still offered near the back of the catalog (some 150,000 of the A model rowboat motors were sold between 1909 and 1928), company advertising really featured the 2½-horse Sportwin, 6-hp Fleetwin, the 12-horse Fastwin, and Evinrude's main attention getter, the 16-hp Speeditwin.

This big motor, which had been introduced during 1927 (as an 8-hp rig) in freshwater and saltwater (with a bronze lower unit) versions, caught most other companies off guard and enjoyed a model year free of high-speed competitors. In 1928 the Speeditwin was joined by a few fast outboards from other firms (like the Elto Speedster and Quad). To most late-1920s boaters, however, it still represented a pretty flashy kicker. Evinrude was again riding high, and Mr. Petrie believed it was an opportune time to sell.

The eager Evinrude buyer was the Briggs and Stratton Corporation. This engine manufacturing outfit (known to almost anyone who's owned a power lawn mower) pumped nearly $400,000 of improvements into Evinrude, cutting sharply into profits. Some Briggs and Stratton officials wanted to retreat from the outboard business and prepared to put Evinrude on the block again.

Briggs and Stratton president Stephen Briggs had other ideas, including the establishment of a multi-companied, General Motors–type outboard firm. With Evinrude already in the fray, Briggs planned to acquire the respected Lockwood Outboard Motor Company. He then arranged a meeting with Ole and Bess Evinrude over at Elto.

Outboarding's first family said, no, they didn't want to sell Elto, which was in the second year of a great sales wave crested by very fast, easy-to-run, twin-cylinder Speedster and 4-cycle Quad motors. Briggs modified his approach, asking if, by chance, Ole had any interest in regaining the commercial right to use the Evinrude name. That query led to a deal which included Elto, Evinrude, and Lockwood. Ole got to be president of the merged companies (in March 1929), which were collectively dubbed the Outboard Motors Corporation (OMC).

Evinrude's Milwaukee plant was the best equipped, resulting in plans calling for all three of OMC's 1930 lines to be built there. Elto had been working on electric starting and was now in a position to share the outboard breakthrough with its new sister brands' deluxe 1930 models. All in all, OMC's divisions were ready for a remarkably bright immediate future. The immediate future, however, was anything but bright.

When my dad was a kid, there was a fellow across the street named Mr. Banker. This guy had done very well in the stock market, burned his mortgage, and paid cash for a 16-cylinder Cadillac touring car. The rest of the money went right back into Wall Street. He had great plans for the bundle sure to follow in late 1929–early 1930. Within a few months Mr. Banker was considered fortunate because, even though his stocks were now

Evinrude

Odd-lot motors were peddled here in the early 1930s to earn money for the company payroll. (Shipyard Museum)

A 1934 Evinrude Lightfour Imperial, featuring engine cowling and rewind starter, helps a proud angler catch a really big one! (Outboard Marine Corp.)

worthless, he still had a home. With no funds for new tires or even gasoline, the big Caddy rested on blocks in the grassy driveway, and Mr. Banker drove a dairy truck to make ends meet.

Just like Mr. Banker, OMC was seriously affected by the Great Depression. Sales fell off instantly, outboard workers were sent home, and the quality Lockwood line was dropped after 1930. Ole Evinrude had his name and $25,000 salary taken off the payroll. Motors made from extra parts (as well as some new/old-stock models, i.e., unsold parts stock used to build new motors) were literally peddled in front of the factory in order to raise enough money to cover drastically reduced employee wages. It was not uncommon in the early Thirties for the OMC plant to operate less than 20 hours per week.

Banks wouldn't loan anything to OMC (which now consisted of Evinrude, Elto, and commonly branded models labeled Outboard Motors Corporation), so Ole kicked in $50,000 from his personal account. Things were very tight through early spring 1933, but Ole and Steve Brigg's company responded with every possible penny-pinching sacrifice.

The firm received another hardship with Bess Evinrude's May 1933 passing. Ole seemed lost without her, but his spirit revived a touch when planning a new concept in outboard design for the 1934 model year.

Having started in 1909, the Evinrude company in 1934 had been in business for 25 years. By this time, all the corporate scrimping began paying off and allowed for the introduction of a pair of Ole's newly designed outboards. These Imperial versions of the 5½-horse Lightwin and 9.2-hp Lightfour were the first truly shrouded outboards. When the optional rewind starter was ordered, the customer really had a modern-looking rig, unlike anything else on the water. In terms of the Depression, the Imperials sold well, and Ole was credited with another fine outboarding idea.

All the acclaim, however, could not make up for his loss of Bess. In this year, 1934, Ole died quietly in his Milwaukee home at age 57, outboard's most respected and best-loved personality.

Ole and Bess's son, Ralph Evinrude, grew up in the midst of outboard history and development. With positive attributes from both parents, young Evinrude began helping out around the factory while still in school. Ralph wasn't offered an automatic royal-family salary but was given the chance to learn the outboard business by working hard in a number of Elto (and then Evinrude/OMC) departments. During the late 1920s, it was Ralph who convinced his folks to build faster outboards. He pushed ahead in the development and testing of the Elto Speedster and Quad (released in late fall 1927), earning still greater responsibility at Elto.

When his dad died, Ralph was asked to serve as Outboard Motor Corporation's president. As it turned out, Ole and Bess would have been quite proud of their son, always leading (until his 1986 passing) the outboard firm in the right direction.

One of Ralph's first official duties was to introduce the 1935 OMC-Evinrude/Elto line. It included a 25-pound, predominantly die-cast, shrouded kicker called the Sportsman. This streamlined, 1 ½-hp motor was the first outboard sold with a reed valve fuel-vapor intake. Many a modern outboard motor subsequent to the Sportsman has used this valve design.

The mid-1930s were relatively prosperous for OMC. In fact, there was even enough extra money to consider the purchase of Johnson, a formidable (albeit faltering) competitor. Although motors wearing Evinrude or Elto decals had been available since the 1930 formation of OMC, most were primarily identified as Outboard Motors Corporation products. The 1935 catalog cover, for example, simply said, "1935 Series Outboard Motors." The OMC logo rested under the words "ELTO" and "Evinrude."

By 1936 Outboard Motors Corporation changed its name to the Outboard Marine and Manufacturing Company, after acquiring the Johnson Outboard firm. This new organization began concentrating on Evinrude and Johnson, leaving Elto to ride out the late Thirties and early Forties as the economy line. Evinrude advertising in 1937 featured Evinrude without much mention of Elto. Gas tank decals, model number plates, and (in most cases) rope sheaves finally dropped the OMC identification and returned to an Evinrude Motors ID. (Although the name changed, the company was and is still referred to as OMC, for Outboard Marine Company. OMMC never caught on.)

In 1938 each Evinrude, from the little 1.1-horse Ranger single to the 33.4-hp Speedifour, had underwater exhaust silencing, hooded powerheads, centrifugal water pump cooling, and copilot steering.

For 1939, Evinrude offered a tiny, ½-hp putt-putt called the Mate. This eggbeater began its retail life at $34.50 (later discounted to $29.95) and weighed about 10 pounds with a full tank of gas! The Mate's powerhead block was cast, from carb to cylinder, in one piece. Most of its sales were likely made to folks who thought the peanut kicker was irresistibly cute. Novel it was, but such is not the province of a very utilitarian product (on

Ralph Evinrude inherited his business and mechanical abilities from his parents. He hounded his folks to make fast outboards, which resulted in the legendary Elto Speedster and Quad motors. In this 1954 photograph, Ralph demonstrates an electric-starting Big Twin 25 that bears his family's name. (Outboard Marine Corp.)

The 1940, ½-hp Evinrude Mate weighed 10 pounds with a full tank of gas. (Shipyard Museum)

About 1940, an Evinrude employee inspects a shipping crate ready for a 5.4-hp, 4-cylinder Zephyr. By the 1950s motors were shipped in cardboard boxes. (Outboard Marine Corp.)

which Evinrude built its strong reputation). When a Mate did start (the minuscule ignition coils and cylinder-piston assemblies were prone to quick wear), a brisk headwind would prove a conquering competitor. Even so, the Mate and her bigger sisters at Evinrude, Johnson, and Elto accounted for 60 percent of America's outboard output.

The long-lived Evinrude Speeditwin (first offered in 1927) was reintroduced in 1939 as the 22.5-hp model 6039. Thousands of these 30-cubic-inch-displacement, opposed-cylinder outboards were sold through 1950. Although usurped by an alternate-firing, 25-horse engine in 1951, a few company press releases included a shot of the Speeditwin. The implication that the old fashioned kicker was still current helped (from 1951 to 1953) move the stock of leftovers.

Another long-produced Evinrude making its (1940) pre–World War II debut was the 5.4-hp Zephyr. This approximately 10-cubic-inch kicker's claim to fame was its quad opposed-cylinder construction. Never meant to be more than a deluxe fishing motor, the Zephyr's four cylinders gave it a smooth-running quality but provided many prospective owners with the mistaken belief that with its two extra jugs it could easily outrace less-endowed 5-horse motors. Most outboard collectors would agree with the alliterative hyperbole that zillions of Zephyrs were turned out (some with silver-colored gas tanks, later ones with blue tanks or decals; a few had weedless lower units) through the late forties.

A typical Evinrude lineup of the prewar era—say, 1941—included the Zephyr, the half-horse Mate, the 1.1-hp Ranger, the 2-horse Sportsman, the Sportwin (a 3.3-hp rig), the 9.7-hp Lightfour, the Sportfour (a 17.4-hp model), the old favorite 22.5-hp Speeditwin, and the big 33.4-horse Speedifour.

By summer 1941 it was inevitable the United States would enter World War II. Many materials crucial to outboard motor production had already been siphoned off to help Britain fight the Axis powers. A 1942 Evinrude model year (minus the Mate and Ranger) was announced in late '41, but not many of these motors were turned out prior to America's December declaration of war. In February 1942 U.S. government officials ordered a freeze on the production of all nonessential civilian items in favor of military goods. Consequently, regular outboard manufacturing ceased.

Actually, Evinrude continued to make motors. It did so for the armed services via Zephyrs and Lightfours (often used to power emergency rubber rafts), as well as Speeditwins and Speedifours for larger craft. The most famous World War II kickers were Evinrude's 50-hp Storm Boat motors. These 60-cubic-inch hulks, designed from the old Elto 4-60 Quad, pushed thousands of troop assault boats to numerous strategic beachheads.

The war finally ended during the summer of 1945. So the next civilian Evinrude model year (after the abbreviated 1942 line) was officially the 1946 offering. Most of these were simply prewar-designed motors wearing postwar serial numbers. Such models as the Ranger, the Zephyr, the Speeditwin, and the Speedifour were in the catalog again. The only relatively new engine in the cache was the now army surplus (188-pound) Storm Boat motor, dubbed Big Four. Many of these 50-horse outboards, along with some Speedifours and Speeditwins, still had the unusual military-style lower unit featuring a tri-element skeg. In addition to the regular skeg fin under the gear case, these rigs had two other skeg "wings" on either side of the gear case. On some of the huge Evinrudes the two-side skeg pieces were cut off. Outlines on the gear case ofttimes served as evidence of the odd skeg's former presence. (A few 1980s heavy-duty commercial Evinrudes had this same arrangement.)

From late 1945 through 1947 there was such a release of pent-up demand for outboards that company officials could have made a profit selling electric mixers treated with Evinrude stickers. While Evinrude engineers were, no doubt, planning new models, motors sold through 1947 were still prewar single-cylinder and opposed multi-cylinder designs. With two exceptions, much of this "old style" line was retained for 1948. Unveiled that year were a 1.5-horse Sportsman single and 3.3-hp alternate-firing Sportwin, each with a silver shaded die-cast gas tank and classic blue Evinrude lettering. They set the stage for the firm's famous Fifties styling.

Evinrude showrooms of 1949 again included the Big Four, as Outboard Marine tried to use up its stock of the powerful, albeit outdated, bulky motors.

For 1950 a pair of alternate-firing, die-cast, blue and silver twins joined the fray. A 7½-horse Fleetwin had no reverse gear,

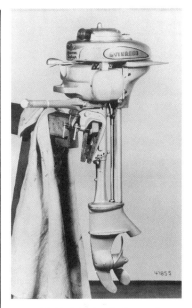

Evinrude's 1940 Zephyr 5.4-hp quad. (Shipyard Museum)

Most of Evinrude's 1950 lineup. The 22.5-hp opposed cylinder Speeditwin, which would be replaced in late 1950, was absent from this ad. It was not a fishing motor.

but could be swung 180 degrees. Neutral was accomplished via a black plastic Duo-Clutch knob that was pulled up (from the top side of the gas tank) when disengaging was desired. This model had its share of shift problems but was well accepted, outselling most other Evinrudes by 1953.

A 14-hp Fastwin also made its 1950 debut. Although displacing some 20 cubic inches, the Fastwin really wasn't all that fast. The 10-horse Mercurys of the day could severely embarrass a Fastwin owner. Actually, the Fastwin's claim to fame is its being the first Evinrude equipped with a remote Cruise-A-Day fuel tank and full F-N-R gearshift.

Fastwin's poor speed record may have caused some concern at Evinrude, but officials were far too busy with a special project to worry about the 14-hp model. The assignment would serve as next year's big outboarding attraction.

Topping the "polychromatic blue" Evinrude marque for 1951 was a revolutionary 35.7-cubic-inch, 25-hp, alternate-firing Big Twin. Not only was this rig some 20 pounds lighter than the old opposed-cylinder, 22.5-horse Speeditwin it replaced, but it was also fitted with a complete (and relatively trouble-free) F-N-R gearshift. The new Big Twin could get a family-size runabout on speaking terms with 30 mph and would sit still for a bit of trolling, too. Unlike its large Evinrude predecessors, the Big Twin had an easy-to-operate twist-grip Roto-Matic synchronized spark/throttle speed control on the steering handle. A 6-gallon, pressurized, remote Cruise-A-Day fuel tank was standard, allowing the powerhead a sleeker look. This motor was clearly the star of the early-fifties Evinrude line.

A well-designed, alternate-firing Lightwin 3-hp was unveiled in late 1951 and quickly became the fisherman's standard. This 32-pound classic wore well-placed carrying handles and made perfect use of Evinrude's famous Weedless-Drive (developed in the

Thirties by Finn Irgens) and propeller. In an updated version this little kicker was still available in the 1980s.

When I was a kid, my neighbor loaned me a bumped-up '52 Lightwin (they seem to run better with a fist-size dent in the tank) for my 12-foot Sears plywood rowboat. That craft loved the little Evinrude, and they seemed perfectly matched to each other. Believing myself to be a junior underwater outboard propulsion researcher, I would jump out of the boat and cling to the side while tugging on the Lightwin's starter cord. She always came to life with about a quarter pull, allowing me to advance the mag/carb lever halfway and be gently pulled (via an old piece of water-ski rope) 25 feet behind the happy pair. Wouldn't the Coast Guard Auxiliary people have loved to witness that wonderful feat?

During 1952, materials needed for the Korean Conflict limited some outboard production, and the '51 motors, minus the 1½-horse Sportsman and 3.3-hp Sportwin leftovers (which were semi-officially part of the 1951 catalog), got carried over another year. The shortages left a few Evinrude dealers without enough products to satisfy every potential buyer.

In announcing their 1953 outboard roster, "Evinrude officials agreed that controls on metals [due to the war] would not be lifted in time to allow the supply to catch up with demand."[5] So the Lightwin, 7½-hp Fleetwin, and Big Twin were continued with little change.

Remember the slow, 14-hp Fastwin introduced in 1950? Evinrude finally received a chance to put the pokey thing to rest through the unveiling of the 1953 Super Fastwin. This redesigned, approximately 20-cubic-inch motor gained an extra horsepower (now 15) and truly had enough zing to pull junior water-skiers and keep up with other outboards in its class. Evinrude engineers chose the Super Fastwin to wear some of their recently developed noise-reduction technology, a water-sealed exhaust and a twin-chambered, acoustically tuned silencer aimed at the "complete elimination of high frequency sound factors." The quieter motor was also equipped with an Auto-Lift hood allowing the operator to un-fasten two clasps and easily raise the port side of the cover. Removal of a pair of screws made it possible to take off the entire hood.

The editor's Evinrude Fisherman 5.5 heads up the Tennessee River in the mid 1950s. (Babb photo)

Both the new Super Fastwin 15 and larger brother Big Twin 25 were finally factory-fitted with shift and speed levers that could (without modification) quickly accept remote (Simplex) controls and steering cables. For 1954 the well-selling 7½-hp Fleetwin (with its shear-pinless Safti-Grip propeller clutch) got a going over and was reintroduced as Super Fastwin's little brother. The new Fleetwin benefited from such modifications as a remote Cruise-A-Day Junior fuel tank and a full F-N-R gearshift. Universal connection points (such as those on Super Fastwin and Big Twin) allowed the easy addition of remote control operation.

Factory-installed electric starting became available for the 25. Powerhead isolation via springs and rubber mounts further quieted the 1954 Evinrude line (except the 3-hp), allowing the motors to be dubbed Aquasonic.

Evinrude catalogs of 1955 quietly noted one rather obscure newcomer called Ducktwin. Simply a Lightwin painted olive drab (and sporting a duck decal), this 3-horse product was aimed at the duck hunter market. It retained a tiny mention in Evinrude sales literature for years. The 1955 15-hp Super Fastwin was still a good motor, but its "Super" designation was dropped.

The pleasantly blue-colored Evinrude line expanded in 1956 with the addition of a 5½-horse Fisherman twin and a 10-horse Sportwin. The top-of-the-line motors went to 30 hp. Joining the Big Twin 30, a more deluxe Lark 30 (with electric starter and designer paint and trim) made its debut.

Things progressed quickly for 1957, with the old 30 moving up to 35 hp and the Fastwin going from 15 to 18 horses (with optional electric start).

All of these models were topped in 1958 with a 50-hp V-4 rig called the Four-Fifty, in plain trim, and Starflite, in deluxe form, with an optional 10-amp, heavy-duty generator. Evinrude's early V-4 engines were huge things nicknamed "Fat-Fifty." Although officially the first U.S.-production V-configured (with cylinders pointing aft) outboard, this model is better known for its heavy fuel consumption. At even half to three-quarters throttle, a Starflite could quickly drink dry a 6-gallon gas tank.

In 1958, some deluxe 35s, called Evinrude Larks, were treated with a boxy powerhead hood. Horsepower designation numerals attached to these grayish-colored covers looked like street address numbers from someone's front porch.

Evinrude celebrated its golden anniversary in 1959 with an attractively styled line ranging from 3 to 50 hp. These power brackets were identical to the previous year's. In honor of its fiftieth summer season, however, Evinrude fitted the 1959 line with blue fiberglass hoods accented in white and golden lettering. (Note: The little 3-horse motor retained an aluminum cowling.)

The "Fat-Fifty" was finally upgraded to a 75-hp model in 1960. Things went well for this big Evinrude until its conventional, two-lever shift/speed control was replaced in 1961 with an electro-magnetic gear changer. Initial difficulties with the Selectric push-button shifter left a few Starflite 75 owners echoing "French" (as in *pardon my*) across North American waterways.

Conversely, folks who swore by the value of mid-size family motors quickly sung the praises of a beefed-up 35 that was promoted to 40 horses by 1960. The Evinrude 40, in standard or premium Lark form, became a true classic of 1960s outboarding.

Throughout the Sixties, Evinrude maintained a solid lineup. OMC's reputable blue motors were typically available in such sizes as 100, 90, 75, 60, 40, 33, 28, 18, 9½, 5½, and 3 hp.

Catering to the ever-growing family-leisure market, Evinrude's rigs represented a good, reliable value. In spring 1967 things got jazzed up just a bit when OMC entered the high-performance outboard arena for the first time since the early Forties. Evinrude introduced a limited-edition kicker called the X-115. (Johnson's version of the same 89.5-cubic-inch powerhouse was dubbed GT-115). This modified edition of the 100-hp model had a few powerhead differences, as well as a "new, slimmer lower unit." Because perennial horsepower leader, Mercury, offered up to 110 horses (in 1967), the flashy X-115 (hp) Evinrude put OMC on top of the power output scale for the first time in years.

Evinrude's appropriate slogan FIRST IN OUTBOARDS recognizes that its success is a result of an honest, hard-working couple who started with nothing more than a "coffee grinder" and a dream. Little did Ole and Bess know their long-ago picnic would be recalled today. Although no one keeps track, it's likely that an Evinrude has played a part in millions of enjoyable outings. Suffice it to say, a certain Evinrude kicker owns a warm spot in many a boater's heart—a memory warm enough even to melt ice cream.

Notes

1. Red Smith, "Views of Sport," *New York Herald Tribune* (11 January 1950).
2. "The Put-Put," *Fortune* (August 1938), p. 55.
3. "The Facts Are, a President Liked His Evinrude," *Antique Outboarder* (January 1972), p. 54.
4. "The Put-Put," op. cit., p. 108.
5. "1953 Outboards," *Boating Industry* (January 1953), p. 80-G.

3

Johnson

Late in 1952 Chicago Johnson dealer W.L. Masters drove to Waukegan, Illinois, in order to get his picture taken near a couple of outboard motors. During that ride to the Johnson factory, Masters no doubt recalled a much earlier trek to Johnson's original South Bend, Indiana, plant. He'd been there in December of 1921 to pick up a motor and sign a paper making him one of the first Johnson dealers. Although it held little historical significance then, the new Johnson franchisee was invoiced for a small, shiny opposed twin wearing serial number 508.

Through good times and bad, Johnson continued to provide outboard motors for its dealers and boating public. The firm nearly collapsed in the early 1930s, but its quality reputation and subsequent acquisition by Evinrude pushed the company to the 1952 occasion attended by Mr. Masters. Someone had found old number 508 and placed it next to a brand-new green 10-hp Johnson Sea Horse sporting serial number 1,000,508. A photographer clicked his camera while the longtime Johnson dealer stood between milestones of one million outboard motors.

The Johnson motor got its name from four Terre Haute, Indiana, brothers, Lou, Harry, Julius (who wasn't officially active in the outboard project), and Clarence Johnson. While the oldest was still in his teens and without much mechanical training, the siblings built a small inboard marine engine. This 1908 homebrew powered a rowboat up the Wabash River to their favorite spot for gathering walnuts.

Scanning the tall black walnut trees must have lifted the brothers' thoughts into air because the Johnsons soon constructed a 2-cycle airplane engine. After an initial attempt at building a predominantly wooden plane to wear the motor, eldest brother Lou restructured much of it with alloy (although the single wood wing remained), enabling him (again, without formal instruction) to make America's first monoplane flight. This 1911 feat prompted the family members to open up the Johnson School of Aviation.

A storm destroyed the airplane enterprise and related engine shop in 1913. Over the next four years the Johnsons pieced together a portion of their building and began producing small, 2-cycle, air-cooled opposed twins of about 1 ½ hp. The motor was supposed to twirl an abbreviated airplane prop and push a rowboat

Johnson bigwigs and staffers take a break to be photographed, in November 1952, with the firm's one millionth outboard motor. No other company had ever produced so many motors. Trim on this 1953 model Sea Horse 10 was painted gold to draw extra attention at upcoming boat shows. (Outboard Marine Corp.)

with air power, but the project didn't make much headway. They tried the propeller on a bike, too, but it proved both slow and very dangerous. Finally, the power plant was adapted to chain-drive the rear wheel of a bicycle. Tests went well, resulting in their Terre Haute shop's rechristening as the Johnson Motor Wheel Company.

The new firm, although not strong on marketing, began peddling motors (and complete motor bikes) to folks wanting inexpensive vehicles. The motor wheel engines worked pretty nicely except when they revved up and burned out their magnetos. A search for better fire power led the Johnsons to the Quick Action Ignition Company in South Bend, Indiana. Quick Action was controlled by Warren Ripple, who took a liking to the motor wheel idea. He helped beef up the Johnsons' young organization, subsequently joining the enterprise responsible for whipping up some 17,000 units. All went rather well until Henry Ford started selling Model T cars for about the same price as two-wheeled, powered transportation. Once the motorcycle market went bust around 1920, Johnson Motor Wheel needed to find another way to sell off those little engines.

Remember that one-lung inboard the brothers concocted in 1908? There had been other, bigger Johnson inboards too. In fact, a pair of the company's specially designed, 2-cycle, V-style, 12-cylinder engines were placed in a homemade runabout. This boat, known as the *Black Demon III* and carrying 360 hp, was said to be the first (circa 1913) craft to attain 60 mph on water.

After the motor wheel project was halted, Lou Johnson must have begun thinking about boat engines again. His brother-in-law, Warren Conover, was looking for something to do, so Lou suggested his relative should take an extra Johnson Motor Wheel power plant, "get an old Evinrude lower unit, make an adapter, and have a nice outfit to fish with."[1]

Although at the time Mr. Conover wasn't too interested in outboarding and forgot the recommendation, he easily recalled what Lou did next:

Johnson

A 1922 Johnson Light Twin. This motor's easy starting and dependability won it many customers. Today the early Johnson Twins rank among the best-running antiques. Later versions (and those fitted with an accessory) wore a basic anti-cavitation plate. When operating their Johnsons in silty/salty waters, owners had to watch for clogging in the simple water pump assembly right above the gearcase. Sometimes referred to as "Water Bugs," these desirable kickers paved the way for the first Sea Horse-labeled Johnsons, which appeared in 1929. The Sea Horse decal on this kicker was mistakenly applied later. (Outboard Marine Corp.)

It was not so very many weeks later Lou came to our home one evening with a big roll of drawing paper and said, "Clear off that dining table. I got something here to share with you." I cleared the table, and he unrolled the drawing of the very first Johnson Outboard Motor, and it was not changed very much until after several thousand motors were built.[2]

Lou had enlisted Purdue University student Finn Irgens to help him with the drafting design. By the late spring of 1921 Conover and Lou, Harry, and Clarence Johnson worked the plans into a prototype. This kicker got tried out in a test tank. Unfortunately, the transom clamps loosened, causing the 2-cycle, water-cooled opposed twin to jump into the soupy drink. Clarence, the youngest brother, quickly hopped in the tank and rescued the outboard, but "swallowed a mouthful of oily water."[3]

Anyone appreciative of progress would verify that motor was worth the dunking. Loosely based on the old air-cooled Johnson Motor Wheel mill, the new, water-cooled Johnson outboard represented a great advance over most competitors. Unlike its 60- to 75-pound counterparts, the 2-cycle, 2-hp (at 2,200 rpm), opposed-twin-cylinder aluminum Johnson was really portable at 35 pounds. The simple Johnson-designed carburetor did not require the operator to possess great mechanical wisdom.

Not only were the little Johnson Light Twins (also called Water Bugs through 1923) reliably easy to start when new, but most, when rediscovered 50-plus years later by vintage-outboard collectors, can be brought back to life after cleaning the fuel strainer and tugging on the starter cord. All this from a motor built during an era when a "good" outboard might be coaxed to run half the time! The totable kicker could be tilted up for beaching (not many others had such a feature), swiveled 360 degrees for complete maneuvering, and came with a one-year guarantee. It was clearly a better outboard, a fact swiftly determined by those attending the 1922 New York Boat Show, where a few of the little motors were placed on display.

Actual production of this Johnson model A began at South Bend, Indiana, in December 1921. Serial numbers started with 500, and five Light Twin/Water Bug motors were considered "pre-production." So number 506 was the first Johnson sold to the public. Each was tested in the nearby St. Joseph River on boats representative of average fishing skiffs. Some 3,000 were eagerly purchased in the 1922 model year.

Positive word spread, and 7,000 of the $140 motors went to happy customers in 1923. Sales were even better the following year. For 1925 a notably lighter 27-pound model J-25 single joined the catalog. This 1½-hp rig also sold well, placing Johnson on the outboard industry's list of major players.

No one associated with other outboard firms had the Johnson brothers' brand of high-speed water travel experience. Understandably then, competitors were pleasantly surprised to learn (in the spring of 1925) Johnson was "wasting time" working on a big, heavy motor. "After all," reasoned industry observers, "successes at Elto and certainly Johnson were completely based on light kickers, not fat, hard-to-lift hulks!"

Johnson's large, 1926 "flop" came in the form of an 80-pound, opposed-cylinder model P-30 Big Twin. While the heavy 6-hp (22.73-cubic-inch) outboard design ignored the scales, it lifted light boats up on plane at 16-plus mph, some 4 to 5 knots faster than most thought an outboard capable. By the end of 1926, tinkering pushed the P-30's rate past 23 mph.

References have also been made to an obscure, very large Johnson circa 1925 vintage. The two-cylinder Aqua-Flyer motor is said to have nearly 50-cubic-inch displacement generating some 15 hp. The big outboard was built into a special Johnson boat for show display purposes. Actual production figures, if any, are unknown.

Johnson was about the only outfit to offer a really quick motor from late 1925 through 1926. Outboard speed caught the public's fancy, and sales of all Johnson models (slower ones included) were brisk. In 1927 the old Big Twin was renamed P-35 and awarded more piston displacement as well as 2 extra horses (to 8 hp). This unit could push a boat over 32 mph! A new 6-hp offering, the K-35 opposed (17.33-cubic-inch) twin, was also introduced that year.

These new models were some of the first to forgo troublesome mechanical water pumps. A pressure vacuum pumping arrangement used propeller suction and forward motion to supply cooling water to the cylinders.

Meanwhile, all the successes caused Johnson to outgrow its South Bend, Indiana, plant. The outboard firm had a bit of trouble competing for workers with nearby Studebaker and other auto-related factories. When the local bigwigs complained Johnson was making too much noise, a piece of land in Illinois on Lake Michigan's shoreline was secured, and the motor company built the industry's finest outboard manufacturing facility. At about the same time Waukegan, Illinois, became Johnson's new home, a small Canadian plant was established for the production of kickers north of U.S. boundaries.

Anyone who has relocated knows that moving can expend a lot of one's energies. Similarly, Johnson's move caused the loss of some headway in the 1928 "big motor" scene. That year Elto officially unveiled its over-22-mph Speedster twin and four-cylinder, 40-mph Quad. These rigs were relatively easy to start and run, and typically performed very well. Evinrude was enjoying a second year of success with its Speeditwin, and Lockwood Ace and Chief models were also setting some racing records.

Unfortunately, Johnson's large 1928 offering came in the form of an impractically classic Giant Twin. Officially labeled model TR-40, this rig weighed in at more than 110 pounds and wore opposed cylinders displacing almost 50 cubic inches. The company had replaced its basic Water Bug/Light Twin A-25 with a restyled 2½-hp A-35 and simply "blew up" the design into the TR-40. It was

Model J-25, 1.5-hp motor, 1925–32.

Johnson

almost as if someone at Johnson had put an A-35 on a photocopier and pressed the enlarge button, yielding a Giant Twin!

In any event, the noisy 25.75-hp monster was faster than previous Johnsons, but provided little all-around competition for motors like Elto's Quad. The Giant Twin found a few customers in 1928. Leftovers were offered in 1929. Thus now it had been Johnson that had underestimated the other companies. Something significant had to be done for 1929.

An advertising agency man named Carl Prell phoned Johnson before the 1929 model year:

> "I've got an idea," said Prell to his Johnson contact.
>
> "Well, we can sure use one," the Johnson man responded.
>
> "How 'bout you call your boat motors by a name representative of mighty waters and creatures exhibiting tremendous strength and stamina?"
>
> Oh, no, I hope he isn't going to recommend something like Ocean Oxen, thought the Johnson official.
>
> "Why not name those outboards"—Prell paused for effect—"something like 'Sea Horse' . . . the Johnson Sea Horse!"
>
> "Hey, that works for us!" came the relieved answer, and the new nomenclature was assigned to the 1929 line.

Fresh off the assembly line with Sea Horse decals were a pair of motors wearing an external, gear-driven (full-crankshaft-speed) rotary crankcase valve. This feature allowed for a greater efficiency in getting gas vapor into the engine. Rotary valves of this type were standard on the new 1929, 13-hp S-45 (approximately 20 cubic inches) opposed twin and the 4-cylinder opposed (approximately 40 cubic inches) 26-horse model V-45. Racing versions of these beautifully engineered kickers were designated SR-45 and VR-45 and checked in with 16 and 32 hp (at 5,200 rpm), respectively.

Lou Johnson, oldest of the Johnson brothers, in his Waukegan, Illinois office. His stern look in this 1932 photo may have been due to the outboard company's financial woes. Motor is a model P-50. (Outboard Marine Corp.)

The new Sea Horse logo appeared on these (and all other '29 Johnsons) looking a bit more like a ferocious dragon than an aqua-equine. No matter, the 1929 Sea Horses (with the exception of the holdover TR-40) were well received, pushing the company up where it wanted to be.

Throughout 1929, Johnson engineering research prospered. An approximately 30-cubic-inch, gear-driven, external rotary valve motor called the P-50 was developed (for 1930 release). This one sported an improved, half-crankcase-speed valve and operated so well the same technology was applied to the proposed 1930 Johnson V-50, 4-cylinder and the S-50 twin. (Leftover full-speed external-rotary-valved S-45 and V-45 motors would also be offered in 1930.)

While testing the four-banger model, one of the Johnson brothers released compression from a pair of cylinders and noticed the V-50 still ran pretty well. As spark plugs in the active bank of opposed cylinders ignited alternately, he wondered if such a firing order was responsible for the smoothness. Further experiments proved that hypothesis correct, and a new set of alternate-firing twins (4-hp model A-50 and K-50 8-horse motors) were developed for 1930 presentation.

Additionally, it was decided to market a line of Johnson boats that could be matched with various Sea Horse outboards. Inventories of boats and motors were stockpiled in late 1929. To let people know about everything Johnson had to sell, company president Warren Ripple pledged a block of the firm's stock and borrowed (from New York investment house Hayden-Stone) lots of promotion-earmarked funds. Six hundred thousand dollars were spent on advertising alone.

The stock market crashed in October of 1929. Even if someone wanted a mated Johnson boat-and-motor combo, he probably couldn't afford one. Johnson had put out huge sums of money, but wasn't taking in much at all. As a result Mr. Ripple lost the security stock to Hayden-Stone, and during 1930, control of the Sea Horses was rounded up by the financiers.

For some reason in 1931 (while Ole Evinrude's company was prudently pulling in the fiscal reins) the bankers let Johnson spend more money improving its existing racing models, adding an

"So easy to operate and maintain even a couple of girls in weird bathing suits can do it," a copy writer might quip. Indeed, the Johnson model J single was a good performer no matter who was at the controls. (Outboard Marine Corp.)

approximately 14-cubic-inch racer called KR-55, along with the obscure, approximately 50-cubic-inch, 50-horse XR-55 opposed, four-cylinder, high-speed rig weighing in at 144 pounds! A few dollars also went to develop an inboard/outboard stern-drive system.

While not commercially successful in 1931, these model SD 10 and SD 11 units (not to be confused with the SD 10 outboard of 1940) were actually 30 years ahead of their time. Wisely, some of the old opposed-twin parts were parsimoniously put together to form the outdated but utilitarian OA (3-hp) and OK (8-hp) two-cylinder outboards.

In 1932 Hayden-Stone had Johnson declare bankruptcy, submerging the once-proud outboard firm into receivership and reorganization. More Wall Street types were sent to Waukegan with financial cures. One new man got Johnson into the refrigerator compressor business, turning out chilly units under its own JoMoCo label, as well as for other firms such as Stewart-Warner.

Small 4-cycle Iron Horse utility power plants were also built at Johnson's Waukegan, Illinois, plant. Hayden-Stone even bought Johnson another factory in Galesburg, Illinois, to handle all the overflow in case the fridge and small-engine business went sky high. Unfortunately, everything kept going through the floor, with the Johnson Motor Company skating in the same direction.

It was probably about this time (1933 or 1934) when a deal—of which so little information remains that it was nearly forgotten—was planned between Johnson and Sears-Roebuck. The famous outboard maker was to provide Sears with a cheap opposed twin based on the model OK leftover motors. A few of these 8-hp opposed kickers were produced, each wearing the Waterwitch ID on its rope sheave plate. It appears that either Sears or Johnson canceled the contract before very many Waterwitches were brewed.

With a "just see if you can do anything with that disaster" attitude, Hayden-Stone kept bringing in and trying out new Johnson managers. The recruits had backgrounds in everything from the military to movie theater and clothes store operation.

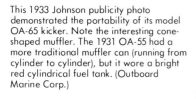
This 1933 Johnson publicity photo demonstrated the portability of its model OA-65 kicker. Note the interesting cone-shaped muffler. The 1931 OA-55 had a more traditional muffler can (running from cylinder to cylinder), but it wore a bright red cylindrical fuel tank. (Outboard Marine Corp.)

None knew much about running an outboard or industrial concern.

Stewart-Warner's association with Johnson (via their refrigerator compressor deal) led the diversified company to make a 1935 purchase order for the ailing outboard firm. Hayden-Stone quickly accepted, even reluctantly agreeing to take Stewart-Warner stock instead of cash.

A few weeks later Stewart-Warner told Charlie Hayden there could be a delay in the proposed transaction while the Securities and Exchange Commission looked into Stewart-Warner's stock values. Knowing the government never does anything fast (except raise taxes), Hayden was extremely aggravated. To make matters worse, he had taken sick and was "laid up in a New York City hotel room in fine temper."[4]

Johnson's chief competitor, Outboard Motors Corporation, had been pinching pennies since late 1929, and its principals, Ralph Evinrude and Steve Briggs, had saved a little extra cash. The pair had often discussed bringing Johnson into the family. Hearing rumors about the Stewart-Warner situation, Briggs headed to Hayden's New York hotel suite.

> "Do you want to buy Johnson?" the ill banker asked.
> "Sure," Briggs said, nodding.
> "I've got to get $10.35 a share for it," said Hayden.
> "OK," came the reply.
> "Well, then, it's yours," Mr. Hayden said in a rather relieved tone.
> And with that, he took a pen, a slip of paper, and wrote: "Steve Briggs and Ralph Evinrude agree to pay $10.35 a share for 80,000 shares (out of 102,000 outstanding) of Johnson Motor Company stock." Briggs scribbled his name on the tiny paper and took a train back to Milwaukee. In telling Ralph Evinrude the news, he smiled. "Johnson is going to be a perfect little gold mine."[5]

The famous company was finally back in the hands of people who knew outboards. Perhaps more importantly, Johnson was now operated by individuals who understood how to manage an outboard firm. Within a year after acquiring Johnson, officials at the newly named Outboard Marine and Manufacturing Corporation (covering Elto, Evinrude, and Johnson) cut Johnson expenses by doing things like "reducing the cost of directors' meetings from $8,000 to $250 annually."[6]

Johnson's expensive-to-produce, 4-cylinder opposed motors were never reintroduced, and by 1937 the firm began securing the position of quality fishing motor maker. In fact, Briggs's supposed "gold mine" prediction had almost instantly come true, as the 1937 Johnson gross exceeded Evinrude/Elto's by nearly $2 million.

Through the close of the 1930s, Johnson continued specializing in smaller fishing engines. In fact, 80 percent of its 10-model 1939 lineup came from motors 5 hp and under. These smooth-trolling "fishin' engines," such as the alternate-firing LT (Light Twin), were highly prized by anglers everywhere.

In 1940 a big 16-horse model SD was introduced. Johnson's first large "hooded" motor wore a fat 2 ½-gallon wraparound fuel tank, giving it the look of a prize pumpkin atop a lower unit. Engineers would soon agree that big outboards needed remote gas tanks. Another hefty Johnson of this vintage came in the form of the model PO. An approximately 30-cubic-inch opposed twin derived from a late-twenties design, this 22-hp kicker long enjoyed a following equaled by the similarly sized Evinrude Speeditwin.

In 1941 and 1942 Johnson updated the LT motors with a 5-horse model TS (TD Deluxe with rewind starting). Also introduced was a 2 ½-hp version called HS (HD). These nice-running outboards received modernization via shrouding. Their sales were quite brisk, and a surprising number are still in use today.

By spring 1942 World War II halted civilian outboard production and started many a GI wishing for the day a trusty Johnson would again take him to a relaxing fishing spot. The famous kicker company issued a wish list brochure promising it wouldn't abandon anyone who had such dreams. It admitted the Sea Horse motors shown in the little catalog were not then available, but "will be manufactured after the war is won. They are substantially the same as those which were discontinued in 1942."

By 1939 Johnson, under Evinrude ownership, had rebounded financially. This company outing included boat rides with Johnson outboards for power. One hopes that the mahogany *inboard* at the end of the dock is not Johnson property! (Outboard Marine Corp.)

The evolution of the Johnson Sea Horse logo.

 1929

 1940

 1958

During World War II, Johnson honored defense contracts with products like modified 22-hp PO motors (model POLR), and water pumps based on the KR racing power plants.

At war's end Johnson did rerelease the HD 2½-, the TD 5-, the KD 9.8-, the SD 16-, and the PO 22-hp models. These products, most especially the two smaller units, sold very well, providing Johnson with a stable catalog offering through 1948. Sea Horses of this vintage began wearing a sea-mist green finish.

Johnson engineers were busy developing a "big" outboard "slenderized" by way of a remote Mile-Master gas tank. Most important, the new motor could be easily shifted into neutral, forward, or reverse. Debuting in 1949, this 10-hp model QD moved an important portion of Outboard Marine and Manufacturing into the state-of-the-art realm. The QD's premier was surpassed only by rival Scott-Atwater's trio of shift motors (4, 5, and 7½ hp), also introduced in '49. Nevertheless, the QD remained Johnson's star through 1950.

A quasi-shift model TN (*N* for neutral) replaced Johnson's old TD. The updated 5-horse favorite resembled its predecessor but had a neutral clutch.

Clear evidence that Johnson and Evinrude had common ownership surfaced with the 1951 introduction of the model RD Sea Horse 25. This instantly popular rig was mechanically identical to Evinrude's Big Twin 25 and contributed a new versatility to outboarding. Ads boasted "25 hp—Yet it trolls . . . and only 85 pounds!" Like many of this era's popular Johnsons, the first Sea Horse 25s sported motor rest wings along and forward of the cowling. The 25 allowed 1951's lineup to be simplified, and the chubby SD and heavy PO were dropped.

An Evinrude-based Johnson 3-hp kicker, dubbed the JW, began its run in 1952. Angle-Matic drive helped prevent the JW from snagging underwater vegetation. Designed to replace the old 2½-horse HD, this junior Johnson linked lots of fishermen and small-boat users with the Sea Horse logo.

Sometime in late October 1952 workers on Johnson's assembly line were instructed to pay close attention to their products' serial numbers. On November 6, a couple of Sea Horse employees pointed at a 10-horse motor shouting, "That's it!" and ran for the foreman.

"Yep, there she is," their supervisor confirmed.

They were talking about the 1 millionth Johnson outboard. The 1953 model QD milestone was subsequently "outfitted with special gold and chrome trim . . . and featured in major boat shows throughout the country."[7]

The year 1954 was when Johnson's cowling wings were moved aft. The 25 was updated and could be purchased with electric starting. (Johnson had last offered that convenience in the

The Johnson model QD 10-hp motor with remote "Mile-Master" fuel tank. The black knob on the lower front cowling shifts this Sea Horse from neutral to forward or reverse. In 1949, the only other outboard company to offer a gearshift was Scott-Atwater. Being a larger firm, however, Johnson got most of the credit for pioneering this convenience. (Outboard Marine Corp.)

early Thirties.) A 5 ½-hp model CD F-N-R shift outboard with Evinrude-influenced features replaced the old reliable 5-horse TN. Sea Horses rated at 3, 5.5, 10, and 25 hp represented the popular green (with white accents) 1954–55 Johnson line.

Rich maroon paint (with white detailing) signaled a change for Johnson's 1956 catalog. Again, Evinrude's influence contributed to the Sea Horse stable via new 7.5- and 15-hp offerings. The old 25 was upped to 30 hp, and came in both regular Sea Horse and deluxe Javelin versions. Like the fancy Evinrude Lark, Javelin served as Johnson's top-of-the-line product. Although always equipped with 6-volt electric starting, the chrome-trimmed Javelin differed only cosmetically from the regular Sea Horse 30 electric.

Javelin's manual-start cord grip was hidden behind a little white cover. When the cover was removed for emergency cranking, sharp edges of the clip, designed to hold it in place, caused salty words to shake from boaters with battery trouble! Such minor inconveniences notwithstanding, the deluxe Javelins were rewarded with a gold paint job (with chrome accents) and upped to 35 hp in 1957. Options included a heavy-duty 10-amp generator. There was also a maroon and white Sea Horse 35. The old 15 was promoted to 18 horses in 1957.

Javelins got tossed from Johnson's 1958 arena, leaving regular and Super Sea Horse 35 models. Top honors in 1958 went to a new white and gold V-4-cylinder hulk dreamed up with Evinrude. The Sea Horse 50, Johnson's version of the "Fat-Fifty," looked as if its 50 horses should perform better than they actually did. Had the motor run fast and consumed fuel slowly, all might have been well. Unfortunately, the opposite was true.

By 1960 the white Sea Horse line had a far superior leader. The new V-4 Sea Horse 75 had a much improved lower unit, was a bit easier on gas, and had an acceptable top end. It came in a two-

A late-1960s Johnson V-4 Meteor. (Outboard Marine Corp.)

lever remote-control version in 1960. Later models were sometimes plagued by bugs in a single-lever-controlled Electramatic, an electromagnetic lower-unit shifter.

Meanwhile, the vintage 35 had evolved into a 40-hp rig available in standard and Electramatic styles. Similar to the old 25s (on which they were based), the 40s became their era's leading family-size outboard.

The year 1964 saw the long-lived 10-horse Johnson dropped in favor of a low profile 9½. More than any other 1960s Sea Horse, the 9½ has an equal share of detractors and enthusiasts.

Few would disagree that the Johnson story is packed with many interesting, innovative, and, most important, dependable outboards. By the way, to illustrate the famous motor maker's accelerated popularity, its 1 millionth kicker from late 1952 was more than 30 years in the making. Johnson's number 2 million, however, arrived much faster, rolling off the line in 1959. By 1968 the 3 millionth Sea Horse presented one of the world's best-loved outboard motor makers with another remarkable photo opportunity.

1. Warren Mason Conover, "Early Johnson Engineering History," *Antique Outboarder* (April 1974), p. 7.
2. Ibid.
3. "Commemorative Edition," *Johnson Jottings*, (OMC, Johnson div. house organ), (1972), p. 3.
4. "The Put-Put," *Fortune* (August 1938), p. 115.
5. Ibid.
6. Ibid.
7. "Johnson," *Boating Industry* (January 1953), p. 82.

Ad touting benefits of being a Johnson dealer.

Notes

4

Kiekhaefer Mercury

Whether some nervous employee in a competitor's PR department did it, no one will ever know. The truth is, however, somebody started a Mercury rumor that has polarized outboarders since the late 1940s. The word was passed: "OK, Mercs might be speedy on tiny, impractical, non-family-oriented craft, but try to pull a skier with one on a real boat, and you'll see those noisy machines have absolutely no power."

The real force behind Mercury grew up on a Midwestern farm. Like Ole Evinrude, another native Wisconsinite, this fellow, E.C. "Carl" Kiekhaefer, was more interested in farm machinery than fields or livestock. Young Kiekhaefer left green pastures for a trade school specializing in practical and automotive electricity. Although this background soon helped him attain chief engineer status at a respectable firm, Carl Kiekhaefer was driven by a desire to run his own shop.

In 1938 the word was that the Cedarburg, Wisconsin, plant, which made Thor outboards, was about to fold. Located in Kiekhaefer's hometown, the Cedarburg Manufacturing Company's facility seemed a likely spot for his dream venture. With financial help from his dad and some townspeople, he acquired the defunct outboard factory and began deciding what kind of product to make.

The old sign saying CEDARBURG MFG. CO. was painted out and relettered KIEKHAEFER CORP. The word MAGNETIC was stuck on the firm's roof, touting Carl Kiekhaefer's expertise in electrical engineering. It also set the stage for the novice company to produce magnetic separators for the dairy industry.

Clean-up operations got under way but the separator idea was short-circuited by the discovery of some outboards in inventory. Kiekhaefer decided to sell them to raise a little capital for some manufacturing machinery.

The 300 or so silver kickers were small Thor singles re-labeled with red Sea King decals. Awaiting their fate, they stood in silent rows on wooden stands winding through the old factory.

Montgomery Ward had contracted Thor for a large stock of the low-cost, badge-engineered (motors that differ from others cosmetically, sold under different brand names) Sea Kings. Customer complaints about the poorly running engines caused the

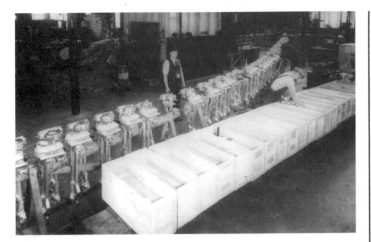

E.C. Kiekhaefer (wearing tie) entered the outboard motor business in 1939. After a mail order company rejected them, he rebuilt and sold these outboards, then went on to sell the Mercury brand to his own dealer organization. (Mercury Marine)

big catalog store to terminate the deal. Already beset by financial problems from the weak sales of Thor motors, Cedarburg was finished off by the Montgomery Ward situation.

Informal inspection of the outboards' fuel-air mixing valve caused Kiekhaefer to question his predecessor's engineering skill. To satisfy mechanical curiosity, the new plant owner postponed his call to the junk man and replaced a random kicker's mixing valve with an automotive-type float-feed carburetor. A factory test tank still holding gallons of oily water was fitted with the experimental Sea King. Three brisk pulls on the starter cord brought the motor to life and Kiekhaefer to consider phoning Montgomery Ward instead of the scrap dealer.

Initially skeptical, the Montgomery Ward buyer soon heard one of his store's erstwhile outboards happily purring with sales potential. The Kiekhaefer Corporation was quickly commissioned to revitalize the idle stock of Sea Kings for inclusion in the 1939 Montgomery Ward catalog. After most of the improved batch had been crated and sent to the Montgomery Ward warehouse, Kiekhaefer finally had time to count his fledgling outfit's receipts and return to the business of coming up with a good product to manufacture.

> "Line two for Mr. Kiekhaefer," paged a secretary. "Montgomery Ward calling long distance."
>
> Oh, no, what do they want? her boss wondered.
>
> "We sold all those Sea Kings," the guy on the phone stated, "and we want you to make us some more."

The old machines that had pressed out Thor/Sea King parts remained usable, so Kiekhaefer and his crew fired them up and satisfied Montgomery Ward's new order. Almost simultaneously, it was decided to print a 1939 Thor brochure and take another step into the outboard motor business.

Someone located the late model Thor's specs, patterns, and

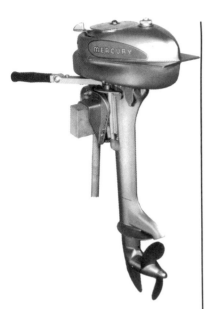

Products such as the 1940 Mercury Single placed the Kiekhaefer Corporation in outboarding's limelight.

castings. Kiekhaefer made a few improvements, such as replacing the mixing valve with a workable carb, and offered a three-cylinder, in-line, 6.2-horse rig, an alternate-firing, 4.1-hp twin, and a 2.4-horse single. Because small motors accounted for most of the industry's business, Kiekhaefer concentrated on his one-lung model. While the lower unit still had Thor's characteristic steel stamping toy appearance, its fuel tank exhibited a new teardrop design. Such styling, complete with little wings and a tail fin, caused it to be dubbed Streamliner. During its brief production run, this kicker was never a common sight. Even so, the Streamliner set the stage for something unique in 1940.

The Cedarburg plant was about 20 miles outside of Milwaukee. Visitors were "welcome for inspection or actual boat demonstrations." Engineering and publicity purposes were served at the factory when Kiekhaefer had his staff run a "destruction test" on a Thor twin. They hooked it to that old test tank and kept it going full speed for an estimated 5,000 miles. Afterward, mechanics "tore it down, and the parts were in fine condition."

Not every employee at the Cedarburg facility was required to advocate Thor motors. Kiekhaefer knew the outboard design he'd acquired with the silent factory represented no long-term asset. So, as some of his staff built up more '39 Thors, the company president and a handful of select engineering associates worked to make their present product line shamefully obsolete.

Late in that final year of the decade, Kiekhaefer's workers were notified that Thor production would be discontinued. Seeing their boss packing things into his Plymouth coupe, numerous staffers wondered if they'd lose their jobs at Thor a second time. Although details were sketchy, rumor soon had it that the plant would actually get busier than ever.

Kiekhaefer's car headed away from the Cedarburg factory carrying a handmade display and a few interesting outboards. Curious service station attendants along the route to New York City might have caught a glimpse of the streamlined silver kickers on the backseat. A blanket protecting the motors could have moved just enough to reveal the word MERCURY on one of the outboard engines' gas tank.

These new models, taking their name from Roman mythology's speedy messenger god, were indeed far superior to the old Thors. Most striking on the 1940-debut Mercs was a "hydrodynamic designed [drive] shaft casing." Unlike most of its competitors, this piece "enclosed the drive shaft, water line, and served as a leak-proof underwater exhaust." Sales literature also claimed the whole unit was "designed like a streamlined airplane strut . . . knifing through water without resistance. The lower unit had no knobs or projections to cause turbulence. Clean, fast, weedless, and by far the strongest ever made."

Additional 1940 Mercury innovations included removable cylinder sleeves and water jackets. These features allowed saltwater boaters to clean the salt scale from the powerhead. Carbon deposits were also accessible for maintenance. A rubber

Rotex water pump eliminated the need for springs, plungers, valves, and other intricate parts found in most competitors' pumps. This facilitated constant cooling without concern for water or corrosion.

Folks attending the Boat Show watched Kiekhaefer highlight these aspects of his small Mercury exhibit. The notable little motors and their inventor's sales presentation netted 16,000 orders! Buyers had the option of the $52.95 Standard Single; the $59.95 De Luxe Single, with streamlined gas tank and powerhead cover; or the $89.95 Twin. Neither the 6-horse, two-cylinder rig nor the 3-hp singles had rewind starting.

The first Merc catalog also included note of a $42.95, 2½-hp single Mercury Special. Touted as the "full-sized motor you want PLUS LOW PRICE," this bargain was probably a relabeled 1939 Thor Streamliner. While its Mercury-like powerhead cowling passed as "new," a "tinny-looking" Thor lower unit kept the Special from being pictured in the 1940 Mercury flyer.

Kiekhaefer's outboard business got off to a good start and grew in 1941. Unfortunately, war clouds forced American officials to tighten the reins on civilian production items. Aluminum supplies for consumer goods, such as outboards, were redirected toward the military. With kicker production nearly halted, Mercury inventories disappeared by 1942.

Actually, the Kiekhaefer Corporation started getting busier. Defense contracting prompted nearly round-the-clock work designing and building "lightweight engines for military chain saws, pumps, compressors, generators, hoists, and target aircraft," according to the Mercury literature. Even a few outboards, wearing metal Kiekhaefer Corporation ID plates on the motor leg, found wartime assignments. Unlike many firms that got tapped by Uncle Sam to make goods completely foreign to their regular merchandise, Kiekhaefer's War Department contracts allowed over four years of research and development in its field of 2-cycle engine technology (ranging from 2½ to 90 hp).

Staffers were constantly reminded to think of ways that this war-products experience could be put to use in a postwar outboard marketplace. Mercury's "new kids on the block" image was kept alive from 1942 to 1945 as even the most vintage (1940) Mercs were only a few years old. This contrasted with other folks' potentially cantankerous 1930s kickers from Elto, Evinrude, or Johnson. When peacetime returned in summer 1945, the Kiekhaefer Corporation was ready with 1946 model-year Mercs.

Immediate postwar Mercs came in 3.2 single and 6-horse twin denominations and were called Comet and Rocket, respectively. "Special" versions of these silver motors wore rewind starters.

By 1947 a trio of new Kiekhaefer models began showing up in a rich, cedar green color. Although two of these rigs (3.6 and 7½ hp) had powerheads based on earlier Mercurys, they (along with a 10-horse big sister) visually outdated a whole crop of predecessors and competitors.

Star of this enviable triangle was indeed the approximately

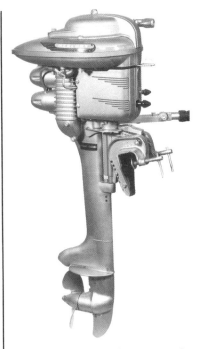

Mercury's 1946, 6-hp Rocket was a good seller for the Kiekhaefer Corporation. Note the ID plate on the motor leg. Early post-war Mercurys were silver, but golden versions were produced for Western Auto to sell under the Wizard name. (Mercury Marine)

This 1947, 7 ½-horse Mercury Rocket KE4 looked almost identical to its bigger brother, the 10-horse Lightning KE7. Both motors set speed records for kickers in their respective classes. The photo shows the original lower cowling, which typically was lost over the years. (Mercury Marine)

20-cubic-inch model KE7 Lightning. Very conservatively rated at 10 hp, the 59-pound Lightning (on a light hull) often made quick work of much bigger Evinrude and Johnson 22-horse opposed twins.

While most outboard firms proudly fitted their products with lots of shiny control panel dials, motor rest wings, and carrying handles, Kiekhaefer built Lightning as sleek as a no-nonsense sports car. Its knifey silver lower unit and beautiful green powerhead, devoid of toting handles, was truly striking. An aluminum ring hugged the bottom edge of the ovalesque fuel tank. The mysterious word *Mercury* (with letters in descending size) was cast into both sides of this piece like teeth partially cloaked in a shark's mouth.

Kiekhaefer's liberal use of ball and needle bearings allowed Lightning to run in rpm ranges dangerous for lesser-engineered outboards. The rather compact green Merc inspired the Michigan Wheel Company to develop special two-blade bronze racing propellers called Aqua-Jet. These props, appropriate for small, planing hulls, made Lightning even faster.

There was something wonderfully strange about the first generation Lightning. It was clearly not the type of motor a respectable family man would long consider. Still, Kiekhaefer's plan to offer an outboard capable of becoming a legend was quickly realized. Non-Mercury dealers scoffed at the glossy green 10s as a hot-rodder's province. Others speculated, "If that's a 10, I sure would like to see a Merc 20 or 25!"

The year 1949 gave curious outboarders just such a view when the four-cylinder, in-line Mercury model KF9 was introduced. This approximately 40-cubic-inch Thunderbolt sported a bright chrome rope-start flywheel slightly above its cedar green power-head covers. Thunderbolt's cowling said MERCURY 25, but like the underrated Lightning, it generated much more zing than advertised. In fact, small print in Kiekhaefer's parts booklets lists this one's horsepower as "25+*." The asterisk refers to a reminder that Thunderbolt's horsepower varies with revolutions per minute. Enigmatically, no rpm rating is given. Adding to the 25's mystique, a "deadman's throttle" grip positioned on the tiller handle was designed to slow the green giant if its operator got thrown out of the boat. The Mercury 25 Thunderbolt was easily 40 hp and could "blow the doors off" craft powered by the larger 50-horse Evinrude quads of the late 1940s.

Carl Kiekhaefer was bugged by the accepted notion that Ole Evinrude had actually invented the outboard motor. Various versions of the famous "ice cream story" (noted in Chapter 2) continually surfaced, honoring Evinrude as the most valid kicker company. So in late 1949 Kiekhaefer hired an investigator to research documents in the U.S. patent office.

Dusty paperwork discovered in Washington predated Ole's ice cream incident and sent the researcher scurrying for the telephone. It seemed that Cameron Waterman was selling outboards before Evinrude ever set up shop.

Seventy-one-year-old Waterman was located in Detroit and invited (along with his wife, of course) by Mercury for an all-expense-paid trip to the upcoming New York Boat Show. There, the elderly gent was honored as outboarding's real inventor. Many prominent outdoors writers and just about all of the New York newspaper columnists were invited, too.

The resulting publicity was a tremendous PR coup for Mercury. The Evinrude people didn't say much. Mr. Waterman smiled a lot, got an official "outboard inventor" plaque and a new 1950 Merc 25. A copy of the plaque turned up years later in a West Coast junkyard.

Leftover KE7 Lightnings were offered through 1949 (and probably later at smaller dealers). The approximately 20-cubic-inch motors were also marketed that year with a few internal updates and convenient carrying handles. Labeled Super 10, KF7, these Lightnings tread water nicely while a hotter "10+ hp*" Merc was on the drawing board. The little one-cylinder Comet 3½ was upgraded a touch and represented a pretty nice fishing engine. Although some of these singles sold in 1949 and 1950, a new 1949 Super 5 twin, priced only a few dollars over the Comet, frequently eclipsed its smaller sister and fast became one of Mercury's most popular products.

Late 1940s economic progress required more space for the Kiekhaefer Corporation. A Fond du Lac, Wisconsin, dairy farm, once renowned for its prize-winning cattle, was acquired and converted into Mercury's new manufacturing, marketing, and training center. By 1951 most Mercs were tagged with their ID plates in a big barn comprising the Fond du Lac plant. It must have seemed strange to see trailer trucks displaying the Mercury outboard logo picking up goods from a siloed structure boasting, in huge letters, CORIUM FARM—HOME OF FAMOUS GUERNSEY COWS.

That old Cedarburg property received the temporary honor of serving as Kiekhaefer's engineering and administrative head-quarters. Once additions were completed in Fond du Lac, the original Thor/Mercury factory's "home office" status quietly ended. Funds were allocated for a parts and service division at Beaver Dam, a research plant at Oshkosh (both Wisconsin), as well as a saltwater test site in Sarasota, Florida.

Meanwhile, racing enthusiasts were squeezing even more miles per hour from their fast Merc-powered boats. Sometime during 1949 or 1950, the factory released a handful of extra speedy KF7-HD (approximately 20-cubic-inch) and (approximately 40-cubic-inch) KF9-HD motors. The *HD* stood for "heavy-duty," signifying these rigs had reinforced castings and larger carbs. HD outboards most likely found their way to promising racers planning a run in some important event such as the New York (City) to Albany Marathon.

Shortly after the HD engines were produced, Kiekhaefer introduced the long (15-inch) Quicksilver racing lower unit. Early versions of this "Quicky" were available for the 10-horse KE7 and KF7, as well as for the 4-cylinder KF9 and subsequent KG9

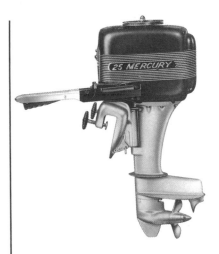

In 1949, big motors produced by other companies lacked rewind starting, so Kiekhaefer officials decided to save time by releasing their revolutionary Mercury 25 Thunderbolt with a simple, rope-start flywheel. The 1949 KF9 was the first 4-cylinder, in-line production outboard. Subsequent Mercs with similar appearance were the KG9, the KG9-1 (with rewind start), and the Mark 40 (on which the side cowling simply read "Mercury"). That squeeze grip on the 40-cubic-inch powerhouse's steering handle operated spark/throttle and would idle if released (or if the driver flipped out of the boat). While most of these rigs were cedar green, some literature shows bare aluminum models. Introductory ads featured a non-ribbed cowl with no lettering. A few KF9s (which apparently had weak crankshafts) and KG9s came through the factory painted red. This underrated 25 was neck-snapping quick. (Mercury Marine)

Kiekhaefer Mercury

HEAVY duty

conversion kits (*for pushing house-boats, barges, big fishing boats and other heavy loads with KE7, K97 and KG7 models.*)

The rugged construction, reserve power and stamina of Mercury KE-7, KF-7 and KG-7 models make them capable of propelling enormous loads. However, for heavy duty work, such as propulsion of barges, houseboats and heavy fishing boats, it is necessary to compensate for abnormally high mounting position of motor by extending lower unit downward so propeller can operate deep enough in the water; also, it is advantageous to use a large diameter low pitch propeller which will develop maximum thrust at low forward speeds, yet will allow engine to operate at normal R.P.M.

Each heavy duty conversion kit contains a special driveshaft housing extension and an extra long drive shaft, plus all parts required to make the conversion. It does not include the propeller

NOTE: For gross loads between 1000 and 1500 pounds, a 9'' x 7'' propeller will be found most efficient. For gross loads over 1500 pounds, a 9'' x 6'' propeller is recommended.

M-50-1191 for KE-7, less propeller	$13.45
M-50-1182 for KF-7 and KG-7, less propeller	18.01
M-50-1132 9'' x 6'' propeller, KF-7 and KG-7	9.90
M-50-1133 9'' x 7'' propeller, KF-7 and KG-7	9.90
M-50-1134 9'' x 6'' propeller, KE-7	9.90
M-50-1135 9'' x 7'' propeller, KE-7	9.90

Heavy-duty conversion kits for Mercury model KE7, KF7, and KG7 model motors.

(featuring a stronger crankshaft). Actually, the Quicksilver unit was really built with a new generation of Merc 10 in mind.

The approximately 20-cubic-inch Super 10 Hurricane model KG7 of 1950 would soon outshine Lightning in Kiekhaefer's crown. (The short-lived KF7-HD was probably a preproduction KG7 Hurricane.) Boaters wanting extra zip offered by a Quicky had to buy a stock motor and then purchase the super-sleek Quicksilver lower unit as an accessory. When a Merc dealer was asked to replace the standard unit with the Quicksilver piece, factory rules authorized him to stamp a little letter *Q* on the motor's ID plate, hence, KG7Q or KF9Q, and so on. Not everyone bothered with this detail.

The 15-inch Quicksilver lower-unit equipped Q motors worked well on racing runabouts, but owners of hydroplanes (tiny boats with transoms shorter than those on utility craft) often placed broken pieces of yardsticks under the motor clamp yoke in order to raise their Mercs to a competitive operating level. Kiekhaefer reps observing this practice prompted the 1950 or 1951 introduction of a new Quicksilver lower unit colloquially known as the Hydro-Short Quicky. This Hydro or H lower unit had only one (instead of two) anticavitation plates and was 2 inches shorter than the old 15-inch Quicky. While the gearfoot design remained the same, a slightly abbreviated drive shaft was used.

Motors mated to the Hydro-Short units came that way from the factory and had an *H* after the model designation. The first H Mercs were the hot Hurricane over-10-hp KG7H and the new approximately 15-cubic-inch 7½-horse Rocket Hurricane KG4H. For the latter, the powerhead was taken directly from the "standard" 7.5-hp KG4 advertised as a fishing engine. Interestingly, in fall 1952 one could select from three 7½-horse Merc "fishin' motors." There was the old reliable 11-cubic-inch KE4, its updated (1953) sister, the Mark 7, and the KG4.

During the mid-Eighties, I purchased a KG4 that appeared to have just come out of the factory packing carton. In late 1952 a gentleman retired to a little lake hamlet in Georgia. As a retirement gift, his familiy went to the local Merc franchise in search of a nice 7.5-horse fishing motor. They had their choice of the functional KE4, a generic Mark 7, and as the dealer stated, a "top-of-the-line seven-and-a-half-horsepower model, KG4 Rocket Hurricane." Wanting only the best for their elderly loved one, a shiny green KG4 was selected.

Although the KE4 and Mark 7 rigs were 11-cubic-inch garden-variety fishing models, the larger displacement KG4 was never made for trolling. It was probably offered on a standard lower unit only to prove the KG4H production run economical.

Well, the KG4's high compression made it nearly impossible for the poor old fellow to rope over. When his son was summoned to get the gift going, the younger man had a tough time, too. Little idling was accomplished on that maiden voyage, and brave bursts of throttle practically stood the senior citizen's 10-foot aluminum jonboat on end! Needless to say, oars were used until the subsequent presentation of a more suitable Sears-Roebuck putt-putt. The sassy KG4 waited out her next 30-plus years in a garage corner.

Carl Kiekhaefer continued bristling at charges his Mercs were simply show-offs' motors. By 1951 Evinrude and Johnson began selling hundreds of their versatile 25-hp twins. Admittedly, Mercury's KG9 (there was never a KG9H) 25-horse rig was much sexier and faster than OMC's offering, but Kiekhaefer's motors lacked one important Evinrude/Johnson detail: a gearshift. Without this function, a bigger outboard became tricky to handle, especially when docking or water-skiing. So, an F-N-R Merc was quickly planned for fall 1951 release. Time constraints, however, allowed only the new "shift" lower unit to be ready for the '52 catalog. As a result, available approximately 20-cubic-inch Hurricane powerheads were mounted on these parts.

The whole product was officially dubbed the Super 10 Hurricane Cruiser, model KH7. Some advertising showed the Cruiser towing a pair of water-skiers or pushing an outboard cabin cruiser. Because the Hurricane power plant got much of its punch from high rpm provided by light loads, outstanding operation under such applications may have been an adman's wish. A good motor, but no real competition for the OMC 25s that had more torque, Merc's Cruiser served primarily as a "transition motor" and was gone by 1953.

A new pair of shift motors was soon introduced, and simplified model designations became Kiekhaefer's 1953 trade-mark. Merc's K nomenclature (as in KE7, KG9, etc.), used since 1940, gave way to motors known as "Mark" something. The two F-N-R engines, bred from the old KH7 Cruiser, were the 10-horse Mark 15 (so-called for its approximately 15-cubic-inch, KG4-type powerhead) and the 16-hp approximately 20-cube Mark 20. These rich green and silver outboards made use of a remote fuel tank system and featured styling so sleek it masked the power plant's capabilities.

Also available for 1953 were a popular 5-horse Mark 5; the updated KE4; a 7½-hp now called the Mark 7 (a brief factory memo offered dealers new Mark 7 ID plates in exchange for KE4 identification, which enabled 1947–52 new/old-stock KE4 motors to be sold as 1953 Mark 7 products); and the old 40-cubic-inch Mercury 25, KG9, renamed Mark 40. Most exotic of the 1953 Mercs was a neck-snapping Mark 40H. Company brochures correctly referred to this kicker as "the winningest thrill mill on water!"

In 1954 a batch of successful Mark 20 motors had their Tillotson carburetors replaced with Carter carbs, were given some strengthened parts, some gold accents, and a side-mounted spark advance lever, and were mounted on a Hydro-Short Quicky lower unit. The resulting Mark 20H kickers became the most popular stock racers in competitive outboard history.

Kiekhaefer's high-volume sales hopes, however, were pinned

The author displays his 1952 Mercury KG7H with Hydro-Short Quicksilver racing lower unit. (Gas tank color should be cedar green.) This was the motor to beat in the early 1950s. Notice that the lower cowling is gone. Most of these covers were removed and discarded by racers wanting a "meaner" look and faster access to engine components.

Early 1950s Mercury ads, ready to go to press.

to the brand-new 1954, four-in-line, 40-horse Mark 50. With a full gearshift (finally!), optional electric start, and remote controls, it clearly did OMC's 25-hp motors one better. A small gold crown affixed to the Mark 50's face signaled Mercury's royal entry into the profitable family-oriented water-skiing/cruising market. This marked the first time Mercury offered a bigger shift motor than did Evinrude and Johnson. While Carl Kiekhaefer owned the company, it was a race Merc would always win.

Appropriately, 1955's big Mercury was labeled Mark 55. Available with electric start (MercElectric Mark 55E), this 40-horse rig's color scheme departed from traditional Merc green, making its debut in a coral tint. Also updated for 1955 was the 20-cube Hurricane, now in the form of a Mark 25 (and electric-starting Mark 25E), wearing an 18-hp rating. A Mark 6 (5.9 hp) made its entrance that year too. (Note: In many fall 1955 Mercury showrooms, you could find a Mark 5, 6, and 7.)

Would there be a Mark 56 in 1956? No. The Mark 55 was simply carried over from the previous year. New in that 40-cubic-inch range, however, was the Mark 55H racer. Those wanting to compete in the 30-cube outboard class were treated to the Turbo-

Four Mark 30H Mercury. A standard Mark 30 (as well as electric-start Mark 30E) provided small cruisers and family runabouts enough zip to handle extended ranges and pull a few water-skiers. It could be equipped with a steering arm for local control. Mark 25s of 1956 were rerated at 20 horses.

The company responsible for those legendary old green motors became increasingly design conscious, offering buyers an authentic Fifties choice of "Two-Tone Merchromatic Colors," like Sarasota Blue, Sand, Silver, Mercury Green (the original cedar green), Marlin Blue, Sunset Orange, Tan, and Gulf Blue.

Kids fond of arguing which motor was truly fastest sent a "Wow, keen!" Mercury's way in 1957. Mr. Kiekhaefer's 2-cycle engine research, begun for the government in World War II, led him to continue with the in-line cylinder format. Six such cylinders, yielding approximately 60 cubic inches of displacement, made up the sparkling new Mark 75E Marathon-Six. Johnson and Evinrude's premium 35s fell far short of this tall kicker's 60 hp. Folks thinking the Mark 75 actually had 75 hp understand why the PR people recommended such labeling.

Along with their great ideas, many famous inventors have embraced a clunker or two. Thomas Edison was long convinced that disc records were simply a flash in the pan compared to his cylindrical recordings.

Similarly, Carl Kiekhaefer held unusual convictions about reversing a big outboard. Perhaps the gearfoot failures of giant kickers like Riley and Fageol caused Merc's father to insist that such powerhouses would always rip up a standard reversing gearshift system. As a result, the huge Mercs were given Direct-Reverse. When backing, this mode actually called for the motor to be momentarily shut off and restarted in reverse! Even so, the Mark 75, with the industry's first single-lever remote control, was quite a machine.

Besides mass-producing the world's first six-cylinder, in-line, 2-cycle outboard, Mercury also put together a few Mark 75H racers. In 1958 a Quicksilver-lower-unit-equipped 75H on a little plywood Aero-Marine Special hydro ($5 plans were available for years from *Science and Mechanics* magazine) "set a new official outboard speed record . . . [at almost 108 mph] returning the title to the United States for the first time since 1937." This honor was held by Mercury into the 1960s.

The late Fifties were a time filled with the essence of "new." Old was getting squarer, outer space would soon be entered, and only items as sleek as rockets were perceived to have a future. Merc designers worked overtime shaping modern powerhead covers. A Trol Twin Rocket, Mark 10 model was fitted with a red top resembling a futuristic fireman's helmet. Engine exhaust shot through the propeller hub.

This 10-hp motor and 22-horse Mark 28 were the first Mercs to receive the "on your mark, get set" look in which the power-head seemed to be leaning forward with lower unit angled out in anticipation. Such a design reduced the possibility of snagging

When competitors Johnson and Evinrude unveiled their 1957 twin cylinder, 35-hp, top-of-the-line motors, Mercury took them by surprise with a tall, 6-cylinder, in-line Mark 75. This Marathon-Six sported 60 cubic inches and 60 hp. The Dyna-Float on the lower unit is a small shock absorber. (Mercury Marine)

In 1964 Carl Kiekhaefer celebrated his firm's 25th anniversary. Shown with a '64 3.9 h.p. single and one-lung 1940 Merc, the founder smiles for a publicity shot.

underwater weeds. Dyna Float shocks rubber-mounted the motor leg for smoother operation. In keeping with the modern theme, these outboards came with spring-loaded, automatic F-N-R transmissions. When they worked, they were OK, but few Merc repair shops enjoyed getting one that didn't. No other manufacturer had such a shifter.

Needless to say, you could always tell a Mercury from its competitors. For 1958 OMC dealers were shipped chubby V-4, 50-horse engines, but Mercury bested its rivals by 20 hp with its lanky new Mark 78E.

Motors from six-cylinder versions to the Mark 6 twin were tested at Kiekhaefer's Lake X. Fabled to be secret, this private Florida waterway was equipped with jump ramps, obstructive logs, and anything else that might stress an outboard. A couple of Mark 75A (60-horse) powered runabouts spent 68 days on Lake X in continuous operation, racking up 50,000 miles each. The boats were refueled, food provided, and drivers switched while in motion. The "record endurance run [meant to represent many years of typical outboard use] . . . at an average speed of 30.3 mph was certified by the U.S. Auto Club." That way, OMC couldn't dispute it.

Although Carl Kiekhaefer successfully augmented Mercury's performance image via factory-built racing models, he was well aware the fast little power plants set few sales records. Johnson and Evinrude produced no competition outboards from World War II through the later Sixties, but were very busy turning out thousands of family-oriented motors. Kiekhaefer aimed for a greater degree of that lucrative leisure market and decided to make 1958 the final year his firm would offer a Quicksilver racer. Consequently, the approximately 30-cubic-inch Mark 30H became the last 1950s' Mercury of its type. Those looking hard enough, however, discovered a tiny scattered stock of leftover Mark 20H, 55H, and 30H rigs through the very early 1960s. The Kiekhaefer Corporation completed the Eisenhower decade still on top of the horsepower hill with their six-cylinder, in-line, 70-horse Mark 78A.

As 1960 Mercurys were ushered in, the well-worn model nomenclature *Mark* was shown the back door. Kiekhaefer borrowed an old Martin motor ID technique in which engines are named with their approximate horsepower and an extra zero. Thus, the 10-horse motor became Merc 100; the new 80-hp powerhouse was called Merc 800, and so on. (Exceptions included the likes of a 22-hp Merc 200 and a 35-horse model known as Merc 300.)

With the updated designations came a complete de-emphasis on exotic color schemes. Most Mercs of the late Fifties and very early Sixties were clean white. By 1962 the first black Mercurys would debut.

Kiekhaefer still had hopes for his big Direct-Reverse models. The 70- and 80-hp motors were offered with this drive system in 1960 and 1961. A gearshift version was available in 1961, and logically, soon replaced direct-reversing Mercs.

The year 1962 became one of the most notable in Mercury outboard history. First, all models got equipped with Jet-Prop, through-the-propeller hub exhaust. (The firm's major boat show displays included a gigantic silver prop turning slowly and blowing colored streamers via a hidden fan attached to the hub.)

Finally, the world's first 100-hp production outboard, the big Merc 1000, was unveiled. Something about all those zeroes captured the public's fancy, and even die-hard Evinrude/Johnson fans (OMC's top motor had 25 fewer horses in 1962) couldn't help but salute Mercury's notable achievement.

Kiekhaefer had decided in summer 1961 to merge his company with the Brunswick Corporation. A recreation-oriented conglomerate with interests in everything from a pop record label to bowling equipment manufacturing, Brunswick was happy to acquire Mercury's expanding consumer marine propulsion niche. This amalgamation brought extra fiscal strength to Merc but quickly placed its iron-willed founder in an environment where he no longer called the shots.

Within a few years, Brunswick deleted the vintage Kiekhaefer Mercury logo in favor of a Mercury Marine nameplate, and in 1970 Carl Kiekhaefer left what was once his organization.

Prior to this departure, a pair of interesting, limited-edition, competition Mercs was introduced. One, the 7.2-cubic-inch Merc 60J, wore a pint-size edition of the old Quicksilver lower unit. It was meant to be raced by kids and petite women and could get a mini hull going 40 mph. The other rig came in the form of a 125-hp powerhouse suitable for rugged, offshore races.

Meanwhile, Brunswick concentrated on marketing a wide range of consumer outboards and MerCruiser stern drives. The big company's methodical promotion was quite successful but lacked Kiekhaefer's "let's take a chance on this one" flair.

Perhaps wanting to do to Brunswick's Mercury what Ole Evinrude did with Elto to his former firm, Mr. Kiekhaefer started a company called Kiekhaefer Aeromarine Motors. While a few Aeromarine kickers were developed for auxiliary sailboat power, and some snowmobile engines were built for Bolens, Kiekhaefer's second dream didn't materialize. The outboard pioneer, who ran a prominent boat motor concern with greater nerve and individuality than anyone before or since, passed away in 1983.

5 | Private Brands

On a Monday morning in 1913 some guy at Sears-Roebuck told coworkers about a very strange sight. He had witnessed two fishermen hang an unusual metal device on the stern of a little rowboat. One angler cranked the thing's top, causing smoke to sputter from the device. It then proceeded to move their craft right past other fishing boats, allowing first dibs on the big ones.

"We'd better look into that," suggested one of the mail-order store's buyers. "Could be something to it. Somebody see who can make a few for us."

The next year's Sears catalog included a genuine Motorgo (built by the Lockwood-Ash Company) rowboat motor, and the private-brand outboard was born.

A private-brand motor is any kicker designed and constructed by one company for sale through some other firm. Breweries often do this type of thing by producing beer (complete with a custom label) for a grocery store chain. Private-brand outboards, like those brewed supermarket counterparts, are generally intended to be a little less chic than their name-brand cousins. Consequently, their price tags are smaller.

The lineage of many private-brand engines is clearly recognizable. Uniqueness in these badge-engineered rigs is found only in a decal, a paint scheme, or a minor, cosmetic cowling feature. Other rigs were made of a major's stock of leftover or obsolete parts. While these models' appearance contained a hint of their better-known kin, they retained a specific distinction.

Outboard makers often viewed private-brand contracts as financial blessings. Not only did such agreements mean the certain sale of a large block of motors, but shelves of theretofore surplus parts began producing revenue. A strong desire to keep the wholesale purchasers happy resulted in some pretty good and attractively priced outboard motors.

The early Sears Motorgo outboards were soon followed by Montgomery Ward's (Caille-produced) Hiawatha rowboat motors. Other vintage marques, such as Sweet, Anderson, Blakely, and (some

Sears ad featuring a Caille-built 1930 Motorgo outboard.

Caille-built) Gray kickers, were most probably private-brand motors. This book's outboard list (see Chapter 11) provides more detail.

By the early 1930s Outboard Motors Corporation, later Outboard Marine and Manufacturing, began taking on private-brand contracts for the likes of Montgomery Ward and Canada's Eaton stores.

During the late Thirties, Thor, a struggling marque in its own right, badge-engineered some Sea Kings. Unfortunately, these poor performers contributed to the firm's demise. A stock of the rejected motors, however, gave birth to the Mercury outboard line.

Scott-Atwater got its start building Champions (originally sold through Firestone stores) and then Firestone-brand kickers.

Waterwitch, Sears's outboard name plate from 1936 to 1945, had numerous origins. The most unusual actually came from the world's most prolific outboard company—Johnson! For some unknown reason, Johnson's Waterwitch contract was canceled after only a few motors were shipped. Information concerning other rare Thirties private brands, such as the little Kingfisher, has been largely forgotten.

It appears the Great Depression created another sort of private brand. Reportedly, a number of outboard dealers, struggling to survive the broken economy, made their own motors from spare parts. Typically, these rigs wore a brand name (like Evinrude or Elto), but didn't look exactly like anything in the current catalog. Any "weirdo" from about 1931 to about 1936 just might be such a concoction. Of course, the outboard manu-facturers were not happy with this practice, but it served as a trade-off for Depression-era bargain motor sales held at factory showrooms.

In 1938 things brightened up a bit, and Outboard Marine and Manufacturing shifted much private-brand work to its Gale Products Division. Montgomery Ward's Sea King and Western Auto's Western Flyer were just two marques to originate at this Galesburg, Illinois, facility.

Post–World War II kicker demand sent OMC's private-brand plant into high gear, and by 1951 the busy factory was cranking out 3-, 5-, and 12-hp motors in seven badge-engineered versions. A few more (short-lived) private-brand contracts, such as Aimcee Wholesale Corporation's AMC Saber, sent the Gale staff into overtime.

During this era, one-third of all outboard motor sales was attributed to private brands. Thousands of that number came from the West Bend Aluminum Company and were marketed under Sears's Elgin label.

The Fifties' "bigger is better" philosophy increased many private-brand offerings to full-range (1.5-hp to over-35-hp) lines. Scores of family runabouts and cruisers got powered by large Elgins, Buccaneers, Sea-Bees, Firestones, and Brooklures. Even so, private-brand horsepower ratings were traditionally a bit lower

WATERWITCH

OUTBOARD MOTORS

Sold exclusively by
SEARS, ROEBUCK & CO.

Logo for the Sears Waterwitch, which was built by Kissel.

The Wizard, circa 1946, built by Kiekhaefer Mercury.

than comparable major-brand models. For example, Gale Products' 1955 top-of-the-line units produced 22 hp, compared to the conglomerate's Evinrude and Johnson 25.

Flashiest of the Fifties private brands was no doubt the Wizard. Made for Western Auto by Kiekhaefer Mercury, Wizards shared Merc's fast "ball and roller bearing power" design. While other private brands' modest literature featured practical aspects of owning a nice, low-priced motor, Wizard's 1953 brochure boasted two world's speed records!

> In races run under supervision of the National Outboard Association at Memphis, Tennessee, a Wizard 10 skimmed the measured mile at 48.8 mph to set a new world's record for class "B" modified service runabouts. A Wizard also won the class "A" race—on the same day [7/20/52]—establishing a new world's record for that classification of 45.1 mph. Both records [were] officially recognized by the NOA.

The pamphlet indicated these Wizards were "modified for racing," which probably means they rode on high-speed Mercury Quicksilver lower units.

The aforementioned records were obtained "legally" in sanctioned events. Racing legend holds, however, that some class "A" racers (officially restricted to outboards with piston displacement less than 15 cubic inches) disguised the "look-alike" 18.34-cube Wizard 10 powerhead under a Mercury (class "A") gas tank. When such a rig was mated to the Quicksilver lower unit, it gave an unfair cylinder-size advantage over those who followed rules. Because this practice was allegedly pulled off below the Mason-Dixon line, such a motor got dubbed a "Southern A."

Unlike most private brands, Wizards were nationally advertised in such publications as *Field and Stream*, *Sports Afield*, *Outdoor Life*, and *True*. Western Auto even commissioned a 16-mm motion picture called *Sea Chasers*. This half-hour film about exciting professionals who search oceans to stock Miami's Seaquarium featured shots of sharks, dolphins, and working Wizard outboards. Civic clubs and sports groups could borrow a copy by writing to Western Auto.

After 1957 the "Medium (pea soup) Green" (with red decals) Merc-built Wizards were no longer marketed, although a few remote, independently owned Western Auto stores had leftovers through the early Sixties. Going out in style were some Wizard Super 10 rigs. They had finally been given remote fuel tanks, upped to almost 20 cubic inches (using the noted Merc Hurricane block), and supplied with special crankshafts from Mercury's recently discontinued Mark 20H racer![1]

No one appears certain why Kiekhaefer stopped Wizard production. Some say growing sales of its name-brand Mercury models simply required more and more manufacturing space. Suggestions have also surfaced indicating Mercury dealers wanted Kiekhaefer-built Wizards off the market. They realized the generic, lower-priced Wizard actually had an uncomfortable number of thoroughbred Mercury features. Private-brand motors were meant for a marketplace somewhat less sophisticated than the marina/boat store clientele. When Wizard began acquiring a reputation, it stepped over a sacred boundary.

Significant line changes in the early-to-mid-Sixties outboard industry affected private-branding. OMC's Gale Products' Gale-Buccaneer closed up shop in 1964. Along with it went the last of its private-brand contracts. McCulloch, which evolved from Scott-Atwater, acted as this era's leading private-brander, producing the final Elgin and subsequent Sears and Ted Williams marques. It even gave Western Auto a late-Fifties–early-Sixties spin with nicely stylized Wizards (featuring PowerBail automatic bailing). West Bend, so renowned for its fine Elgin contributions, eventually made some Wizards and then sold out to Chrysler.

Large auto-related retailers (Firestone, Goodyear, and B.F. Goodrich), once eager to market a complete line of private-brand kickers, decided to get back to basics. As a result, they either dropped their outboard line entirely, or went with a drastically reduced offering of a couple of fishing motors. When the latter occurred, a small company, such as Clinton or Eska, usually gained the contract. Remaining late 1960s private brands were largely the province of minor producers. Single-cylinder, air-cooled Tecumseh powerheads were the standard fare.

By the mid-1970s foreign-made kickers appeared at large American retail chains. Additionally, major U.S. outboard firms, such as Mercury, began obtaining Japanese motors to sell under their own and subsidiary (such as Mariner) labels.

Over the years, parts and service problems have plagued private-brand owners. Many major brand's franchised repair departments prejudicially view such rigs as troublesome orphans. I recall visiting a busy big-name outboard dealership when a man carried in a private-brand rig that "wouldn't idle too good." The shop's three mechanics rolled their eyeballs. After superficially examining that 5-horse twin, one technician recommended, "Do yourself a favor; go into our showroom and trade up to a real motor!"

In reality, of course, private-brand kickers are as authentic as any brand-name motor. And most importantly, since 1914 they have been responsible for an impressive amount of outboarding pleasure.

1. Lawrence Carpenter, "Antique Corner—Wizard," *Trailer Boats* (January 1989), p. 164.

Notes

6

Hot-Rod Outboards

Just a few years earlier, Jim Bouton would not have noticed the young woman who was watching a beautiful mahogany inboard being launched. As she stepped into the expensive runabout, Jim studied her gently curving blue swimsuit . . . but only for a moment, as the 15-year-old boy was much more experienced critiquing a boat's lines. And this brightly varnished craft looked like a million!

The young lady's companion whispered something to her. They laughed, and a hefty-sounding marine engine came to life. Higher points of a slight chop choked the inboard's exhaust, creating a deep, slow, oscillating murmur. The blue one-piece shifted a touch as its wearer and the smiling fellow at the wheel glanced aft. Sun sparkled off the mahogany sheen while the fancy boat slowly backed out of the marina.

Jim recalled being cautioned against showing off, but this was different. He sprinted carefully on the long, floating dock. His boat, neatly moored to the end section, was a well-built, homemade, plywood utility. The 10-footer received power from a big, late-model '51 Scott-Atwater 16-horse twin.

The rich green outboard motor needed five pulls as nervous anticipation caused its operator initially to forget the closed fuel valve. Soon, however, each boat was under way, and Jim was quickly approaching his challenger. The girl leaned toward her friend, said something, and pointed to Jim. The inboard picked up a little speed and maneuvered to within 25 feet of its smaller counterpart. When the two decks were even, both drivers instinctively saluted and poured on the coal.

A small lever on the mahogany rig's steering wheel roared the bigger boat over the water's near perfect surface. Auburn hair danced on the woman's head. Jim squeezed his throttle handle until the silver lever made contact with its backstop. The Scott-Atwater sang while skimming its owner a few inches past his competitor.

Crouching lower let Jim's pumpkin seed of a boat overcome enough resistance to keep the boy "king of the lake." The couple's smiles became a bit less confident but were included with polite waves. Their regal runabout veered off toward an island.

Later, Jim noticed them tie up and head over to his portion of dock.

"Well, you sure embarrassed a seven-thousand-dollar boat and her smug owners," the young man joked.

"It's a beauty anyway," Jim responded.

"How'd that old Scott get so fast?"

The boy hopped into his tiny craft and slowly raised the motor. As its prop broke through the quiet surface, the inboard man smiled again.

"Oh! So that's it!"

"Yeah," said Jim, smiling. "A special Green-Hornet racing lower unit with a high-speed Michigan prop."

"Sure puts a wild streak in a family outboard!" the man conceded.

"It helps me be the fastest around here . . . for now, anyway, until someone gets a hotter motor."

"Seen any hungry Merc Lightnings, Thunderbolt four-cylinder jobs, Champ Hot Rods, or Martin 200s?" he asked.

"Not here," the boy said thoughtfully. "Not yet."

The inboard skipper issued, "Good luck," and walked toward the restaurant. The pretty young woman in the blue swimsuit smiled too, and Jim Bouton wondered if he and his Scott-Atwater would ever have another day like this.

Apparently, the first real outboard race (albeit a verrrry slow one) occurred on Lake Pewaukee, Wisconsin, in the summer of 1911. A field of contestants piloting bulky, flat-bottomed rowboats putt-putted toward the finish line. An Evinrude won—basically because *all* the skiffs were powered by that well-known brand.

This victory gave the young outboard company enough confidence to order a specially engraved Evinrude Cup and stage its own race. Unfortunately, the April 1914 four-mile event didn't provide that firm with any usable publicity. Some entrants from California showed up with a "hot" 1913 Waterman Porto motor and won the Evinrude trophy.[1] Even so, Waterman folded a few years later, and the defeat was largely forgotten.

Through the early 1920s there were, no doubt, hundreds of informal outboard races. Many were simply the product of one

A 1930 Evinrude Speeditwin racer with twin carbs and steering handle. A rare rig! This model 177 wore carburetors from the 1929 Lockwood Racing Chief. Evinrude's limited edition racer was made for a "few hundred American sportsmen."

Battery-fired 1928 Elto Speedster about to be started. (Shipyard Museum)

angler betting a beer his eggbeater-powered fishing tub would reach shore before the other fellow's. Kids with access to dad's new twin-cylinder Koban or Ferro single probably put such early rigs to competitive use too. And there were even a few contests between outboard and manually driven boats, with the motor *usually* winning!

The swiftest outboard boats of this era (the first few years after World War I) were actually square-stern canoes. Because their thin hulls displaced less water than did wide rowboats, these craft had some speed potential. Elto's mid-Twenties Ruddertwin could push a canoe at 10 mph.

That was, indeed, fast in outboarding circles . . . until Johnson's preproduction 1926 Big Twin P-30 was tested in the summer of '25. This 6-horse rig got its boat and driver up on plane achieving 16.15 mph. Other motor makers (and boat companies) took note, and new outboard speeds were racked up almost daily.

Evinrude countered with its 1927 Speeditwin, an 8-hp kicker that doubled in power the following year. Johnson's 1928 TR-40 (*R* for racing) Giant Twin became the world's largest piston displacement (at 50 cubic inches) opposed twin, aiming its bulk at being fastest too. Lockwood also entered the speedy fray with nicely engineered Ace and Chief motors. Caille introduced racers, some with twin carbs and tractor (propeller in front) lower units.

In my view the first real hot-rod motor was unveiled in the fall of 1927 as the 1928 Elto Speedster. This mechanically straightforward beauty was one of the first to employ a sleek lower unit and aggressive two-blade, high-speed prop. It had to do 22-plus mph or it didn't leave the factory. While not competitive in organized events, the Speedster was, arguably, the first "Corvette" of the outboard world.

The Speedster's big, four-cylinder brother (actually components from two Speedsters) was the Elto Quad. Also introduced as a '28, the Quad took its industry by storm and beat everything in sight.

For 1929 the Speedster and the Quad came in an H, or high-speed, version. Quads were breaking 40 mph. Compare this figure with 1925's 16.15 mph!

In 1929 Johnson rebounded in racing circles with its four-cylinder, approximately 40-cubic-inch V-45 and VR-45 racer. An approximately 20-cube opposed twin with S-45 and SR-45 designations also made Johnson catalogs that year.

With all this new equipment, races were springing up from coast to coast. Many were sanctioned by the American Power Boat Association (APBA) and the National Outboard Association (NOA). Specific motor size classifications were developed to ensure fair competition. Although the categories changed a bit, they may be identified in the accompanying table delineating classes.

Motor Size Classification

Class	Motor's Cylinder Displacement
M (or J)	up to 7.5 cu. in.
A	up to 15 "
B	up to 20 "
C	up to 30 "
D	up to 40 "
E	up to 50 "
F	up to 60 "

(Please note: When a kicker is referred to as, say, a 20-cube model, it is typically just under that mark. For example, the famous 1950s Mercury Hurricane class "B" engines check in at 19.8 cubic inches.)

Testing a 1928-29 Elto Speedster near the Milwaukee Elto factory. (Shipyard Museum)

The Elto people kept bumping up their Quad's displacement from 40 to 50, and finally to 60. This class "F" Quad, dubbed 4-60 (four cylinders, 60 cubic inches), gained an instant following and remains the granddaddy of all big outboard racing machines.

Johnson tried hitting the 4-60 with a 50-cube, four-cylinder XR-55 (1931) but made little impact. Johnson's greatest Thirties racing contributions consisted of its alternate-firing KR, as well as the (updated) SR and PR opposed twins. Throughout the late 1940s (and in some cases mid-1950s) they dominated class A, B, and C racing, respectively.

Many of the aforementioned motors saw service on the sterns of collegiate racers' boats. Numerous schools, such as Syracuse University, sponsored teams (drivers usually purchased their own outfits) which challenged other scholastic outboard enthusiasts. Begun in earnest during the late Twenties, this intercollegiate event had faded out by World War II.

Just about every outboard maker engaged in manufacturing high-speed rigs poured loads of money into a few promising motors. These expensive kickers went to "factory drivers" paid to "win one for the public relations/advertising department." Every time a race was won by a certain outboard, its maker could use the victory to sell more products. Most of these sales were related to small fishing motors, but the race glory definitely played a role. In any event, racing engines were constantly being factory-modified.

The late Dick Hawie, who knew more about outboard racing history than just about anyone, once told me, "In those days, as far as I can tell from the racing rules, only 25 motors [of a specific model] had to be made to get the motor approved. If the motor wasn't making it on the racing circuit, it is possible some of the 25 were [quickly] modified by the factory to make them go faster, and they then became a part of the new 25, but the model and serial number weren't changed. [Rules mandated] the factory had to have 25 motors for sale, but they did not have to sell 25. In 1930 there was also a Division IV for factory drivers who could

A winning driver poses with his trophy and a 1930 Elto Quad. (Shipyard Museum)

A cedar strip boat with a 22-horse Johnson PO.

race 'non-stock' motors, so who knows what some of the 'approved' racing motors actually looked like?"

Dick was addressing a question raised by an unusual 1930 model 177 Evinrude Speeditwin racer I had added to my outboard collection. That was in 1987, when about five model 177s were known to exist. Two were only 12 serial numbers apart, and yet all five are noticeably different!

Spending needed cash on racing programs just to keep up with some other company that was consuming funds trying to keep up with the first firm, with the ultimate goal of promoting 3-horse fishing engines, started to lose its appeal among outboard companies. Eventually, they got together and agreed to limit these practices. Money spent on "factory drivers" and equipment was then channeled into more lucrative consumer motor areas. But sometimes there was a little something left in the budget for an occasional new racing model.

Elto/Evinrude's 4-60 was joined (circa 1936) by a new Speeditwin racer with hexagonal cylinder heads (so it could be secured to its cylinder better, with six bolts instead of the typical four). This class "C" Hex-Head Speeditwin had battery ignition and used Johnson's external-rotary-valve technology. Such engineering was the by-product of Elto/Evinrude acquiring Johnson in 1936.

The 4-60 and the Hex-Head Speeditwin had a baby sister in the form of the tiny, 7.5-cube, class "M" Midget Racer. Although the little Evinrude could be lifted with one hand, it powered many hydros (piloted by kids and petite women) over 40 mph!

Many of the Thirties motors, from class "M" to "F," picked up extra rpm after being converted to run on alcohol (methanol) and castor oil. The "alky" outboards sounded more like model airplane engines than boat motors.

Johnson made racers through 1936. Remaining Elto/Evinrude racing rigs were built until 1940. Meanwhile, 1939 saw the introduction of the model 6039 Evinrude Speeditwin. This 30-cubic-inch motor not only served in World War II, but returned after the war and stayed in Evinrude catalogs through 1950! The model 6039 was designed to be a pleasure, or regular-service, motor and had little of the gadgetry claimed by its Hex-Head cousin. Still, the 6039 became a hot-rod motor used on light family runabouts. Additionally, this classic received some homebrew tinkering (new pistons and higher compression, etc.) and became a star in an outboard racing class called "C-Service." Some of these old-timers are still being raced today!

Johnson marketed a similar-sized motor called the model PO. It, too, was long-lived (1937–1950) and was often used as a hot-rod engine.

Following the war, outdoors enthusiasts bought fishing and family outboards like crazy—or, at least they would have, had there been enough to go around. Almost every motor company had real orders to fill and no time to spend on kickers not sought by the general public. So Outboard Marine & Manufacturing Company, the last outfit to make racers, concentrated on the most popular outboard models and offered no postwar-era racing products.

This vacuum pulled small firms into the picture. Names like Clyde Wiseman, Starnes, Fuller, Marshall Eldredge, and Randolph Hubbell began producing newly cast parts designed to keep the prewar racers operable.

A war surplus pump (made by Johnson for the U.S. Navy) had some characteristics of the old class "A" KR and was quickly discovered by racing nuts. These folks used some new and used parts and lots of basement workshop ingenuity to turn the "pumpers" into competitors.

The Hubbell shop in California eventually made enough new/old-style outboard parts to offer nice copies of 1930s Johnson PR, SR, and KR motors. Typically, these rigs burned a fuel mixture of alcohol (methanol) and castor oil, and required some mechanical expertise to operate well.

There was a need for a "stock" motor a kid could take out of a box, put on his homebrew hydro, gas up, and pull the cord to go fast. Kiekhaefer Mercury was cruising for some publicity and answered the call.

Since 1947, Merc's KE7, 20-cubic-inch Lightning 10 had been attracting lots of attention. The firm's 11-cube KE4, 7½-hp Rocket was also somewhat quicker than the average fishing motor.

Mr. Kiekhaefer noted some outboard hot-rod nuts fooling around with his products in hopes of a few more miles per hour. He soon sent some Mercury staffers on a similar quest, resulting in developments like the "Quick Silver" (early literature breaks it into two words) racing lower unit. When mated to a KE7 or subsequent KF7 Lightning, this piece put stock outboard racing within the reach of a whole new generation of boating enthusiasts.

The Kiekhaefer Corporation wasn't the only organization working on a stock racer. During the summer of 1949, Martin unveiled an 11-cubic-inch Hi-Speed 60. A modified version of its cornerstone 7.2-horse, alternate-firing fishing twin, the Hi-Speed 60 was truly stripped for action.

In addition to a choice of hot, two-blade props, this rig featured enlarged intake and exhaust ports, mechanically "broke-in" powerhead, Tillotson carb rigged for remote throttle control,

A rare sight for the era, the 1950 Martin 60 Hi-Speed could pull 16-plus horses from its 11-cubic-inch displacement. Martin called its little streamlined racing lower unit the Torpedo.

faster intake poppet-valve timing, copper-clad head gaskets, high-compression head, ball and needle main bearings, steel rods with needle bearings, steering bar, and Torpedo lower unit (with water scoop instead of pump). Martin would sell you the entire Hi-Speed 60 package, or simply provide the racing powerhead, mag, and carb.

Strangely, Martin also marketed that special full-race powerhead on the standard Martin 60 fishing lower unit! Not only would such an engine, equipped with open exhaust (at rest you could look right through the ports and view pistons and rings), scare the wits out of every nearby fish, but trolling speeds would frustrate the poor power plant into stalling. Why anyone would want a high-performance engine on a low-performance lower unit is a question suitable for a psychiatry convention!

Had this cutie's displacement been 7.5 cubic inches (for class "J") or closer to 15 (attaining class "A" status), the Martin Hi-Speed 60 might have become an important 1950s racing factor. At 11 cubic inches, it was neither fish nor fowl.

Here is a quote from a 1987 letter I received from outboard racing historian Dick Hawie:

> This motor is a strange displacement, 11 cubic inches. The Hi-Speed "60" had open exhaust, so it really didn't fit any APBA class. It wouldn't fit stock classes with that open exhaust, and the class "A" alky KR motor had a bigger displacement of 13.96 cubic inches . . . three inches more! It's pretty hard to beat cubic inches. I don't know why Martin made the attempt. I doubt many were sold. One of their ads boasted all kinds of wins, but this was in 1949 in local [non-sanctioned] races where, I suspect, the rules didn't allow other motors. It's hard to believe a poppet valve Martin Hi-Speed "60" could compete with a rotary valve KR in circa 1950 APBA racing.

Incidentally, some of these interesting kickers were converted to alcohol fuel. Even so, the little Martin Hi-Speed 60 was never a common sight and is a very rare motor today.

Actually, its largest exposure was in the form of a few grainy photos perpetually seen in *Science and Mechanics* and *Boat Builder's Handbook* magazines. From the early Fifties through the Seventies those publications often included plans for an 8-foot hydro called Yellow Jacket. The first Yellow Jacket had been tested with a Martin Hi-Speed 60. One of the last issues of the *Boat Builder's Handbook* (late 1970s) still ran the Yellow Jacket "craft prints" and accompanying shots of the small Martin. It even informed readers what kind of fuel mixes to use (gas- or alcohol-based), all for a motor that had been scarce as hen's teeth for years.

While studying some rather obscure outboard specifications, I noticed a listing for a Martin Hi-Speed 100. This may have been a misprint (or jumping the gun by someone in the advertising department), as no one else seems to recall a racing version of Martin's 13.15-cubic-inch, 10-hp job.

Martin's first racing motor was like the mouse that roared compared to rigs being generated by Mercury. Their "full-jeweled" (ball, roller, and needle bearings throughout) powerheads with Quicksilver lower units were fast becoming standards in stock outboard racing. In 1950 a specially designed 14.89-cubic-inch, model KG4H (called Rocket-Hurricane) was placed in class "A" competition, quickly jumping the old Johnson KR-generated mile straightaway record from 54 to 61 mph.

The famed Merc Lightning's racing successor, Super 10 Hurricane, model KG7H also joined the high-speed set in 1950. Introductory ads warned: "Look out! Here comes a Hurricane!" The copy then asked: "Want thrills? They're all yours when you rocket out of the pits with a Super Ten Hurricane. And with the Quicksilver lower unit, you'll have the combination you need to win."

Among others, an official with the Italian Navy responded to such plugs. He ordered a fleet of Hurricanes and race boats which were used in certain training exercises.

A larger version of the Quicksilver lower unit was developed for the big 4-cylinder Thunderbolt 25. It soon brought class "D" competition back to life.

May 1952 noted the start of a new magazine geared toward boat racing buffs. Although some inboards and family craft were featured, *Boat Sport* focused on outboard racing. The first issue included an in-depth article on building up a class "A" Johnson KR engine. Most of the articles were handled by veteran outboard racer and boating writer Hank Wieand Bowman and his wife (also with firsthand knowledge of the topic) Blake Gilpin. *Boat Sport* served an audience few other publications courted. Unfortunately, its actual target readership was never broad enough to capture high circulation. After being modified to the more general *Aqua Sport* (bringing in quasi-related subjects like water-skiing) in 1958, it quickly faded from local magazine racks. Mr. Bowman later died in a boating mishap.

Champion Outboard Motors Company began producing a Hot Rod Special in 1949. The 7.9-hp, 12.41-cubic-inch racer never enjoyed much distribution, but was upgraded to 8.5 horses in 1951. Two years later these original Hot Rods were replaced by a line of (9.66-cubic inch) "J," (14.96-cubic inch) "A," and (19.94-cubic inch) "B" racers. Nobody denied Champion made some very nice motors, but most buyers continued jumping on Mercury's stock outboard bandwagon.

A couple hundred Quicksilver-style racing lower units were manufactured by Chris-Craft for its 10-hp motor. Although extremely fast, the motor was discontinued in 1953.

Following false starts in 1951 and 1952, Martin Motors came out with what I believe to have been the ultimate hot-rod outboard. The 1953, nonshift, 19.94-cubic-inch, class "B" Martin 200 Silver Streak featured a beautifully designed Torpedo lower unit. A switch on its control panel shifted fuel input from integral to the remote, Cruise-More tank. The 200's steering handle with

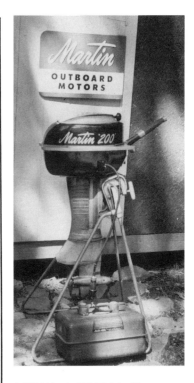

A 1954 Martin 200 (20 hp) with remote, Cruise-More tank.

ribbed red plastic grip could unplug, allowing the motor to accept a plug-in remote speed-control assembly.

This motor was produced with three separate buyers in mind. Outboard cruiser owners were targeted with publicity photos of a 200 (equipped with three-blade power prop) stepping lively on the stern of a well-laden cabin boat. Amateur speedsters noticed 200's sleek lower-unit gear case and nearly 1-to-1 gear ratio. A quick glance confirmed this unit to be far more streamlined than Mercury's standard issue counterpart. Its powerhead was just as healthy as any similar-sized Kiekhaefer product. Martin also hoped to generate some stock racing sales. In early 1954 *Boat Sport* declared

> None of the stock runabout and hydro enthusiasts have any doubts about the Martin "200" class "B" stock motor having plenty of punch. . . . It should be a real threat [for Mercury] in '54.[2]

It had taken over a year from the motor's introduction for some good racing propellers to be developed. And, even with serious high-speed accessories like streamlined gear-case cap and 3-inch-shorter exhaust housing (circa spring 1954) few Martin 200s got into circulation. By that time, company officials had lost interest in the project (the racing accessories actually had been spearheaded by a large Martin dealership), closing up shop for good by fall of 1954. Boatbuilder and outboard racer Harold Kelly, who tried the 200 for *Boat Sport*, had truly expected to see the Martin "winning plenty of races."[3]

Alas, the most notable speed contests these black and silver outboards won consisted of fast price reductions instituted by jilted Martin dealers wanting to get rid of 200s quickly. The 200's demise meant Mercury had been saved from another challenger.

Because it could pass as a "regular" motor, the 200 was arguably the best example of an authentic hot-rod outboard. Where a young fellow would have difficulty convincing his father to purchase a KG7H Mercury for the family's aluminum rowboat, the Martin (with its maker's "good fishin' motor" reputation) just might appeal to dad's sense of the practical. But when that svelte lower unit hit the water and the starter cord brought the 200 to life, "old Pop" would get a few surprises. More importantly, so would the kids hanging around the dock!

The Kiekhaefer Corporation bettered its original KG7H Hurricane with the 1954 Mercury Mark 20H. Promotional literature touting this striking green and gold class "B" powerhouse promised "the speed happy combo" of race-minded powerhead and Hydro-Short Quicksilver lower unit would "rocket you so far out in front you'll be lonesome!" Early 20H owners soon had lots of company, however, as the compact Mercury product became an instant standard in class "B" stock outboard competition.

When the Kiekhaefer Corporation introduced its new 1954

Mercury Mark 20H class "B" stock racing outboard, all of the old Merc "B" engines (namely the KG7H) became obsolete. Try as they might, few KG7H motors could match the extra 4-to-5-mph push offered by the new Mark 20H.

Understandably, racers with pre-1954 Merc "B" rigs were not happy to be left in the land of obsolescence. As a result of this anticipated discontent, Mercury came up with a plan designed to rescue at least some of its old customers.

Kiekhaefer Mercury canceled all 1954 production of its popular 15-cubic-inch, class "A" KG4H engine and, instead of offering a complete "A" motor, marketed only a do-it-yourself "B"- to-"A" conversion kit. With such a package, one could change a 20-cubic-inch KG7H into a (still competitive in 1954) 15-cubic-inch KG4H. In this way all of the 1954 KG4H motors would be born in a home or local Merc dealer workshop.

The kit consisted of a cylinder block, piston set, ring and pin assembly, gasket set, various screws and washers, cowls, protector rim, and a new KG4H serial-number–ID plate. The folks at Mercury would not sell a kit with the new KG4H serial-number–ID plate until the old KG7H plate was sent back to the factory for cancelation. Incidentally, the conversion cost $72.87 (excluding labor) and took about 2½ hours to complete. Somewhere, there must be a record of a block of 1954 KG4H serial numbers assigned exclusively to these do-it-yourself, converted Mercs.

By spring 1955 Mercury's influence had spread to a rather unlikely ally. Randolph Hubbell, the California fellow who made 1930s design racing parts and associated motors, started selling kits mating Johnson SR ("B") and KR ("A") alky powerheads to Merc Quicksilver lower units. Revised APBA rules allowed the use of any approved "stock" lower unit. The Quicky was recognized as a better design than older Johnson types. Hubbell conversions were meant for those wanting to keep their Thirties-style powerheads somewhat competitive. Via this setup, Mr. Hubbell hoped to revive the shrinking stature of the class "A" KR. He continued trying through the early 1960s with a KR alky engine sporting battery ignition, Merc fuel pump, and tuned exhaust pipes, all atop a Quicksilver lower unit. In reality the vintage KR design, regardless of numerous accessories, had already seen its best days.

Amidst slowing sales of its regular motors, the Champion company decided to make a final push for greater class "B" racing honors. In so doing, however, the firm's newly designed 1956 Pacemaker Hot Rod, model 6N-HR, stepped on a few Mercury (Mark 20H) toes. The blue Champs began winning the small number of races they entered, gaining few friends at Kiekhaefer. Impartial buffs agreed the '56 Hot Rod had great potential. Individually "hand-built" at the factory, there were some internal differences from motor to motor. Racing Commission inspectors felt that violated the spirit of "stock" engine rules and disqualified various Hot Rod victors.

An ad from outboard hotrodder Randolph Hubbell.

A well-worn 1951 Evinrude Big Twin 25 hp rests a little prouder on a forward-only racing lower unit, maker unknown.

Kiekhaefer took advantage of Champion's downtime to introduce a tuned-exhaust Howler drive shaft housing for its slipping Mercury Mark 20H. It gave the Mark 20H an edge, and Champion was not allowed, by racing dictates, to follow suit.

Champion's management said 750 Hot Rods were "scheduled for production in 1956," so there would be plenty for everyone. It's unknown if that goal was achieved, but the cleverly engineered class "B" rig, which couldn't seem to get a fair shake, was available through 1958 when Champion quietly closed its corporate doors.

The December 1956 issue of *Boat Sport* introduced Mercury's entire 1957 line. Notables included the class "D" Mark 55H (which evolved from the Mark 40H and older KF9/KG9) and the new 30-cubic-inch Mark 30H. This latter motor quickly revived stock class "C" outboard events. That magazine ad also answered a popular Mercury-nut question: Was there actually a high-speed version of the early six-cylinder, in-line Mark 75? Yes! At the bottom of the page was a picture of a tall powerhead on a short Quicksilver lower unit. The front cowl reads MARK 75H. Its ad copy identifies the big rig as a "competition model of the Mark 75 (60 HP, 60 cubic inches) now entering competition with the promise of breaking most existing records." It was not the type of kicker you'd casually affix to your rowboat, but an interesting (and very limited production) outboard, nonetheless.

Although not intentionally, OMC entered the Fifties stock racing scene. The "36" class, named for its engines' approximately 36- (35.7-) cubic-inch displacement, gathered regional support. Racers usually ran Evinrude Big Twin 25- or 30-hp rigs, as well as Johnson and Buccaneer clones. For some reason the Johnson Sea Horse 30 (identical to the other, similarly endowed OMC products) held most of this category's 1- and 5-mile straightaway speed records.

It was reported (in 1955) that about 6,000 Americans participated in formal outboard racing.[4] Consistent with such a low figure was Champion's assumption that 750 of its Hot Rod models would sufficiently fill the marketplace. With only a few thousand potential racing-motor customers, it's clear that outboard makers would go broke constantly catering to them. The small sales volume, coupled with the relatively low prices the market could bear, left big manufacturers little hope of profit. Mercury, which had enjoyed surviving all other challengers, discontinued stock outboard racing motor production by 1959.

Fast foreign kickers began infiltrating American racing. In the early Sixties only one major, McCulloch, had new U.S.-built factory racers in the catalog. But these were the likes of a class "F" McCulloch model 590, a three-cylinder, triple-carbed heavy-weight with a sleek lower unit but electric starting. Such would never be within reach of the average weekend racer.

In reality all the attention that was paid to Merc's Quicksilver models, Champ Hot Rods, alky motors, and the aforementioned McCullochs, was centered in very small pockets. Although my

Above: Late 1940s Aqua-Jet propeller ad.

Left: Michigan Wheel's offerings for early Mercs.

12-year-old colleagues and I spent hours discussing the merits of, say, a Mark 30H over an Evinrude 4-60, none of us had ever actually seen either one. If you didn't live near a sanctioned race locale or know some retired racer who retained his old rig, all outboard hot-rodding was pretty much left to the imagination.

Perhaps one young boater in a hundred was lucky enough to have a dad who'd help build a real hydroplane. An 8-foot model called the Minimax could be constructed from a pair of 4-by-8-foot sheets of marine plywood. While not suited for strenuous competition, the Minimax was probably the most used hot-rod boat of all time. Its plans appeared in just about every *Popular Mechanics*–type magazine of the Fifties and Sixties.

Even with such a craft, however, few dabbling hot-rodders had an alky KR or full race Merc Hurricane at their disposal. Power more likely originated from a 7½-hp Evinrude Fleetwin.

Back in the late 1940s and early 1950s there were probably many would-be outboard racers who dreamed of owning a fast Johnson PR, a Champion Hot Rod, or a Mercury KG9 equipped with a Quicksilver lower unit. Undoubtedly, however, most of these junior outboarders' activities were the product of a homemade plywood boat pushed by the family Scott-Atwater 7½, Sea King 12 hp, or 10-horse Johnson QD.

Sensing a market for a quick, inexpensive "hop-up" device for the garden-variety outboard, the Michigan Wheel Company introduced its Aqua-Jet (AJ) racing type propellers.

The original AJ prop was a semi-custom piece designed for the KE7 Mercury Lightning. A Michigan catalog (circa 1950) indicates:

> Aqua-Jet propellers are super deluxe racing wheels, virtually custom-built to fit the specific individual motors on which they are to be used, yet priced to sell at practically the cost of a stock propeller. [For example, the 2-blade, 8¾ × 10½-inch bronze AJ prop for a 1949–50 Sea King 12-hp motor was priced at an affordable $12.] Their design is such that no cutting or rebuilding of the lower unit is necessary.

A tired old 1955 Scott-Atwater 16 perked up by a Green Hornet racing lower unit. This piece has only forward gearing, so the shift lever on the side of the motor no longer has any function. The Bail-o-matic is also disconnected. Reportedly, a Scott-Atwater Green Hornet racer prototype was worked up at the factory. This Class "B" competition motor wore the Green Hornet high-speed lower unit as well as dual carburetors.

The Michigan Wheel Company tested various AJ high-speed prop designs on boats and motors of all sizes. Summer testing was done at a lake in Michigan, winter testing on a body of water in Tennessee. Test boats were driven an average of 150 miles per day. Photos of the early post–World War II test craft include shots of Evinrude Speedifour powerhead Whirlwinds, a small Thomson runabout with a 7½-hp Scott-Atwater, and the like. Each boat, including a light, Aero-Craft aluminum rig pushed by a generic-looking Elgin 7½, was equipped with a center wheel deck, a steering wheel, a dead man's (racing) throttle, a speedometer, and an electronic tachometer.

Apparently, these boats, motors, and test gear received quite a workout. Some styles of AJ props pushed these rigs through their paces for up to six weeks before the Michigan Wheel engineering and field staffs were satisfied with a prop's pitch/diameter and design. When mounted on an outboarder's properly recommended motor and associated light hull, the Michigan Aqua-Jet prop gave its owner an extra punch unavailable with the engine's original stock propeller.

Today, the AJ prop is, perhaps, one of the easiest-to-spot vintage outboard parts. Typically, these two-blade, highly pitched, bronze wheels are seen hanging on nails in the parts departments of many a small boat shop. Because these "new old-stock" units do not fit on many of the new motors, the prices are not too unreasonable. When polished, an AJ prop can really dress up a restored outboard's appearance and performance.

Most AJ propellers have an ID number (such as AJ47) on the end of the hub (where the prop nut goes). In order to match the prop with an appropriate motor and boat, you'll need to check the ID code found in old issues of the Michigan Wheel catalog. Unfortunately, this literature is no longer in print. Sometimes, however, a long-time Michigan dealer has one stacked away among his sundry parts books.

In the search for vintage accessories, every once in a while somebody will turn up with a nifty one such as the Scott-Atwater Green Hornet lower unit.

During the 1930s, the Scott-Atwater Company began producing small outboards for the Champion label. Following World War II, the firm marketed motors under its own Scott-Atwater name. Business was brisk, as countless returning GIs turned to fishing and boating in their quest for the American Dream.

The outboarders of the immediate postwar period hungered for any kind of engine they could get, and most were satisfied with the proverbial "fishing motor" of 7½ hp or less. This low-horsepower environment started to change in the early 1950s. Many outboard companies that had no midsize or large models in their catalogs were soon perceived as "limited lines," and by the end of the decade went the way of the wind.

Scott-Atwater, anxious to shed its "small motors only" image, introduced a 19.95-cubic-inch twin in 1950. This rig was rushed off the drawing board and into production so quickly that it caught even the company advertising department off guard. Early ads for the large 1950 Scott (later known as the 16-hp model) did not include an exact horsepower rating. The ad copy simply read, "Over 15 HP—to be certified."

But by 1950 Mercury had already introduced its super-fast, over-25-hp, four-cylinder Thunderbolt. And Evinrude and Johnson were only a year away from marketing their dynamic Big Twin 25-hp engines. So Scott-Atwater needed a quick, inexpensive way to stay at least partially in tune with outboarding's higher speed market.

Their second means to such an end was heralded in a tiny section of the *Scott-Atwater Accessories Catalog*. There at the bottom of a page appeared a depiction of a Johnson PR-type racing lower unit. The associated copy read as follows: "HIGH SPEED NON-SHIFT LOWER UNIT specially designed to step up speed of the Scott-Atwater 16-HP motors. Increases speed 5 miles per hour or more. For use only with light, easily planed boats. Has 13[-to-]17 gear ratio. Water pump drag is eliminated by water scoop at rear of propeller. No machining required for installation."

Interestingly, the part numbers indicated that there were two different high-speed lower units. One was for the 1950 through 1952 16-hp motors, and another for the 1953 through 1955 Bail-a-Matic models. Both units called for a two-blade, $8 \times 10\frac{1}{2}$, bronze racing prop.

The October 1953 issue of *Boat Sport* magazine contains an article entitled "Big-Twin Hop-Up," which features a modified Scott-Atwater high-speed lower unit adapted to an Evinrude 25. The article refers to the Scott piece as the "16-HP Scott-Atwater TORPEDO lower unit." (Actually, *Torpedo* was a Martin term used in connection with its Hi-Speed 60, and "200" gear casing.) The official Scott literature calls the accessory the "GREEN HORNET LOWER UNIT." The Green Hornet name is certainly a natural, since the Scott-Atwaters of the day were painted a rich green color. Oddly enough, both of the Green Hornet units that I've seen were plain silver—bare aluminum!

The unit that I was finally able to track down looks a bit different than the Johnson PR-style piece shown in the 1955 *Scott-Atwater Accessories Catalog*. It is the earlier, 1950–52 model. Apparently, it had been sitting in the factory parts bin and was discovered (along with another one which was sold to a Minnesota man) when the McCulloch Corporation sold off all the old Scott-Atwater/McCulloch outboard stock.

Unfortunately, there isn't much remaining performance information about the 16-hp Green Hornet racing setup. A fellow who once worked with Scott's parts department said the attempt to compete with the likes of Merc and Champion was simply a "failure from the start." Other than that, the small number of tales I've heard regarding the rare lower unit typically concern its adaptation to an Evinrude or Johnson 25. My guess is that the very few 16-hp Scotts (or the badge-engineered Firestone or

Corsair 16 models) equipped with a Green Hornet racing lower unit belonged to a fortunate handful of amateur hot-rodders, young people who, no doubt, were related to the local Scott-Atwater dealer.

Hubbell and other tiny, now-forgotten specialty shops made similar lower units for other garden-variety motors like the Evinrude Big Twin 25. In automative terms, these pieces turned a four-door Ford sedan into a Ferrari—if only in the mind of its owner and a few curious young spectators.

Notes

1. Robert J. Whittier, *The Outboard Motor and Boat Book* (Concord, MA: Voyager Press, 1949), p. 12.
2. "Martin '200' a Real Threat for '54!" *Boat Sport* (February 1954), pp. 20–21.
3. Ibid., p. 33.
4. Hank Wieand Bowman, *The Encyclopedia of Outboard Motor Boating* New York: A.S. Barnes and Co., 1955), p. 312.

7

Outboard Accessories

True or false? A well-known kicker company actually marketed a thing with wheels on which groceries or its motors could be mounted. While this question will probably never pop up on a TV game show, the answer is yes, and it was called the Evinrude Cart. That early 1920s wooden device, wearing 16-inch, rubber-tired spoke wheels, was, in the words of Evinrude's sales literature, "designed particularly for those who want to haul their motor (or other stuff) a considerable distance." Even though it had a "staunch axle," a 2-hp Evinrude single was the cart's carrying limit. An optional canvas motor cover would make onlookers more curious. The aforementioned buggy was just one of many offerings in a vintage catalog of outboard motors and accessories.

Circa World War I, Evinrude (often collaborating with outside suppliers) realized a proprietary accessory line provided another way to put food on the table. Many of the first ancillary outboard items were simply updated parts for retrofitting older motors. Primary examples included flywheel magnetos (replacing the entire battery ignition system), reversing lower-unit attachments, and rope-start sheaves. Those wanting kits converting a regular-shaft Evinrude rowboat motor into a short, through-the-bottom-of-the-craft canoe motor had such an option. There was also a vice versa kit for folks fed up with power-canoeing. Instructions with the rowboat-to-canoe package suggested purchasing a special "outboard canoe exhaust" system piping motor fumes through the canoe's side.

Various motor stands.

A 1920s Evinrude stove ad.

Prevent Fires!

Use a real, he-man Camp Stove! Evinrude in developing the Evinrude Camp Stove, drew on the full, ripe experience gained through years of serving sportsmen well. We offer a Camp Stove 100 per cent safe, a camp stove with a blue gas flame so much hotter than ever achieved before that it amazed even skeptical University Engineering Laboratories, a camp stove that is a model of compactness and practicability.

We are proud of the Evinrude Camp Stove—three seasons beyond experiment. As safe a buy as a key of ten-penny nails or a dozen league baseballs. Buy it! Try it! Write for Booklet.

EVINRUDE MOTOR CO.
CAMP STOVE DIVISION
Milwaukee   Wisconsin

Stove, utensils and all fit snugly in it's carrying container

A complete kitchen is on hand

Some early Evinrude owners suffering from pounding headaches bought a "maxim silencer" muffler baffle. A few extra bucks netted a deluxe water-cooled version which, according to company literature, caused hot gases, led through water jackets, to say simply "puff-puff" upon emission. Speed demons could activate the unit's "cut-out." Outboard buffs buffeted by their motors' hitting bottom were targeted for a tilt-up attachment. Without such an accessory, early Evinrude-powered boats could not be beached completely. Anyone finding an Evinrude rowboat motor wearing a 14-gauge brass rudder (clamped over the drive shaft tube) has a nice factory-authorized accessory.

Proud Evinruders could consider a wooden motor stand, gray motor enamel, and motor polish to keep that kicker "clean and bright." Evinrude grease and lubricating oil (with "full directions on each can") were always the "proper density for Evinrude motors." The latter substance "prevented carbon deposits."

Occasionally, a vintage outboard surfaces in its own special protective case. For the 2-horse rowboat motors, Evinrude offered a "full length" white pine shipping case, as well as a trunk. Covered and lined with "vulcanized fibre," the (38-inch by 13½-inch by 17½-inch) Evinrude trunk was built of "3-ply veneer lumber, securely bound in brass and fitted with a high grade lock." It could be conveniently checked on a train as baggage or lashed to an automobile running board.

Some pioneer gadgeteers equipped their rowboat motors with an Evinrude "magneto-electric lighting system." An extra coil, a switch, 32 feet of waterproof wire, and a searchlight (on a stand)

"Official" outboard accessories included brand-name engine oil.

got power from the kicker's mag. "Unusual weather conditions due to dense saltwater fogs of the ocean" called for the use of the magneto Booster. Its dry-cell battery, enclosed in a waterproof case, was wired to the magneto coil and could be switched on if the mag didn't have sufficient zing.

Through the years, most outboard companies pushed at least a page or two of "official accessories" aimed at helping the outboarder get more utility from his motor. Scott-Atwater offered everything from remote control and its own brand of 2-cycle motor oil to the obscure Green Hornet high-speed lower unit and racing throttle kit for its 16-hp twin. Private brands like Elgin, Sea King, and Wizard marketed a handful of accessories. Gas cans, engine covers, oil, and shear pins were chief among them.

Martin published a four-page accessory flyer offering standard outboarding fare. Items like motor safety cables ($1 for regular and $2 for the deluxe, stainless steel version) and canvas engine carrying bags graced its 1948 cover. The Upland Manufacturing Company of Upland, Indiana, made Martin some chubby outboard covers. If trouble struck, these items doubled as life jackets. Generic storage stands, also produced by an outside firm, were offered in three sizes ranging in price from $2.98 to about $12 (for the one with wheels). Saltwater boaters could get a special "Martin designed cooling system flushing attachment." The dollar-and-a-half rubber tip screwed into a garden hose and was stuck into a lower-unit water-intake port.

Martin 60 owners with high transom craft had the option of a $10, 5-inch "lower unit extension set." Those taking pride in their National Pressure Cooker Company–produced kickers were invited to brighten up for the new season with a complete Martin decal set. At 20 cents each, it's a shame they're not available today!

By the mid-1950s Mercury's Quicksilver accessory line had developed into a nice sideline for its dealer organization. Because Mercs were never as generic as other brands, accessory catalogs featured many interesting, uniquely Mercury items. Chief among them were the Quicksilver racing lower units and high-speed, two-blade propellers.

Although a standard (family runabout) front-mount steering-cable motor bracket was offered, rear-mounted racer's steering bars were prominently touted. They could be quickly bolted to any Merc competition model. In any event the Kiekhaefer Corporation pioneered hydraulic steering and pushed its Ride-Guide system for single- or dual-engine installation. Wheels came in a choice of such shades as "Marlin Blue," "Desert Sand," and "Sunset Orange." Regular (rope and pulley) steering wheels received less catalog space.

Steering handles with twist-grip speed control could be purchased for the big four-cylinder Mercs of the day. Dual-lever Quicksilver remote controls were marketed to boaters desiring "armchair comfort . . . fingertip control" of shift, throttle, and electric starting. Single-lever units debuted in 1957. A fuel-pump conversion kit adapted one-hose tanks to the older (Mark 50)

Handy Shear Pin Kit
Six shear pins and two cotter pins in transparent plastic capsule with metal cap.

Here's a dandy little metal-capped transparent plastic tube containing six shear pins and two cotter pins. Keep one in your tool box or tackle box; it may come in handy. . . . . .35¢ ea.

Mercury's dandy little shear pin kit sold for 35 cents.

A generic ad for Mercury outboard accessories.

Twist Grip Throttle Control

Just a "Twist of the Wrist" is all it takes to control the speed of the boat when your Mercury is fitted with this steering handle incorporating the ingenious twist-grip throttle developed by Kiekhaefer Mercury engineers. It's simple and reliable; a rotatable grip is connected to the throttle linkage through a flexible control cable. Handle can be set in vertical carrying position without upsetting throttle adjustment.

For safe, sure, split-second, one-hand control of Mercury Horsepower in any emergency and under all conditions of operation, the twist-grip throttle is ideal. It can be fitted to KE-4, KE-7, KG-4, KF-7 and KG-7 models. Handle bracket supplied with kit is adapted to use of steering bar. Kit includes all necessary attachments and fittings. M-60-588............................ $10.50

Keep the stern of your boat
SPIC and SPAN
with this mercury drip pan

Every outboard operator knows that, over a period of time, even the most neatly kept boat will eventually show the deteriorating effects of gasoline and oil drippings. You can keep the stern of your boat spic and span with this nicely finished aluminum drip pan which attaches to the transom and is provided with a drain tube leading to the outside of the boat.

An additional feature of this drip pan is the rib at the top edge, designed to prevent motor from coming off of transom if clamp brackets should accidentally work loose during operation. M-60-5034................................$4.63

More Mercury accessories: "Twist of the Wrist" throttle control and aluminum drip pan.

This OMC accessory made it possible to control steering and throttle at the motor.

STEERING HANDLE

For 28 H.P., 33 H.P. and 40 H.P. motors (except electric shift). Permits steering and throttle control at the motor. Installation instructions are furnished.

Part No. 377949 $11.00

pressurized system. Cooling system flushing attachments were available for a wide range of Merc motors.

Fastidious boaters could keep leaking fuel from gumming up their hulls by getting an official Quicksilver aluminum drip pan. Sort of a cookie sheet bent at a 45-degree angle, it attached to and protected the transom. The Merc got clamped over it. The unit's top rib would catch the clamps should they vibrate loose. Lots of utility for $4.63!

Older Mercurys sporting integral gas tanks could be fitted with an interesting "fuel transfer cap." This piece resembled its standard counterpart except for a horizontal, ¼-inch hose-fitting on top. A tube running from this fitting to an ordinary gas can refilled the motor's tank whenever the auxiliary gas can was pumped or raised above the kicker. A check valve prevented overfilling. Marathon racers used these $2.95 items religiously.

Truly one of the nicest Merc accessories was a custom motor stand. Constructed of heavy cast iron, the black and silver (some were all black) unit featured a prominently embossed Kiekhaefer Mercury logo. They were equally at home with a one-lung putt-putt or a six-cylinder giant.

Mercury nuts, especially those who raced the legendary power plants, were asked by the accessory catalog to "wear the emblem and fly the pennant." Deck pennants, sweatshirts, hats, and $1.25 T-shirts were marketed. Mercury's famous logo, in 65-cent and $1.15 sizes, could be sewn on an enthusiast's clothing to "boost his motor." Championship hydroplane racer Bill Tenney bought one of the bigger emblems. He gained worldwide outboarding notoriety with a very fast 1930s-era Johnson model SR. That aforementioned accessory patch was added to text carefully embroidered to his racing togs. The results read something like I HAVE NOT YET SUCCUMBED TO KIEKHAEFER MERCURY!

Evinrude, Johnson, and Gale Products outboard owners of the 1960s could yield to desires to dress up their motors via genuine OMC accessories. Among the featured gear were single and traditional two-lever remote controls. (Evinrude's was dubbed Simplex, while Johnson's said Ship Master.) Gadget-minded, large-horsepower skippers could choose from generator, electric starting, power tilt, and radio-noise-suppression kits. Operators of the little 3-horse OMC twins were offered a $9.75 fuel pump kit, allowing the integral tank to be retired in favor of a heftier remote unit. A lengthy, 15-inch lower-unit extension package was also available for the 3-horse. Five-horse OMC products used in the fall or in cold climates could be fitted with a $2.80 thermostat so the motor would warm up rapidly. Many salty, sandy, or silty water outboarders had the option of OMC's chrome water-pump kit, said to resist damage from foreign particles. Of course, an assortment of auxiliary fuel tanks, hoses (up to 100 feet!), official OMC lubricants, engine cleaner, and rust preventative were offered. A clever "spare propeller kit" was marketed on an almond-shaped base. This handy rig (which mounted in the boat) included everything, from pliers to prop nut, for a quick emergency wheel change.

Most universal of all OMC accessories were its classic engine stands. Although lightweight, they were very sturdy. Their aluminum tube legs pulled out for easy transport. Today, both regular (for motors up to 40 hp) and jumbo-size OMC stands are favored among outboard collectors.

Outboard makers were not the only firms producing motor accessories. In fact, dozens of "factory-authorized" pieces (such as Evinrude Cruise-A-Day fuel tanks) were built by outside sources. Most frequently these were motor stands, locks, remote controls, and lower-unit–mounted trolling plates.

Many times, some little "aftermarket" company pioneers technology eventually adopted by the majors. A tiny Midwestern outfit offered electric starting kits (linking starter motor to flywheel via a bicycle chain and ratchet) for OMC 25s a few years prior to the concept's 1954 "factory equipped" reintroduction. Small, belt-driven DC generators were also available.

Circa 1948, another pint-size manufacturing concern worked up a steering handle twist-grip throttle control for early Mercury Rockets and Lightnings. Merc began adopting this principle in 1952. Mercury 10 owners could also acquire the Tescher Automatic Fuel Pump and install a remote gas tank. Similar kits were available for the Evinrude Fleetwin 7½ hp and Martin 100 (10 hp) outboards. This pump employed a safe, nonpressurized, single-hose system some years before the big firms decided that that process was best.

The Quincy (Illinois) Welding Works sold hop-up accessories directly and through Mercury distributors. Lucky motor buffs may still find an old Merc sporting a Quincy exhaust stack, manifold cut-out shutter, or other items.

Perhaps one of the most elusive pieces of this genre was designed for Johnson, Evinrude, and Gale Products (Buccaneer, Sea King, Sea-Bee, etc.) 35-horse models. In 1958 a small Bartlesville, Oklahoma, company marketed JET-PAC Dual Carburetion for the aforementioned outboards. Apparently the second carb mounted on the cylinder assembly and added "5 HP with no increase in fuel consumption."

Collectors who gobble up outboard accessories might like to find a juice-can-sized device hooked to their motor. Labeled Retriev-a-Buoy, this canister was clipped to the kicker's transom clamp thumbscrew or bracket-mounted to the steering arm. If the outboard ever fell overboard, Retriev-a-Buoy's airtight cartridge on a 120-foot nylon line would float to the surface. The submerged motor could thus be rescued.

Those who save old motors should keep an eye open for their pastime's associated products. A vintage putt-putt dressed with some official accessory is truly double the treasure.

8

Where Have All the Old Outboards Gone?

Down South a fellow noticed the strangest looking tree. It had three large trunks originating at a lumpy, rooty base. Wedged between and grown firmly into the rough trio was a knot or something shaped like an outboard motor. No one seemed to be home, so the curious individual jumped a rickety fence for a closer inspection.

Suddenly, an elderly lady appeared in the yard and verified the "bump" in the tree's middle was indeed an Evinrude motor. Her late husband had, years ago, leaned it there. Over time the tree had grown around the outboard. She said the leaves were a nuisance and anyone having the tree completely removed could take the Evinrude free of charge.

Up North lived new owners of an old lakeside cabin. All fall they'd been feeding a stony fireplace with cordwood found on their recently acquired side porch. During one quick evening trip to the chilly veranda, four or five logs were gathered. A cold, medium-size stick for kindling seemed stuck to the floor. Hearty tugs were exercised, toppling the surrounding wood onto the ground. That man fetching fuel for the fire was surprised to be grasping a contraption complete with copper gas tank. It was a 1913 Waterman outboard, buried under chopped wood for nearly half a century.

Not every motor lives long enough to create such tales. The vociferous scrap drives of World War II and the Korean Conflict claimed tons of early examples.

As a kid, I witnessed a frustrated fisherman echo discouraging words across our lake. His ancient Sea King single had caught fire in the sunset, and he finally claimed victory over the perpetually balky eggbeater by loosening its lone transom clamp and waving "bye-bye." If waterways had rubber drain plugs that could be pulled up, we'd all find a tremendous stockpile of rusty relics.

Best Bets for Locating ID Numbers

Brand	ID Number Location
Champion	Many post-World War II Champ products are identified by small transom clamp bracket ID plates.
Elto	Earlier models: Fuel tank should have metal ID plate. Serial number also stamped into engine block. Later models: Small ID plate should be on transom bracket or steering arm support.
Evinrude	Many early models had alloy tags soldered into gas tank. Look for some model numbers stamped into front of engine block. Identification is also found on plate mounted to steering arm or transom bracket. (Note: On post-1929 Evinrude, Elto, and OMC motors, model number is first three or four digits of designation. Serial number occupies the figure's remainder. Thus, Evinrude #1770015 is the fifteenth motor in the model 177 series.)
Johnson	Early Johnsons featured rope sheave plate IDs. Vintage electric-start models (i.e., the VA-50) had model stamped into the starter motor cover's thin rim. Most Johnsons had serial number stamped into the block. Motors that had rewind but no rope sheave plate sported the ID and the model designation on the block. By the Fifties, most Johnson numbers were put on transom bracket plates.
Lockwood	Rope sheave plate usually tells the story.
Martin	Look for a small plate on steering handle or (Martin 200) on motor leg.
Mercury	Early Mercs had some numbers placed on rope sheave. Throughout the years some got tagged on motor leg. Most of the classic "green" models were ID'd on the tank rim plate. (KF9/KG9 plates were put on front cover.)
Scott-Atwater	The important numbers are usually found on a transom bracket plate.

Each outboard maker had its own model and serial number code. Some, like the Koban (noted in the motor list chapter) and post–World War II Scott-Atwater, revealed the kicker's year through its numbers. For example, a model *473* is a 1947 Scott-Atwater. A *509* comes from 1950, and so on. Model numbers from 1952 through 1957 had the final two digits of the year reversed in the last pair of the four-numeral model designation (e.g., 37125 would be a 1952 motor). Just like life, there were exceptions to these and other manufacturers' ID rules.

For decades boat shops and marinas were great places to locate classic outboards. Establishments with questionable storage sheds featuring broken windows provided obvious havens for wayward motors. By the late 1970s, however, the pleasure-boating industry became so upscale that those little old boat and motor places, if occupying some key waterfront locale, were revamped and divested of their iron goodies. Most of the legendary one-man motor repair shops simply went the way of the wind. Tiny "junque"-filled outboard dealerships, usually the home of some second-string brand, have also become a rarity.

A spring 1975 college outing led me to Boston. There I spied a time-worn outboard store which turned out to have a cellar full of old motors. Minutes later and $35 lighter, I carefully walked upstairs with a nice little Clarke Troller. My vow to return for other classic iron was thwarted that summer, however, when urban renewal flattened the place. No one seemed to know what had happened to the proprietor and his classic kickers.

Even when it's impossible to locate a remarkably run-down rural boat shop run by some guy with poor sentence structure, don't assume that the old motor stream has dried up. While many models are scarce, enough old "bread and butter" outboards still exist for everyone to enjoy.

Actually, the best place to find old kickers continues to be the outboard dealership. Usually, antique motors displayed in a marine outlet are not for sale, but their presence often sensitizes customers to the fact that vintage rigs shouldn't be discarded. By the same token, marina owners need floor space for stuff normal people buy, and they can't accept every old putt-putt coming through the turnstile. As a result, the local boat place is a good spot to obtain castoffs, or at least good old-engine leads.

A local radio station swap-shop show and weekly paper's classified sections always provide outboard collectors paths toward old iron. Amidst badly spelled ads for FREE HOUSE BORKEN PUPPIES and SIZE 14 WEDDING GOWN, NEVER WORN, a WANTED—OLD OUTBOARD MOTORS request may command attention.

Serious engine enthusiasts sometimes spend a few dollars printing up their desire on business cards (or on photocopied slips of paper). You never know who'll see one of these cards posted in a restaurant, shopping mall, or laundromat. They also can be handed out at gas stations, junkyards, hardware stores, small engine repair shops, and the like. The more folks who know you're nuts about old motors and think you'll actually pay cash for Uncle Waldo's corroded fishin' engine, the faster your collection will grow.

Unlike classic cars, aged outboards take up little space and have been stacked away in peculiar places. While waterside communities hold the best discovery bets, old motors have even popped up at flea markets held in desert towns. Throughout burgs with more grass, lawn sales frequently provide point-of-purchase eggbeater opportunities. Of course, the Antique Outboard Motor Club (see Chapter 10) also gives hope to motor seekers.

The author's "business" card advertises his hobby.

Peter Hunn
COLLECTOR OF OLD OUTBOARD MOTORS

WILL BUY PRE-1960 MOTORS. PARTS. CATALOGS. ACCESSORIES. ETC.

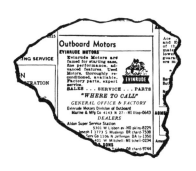

Old phonebooks are a good resource for tracking old dealers.

Although they don't usually grow on (or in) trees, vintage kickers yet to be found are out there, and in the craziest locations.

"My neighbor is in big trouble and could really use your help," a business associate told me. He recounted the story, one heard all too often, and I sprinted for the car.

"You're here!" the distressed fellow exclaimed as I pulled into his driveway. "It's hidden in the garage," he whispered.

While walking toward the building, the guy recounted how his compulsive behavior at a bar and subsequent weekend auction had placed him in authentic hot water.

"Bought myself an old outboard motor and a heap of yelling from my wife! If you'd just give me what I got in it and get the stinkin' thing outta here quick, I could probably patch things up with her."

The poor fellow's rather violent-looking spouse gave us the evil eye from a back-porch vantage point. She was aggressively operating one of those pulley clotheslines.

"Are you at all interested in the motor?" the desperate man asked. "See, I've been sleeping on the couch since last Saturday."

He paused briefly to rub his lower back while I inquired, "What kind of outboard is it?"

"Oh, someone said it's a Clinton . . . a 4-cycle, cylinder electric-starting Clinton. But actually," he stated, crestfallen, "I don't know and wouldn't even know where to look."

Typically, Clinton specialized in small, garden-variety, 2-cycle, single-cylinder kickers. Such a mysterious assessment, coupled with an electric-start description, really threw me for a loop! It must have had the same effect on a few other old-motor nuts who phoned prior to my arrival. The generic Clinton ID had kept them away.

Well, the strange Clinton turned out to be a Johnson VA-50, a very limited-production, electric-starting model dating back to 1930. The deluxe rig was meant to be mated to a classy Aqua-Flyer boat and today represents the rarest of four-cylinder Johnsons.

My glowing account brightened the fellow's face, and he was, no doubt, about to boost the asking price significantly. As fate would have it, however, the wife's other clothesline pulley was hooked to the garage. Its sharp, vicious-sounding squeak startled the fellow into divulging he'd actually paid only $10 for the old engine. That unlubricated squeal prompted my host to offer free, next-day delivery. The VA-50 was the first misidentified putt-putt I'd taken on for humanitarian reasons.

In retrospect, that unusual Johnson might have produced a greater interest level had the contraption been properly advertised to collectors. But as its erstwhile owner noted, ready knowledge of make, model, and year was the critical factor he lacked.

My first vintage kicker, assumed to be a 1922, was later identified as a '28. The misidentification was corrected only after writing the manufacturer with a model number.

Nowadays, letters to most old outboard firms will come back "address unknown." The remaining companies seldom have the archival staff eager to research aged motor topics. As a result, the ability to locate basic outboard data is crucial to enjoying vintage motors.

Few companies set out to hide the identity of their products. A well-running outboard emblazoned with a bright gas tank decal held great promotional power. Unfortunately, these labels were often worn away by years of having fuel spilled on them. If your rig still sports a decal, though, you've probably got a good idea as to its manufacture.

Model and serial numbers are very important, and on many kickers may be found stamped into the flywheel's rope sheave plate. Regrettably, many a rope sheave, removed to inspect or service the magneto, got dropped overboard or was simply misplaced. Because plates from other motors would sometimes fit, there are plenty of old kickers wearing incorrect identities.

Some companies wisely stamped the serial number (and model) on the engine block. (Be careful not to confuse them with casting part numbers.) If those digits disagree with the rope sheave (or fuel-tank-based ID stamp), something got switched somewhere.

Remember, most of these motors came from a time when people went to great lengths to repair, fix up, or modify a tired engine inexpensively. Typically, money was scarcer than time. If a part that would *sort of* fit could be scrounged for a few dollar there were plenty of tiny machine shops and backyard me willing to complete the job.

I once found a battery-ignition early-Thirties El elaborately fitted with a 1929 Johnson V-45 flywh It sure looked weird, but it apparently worked category was a bargain-basement Sears W some talented tinkerer had equipped w shifter—years before such mechanis available.

Owners of racing motors we offenders, as provocative modificatic part of the fun. If some guy's champio been treated with a purple cylinder head modifications would soon proliferate. By the mufflers probably got tossed. In any event, w service motor or racer, a little enjoyable detectiv usually reveal a rationale for the refitting.

In 1925 the Johnson people gave their outboard model designations a logical -25 suffix (e.g., A-25, J-25). They added five to that figure in 1926, so new model designations were suffixed with -30 (e.g., P-30). This "plus five" practice continued through 1936, when an -80 suffix was issued. Most 1937 Johnsons wore a -37 suffix; 1938s a -38; and '39s a -39. It was -10 for 1940 and, typically, -15 in 1941.

Again, there were numerous violations of this rule. Some A-35 (1927) Johnsons, for example, were 1928 motors. There were also pre–World War II Johnsons designated model 100, 200, and 300, not in keeping with the suffix system.

The letter *B* in a Johnson model name (such as PB-30) usually signified a bronze lower unit (suited for ocean use). There was a model B Johnson, however, that sported a standard aluminum lower unit which *b*olted to the boat instead of being affixed via transom clip thumbscrews. Getting back to the high seas, 1920s Evinrudes containing an *S* in their model names (e.g., TS, NS) were bronze lower unit versions meant for saltwater applications.

Johnson and Lockwood stamped an *R* in the model description of their racing outboards. The fast version of Johnson's alternate-firing twin K was dubbed KR. Please note, however, that Johnson made a military version of the 22-horse PO called POLR. It was *not* a racing engine. Post–World War II Sea Horse 25s model RD rigs were not racers either. So not everything fit into the "R = racing motor" lexicon.

Elto's high-speed models often had an *H* stamped after the serial number. Merc's H outboards were racers, too, but that *H* stood for the Hydro-Short streamlined lower unit.

About the only quasi-universal nomenclature was the *L*. Typically, such a designation at the conclusion of a model description signifies a *l*ong-shaft lower unit.

Some kickers, especially old, private-brand, catalog store models, are now virtually devoid of ID. And more than one old-outboard enthusiast has encountered a real mystery motor. Fortunately, such challenge is another enjoyable aspect of the antique outboard hobby.

Be advised there are still a number of homebrew rigs out there. Few are more than a discarded lower unit fitted to a lawn mower or garden tractor engine. Even though none existed commercially, both John Deere and Wheel Horse outboards pop up occasionally.

In any event, keeping this info at hand may allow you to help a troubled neighbor getting static for bidding on some dusty old Johnson PBL-30. You'll quickly deduce it's a 1926 *l*ong, *b*ronze-shaft, and will drive away with a classic little outboard gold mine!

"Oh, it's you again," the busy outboard dealer sighed into his multi-line telephone.

An elderly woman's feeble voice stated, "Yes, I'm

How much is it worth?

calling for the old motor appraisal you promised me."

"OK, ma'am," the marine store proprietor said, while reaching into a bottom desk drawer for a dusty booklet. "What kind of outboard you say it is?"

"Well . . . there's a little sign on it that looks like it says Buccaneer."

"OK, any numbers on it?"

"Well . . . there's a 12. Twelve horse . . . power."

"OK, what year?"

"Oh, my goodness, well . . . my late husband bought it the year President Eisenhower . . . right around 1953. What do you feel it's worth?"

"That's hard to know, ma'am, but this 1960 used outboard motor guide I'm looking at says a good one would have brought sixty-five bucks back then. 'Course that was years ago."

"So you're saying it has increased in value?"

"Uh . . . well, you know how much prices have gone up on antiques. Some of that old stuff probably sells for 10 times what it's worth."

"Ten times you say?"

"I guess. . . ."

"Thank you, young man," said the widow.

That phone call helped her decide that anything less than $650 for the weathered Buccaneer would be an insult to her husband's memory. Because nobody wanted the motor at anywhere near that price, it was a recollection she long held.

Although there are some classic outboards which command a good dollar, most contain greater sentimental than monetary value. Back in the Sixties only an exceptional kicker would bring more than $15 to $25. Five-dollar motors were commonplace. Many overloaded dealers would calculate a "scrap" price, selling you the kicker and loose parts by the carload.

Thirty years later, a few $500-plus motors have been noted, but their $10 counterparts are still available (especially from bulging collections). For most tinkerers, it's the reasonable-ticket aspect of old outboarding which makes such a pastime enjoyable.

Perhaps you'll feel this chapter is geared more toward the buyer than the seller. But for quite some time, there have been more old outboards looking for homes than people interested in housing them. Until this supply and demand quotient shifts, antique motors can fit into most any budget.

Without insulting the owner, an old-outboard seeker should ask the following questions:

1. *Is it a "freshwater" motor?* The majority of engines used in salty waterways have seriously corroded parts. Unless the saltwater motor has been flushed regularly, is a special bronze-lower-unit

saltwater model, is otherwise scarce, or was owned by a past President, it might not represent a good buy.

2. *Does the motor have all its parts? Are there any damaged, cracked, or broken parts?* As in automotive circles, the sum of an outboard's parts is often greater than its total price. The innocent-looking $25 motor, missing a rewind starter assembly, propeller, and gas cap, isn't really a $25 engine.

3. *Can you rotate the flywheel?* If a motor is stuck, chances are its piston(s) are bonded to the cylinder wall. A complete overhaul may be required. Note: Should the motor "turn-over" with some resistance, or do so with lots of play (from side to side) in the crankshaft, major repairs are likely to be needed.

4. *Is there good compression?* With a finger-tight spark plug and lubricated piston-cylinder assembly, a promising motor will demonstrate some compression "bounce."

5. *Is there any spark?* Don't ask the seller to hold the plug wires while you pull the starter cord. Although, if you do ask and he refuses, chances are that motor has run in his lifetime. Ask to remove the spark plug, ground it against the cylinder, and quickly rotate the flywheel. You should see a spark jump between the plug's gap. (Battery-ignition models require a 6-volt DC source.)

6. *What is the condition of exterior finish, including decals?* Because a "nice, original" condition motor is considered more valuable than a restored rig, everything from faded paint to gasoline-worn starting-instruction stickers comes under consideration here. More than a few vintage putt-putts have been brush-stroked red by some well-meaning fixer-upper. If authenticity is your goal, however, three coats of house paint will not make your job easier.

7. *Is there original equipment or accessories?* Find out whether the owner retained any instruction booklets, sales literature, a motor stand, the original packing case, and so on. The answer is usually no, but it never hurts to ask.

8. *Does the outboard run?* Remember, every motor "worked the last time it was used," so don't get caught up in that infamous play on words. Someone with an operating engine will usually provide a brief demonstration. Even if the thing is "fired up dry" (on a sawhorse) for 5 or 10 seconds, you'll know it has compression, spark, and quasi-complete carburetion. Multi-family mouse nests under the cover can also tell you something about this topic.

9. *Do you really want this particular motor?* This is a very subjective question not always easy to answer. I usually ask myself, If the old motor doesn't fit in with the rest of my valuable equipment, can I pass it along to someone else for the same price?

When purchasing an old outboard, never attempt stealing the thing through intimidation. Comments like "What a piece of junk!" or "You called me out here to see this?" will leave a sour taste. A better way to soften the reality that the seller's '51 Martin isn't the only old kicker known to exist might be to show a snapshot of

Motors from bygone days, ready to come out of retirement.

some rigs in your collection. Perhaps point out that although it's a nice example of a vintage motor, there are some parts missing and it has an incomplete decal. The seller will sometimes take exception to such assessments, but remember that aforementioned widow. She wasn't selling a tinny eggbeater as much as offering a cherished memento. You may see a bashed-in gas tank; the seller visualizes Uncle Louis sputtering to some long-forgotten dock with a full stringer of perch.

Speaking of fishermen, there are plenty who'd gladly pay $200 for a nice-running old outboard that is worth $50. Because a new 5-horse fishin' engine can produce sticker shock, a good vintage model is typically worth more to an angler than it is to a collector.

In deference to the average-condition kicker, super-nice motors make me nervous. Because I fear "scratch and dent" incidents, primo motors in my collection seldom see water. Come to think of it, beat-up Elgins, incapable of idling on both cylinders, have provided a more relaxing brand of fun than my "nearly mint" originals. Everybody approaches old outboarding differently, but it seems the hobby is best supported by a rig (albeit hopelessly weathered) receiving regular exercise.

Placing an exact dollar value on old motors is very difficult. Obviously, the person wanting a certain outboard the most will pay the highest price. Anyone who has spent a bundle, however, knows that the weekend after you do so, some guy in your church will clean out his basement and present you with one just like it!

Sellers claiming they've just turned down 10 grand for their motor often sing a new tune when you demonstrate that your collection contains three similar models . . . and then ask for the $10,000 bidder's phone number.

As previously noted, well-cared-for, original-condition motors top the value list. Although such popularity is cyclical, good 1950s models command interest. Factory racers and hot-rod motors are prized by collectors. Outboards wearing a lot of brass parts receive attention. Very old (pre–World War I) examples are also popular with some antique buffs. In general the big brand old-timers seem to generate the most conversation. Because many Johnson, Evinrude, and Mercurys were sold through the years, lots of people remember them and seek such products today.

Finally, the tiny ½-hp eggbeaters and novel Clarke Trollers often bring buyers. These motors are easy to handle (but seldom run very well) and produce a focal point in a showroom or basement display. Conversely, huge rigs like Johnson's TR-40 Giant Twin and the Cross Radial have their following.

Old outboards probably shouldn't be purchased only as "big investments." Although it's been tried, no one having done so has received recognition from Wall Street. A vintage kicker is best acquired by someone who will obtain pleasure from its history, repair, care, and use. Pride demonstrated by new owners of everything from rare twin-carbed racing engines to garden-variety Scott-Atwater singles is the fuel that makes the antique outboard world go round. Here, fortunately, value is predominantly in the beholder's eye.

Parts department

In 1929 the Detroit-Parks Airplane Company built eight model P-2A Speedster biplanes. Years later, author Richard Bach acquired an operable member of this tiny production run and did a bit of old-fashioned Midwestern barnstorming. During that 1966 recreation, he met a friend in Palmyra, Wisconsin, who asked to give the rare plane a try.

Unfortunately, upon landing, the friend cracked up the vintage craft. Pushing the damaged biplane to within 10 feet of a little hangar, they set about making repairs. But it was no use. A wing strut, 100-percent unique to the original eight P-2A airplanes, was hopelessly shot.

An old guy watching from the nearby weathered hangar called out, "Need any help, fellas?"

Mr. Bach shook his head, saying, "Not unless you have a left wing strut for a 1929 Detroit-Parks Speedster biplane model P-2A!"

The onlooker began rummaging through his hangar and soon emerged with the factory-original replacement part.

It surely would be neat if that kind of thing always happened to everyone. How rewarding it would be simply to head to the local outboard dealer and pick up, say, a crankshaft for some 1940 Clarke Troller 2.7-hp twin . . . or even gaskets for a 1961 Evinrude.

Fortunately, there are times when critical parts do show up. They usually appear in one of four ways:

1. *New/old stock.* These new, but obsolete, components have been sitting around (taking up room) for years. Because they're small, new/old-stock stuff can hide in most any shop.
2. *Used.* Often a result of a "parted-out" motor, used parts run a close second to new, more difficult to obtain pieces.
3. *Reproductions.* A few critical outboard parts are now being manufactured by old kicker buffs. Included in this category are decals, Elto Speedster timer cam bushings, and the like.
4. *Parts motors.* Some old outboards are simply too shot (or salt-ridden) for restoration. Generally available for a few bucks, these "junked car" counterparts frequently contain pieces usable on similar models.

The Antique Outboard Motor Club's *Newsletter* (mailed eight times annually) is a great tool for parts searchers. Members can place free ads, while nonmembers pay only a nominal fee. The publication's readers hold literally tons of old outboard parts from 1910 to 1970. Like the old fellow in the airplane hangar, many AOMC people enjoy surprising kicker fixer-uppers who believe they're stuck.

Anyone looking for old Mercury parts may have some luck at the following:

Grubb's Marine (member AOMC)
402 Walnut Street
Spring City, PA 19475
(215) 948-8855

Outboard Service Co.
2511 N. Rosemead Blvd.
S. El Monte, CA 91733
(213) 444-5912

Evinrude, Johnson, and Gale products may be sought through the following sources. (Please be advised addresses and parts availability are subject to change. The listing does not represent the author's endorsement.)

Twin City Outboards
3303 ½ Nicollet Ave.
Minneapolis, MN 55408
(612) 827-8281

Fairwind's Marina
R.R. #6-1000 Fairwinds Dr.
Annapolis, MD 21401
(301) 974-0758

Clawson Boats & Motors
7805 Manchester Ave.
St. Louis, MO 63143
(314) 645-6666

Jernigan's Marine
1701 East Street
Ludlow, MA 01056
(413) 583-4053

Wonderland Marine West
5796 E. Grand River
Howell, MI 48843
(313) 229-9531

Lakeside Marine
Hwy. 90 W., Box 24E
Del Rio, TX 78840
(512) 775-2567

Paul's Hobby Outboard
P.O. Box 724
Zephyr Cove, NV 89448
(702) 588-2012

Thurston Enterprises
Rt. 3
The Weirs, NH 03246
(603) 366-4811

Bird Island Marine
75 Bird Ave.
Buffalo, NY 14213
(716) 883-5233

Hi-Skipper Marine
377 Sweeney St.
N. Tonawanda, NY 14120
(716) 694-4311

Thurow's Lawn & Marine
S92 W27825 Hwy. E.S.
Mukwonago, WI 53149
(414) 363-7711

American Outboard Motors
Rt. 1, Box 113
Cordova, MD 21625
(301) 822-1740

Zinner's Marine, Inc.
32895 S. River Rd.
Mt. Clemens, MI 48045
(313) 465-5558

Sea Way Marine, Inc.
2940 Southwest Avalon Way
Seattle, WA 98166
(206) 937-7373

Tom's Sport Shop
North Main
Kewaunee, WI 54216
(414) 388-3262

Engine Blade & Prop
3524 W. National Ave.
Milwaukee, WI 53215
(414) 671-0533

Dave's Outboard
Rt. 1, Long Lake
Sarona, WI 54870
(715) 354-3430

Raymond's Boats & Motors
Attn: Parts Manager
Rt. 1, Box 30
Gravois Mills, MO 65037
(314) 372-5115

9

Care, Repair, and Operation

Ole Evinrude never expected anyone to run old outboard motors. Although the famed inventor strived for top-quality kickers, early 1930s catalog rhetoric had him proposing a good Evinrude/Elto might last 10 years. Decades later, scores of Ole's products (along with lesser-known brands) are still operable. True, most hold semi-retired status, but more than one ancient kicker is quite ready to serve its proud owner. Accounts of easy-starting, useful antiques need not be mythical.

No top-notch Boy Scout would ever coerce an elderly lady to cross the street. Similarly, after scouting a vintage outboard, the kicker enthusiast should never force any of its old parts. Jammed or corroded pieces (such as choke levers) often break under pressure. For example, long-inactive timer mechanisms on battery-ignited motors (such as Eltos) can crack from flywheel motion. New owners of inoperative Elto speedsters, Quads, and the like would do well to remove the timer prior to powerhead work.

After an outboard acquisition, perhaps the first order of business should be the wiping away of loose grease and dust. Take out the spark plug(s) and squirt in a little oil. The flywheel should rotate smoothly. If something feels stuck, dismantling is probably in order, as damaged piston(s), rod(s), or piston ring(s) are likely culprits. If the piston is seized in its cylinder, removal is not always easy. Subsequent honing of the cylinder wall, along with piston repair or replacement, is usually necessary too. Liberal use of penetrating oil may help.

It is hoped that a stuck piston has its crown close to the spark plug hole. If this is the case, a grease gun with its hose securely fitted through a discarded spark plug base can be used to free the piston. Grease pumped into the space between the piston crown and cylinder head often loosens the works. Sometimes, however, this process takes days. If the cylinder ports are exposed, other piston removal measures must be taken.

Please be advised that a lodged flywheel doesn't always involve the piston-cylinder assembly. Perhaps the engine bearings are damaged or seized to the crankshaft. More typically, the lower-unit gears are broken, rusted, or corroded stuck. Removing the kicker's lower extremities should help prove such a hunch.

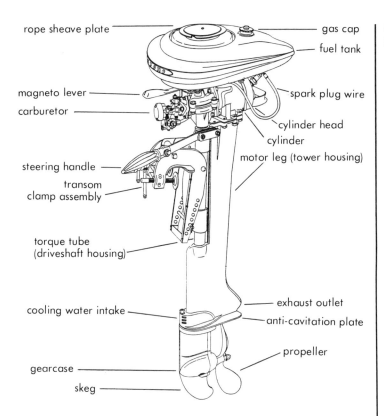

rope sheave plate

gas cap

fuel tank

magneto lever

spark plug wire

carburetor

cylinder head

cylinder

motor leg (tower housing)

steering handle

transom clamp assembly

torque tube (driveshaft housing)

cooling water intake

exhaust outlet

anti-cavitation plate

propeller

gearcase

skeg

General identification of outboard motor parts.

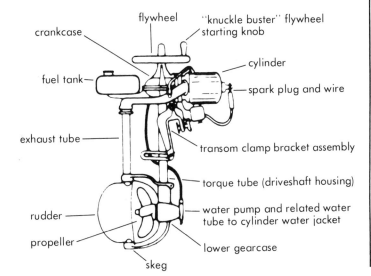

flywheel

"knuckle buster" flywheel starting knob

crankcase

cylinder

fuel tank

spark plug and wire

exhaust tube

transom clamp bracket assembly

torque tube (driveshaft housing)

rudder

water pump and related water tube to cylinder water jacket

propeller

lower gearcase

skeg

Rowboat motor parts.

Barring a stuck engine, the ignition system can next be checked. Most every kid goes through a nasty stage during which he asks some first grader to grip a spark plug wire while the flywheel is aggressively twirled. Because most of us former grade-schoolers have had such initiation, there's no need for further magneto function explanations. Suffice it to say, a good mag should produce a hot spark. An extracted spark plug connected to the ignition wire, and with its threaded end grounded to the engine block, will serve as a willing test volunteer. Following that exercise, reinsert the plug, always reattaching the wire(s), and spin the flywheel again. A healthy "compression bounce" is the desired result.

If an old outboard turns over smoothly, has compression as well as spark, and is reasonably complete, chances are it will run. Prior to firing up the old gal, however, it might be wise to inspect the fuel system.

Not a single owner's manual recommends leaving fuel in a stored outboard. Nevertheless, few vintage motors are acquired without containing at least a little "antique gas." The results range from lacquer-like residue in fuel strainers to half a tank of molasses-style goo.

Even kickers with reasonably clean tanks may be plagued with enough glop somewhere in the system (and it doesn't take much) to conk out a mile offshore. Often the tank can simply be drained and its fuel filter screen removed and blown clean under air pressure. Gas lines, fuel shut-off valves, and water lines should also be revitalized in this manner. Some auto parts stores sell a "sloshing compound" which, when rinsed around in the tank, coats that important container with a new inside surface.

If, after drying out the tank, potentially troublesome particles remain, you might want to loosen things by inserting a handful of pebbles and carefully shaking it.

"Newer" old outboards sporting remote fuel tanks present a different challenge, as gauges and rubber hoses come into play. Many buffs purchase a modern plastic gas tank for their prized 1950s and 1960s kickers. Owners of the earlier, more complex pressure-type remote tank have a little more checking to do. Special gaskets serving to keep the works airtight must be checked to ensure a good seal. Springs, check valves, and diaphragm assemblies need examination too. Some say a good pressure tank can be worth more than its corresponding motor.

Once it's evident that clear fuel may freely flow to the powerhead, carburetion becomes the focus. No matter what type of carburetor or mixing valve an old outboard wears, it must be clean. Dirt, sand particles, and ancient gas-oil residue love to live in these vital components and provide trouble for their hosts. When dismantling is required, pieces should be safely placed in a pie plate or jar. Take note of things like "what goes where," order of reassembly, and number of turns a needle valve is raised off its seat. While this sounds elementary, it may save you from putting the thing back together and having leftover parts, or wondering about the correct slow-speed needle valve setting! (Note: When these valves look totally out of whack, half to three-quarters of a turn from closed may get the motor going.)

Obviously, float-type carbs require their floats to float. Tiny holes in a metal one, or sogginess in a cork-style, will cause trouble. (A touch of solder on the former, or a coat of lacquer after drying out the latter, may help.)

Springs for poppet-valve-type carburetion need to give proper tension. Gaskets for the carb body and valve fittings must also be within acceptable tolerances. (They're usually OK if they don't leak.)

Upon successfully reattaching the spruced-up carburetor to its engine, the whole rig is almost ready for a try.

Even though it may not seem like much fun, the lower-unit-gear grease situation needs attention. It is hoped that seals on the propeller shaft, air vent, and grease inlet port are sound and haven't accepted any water. (If this has happened and the motor was left in the cold, look at the seals for signs of cracking.) Select a gear grease appropriate for nonshift (e.g., Lubriplate #105) or shift (less viscous) lower unit. Remove the grease port and air vent screws, then squeeze the grease into the motor until it starts coming out of the vent. Air and water may be emitted as well. The point is to fill the lower-unit gear cavity completely with lubricant. Should lots of grease ooze onto the prop shaft, the seal isn't adequate.

Once the bottom is properly lubed, the kicker can be fueled up. When these rigs were new, leaded gasoline was commonplace. In the absence of such old-time fuel, many antiquers argue whether regular or premium unleaded gas should be used. It's a controversy destined to continue, but many seem satisfied with no-lead (nonalcohol additive) regular. Besides, the average present-day stuff is probably better than the hodge-podge fuels of the 1920s and 1930s.

Outboard oil also brews controversy here, as the good old-fashioned SAE 40 "black gold" 2-cycle stuff is now a rarity. Again, many old kickers got weaned on a diet of straight 30-weight automotive oil and regular ethyl gas, though 30-weight was never designed to burn the way special 2-stroke lubricant is. Considering this ingredient, plus a few pine needles thrown in for good measure, it is amazing the poor eggbeaters ever made any noise.

Check with your local marine dealer on this one, but dozens of classic rigs do fine with present-day outboard oils. Please be advised, however, that a modern 50-to-1 mixture ratio is unacceptable in vintage putt-putts. Use the new type of lubrication (such as is available at Mercury or OMC dealers) but mix it only in accordance with the motor's *original* recommendation. For example, a 1949 horse-and-a-half Royal needed one-half pint of oil per gallon of gasoline. Even with modern-ratio oils, it still does! Do not scrimp on such lubrication. In fact, running a bit "fat" on oil is a common antique-outboarder practice. A little extra exhaust smoke is better than a stuck piston.

ONE OF THE BEST OUT-BOARD SALESMEN IS AN OLD OIL DRUM

And with present day lightness of the Ranger motor, every dealer should put this salesman to work.

Years ago, some folks wanted to see their prospective kickers in action before buying them. Dealers used to lug the outboards to the trusty test tank oil drum for such demonstrations, as this 1940s test tank promo illustrates.

Some years ago many old-outboard club members watched as a fellow enthusiast blew up a beautiful Lockwood Chief. Later, three sad words told the story: "Not enough oil."

Having been gassed up, the outboard is ready for an experimental run. Whether on a boat or in a test tank, make certain its transom clamp thumbscrews are properly tightened. Outboarders who forget make many voluntary contributions to Davy Jones's locker. Similarly, the flywheel nut warrants last-minute attention. A loose example may quickly prompt the old *fly*wheel into self-definition. Many late-Twenties Eltos had KEEP FLYWHEEL NUT TIGHT stamped onto their tops. Ignoring that warning could result in serious injury to operator, passengers, boat, or motor.

Open the gas tank air vent (except in remote pressure tank applications) and fuel valve. If gas begins leaking, there's probably a carburetor problem. It may be something as simple as a stuck float. Sometimes the carb float has slipped up or down the pin on which it's mounted. Numerous old-outboard firms "notched" their float pins at the proper position. On some vintage rigs the float pin can be seen rising from the top of the carb body. Perhaps desposits have gummed up the valve seat at the pin's bottom. Priming may be facilitated by holding down this pin until a little fuel leaks from around the pin's hole.

Engage the choke on a cold motor so equipped. Magneto rope-start rigs usually need their mag lever at the "start," or just past center, position. Timer-lever placement on battery-fired motors differs from model to model (between the 8 and 9 o'clock positions on an Elto Speedster).

Now comes the fun of pulling that starter cord or rotating the flywheel knob clockwise (on most models; Elto "knucklebusters" get their flywheels bounced against compression, counter-clockwise). The rope may require lots of use, so a healthy length with a good end-knot is best. (Great advice from one who tried to yank a stubborn 1947 Sea King 15.2-horse Giant Twin with a watery piece of clothesline lashed to about a foot of broken driftwood!)

As soon as the motor starts (and some of them do!), it's very important to make sure the water-pump system is supplying the cylinders with adequate cooling. Typically, there's an outlet pipe on the cylinder (which may run into the muffler) or a small water detection port in the lower cylinder block or on the motor let for just such inspection. A good stream of H_2O should be visible. Exposed cylinders may be touched for further evidence. Some kickers, such as Elto service Speedsters, have no water jackets on the cylinder ends. These places get quite hot. Watch out, too, not to come in contact with the muffler or an exposed spark plug terminal.

Never continue operating an outboard (unless, of course, it's air cooled) that isn't receiving proper cooling water. Small cams, springs, and ball bearings in check-valve-type pumps are extremely vulnerable to foreign objects. All such matter should be removed.

Also, look for weeds or any obstruction affecting the water intake. Of course, all water intake lines should be clear. Old rubber water-pump rotors are susceptible to wear and problems from prolonged disuse (or being rotated in the wrong direction). If faulty, such components require replacement.

Once it is clear the motor is running "cool," carburetion adjustments should allow the old eggbeater to smooth out. No matter how fancy the carb is (whether it sports high and low speed settings, or just has a single adjustment screw), its metering valve(s) may be positioned rich, yielding a mix of more fuel than air, or lean, for less gas and greater air content. The object is to set the fuel-to-air ratio at a point which causes the engine to fire evenly.

Owners of "modern" old motors featuring a nonpressurized remote gas tank may discover the rubber diaphragm in their fuel pump has weakened. This disorder's symptoms frequently mimic those of carburetion troubles. A motor operating long enough to receive carb adjustment certainly has promise.

What can come next is merely a matter of one's hobby preference. While some vintage-outboard buffs are perfectly satisfied with a kicker fixed up just enough to run OK, others find pleasure in a second level of fine tuning.

Flywheel magneto models may be examined better upon removal of the flywheel. If an integral puller isn't built into the flywheel nut and rope sheave plate, an external tool probably will be needed. A light tap on the top of the crankshaft, preferably buffered with a piece of wood, sometimes frees a moderately stuck flywheel.

In models made before the late 1930s, most flywheel-mounted magnets would lose their power over time. Should the magnets on the inside of this flywheel have trouble attracting a screwdriver, chances are they need recharging (at well-equipped repair stations). Alnico magnets, developed just prior to World War II, have a better record and most examples are sufficient today.

The magneto plate, which usually includes a speed lever, serves as a bed for parts such as the coil, the capacitor or condenser, and the breaker points. Being careful not to break any wires (unless the system is totally defunct), clean these components. It is likely the points are worn, pitted, or misaligned. A very thin, fine file or extremely fine sandpaper can be used to dress the points' surface. These faces are usually made of hard tungsten steel. Even so, a strong abrasive will cause damage. After revitalization, the points must be adjusted to open at a specific (ofttimes 0.020-inch) gap measurement. A feeler gauge, similar to the instrument used to set a spark plug's gap, is a key tool here, too.

Operable condensers over 50 years old are not uncommon. But a suspect condenser (also called a *capacitor*) can be checked by any shop equipped with basic electrical test gear. Likewise, coils on motors producing weak or no spark should be tested.

Breaker point maintenance.

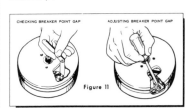

"WE'VE DROPPED IT 35 FEET... LAID IT ON THE OCEAN FLOOR FOR 6 WEEKS... AND LET IT RUN 250,000 HOURS WITHOUT HARM. NOW FOR THE FINAL TEST... A TYPICAL OUTBOARDER WILL ATTEMPT A MINOR ADJUSTMENT!"

A 1954 Mercury comic. (Mercury Marine)

Although substitute condensers are available for almost any old outboard, replacement coils are not always easily found. Fortunately, many are still in acceptable shape. Most old coils were filled with tar. This glop has to be melted out in order to gain access to the actual wire windings and spark plug lead(s). Many battery-ignition Elto coils also house the condenser. (There was an aftermarket version with a side-mounted capacitor.) In any event, heating up the tar with an infrared lamp and digging out the troubled components is best left to a gloved individual with lots of patience. Occasionally, when another outboard-type coil is unavailable, a motorcycle version may be adapted. Consulting electric motor shops or automotive ignition professionals could bring other answers.

Complete powerhead disassembly is not always a mandatory part of old kicker revitalization. When everything feels and sounds like it's within tolerance, many outboarders simply leave well enough alone. On water-cooled models, however, any suspicions of problem water jackets should be investigated. Freeze plugs on many cylinders can be knocked out for access. Numerous small, pre–World War II Johnsons will accept a penny as a freeze plug replacement. Radiator and auto repair shops may be able to provide other size plugs.

Actually, prior to punching any freeze plug, removal of the cylinder and (in models so equipped) cylinder head should lend insight into a water jacket's condition. Those that are stopped-up must be treated. Pipe cleaners, wire, screwdriver blades, or any workable scraper will aid in scale, rust, and corrosion eradication. At this time carbon deposits (in cylinder ports and head) may also be eliminated. Be careful not to score the cylinder walls. Blasts from a service station's air hose complete this vital job.

Outboards that always leak oil and/or gas at the cylinder head, or where the cylinder mates the crankcase, probably need new gaskets. Residue on surfaces between crankcase sections or crankcase and lower unit could indicate gasket trouble. Very important crankcase seals may also require attention. Bad seals not only allow fuel out, but let superfluous air in, interfering with proper crankcase pressure. Before further action, however, make certain that all pertinent nuts and bolts are tight.

Some say every vintage motor worth its salt has a gas tank dent or two. Even-tempered folks consider these to be badges of legitimate service. Perfectionists are not quite so content with cosmetic shortfalls and desire remedies.

Small dents and dings can be filled with auto body compounds. Larger depressions sometimes yield to taps from a tool positioned through the fuel cap opening. A ¼-inch hole drilled in the dent's center will accommodate a bolt which provides a pulling "handle." Reseal the hole with plastic filler or take the tank to a welder and have the hole welded shut.

Bashed-in tanks, especially the old "wrapped around the flywheel" style, may be cut open to allow repair access. After rejuvenation, the severed portion (typically, under or in front of

"Me Tarzan, you Johnson Sea Horse"; Johnny Weissmuller at a 1933 catalog photo shoot. The 21.4-hp model P-65 was fresh off the assembly line, but it already had a small dent on the side of its gas tank. An old kicker with a "mint" tank is a good find! (Outboard Marine Corp.)

the tank) can be welded back into place. Of course, prior to any fuel tank work, the container must be completely free of flammable residues. Sometimes such work requires that the tank be filled with sand. Logically, the process is best left to experienced welders.

In rare instances, a "soft" dent can be popped out by applying air pressure into the gas tank. Again, improper implementation can be very dangerous.

Nothing dresses up an old-outboard fuel tank like a colorful decal. Regrettably, sun and gasoline have claimed much of this original equipment. While new/old-stock stickers are virtually nonexistent, ambitious members of the Antique Outboard Motor Club have reproduced the most popular versions. They are offered for sale through the club publications. (See Antique Outboard Motor Club in Chapter 10.) "Unauthorized" banners for less common brands (or on motors not destined for restoration competition) are often concocted with stick-on lettering or hobby paints.

Concerning color, newer motors should wear only tints matching or close to their original. Finding such shades is not always easy, but stores offering a wide range of automotive paints represent the best source. For example, the nearly impossible to duplicate Mercury cedar green turned up in a Chrysler-product truck color. Unfortunately, these offerings are subject to change.

Late-1940s shear pin guide.

On older bare-aluminum outboards, purists don't like silver paint applied to parts on which there was none originally. Exact identification of every piece painted silver at the factory, however, is a source of controversy. Nevertheless, top-drawer restorers don't appreciate poetic license.

External, nonpainted aluminum (or brass) components can be buffed bright. Pitted lower units can benefit from this treatment, although severe pocks may necessitate filler. Care should be taken not to overbuff any thin or plated surface.

During the early 1970s, lots of old bare-aluminum motors were beautified with a German-made product called MET-ALL. Any aluminum polish recommended by a reputable cycle shop or auto parts store will fill this need.

Finally, a vintage eggbeater's propeller needs consideration. A few enthusiasts have two props for their favorite rigs. One is a "mint" display version, and another is for actual use. Without getting so fancy, it's still important to swing a wheel that is devoid of serious damage. Bad propellers can create powerhead problems. Nicks should be filed down, and improper bends need rectification. Large outboard repair stations are sometimes equipped with pitch blocks used for returning beat-up props to proper shape. By the way, if your motor's former owner was a "citizens for the use of nails instead of shear pins" supporter, become "right wing," and replace that rusty spike with the factory-authorized component! It could save much aggravation.

Whether an antique outboarder has elected to totally restore his motor, or simply pay attention to its mechanicals, the classic sound of vintage cylinders firing provides an instant reward. Don't be surprised at the attention such a rig will attract, either. Surely, if Ole Evinrude were around today, he'd call to Bess and say, "Look! That person has one of our first motors . . . and it still runs!"

10

The Antique Outboard Motor Club

"Oh, no!" moaned my cousin Jim, "someone's coming! Quick! Hide this magazine in your shirt!"

I stashed the publication on my person just as Aunt Sarah opened the door.

"Why don't you boys get some fresh air?" she suggested.

As I began following my young relative, that questionable magazine slid down to the top of my socks. Only an exaggerated limp prevented its untimely appearance.

"Is your leg all right?" Aunt Sarah inquired.

"Sure it is!" Jim chimed in with a slap on my shoulder. "Pete just has an old football injury."

"Your cousin Peter plays with old motors, not footballs," she reponded suspiciously.

"Well . . ." I stammered, "I played football once and got tackled."

After we were safely outside, Jim rewarded my ad hoc clandestine cooperation by explaining the hot pages were "sorta borrowed" from a friend's dad. The magazine's ownership then passed to me with a blessing, "There're some pictures in there I know you'll love!"

My cousin was right on target. Those photos were, indeed, eye-opening. They also defeated my fears that I was the only one who thought about such things. After being shown the magazine, my folks expressed shock.

"You mean to tell us," they gasped, "*Popular Mechanics* actually found other people who collect antique outboard motors!"

The famed publication's March 1966 issue not only featured old kickers, but introduced an organization called the Antique Outboard Motor Club. In those days membership was $5. I promised to do extra chores as my skeptical mom wrote out a check. It was a wise use of five bucks.

The Antique Outboarder, house organ of the Antique Outboard Motor Club, Inc.

The idea for an antique outboard club probably got its start in a Florida Ford dealership. Assistant service manager George Ralph enjoyed pre–World War II kickers and often compared his hobby to vintage car collecting. Old car clubs were flourishing, and members paid dues, and bought publications and promotional materials. Mr. Ralph believed outboard collectors would do likewise.

During the spring of 1959, he formed the Antique Outboard Motor Club of America. A local advertising agency helped prepare ads aimed at acquiring membership. The desired enrollees were supposed to establish club chapters and pay small annual royalties for this affiliation. By 1962 one of the modest ads appeared. Unfortunately, only about 50 motor buffs replied. A few short club magazines were published, but none were printed after 1963. Subsequently, the Antique Outboard Motor Club of America faded out.

One of that outfit's disappointed members was a graduate student named David Reinhartsen. On a semester break he visited club founder George Ralph, only to discover there was little hope Ralph's club would be reactivated. Taking names from the old outboard magazines, Reinhartsen contacted a handful of collectors and decided to start a new organization. This one, called simply the Antique Outboard Motor Club, meant only to help anyone interested in vintage kickers, and had no profit motive.

During the formative years, Reinhartsen and his wife, although busy with other things, handled most of the club's workload. A better brand of magazine was introduced. Soon a few other buffs pitched in, allowing the Antique Outboard Motor Club continued growth.

Today, several thousand enthusiasts from coast to coast and around the world are members. Many participate in various indoor swap and outdoor "wet" meets. Some contribute articles to the quarterly *Antique Outboarder* publication, or buy and sell old motors and parts through the club's regular newsletter.

A.O.M.C. logo.

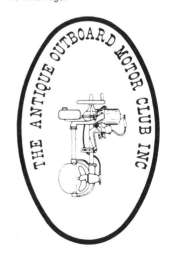

A display of restored Johnson outboards at an Antique Outboard Motor Club Meet. Some enthusiasts like to find "basket case" outboards and turn them into beauties like these.

Anyone who enjoys this book and its topic would be very happy with membership in the Antique Outboard Motor Club. Most AOMC people vividly recall how singular they felt before realizing there was a whole club full of folks sharing their unique interest. As a result, veteran members helping new ones is commonplace. Whether you're seeking a propeller for a '56 Firestone 5-hp or need starting instructions for some battery-ignition kicker, the best source has long been this fine club.

From time to time, the AOMC address changes with a shift in officers. Should you desire more information, write me in care of the publisher. Or, better yet, contact the Shipyard Museum, 750 Mary Street, Clayton, New York 13624. This excellent Thousand Islands–area repository (which has an extensive old-outboard display) can give you the Antique Outboard Club's current mailing address.

11

The Big List

In 1951 Edwin Hodge composed a doctoral dissertation for Indiana University. His scholarly work, entitled "A Study of the Outboard Motor Industry," contained a historical listing of U.S. outboard manufacturers. That interesting roster was updated by Jim Webb and Robert Carrack in their 1967 *Pictorial History of Outboard Motors* and has received revisions from members of the Antique Outboard Motor Club.

Based in part on the aforementioned works, the following list attempts to identify all known American brands of gasoline-powered outboards. Engines from the beginning of the industry through the early 1960s are included. Many of the entries outline producers from the World War I era. A majority of their machines were of the 2-cycle, forward-pointing, single-cylinder variety. More often than not, each gave about 2 hp via a modest (under 1,000) rpm rating. Most were rather obvious copies of Ole Evinrude's already famous rowboat motor.

When you think back to the late 1970s consumer scene, you'll recall everybody trying to break into the promising home computer market. Dozens of companies quickly put a little computer into production, or more commonly, marketed a relabeled model from someone else's factory. Many of those early junior electronic setups, with their modest keyboard, cassette player drive, and $89 black-and-white TV monitor, looked about the same. By the late '80s the normal business shakedown had converted most pioneer home computer firms into a footnote in American business history, and assigned remnants of their first-generation wares to the trash, or more mercifully, neighborhood lawn sales.

Similarly, the years 1913 to 1919 saw many manufacturers taking a chance in the growing outboard motor marketplace. While a few companies came up with original designs, the majority either duplicated (with the possible exception of adding rudder steering) Mr. Evinrude's early motor, or marketed a batch of badge-engineered outboards produced by some other oufit. In any event, those not wholeheartedly committed to weathering economic storms in which supply was usually far greater than demand silently submerged.

After World War II, the economy strengthened, and many people seemed to be interested in buying a lot of outboards. To fill this need, the majors strengthened their lines, and dozens of small companies entered the field. This flurry of activity continued through most of the 1960s. (Note: As a result of this activity, acquisitions, and badge-engineering as well as public preference, many outboards were known by several names. In the Big List, these other monikers appear in parentheses after the engine's proper or most common name.)

Rather than preface this directory with a list of excuses, suffice it to say, the more I researched, the greater my "content confidence" was shaken. There are probably some outboard examples that escaped my typewriter. Should you come across something not listed here, I would be most happy to receive your correspondence via the publisher.

Admiral

Boaters who valued their feet were, no doubt, swayed by Affiliated Manufacturers Company advertising. The Milwaukee concern said its Admiral detachable rowboat motor would "fit any boat like an old shoe."

The Admiral, which looked quite like the Anderson and some Blakely models, was available with either a gear-driven magneto or battery ignition. An underwater exhaust tube could be substituted for the "can" muffler at no extra charge. The lower-unit gear case was said to be "small and streamlined" and contained the water pump. Rather than use a shear pin or key, the propeller was taper fitted.

Like the Anderson and some Blakelys, the Admiral sported a relatively prominent, unusually shaped skeg, called a "skag [sic] rudder" (but the motor was not rudder-steered).

Affiliated Manufacturers had its foot in the outboard industry door between 1914 and 1916.

Aerothrust

Aerothrust outboards were not designed to get wet! That is to say, their props were like airplane propellers and pushed boats by means of air thrust.

A 1919 Aerothrust Engine Co. advertisement.

It appears the Chicago-made motors debuted in 1915 and were not produced much after 1920. (One source does indicate Aerothrusts were built through 1925, but research into old advertising conflicts with the report.)

These products, generally in the form of 2-, 3-, or 5-horse twins, were air-cooled and available with either battery or magneto ignition. Some Aerothrusts came through with the crankcase and both (opposed) cylinders cast in a single assembly. A front-mounted flywheel got "turned over" with a removable hand crank. Once the engine started, the operator was to pull the crank from the catch fitting, adjust the float-style carb, and prepare to get whisked away.

During its production run, Aerothrusts were equipped with two-blade props composed in various formats. Some looked like a pair of laminated wooden paddle blades, while others had a sharper appearance and were fashioned of alloy.

A few Aerothrusts never saw liquid waterways but were mounted on 45-mph ice sleds.[1]

First produced in 1954, the Air-Boy consisted of a small air-cooled engine driving an airplane-style prop. Air thrust from the propeller pushed the boat. Airboats, Inc., of Denver made the Air-Boy through the 1960s. The single-cylinder machines were available in 2-, 3½-, 4-, and 5-hp denominations.

An early attempt to market a fan-prop type outboard rig came from the Kemp Machine Works in Muncie, Indiana. The Airdrive was sold from 1918 through 1922. Some advertising called this one the Kemp.

Another Fifties private-brand outboard, the AMC Saber, was produced by Gale Products for Aimcee Wholesale Corporation, New York, New York.

The AMC Saber made its debut in 1955 with 3-, 5-, 12-, and 22-hp models. For 1956 the 22-hp was replaced with a 25-hp. Even so, officials at Aimcee decided the AMC Saber marque just couldn't cut it and discontinued sales at the close of the year.

The 1896 American outboard is covered in Chapter 1, page 3.

Not to be confused with the 1896 American outboard, this rig, built in Detroit by the American Engine Company, generated 2 hp at 900 rpm. Most models had a gear-driven magneto and rudder steering. The flywheel-knob-start, 62-pound single was produced between 1913 and 1918.

Would you buy an outboard requiring no carburetor, no valves, no magneto, nor even a single spark plug? What if this motor, minus said troublesome components, sported one cylinder and a pair of pistons? Sound weird? Well, such an outboard, a diesel, was actually made.

A Kemp Machine Works "Airdrive" ad from 1919.

Air-Boy

Airdrive

AMC Saber

American (1)
American (2)

American Marc

Around 1959 American Marc, Inc., of Inglewood, California, advertised a line of diesel outboards ranging from 7½ to 22 hp. Early ads, however, showed only the American Marc 10 (not to be confused with the Mercury Mark 10 of similar vintage). The single-cylinder, opposed-dual-piston model produced 9¼ hp at 3,500 rpm. The lower unit was reminiscent of a Merc or Oliver, and its twist-grip steering handle looked 100-percent Mercury.

The California company's prototype may not have actually gone into production, as subsequent literature covering its restyled AMARC 10 identified the motor as "the first diesel outboard."

Although the AMARC 10 could go without parts vital to gas outboards and could cruise "twice as far as a gasoline engine of comparable size on the same amount of fuel," its unconventionality kept customers away. Even in its faint heyday, the AMARC 10 was a rare sight. It was much more so after being discontinued in the early Sixties. (It should be noted that American Marc, Inc., also marketed its own line of boats in lengths from 14 to 30 feet.)

Amphion

Most companies without aggressive sales organizations seldom put a dent in the marketplace. Such was the case with Clarence Allen's Milwaukee, Wisconsin, outboard business.

Allen knew Ole Evinrude and admired the success of Ole's rowboat motor. Consequently, he decided to build a couple of small inboard marine engines, and in 1915 mounted an in-line, alternate-firing twin on an outboard lower unit. (This represents one of the earliest alternate-firing two-cylinder outboards.) The strange-looking rig, called "Amphion," was on the market (so to speak) until 1919.

Unfortunately, Mr. Allen lacked a strong dealer network, and his biggest orders were said to have come from "one enterprising salesman who'd load up his Model T Ford truck and go to nearby Wisconsin lakes and peddle the Amphions."[2]

In 1926 Allen advertised a weird-looking 3-to-4-hp model "D.O." outboard. Its odd appearance was a primary result of the cowl-like rudder covering most of the prop area. This feature was identified as the McNabb Kitchen Rudder and was said to lack "freakiness."

A short time later Allen sold all the remaining Amphions, patterns, tooling, and parts to fellow Milwaukeean A.J. Machek. This guy assembled some of the motors, and a few more Amphions made it to the waterways. The firm was sold at the close of World War II, and the Amphion stuff (tooling, patterns, etc.) was donated to the shop department of a Wisconsin high school.

In the 1960s a member of the Antique Outboard Motor Club found some old Amphion goods, including what turned out to be a late Twenties unfinished Amphion Dreadnaught kicker. After some machining, adjusting, and balancing, the opposed twin went to work. While not the smoothest or lightest 6-hp of its day (circa 1928), the Dreadnaught's horseshoe-shaped gas tank is not afraid to sport a beautifully cast oval Amphion logo, reminding us of its company's interesting place in outboarding history.

This 1914–18 vintage 2½-hp rowboat motor was available in either battery or gear-driven magneto models. The Anderson, complete with its ornately shaped skeg, looked a lot like the Admiral and Blakely. It was made by the Anderson Engine Company of Chicago.

"Pull the starter," says an Aqua-Jet ad, "and you're on your way to fishing spots you could never reach with an ordinary motor." This jet pump outboard from Farrow Manufacturing Inc., of Elmore, Minnesota, used a single-cylinder, air-cooled Tecumseh powerhead and was easily carried by means of handles both front and back. The Aqua-Jet water intake was "covered by a shield which kept debris out and allowed an unrestricted flow of water in." The 5-hp rig was advertised as the motor that "would take you where you want to go"; however, its mid-Sixties production went but a few years.

Most remembered for a 1916 acquisition of the pioneer Waterman outboard firm, the Arrow Motor and Machine Company (sometimes called Newark Motor and Machine) had been marketing its own kickers for two years prior to absorbing Waterman.

Arrow's main offering was a flywheel-knob-start, 4-hp, opposed-twin-cylinder model with adjustable propeller. As a special "anti-backfiring" feature, Arrow cylinders were drilled with double ports.

Also originating in a Newark, New Jersey, factory were the National and Federal twins. Because of the similar venue and like appearance, I'll bet there was some connection between the three motors.

Although Arrow's mechanical claim to fame was its two-cylinder status, some dusty listings mention a 2½-hp Arrow single.

It is generally believed that Arrow and sister line (as of late 1916) Waterman went totally out of business in 1924. Apparently, however, ownership eventually passed to the Pausin Engineering Company of Newark, and a small stock of motors was still available into the early Thirties. Reportedly, Pausin was getting requests for Waterman (and possibly Arrow) outboard replacement parts through the 1940s.[3] Some of these requisitions came from exotic ports in Africa and China.

The 1960s-vintage Arrow linked "Canada's finest outboard with the famous [air-cooled, 2-cycle] American-made Tecumseh power plant." Painted in "heat- and gasoline-resistant off-white," these rigs wore a front-and-back carrying handle assembly.

Rather than the typical "pin"-style motor angle adjustment, Arrow's transom bracket had a knob on the end of a bolt which could be tightened into the proper position. The transom clamp bracket's height could also be adjusted. Its collar, securing it to

Anderson

Aqua-Jet

Arrow (1)

A 1907 Waterman outboard.

Arrow (2)

Bantam

Barracuda

This air-cooled, 4-hp Barracuda "standard" outboard, circa 1960, was picked up at a swap meet. This rig is identical to various Mono, Eska, and My-te models.

the motor leg, slid up and down. This allowed the operator to obtain the desired lower-unit length.

Arrows were identified with Indian names and wore such model designations as Iroquois (3 hp), Mohawk (4 hp), Seminole (5 hp), Mohican (6 hp), Navajo (7½ hp), and Apache (9½ hp). Arrow, primarily a Montreal, Quebec, firm, also maintained an office in New York, New York.

Not much is remembered about this 1946 offering from the Bantam Products Company of New York City.

Imagine that it is early August, 1961; a fellow walks into a New Jersey Mercury dealership looking for a fishing motor bargain. The proprietor quickly shows him a shiny new 6 horse Merc but is met by an objection:

> "No, no! Too expensive!"
> "Well sir," the outboard dealer says, "over here, we have a nice little economy model. . . ."
> "How much?" the customer interrupts.
> "This 5.1-cubic-inch single lists for $92.50."
> "Still too much!" the customer retorts.
> "Wait a minute sir. I quoted the suggested retail price. *Today* this particular gem happens to be *on sale* for . . . only $76.00."
> "Seventy-six, you say?"
> "Just 76 bucks; yes, sir."
> "I'll take it and pay cash," comes the reply. "Now what kind of kicker did I just get?"

Actually, I don't know if the original owner of Barracuda outboard motor, serial number 4705, was a true skinflint. I concocted this hypothetical scenario based upon a nearly forgotten sales slip. It is likely, however, the 4-hp Barracuda was purchased largely on the basis of price.

Accompanying literature from the Barracuda Outboard Company of Aurora, Illinois, boasted that its product is "a machine of the finest quality . . . found to be in perfect mechanical condition." Even so, the firm warned: "Do not contact us if you experience engine difficulties." Of course, that's because the Power Products Corporation (lawn-mower–type) engine could be serviced at any one of the many local small engine shops authorized throughout the U.S. and Canada.

Identical to other low-priced brands (such as Mono, Eska, My-Te, etc.), Barracuda featured an air-cooled powerhead and water-cooled lower unit exhaust assembly and engine base. Standard (with small cylindrical, exposed fuel tank), and Deluxe (wearing a plastic powerhead shroud) versions were available. By mail, the little outboard concern also offered (for 30 days after motor purchase), "a rugged chromium-plated" storage stand ($4.95), as well as a spare, $2.50 prop (plus 50¢ postage). A white "Barracuda" decal (typically on a blue engine) distinguished this mini-marque from its previously noted and very similar competitors.

Whether the Barracuda Outboard Company really built the lower unit and attached the powerhead is a mystery. Perhaps the entire package came from another source with Barracuda simply acting as a private-brand marketing agent.

One thing for sure is the likely existence of other such tiny brands not presently known by the author. The Barracuda was yet another cute, lightweight, which served a limited, but valid, boating public.

See the listing for Fageol.

A relatively rare marque, known for its air-cooled, 2-cycle power-head, was the Bendix. Produced by the Bendix Aviation Company of Newark, New Jersey, the Bendix Eclipse outboards were actually built in the firm's South Bend, Indiana, facility.

Two basic powerheads were available: a 2 ¼-hp single, and a 4 ½-hp opposed twin. Usually a tiny ID plate riveted to the transom bracket assembly carried easy-to-interpret model codes like TMD (Twin-Magneto-Deluxe), SMD (Single-Magneto-Deluxe), SM (Single-Magneto), and SB (Single-Battery). An *L* indicated "Longshaft."

The Bendix outboards were marketed from 1936 to about 1940. Parts were supplied through the early post–World War II years.

Around 1938 Bendix worked up a high-horsepower prototype. It was a four-cylinder, in-line, air-cooled machine requiring a good-size flywheel/cooling fan. Technicians ran the big Bendix in the shop, but for reasons lost to time, the approximately 15-hp outboard never saw production.[4]

It is not uncommon for a wayward Bendix to be discovered minus some of its skeg. This component was a rather thin casting that broke easily with carelessness.

Bendix production ceased in 1940. Bendix owners with motors needing parts or service were directed to Pozgay Welding Works on Long Island, New York.

The Blakely Engine Company of Muskegon, Michigan, was in the outboard business from 1914 to 1918. During that run, it offered a standard, battery-ignition rowboat motor with above-water "tin-can" exhaust, as well as a deluxe, gear-driven, magneto version sporting a below-the-waterline exhaust tube. Some of the basic rigs were offered for $39.50 "while they last." Both of the aforementioned models looked nearly identical to the Admiral and Anderson singles.

It should be noted that Blakely also marketed a 1916 flexible drive shaft model that was clearly a relabeled Gray Gearless outboard from Detroit's Gray Motor Company. Whether or not Blakely actually built their own rowboat motors is certainly open to speculation.

Bearcat
Bendix

The top on this streamlined, air-cooled 1936 Bendix got "flipped" so the operator could wrap the starter rope around the flywheel. Once this battery-ignition kicker started, adjustments to a choke lever dangerously close to the flywheel required strict attention. Not a motor for OSHA inspectors!

Blakely

Bourke-Cycle

A couple of motors with weird mechanical properties appeared briefly on the outboard racing scene in late 1954. These 2-stroke engines, affixed to Mercury class "D" Quicksilver high-speed lower units, came from B.R. Bourke Research of Portland, Oregon.

The Bourke-Cycle outboards had only two moving powerhead parts: the piston/connecting-rod assembly and the crankshaft. Glow plugs, rather than spark plugs, were fired by battery ignition. Motorcycle-style cooling fins covered the cylinders. The Bourke engines had no flywheel and were available in two sizes: the two-cylinder Bourke-30 and a four-cylinder rig called the V-4-60. "The single throw crank of the 2-cylinder model had no connection to the pistons, and the engine functioned more like a high pressure turbine than like a reciprocating engine."[5]

Bourke claimed its approximately 30-cubic-inch twin could do 15,000 rpm and produce 114 hp! Reportedly, the first Bourke experiments were done in the 1930s through an Evinrude racing lower unit whose gears the Bourke tore up.

Brooklure

Spiegel, Inc., the famous Chicago-based mail-order house, decided to get into the outboard business in 1950. Motors wearing the Brooklure label were manufactured by Outboard Marine's Gale Products Division, of Galesburg, Illinois.

Over its production run, Brooklure outboards came in sizes from 1½ to 25 hp. Records show the 1958 Brooklures made up the last of their line.

Buccaneer (Gale)

In the late Forties Outboard Marine and Manufacturing, producer of Evinrude, Johnson, and half a dozen private-brand outboards, saw another niche it might fill. Wholesalers serving sporting goods and hardware stores sought a small line of low-priced outboard motors they could offer their clients. Many of these retailers were already in someone else's Evinrude or Johnson franchise area, and they wanted just a simple outboard that could be added to their outdoor-related inventory and sold informally.

Because Outboard Marine's Gale Products Division was already building a series of 3-, 5-, and 12-hp generic kickers, a decision was made to badge-engineer another brand for direct sale to the aforementioned wholesalers. The new line was dubbed Buccaneer and was debuted in 1950.

Over the years the brand name was changed to Gale, with Buccaneer becoming a model designation. Like many of its private-brand sisters, this product offered boaters on a budget their first opportunity to own a reliable outboard.

The last Gale Buccaneers and more deluxe Gale Sovereigns were marketed in 1963. This line included motors from a 3-hp single to a V-configuration, four-cylinder, 60-horse job.

Buccaneer's freebooter logo.

Bundy

The Detroit-based Bundy Tubing Company imported a line of outboards from its Milan, Italy, subsidiary. Bundy motors were actively marketed in the United States from about 1961 to 1964.

I have heard tales of brand-new, new/old-stock Bundy 40-horse outboards (complete with fuel tank and a few spare parts) being offered in a Connecticut marina as late as the mid-1980s. Although clearance-sale priced comparable to a fishing motor, these particular "never been run" rigs drew little more than customer conversation.

Burroughs

"Let Burroughs Row for You," suggested 1916 ads for the Time Manufacturing Company's new single, forward-pointing-cylinder rowboat motor. The Milwaukee firm (with a factory in Oostburg, Wisconsin) said its knob-start, rudder-steered rig was "so powerful that you can go anywhere and pass them all." A fancy-looking variable-pitch prop mechanism may have caused its producer to believe its motor could give small boaters a life in the fast lane.

Although the outboard "typified 100% efficiency, being as nearly troubleproof as human ingenuity permitted," the public's satisfaction with other motors caused the Burroughs marque to fade after 1918.

Burtray (Walnut, Water Sprite)

At least two years before Ole Evinrude began seriously marketing his rowboat motor, the Burtray Engine Works of Chicago quietly introduced a primitive but relatively practical outboard. The Burtray wore a vertical, air-cooled cylinder, sight oiler, and Lunkenheimer valve-lift-type carb. On the prominent flywheel (positioned horizontally over the transom clamps) was mounted a large wooden starting knob. The Burtray's gas tank, sitting vertically next to the cylinder, looked like a "family-size" flask. The battery-fired power plant rested atop a cast aluminum lower unit and swung a hefty 12-inch, three-blade prop reminiscent of an electric fan. An adjustment allowed the Burtray operator to change the outboard's transom angle easily. Although the Burtray had an exaggerated skeg/rudder, encompassing a good portion of the lower unit, the motor was pivot-steered like its present-day counterparts. First available in 1907, the Burtray had been discontinued by the close of the 1909 boating season.

A motor called the Walnut (bearing properties nearly identical to the Burtray) also appeared on the scene a couple of years prior to the Evinrude. One wayward Walnut was discovered in the 1950s by a prominent Connecticut outboard collector. That machine differed from the Burtray only with respect to being minus the skeg/rudder and the metal shells covering the upper and lower bevel gears.

The Walnut Machine and Brass Foundry Company of Toledo may not have placed shells over its outboards' gearing, or the coverings simply may have been missing from this particular machine; the issue is open to question.

No one would blame you for wondering if the Walnut and the Burtray, being so distinctively designed for the day, were dreamed up by the same guy, or actually came out of a common factory, or something of that nature. Coincidentally, the Walnut lasted for the

Caille

Two views of a 1930 Caille Class "B" 5-speed outboard. Raising or lowering the steering arm bracket would "shift" the propeller pitch through five speeds: reverse, neutral, and three forward speeds. Steering arm motion swiveled only the lower unit, not the powerhead. These motors were dubbed Caille Red Heads in honor of their red gas tanks.

exact length of time as the Burtray, silently fading from the early outboard marketplace in 1909.

To add to the interesting confusion (which may never be straightened out), another Chicago firm offered a detachable boat motor it sold as the Water Sprite. That model was available only in 1910 and strongly resembled both the Burtray and Walnut!

A fellow named Sidney Helm was probably the most unusual Caille outboard owner. In 1925 he bought a direct-drive Liberty twin model, affixed it to a floating mattress, and putt-putted over 200 miles from Keokuk, Iowa, to St. Louis.[6]

Without anticipating such antics, Adolph and Arthur Caille formed the Detroit-based Caille Perfection Motor Company. This was in 1910, and the chief product was to be inboard marine engines. The brothers had been in other businesses together for nearly 20 years. Successes making coin-operated phonographs, scales, and slot machines provided capital for the marine engine concern.

By 1913 outboard production was begun, and it didn't take long for the kickers to eclipse Caille's interest in its inboard line. Even Montgomery Ward bought some early Caille outboard motors for resale (under the Hiawatha banner) in its mail-order catalog.

Early on Caille set its agenda with distinctive-feature outboards. The Liberty single's and subsequent Liberty twin's long, direct-drive shaft was easily recognizable. The firm also came up with a five-speed, adjustable propeller system said to offer neutral, reverse, and three speeds forward. In the mid-Teens Caille bought some prominently labeled magnetos from Evinrude. Consequently, these models could be mistaken for Evinrude rowboat motors.

When outboard racing began attracting national attention, Caille joined the field with such motors as the "Flash" and "Streak." Some of these wore tractor lower units (pulling props mounted in front of the gear housing) and dual carbs.

Caille powerheads remained stationary on the boat, as the tiller handle steered only the lower unit. On the bigger twins this arrangement lessened the effects of engine vibration but made high-speed (high-torque) steering a muscleman's province.

The Caille organization quickly built a quality reputation and advertised in upscale publications such as *National Geographic*. The firm's early Thirties "Red Head" (with bright red gas tank) outboards, some with the five-speed prop feature, enhanced that swanky image.

Meanwhile, impecunious boaters desiring Caille craftsmanship could pay a little less for the firm's product sold under Sears's Motorgo label. (A Caille-style motor minus flywheel rope sheave plate labeling is probably a Motorgo.).

By 1932 the Depression had taken its toll on Caille. In an effort to weather the storm, company officials pushed their more basic outboards. A good example of this redirection came in the form of the model 79, so named for its modest $79 price tag. A few other Cailles were renamed to reflect their attractive sales price.

Early the following year control of the once proud, family-owned outboard maker passed to a large holding company called Fuller Johnson. This outfit "owned a number of important manufacturing companies in the east and middle west," and "predict[ed] a bright future for Caille."[7] Unfortunately, that forecast was off the mark. From 1933 to 1935 Fuller Johnson did little to spark up Caille's line. The marque's catalog offered pretty much the same motors for three years, and Caille outboard production was quietly discontinued by the end of 1935.

Vintage motor buffs may be interested to know that the Caille Motor Company, although long out of the kicker business, was still operational (in Minerva, Ohio) during the 1950s.[8]

Cal-Jet

While writing this chapter, I showed it to a fellow anxious to see his old outboard in print.

"Where's the listing for Cal-Jet?" he asked.

"Uh-oh, never heard of it," came my reply.

Seems back in the mid-Sixties a coworker offered this gentleman a brand-new, genuine, gasoline-powered fishing motor for $50! He was directed to an evening rendezvous behind some guy's house (in the nearby Syracuse, New York, area). Fifty bucks were produced, prompting a backyard wholesale entrepreneur to open his garage door.

Reportedly, the place was filled with Cal-Jet outboard motors. Memory indicates the small, approximately 3½- and 5-horse, jet-thrust kickers were powered by single-cylinder, 2-cycle, air-cooled engines (probably Tecumseh). Not much more came to the erstwhile Cal-Jet owner's mind.

The rig's name leads one to speculate that the little motors were a product of some California company. Incidentally, three Cal-Jet models, Jetmaster, Ramjet, and Econojet, streamed out of the factory.

Campbell

Among the many Minneapolis-built outboards was the 2½-hp "Baby Campbell" rowboat motor. Campbell Motor Manufacturing Company specialized in marine, inboard engines up to 125 hp, but offered "immediate shipment" and "special prices" on its "absolutely guaranteed" rudder-steered outboard motor. The Campbell's cigar-box-shaped gas tank looked a bit larger than those of its contemporaries. The company was always looking for "agents" to sell the "Baby Campbell" during its 1914 to 1918 production run.

Cary Jet

Cary Enterprises of Huntington Station, New York, entered the jet-thrust outboard field in 1963. Its fishing-motor-sized product with its Italian-built powerhead was offered for only a few years.

Champion

The Champion outboard label was founded by a guy out in his St. Paul, Minnesota, workshop. Sig Konrad's 1926 Champions (and the less expensive Monarch motors) were the first Champ outboard

Circa-1935 Champion logo.

New Home of Champion Motors
MORE THAN 4½ ACRES UNDER ONE ROOF . .

Post-World War II Champion factory.

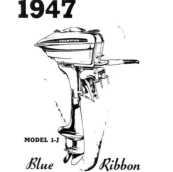

1947

MODEL 1-J

Blue Ribbon
CHAMPION

Champion began producing the Blue Ribbon line of motors in its own plant after an agreement with Firestone retailers expired.

products. Champions bearing low serial numbers (yes, they started with #1) were of the water-cooled, 2-hp, single-cylinder, 2-cycle variety. They had a small, square exhaust housing leading to the lower unit and timing marks you could use to realign (in the event of hitting an underwater obstruction) the keyway-less flywheel and crankshaft.

A rather deluxe 4-cycle, water-cooled Champion was produced in limited quantities. This model featured a dipstick and a pair of spark plugs in its single cylinder. Should one plug foul, the spark wire could be moved in order to give the other one a try! Much of the early Champion output was sold close to home by a St. Paul boating store.

In 1935 Mr. Konrad decided to leave the outboard business and let the Champion name go to Earl DuMonte (who hoped the marque would someday make him a millionaire[9]) for $500. Another fellow, Stanley Grey, became a partner in the new venture.

DuMonte, a veteran outboard racer, moved his new Champion Outboard Motors Company a few miles to Minneapolis. Actually, the young firm had no way to make motors and existed only as a sales organization offering Scott-Atwater-built outboards, primarily through Firestone retailers.

The Scott-Atwater "Champion" engines date from 1935 to 1942. Firestone's agreement began around 1939 and ended with the United States' entry into World War II. During wartime the Champion folks envisioned newly designed kickers constructed in their own factory.

Following the war a new production facility was built. Ralph Herrington, a top Scott-Atwater engineer, joined Champion, and the firm's dreams of independence began to be realized. Within a short time a small line of new Champion Blue Ribbon motors was rolling off the assembly line.

The late Forties saw great consumer acceptance of the well-built, reasonably priced motors. To expand the line, private-brand versions called Majestic and Voyager were introduced around 1949 or 1950.

Also at this time DuMonte unveiled his pride and joy, the Champion Hot Rod special stock outboard racer. The Hot Rod has been compared to the old Johnson KR racing engine of the 1930s, but featured state-of-the-art improvements. Its gear ratio, 14 to 19, was superior to the KR's 12-to-19 figure. The Champion also wore a more sophisticated and streamlined lower unit. Because the Hot Rod's prop turned opposite of the KR, special propellers had to be developed and tested.

By the mid-Fifties a few of the available Hot Rods showed up to compete in class "B" (approximately 20-cubic-inch displacement) races. Quickly, the "B" Hot Rods began to embarrass owners of high-speed Mercury rigs. Postwar Mercs had enjoyed an easy dominance of the stock outboard racing scene and were not too happy with DuMonte's buzzing challenger. Some say politics came into play, causing victorious Hot Rods to be dismantled by inspectors and then disqualified on construction technicalities. In the face of this battle, race officials gave Mercury permission to replace the veteran Quicksilver drive-shaft housing with a tuned exhaust "Howler" unit. This gave the Merc 20-hp high-speed jobs an advantage over the pretty blue Champions. (The Champs weren't allowed to modify the exhaust.) Also in competition were class "J" (9.66-cubic-inch) and "A" (14.96-cubic-inch) versions.

By 1955, with all the unfortunate Hot Rod setbacks, sales of the service (fishing/pleasure motor) Champion lines also began to slow. While the major manufacturers could sell you a 25- or 40-horse outboard, Champion's top offering registered just 16½ hp. Admittedly, this approximately 20-cubic-inch "Blue Streak" twin (sister to the Hot Rod) was a good performer, but it didn't have nearly enough zing for family cruising or serious water-skiing.

In order to stem the tide while deciding whether to retool for the expensive production of bigger motors, Champion modified the prop rotation on a small stock of 16½s. By matching a standard-rotation 16½ with a counter-rotating version, the pair (complete with Y-shaped gas tank hose) could be marketed as a Tandem 33. As it worked out, the pair idea didn't catch on well enough to give Champion a marketable "full-line outboard maker" image.

This failure again raised the urgent question: should Champion spend the money to develop bigger outboards? It had just put out a sizable sum for a new factory in 1955. The company bank account answered "no," leaving the firm with few viable options. As a cold economic result, the 1957 Champs were the last (although some late '57s were called '58 models).

By early 1958 the Champion name and patents were sold to Western Tool and Stamping. Western figured it could save the well-known marque and built some very contemporary, 25-, 50-, and 75-hp prototypes. (These looked a little like the big West Bends or Scotts of the day.) Alas, money again became an issue, and the powerful Champions never saw the showroom. The brand's trade name and all remaining outboard assets were then sold to a small manufacturing firm in the summer of 1962.[10]

Incidentally, all of the Hot Rod stuff had been sold to Swanson's Outboard Service of Crystal, Minnesota. For many years Lyle Swanson built Hot Rods from old stock, and subsequently, newly manufactured parts. The racer was renamed the "Swanson Hot Rod" and was available new into the 1970s. By the mid-Eighties a redesigned "Hot Rod" (which won many races) was available from a firm that had purchased the Swanson interests. At about this time a garage full of new/old-stock Champion fishing-motor parts (since 1958 they had gone from one small firm to the next) were advertised for sale.

In retrospect it is interesting to note some of the many cleverly nutty promotional stunts staged during Champion's heyday. For example, two Midwestern fellows, one seven and the other eighty-three years young, were taken to a little Minnesota lake in June 1947. Neither had ever operated an outboard, but after basic instructions, both easily passed the "One-Pull Test"

Champion's 1955, 16½-hp Blue Streak. The factory would also sell you a pair of these motors with counter-rotating props, under the name Tandem 33.

This 1955 Champion Midget Hot Rod's 9.66 cubic inches could push a small hydro to 40 mph-plus.

with a Champion. The following year Champ employees placed one of their motors in a specially designed steel hoop. They started the outboard in –21-degree weather and rolled it down an icy road. When the hoop stopped, the Champion (now upside down) was still running. The promo tricks took a wrong turn, however, when a motor that was supposed to be dropped from an airplane into a lake was ejected too soon. The engine landed, gas tank first, on a farm!

Chris-Craft

Chris-Craft
10 h.p.

Chris-Craft
5½ h.p.

THE CHOICE OF EXPERTS

Chris ★ Craft

OUTBOARD MOTORS
2000 BEVERLY, GRAND RAPIDS 9, MICH.

A 1951 Chris-Craft ad.

In the late 1930s Jay W. Smith began work on an outboard motor design. Ordinarily, a fellow with a common surname involved in such a project wouldn't seem too significant. This Smith, however, was the son of Chris Smith, the master boatbuilder responsible for the legendary Chris-Craft inboards.

The younger Smith observed post-Depression America seeking recreation but understood that not everyone could afford even the smallest mahogany-decked Chris-Craft. Consequently, the firm planned for a line of outboard-powered craft, the most modest of which (an 8-foot pram) sold for $42!

To power these new Chrises, while keeping the customers in the family, the famous yacht producer offered a couple of newly designed outboards of its own. The rich blue Chris-Craft motors came in the form of a 5½-hp "Challenger" (introduced in 1949) and 10-horse "Commander." Beginning in 1950 these products, aided no doubt by their famous nomenclature, sold rather well, and some 15,000 were manufactured in 1950. The firm was rumored to be planning an expanded outboard line featuring larger power motors.[11]

Chris-Craft outboards were nicely built and performed very satisfactorily. The 10-hp model was comparable to similarly rated Mercury Lightnings and Hurricanes. Some said the design comparisons were too coincidental and talked of possible litigation.

Suddenly, perhaps to avoid the courtroom, the attractive Chris-Craft outboard line was discontinued at the end of 1953. A short time later the Grand Rapids–based company sold its outboard division to the folks who made Oliver farm tractors.

Chrysler

Chrysler Motors Corporation had been in the marine inboard engine business since 1927. By 1965 the famous auto firm saw its chance to expand via a pair of purchases. It acquired the Lone Star Boat Company and bought West Bend's outboard division.

The first Chrysler kickers (or the last West Bends, depending how you view it) were the 1965 "West Bend by Chrysler" models. While most of the subsequent 1966 Chrysler line came from West Bend's vintage drawing board, Chrysler engineers came up with new three-cylinder, 75-hp, and four-cylinder, 105-hp outboards. Over the years several Chryslers, including the 105, were also offered in racing versions (complete with exhaust stacks!). The motors, with the distinctive white with blue and gold accents, sold rather well.

In some cases the outboards drew more customers to Chrysler Corporation showrooms than did the autos. In the late 1970s, with Chrysler, Dodge, and Plymouth on the verge of bankruptcy, management decided to sell the outboard division to the Force people. During Chrysler's tenure building outboard motors, their plant in Barrie, Ontario, filled Canadian orders.[12]

> An amazed-looking guy quickly entered a small, main street, upstate New York shop. The proprietor could already guess what was to come next.
> "Is that little outboard in your window display for sale?" the fellow asked.
> "No! And you're only the twelfth person today to ask me!"

That diminutive old motor was a Clarke Troller, produced in small quantities between 1937 and 1941. It was the brainchild of one D.R. Clarke and his Clarke Engineering Company in Detroit. At 10 ½ pounds and just 21 inches high, it certainly was the most portable of all outboards.

Reportedly, a balky conventional outboard led Canadian-born Clarke to invent his own kind of motor. Indeed, the Clarke Troller represents the pinnacle of individualist thinking. The top of the unit contained the coil, fuel metering device, and gas tank. (Some models had a one-piece tank, while others were fitted with a tank made of a pair of castings.)

New York outboard collector Phil Kranz, who is knowledgeable about Clarkes, explains, "The motor incorporated several unusual engineering features. The powerhead operated completely underwater (facilitating simple water cooling) and there were no bevel gears, as the crankshaft was also the propeller shaft. The rope starter sheave was on the propeller end of the crankshaft, with the motor tilted out of the water for starting. There was no magneto, so a battery was used to provide electric current to the coil. The motor was made largely from polished aluminum castings."[13]

In all candor, the Clarke approximately 1.2-hp power plant was equal in zing to a model airplane engine and even used the tiny Champion (⅜-inch-thread) spark plug popular with modelers. While the Clarke's parts were fabricated in the United States, actual construction took place in both Detroit and Toronto.

The motor sold for about $35, and came complete with a canvas carry-bag. Accessories included a canoe bracket, a 6-inch-long shaft extension, and a strange clock-spring thing hooked to a rod. This item, called a "chicken starter," would be wound up, cocked, placed over the prop's starter sheave, and released. The bronze prop on some Clarkes had a variable-pitch feature. No matter what the propeller adjustment was, however, once a running motor was eased into the water, it usually quit—a victim of too much theory and not enough power.

Clarke Troller

A 1939 Clarke Troller advertisement.

Hoping to curb some of his machine's capriciousness, Clarke announced the advent of a twin-cylinder version. Few of these have surfaced.

From a collector's point of view, the Clarke is a gem. In fact even folks who don't know they like old outboards enjoy looking at one of these trinkets of the waterways.

Clay

Most likely a forward-pointing, single-cylinder rowboat motor, the Clay came from Cleveland in 1914.

Clinton (Chief, Peerless, Apache)

Clinton Engines Corporation, of Maquoketa, Iowa, along with its predecessor, Clinton Machine Company of Clinton, Michigan, had been marketing single-cylinder, air-cooled saws, mowers, and inboard marine engines prior to its 1955 introduction of a low-priced outboard motor. (Early Clintons were distributed by Fageol.)

The Clinton outboards, available through the years in almost every color from light green to gold, were just about the simplest, dependably understandable motors you'd find anywhere. Clintons bore model names such as Sprite, "J-9," Peerless, Apache, and Chief.

A member of the Antique Outboard Motor Club drove five hours to follow a lead on "an old Chief with a red gas tank," assuming it to be a rare 1929 Lockwood Racing Chief. He came home with a garden-variety Clinton!

Some Clintons were available with a red, remote, 3-gallon fuel tank, a lower unit whose shaft was 5 inches longer, a neutral gear,

Left: In an effort to economically devise another private-brand marque, or to modernize an existing power plant, Clinton made use of shroud styling. This late-1960s Sprite used the famous little Clinton lower unit also worn by the likes of Eska and Mono. (Clinton Engines Corp.)

Right: This 1969 Clinton Chief 350 delivered 3.5 hp. Over the years, similar-looking outboards with various color schemes and model names (such as J-9 and Apache) left the Clinton factory. The Starling-Jet water thrust outboard version of this rig wore a jet lower unit. (Clinton Engines Corp.)

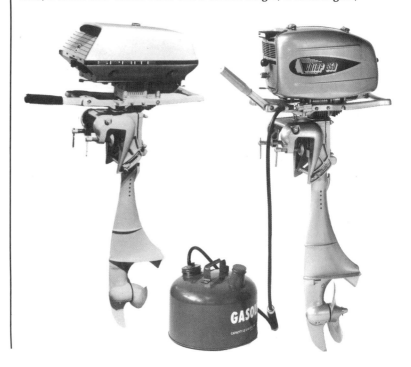

Left: A simple 2-cycle, lawnmower-type powerhead with small cylindrical fuel tank on a lower unit comprised the first (mid-1950s) Clinton outboards. These budget-priced kickers, like the 2-horse, 1971 model pictured here, represented a reliable motor value. They became an important part of Clinton's outboard business, and were private-branded by a number of other firms as well. Parts and service were always as near as the local small engine shop. (Clinton Engines Corp.)

Right: By the mid-1970s, Clinton labeled their smaller kickers with cubic centimeter (CC) as well as horsepower ratings. They produced outboard products designed to compete with low-priced imports. (Clinton Engines Corp.)

and a lighting coil. The latter feature developed 42 watts at 4,000 rpm and could fire a 6- or 12-volt trouble light when connected via the optional "handy plug-in receptacle on the control panel."

Generally in the 3-to-5 ½-hp range, Clinton outboards were also wholesaled to a number of other firms that marketed them under their own private-brand labels.

By the early 1980s Clinton signed a temporary pact with rival Eska agreeing to limit the sale of Clintons in certain markets.

There used to be an old fisherman near my summer place on Lake Champlain who every evening faithfully outboarded to a distant fishing spot. Curious about the brand of his busy-sounding little fishing motor, I finally asked.

"Uh, it's a *good* one," he responded, subsequently admitting he forgot who had made it.

Later I discovered it was a Clinton and realized that not everyone needs to buy a motor from one of the big manu-facturers.

Columbian (Cullen)

"Unlimited enjoyment at very little expense" is essentially what the Cullen Motor Company of Chicago offered its outboarding customers from 1913 to 1918. Like many of its contemporaries, the 2-hp (at 900 rpm) Columbian (also labeled Cullen) resembled Ole Evinrude's standard rowboat motor. The later Cullen (or Columbian) models had a flywheel magneto.

In the final production year the Cullen Motor Company equipped its outboards with an aluminum piston, thus "reducing the weight of the motor . . . and its vibration while running." The firm advertised its pride in marketing the motor "with a get-there come-back reputation."

Commando

See the listing for Milburn.

Commodore

Essentially a relabeled 2-hp West Bend fishing motor, the Commodore was available around the time President Kennedy took office. Bigger Commodore-brand outboards came in such sizes as 7½, 10, 18, and 40 hp.

Continental (1)

Added by late 1932 to the long list of former Detroit outboard makers was the Continental Motors Corporation. It had begun production in 1926. This outboard is not to be confused with the small post–World War II single from California.

Continental (2)

See the listing for Milburn.

Corsair

In 1948 Scott-Atwater began producing a line of private-brand outboards for the Corsair Outboard Motor Company, of Minneapolis, Minnesota. The outboards were distributed by both Skelly Oil Company and Pure Oil Company. When Scott was acquired by the McCulloch people in 1956, the new management briefly continued the construction of Corsairs. The line was discontinued in 1957.

Crescent

Direct from the "maybe, who knows?" department comes an early World War I–era rowboater called the Crescent. Actually, this listing was almost omitted, but a fellow old-outboard collector is pretty sure he saw an old brochure—somewhere—advertising such a forward-pointing single. The motor was said to have been built by a long-forgotten outfit in Scotia, New York. For years a river bend in that community has been known as the "crescent." Perhaps there's a connection?

Crofton

See the listing for Fageol.

Cross (Cross Radial, Sea Gull)

A family business on Detroit's waterfront, the Cross Gear and Engine Company had roots in the manufacturing of brass marine accessories. The firm branched out into the production of inboard engines and by 1928 began building a 73-cubic-inch, 35-hp outboard called the Cross Radial. The giant, 4-cycle kicker got its name from the powerhead arrangement with "5 cylinders placed radially around the shaft, the axis of the cylinders being horizontal." Not designed for fishermen seeking a trolling motor, the 135- to 160-pound Cross Radial appealed to a few high-speed enthusiasts desiring an outboard larger than any other. Either a tractor or pusher lower unit could be furnished, and "the gear ratio could be made suitable for racing or ordinary service."

Cross Radial owners filling the 3-gallon (around the flywheel) gas tank and 1-gallon oil reservoir were ready to be treated to "lightning acceleration." Those behind the big outboard were treated to a roar, as no muffler was used. Speeds of 45 to 50 mph were targeted by the manufacturer.

The Cross firm recognized that its water-cooled radial model (which soon had been beefed up to 50 hp) was not for everyone. Consequently, in 1931 it introduced an outboard motor promised to be "smooth, alert, simple, perfect for your wife and kiddies to handle." This gentler offering came in the form of the 40-cycle, 29.68-cubic-inch "Sea Gull 29." The masculine-looking, two-cylinder motor, in service form, generated between 20 and 25 hp.

Its racing sister with twin carbs and battery dual ignition (two spark plugs for each cylinder) wore a gas tank with a pair of filler caps. As on the service Sea Gull 29, about three-quarters of the tank held gasoline, while the other quarter was an oil reservoir.

Most old-motor enthusiasts agree the Sea Gull 29 racer, complete with ultra-streamlined lower unit, was one of the most beautiful motors ever produced. The 76-pound rig had aluminum pistons and no-nonsense open exhaust stacks. Racers were rated at 28 hp at 6,000 rpm.

Although of the opposed-cylinder configuration, Sea Gull 29s were alternate-firing engines. Believing people would be fired up to buy these motors, production was said to have been increased 300 percent for 1932. (Of course, that wasn't too difficult in light of small 1931 production runs.)

Cross Radial and Sea Gull 29 motors were built through 1933. The previous year the outboard division (renamed Cross Motor Sales Corporation) told prospective dealers that the Cross franchise would "be even more valuable in the years to come!" Early Thirties economic troubles got the better part of that claim. The business was reduced to three members, and no new Cross outboards were marketed after the close of 1933.

The once-ambitious firm sold its outboard interests to the Detroit Outboard Products Corporation of St. Clair Shores, Michigan. Although the racing twin and radial designs were permanently retired, this new organization resurrected the Sea Gull 29 service model as a 1940 motor called the Detroiter.

Cunard

A rowboat motor marketed by Russell A. Reed of New York City, the Cunard was available during 1916. The single-cylinder kicker was rated at 2 ½ hp at 675 rpm.

Cyclone

It's hard to believe anyone would have the nerve to name an approximately 2-hp motor the "Cyclone"! That's just what the folks at the Bellevue Industrial Furnace Company did, however, when labeling their "new patented detachable rowboat motor, specially designed for fishing and pleasure trips."

The water-cooled, forward-pointing, single-cylinder engine wore a knob-start flywheel, a tin-can muffler (positioned under the gas tank), and a reversing lower unit. Both sides of the cylinder had spacers and wing nuts holding brackets connected to the transom clamp assembly. You could loosen the wing nuts, tilt the motor angle, and retighten after reaching the desired position.

Filled with the usual exaggeration of the day, Cyclone brochures claimed its special features would drive an ordinary rowboat about 11 mph. (I bet "about" is the key word here!) The literature also made it clear that anyone who attempted to steal the company's patents, such as the mysterious "non-vibrating device," would not escape prosecution.

One of the many "troubles [that would] cease when you own a Cyclone" was fouling by water vegetation, as the outboard wore a weedless prop. Actually, this wheel looked very much like the useful weedless props of post–World War II Evinrude/Johnson 3-hp fame. The propeller could be replaced with an accessory pulley "for running different kinds of machinery." (Coolant water would have to be supplied by a garden hose.)

The Cyclone was advertised at around $100. Apparently, few customers with money to burn felt the Detroit-based furnace firm's offering was hot enough. Although little Cyclone information exists today, it appears the outboard was made around 1914.

I can't help but wonder if George Thrall (the Detroit boiler factory owner who was said to have helped develop the early Waterman) had something to do with the Cyclone.

Davis (Experimental)

The Davis outboard was a 1930s prototype. Its water-cooled, 4-cycle, five-cylinder, radial-type powerhead got mated to a Caille lower unit. The 29.96-cubic-inch Davis was said to develop 27 HP at 6,500 rpm. Although William Morris Davis worked up an operable outboard and spare powerhead, his plans to produce the class "C" racer never went any further.[14]

Detroit

Logically, the Detroit was produced in its Michigan namesake. The front-pointing single with a knob-start flywheel was offered in both 1914 and 1915.

Detroiter

When the "new" Detroiter was introduced as "1940's outboard sensation," the poor thing was already about 10 years old. Although modified here and there, the 18-hp Detroiter was obviously a reincarnation of the old 4-cycle Cross Sea Gull 29.

Convinced boaters would love to say "good-bye to chatter, stink, and stalls" of 2-cycle outboarding, Detroit Outboard Products (based in St. Clair, Michigan) purchased the rights to the early Thirties Cross 4-cycle kicker. As had been said of the Cross in 1931, it was claimed that the Detroiter would give performance equaling "the smoothness of the modern motor car." Detroit Outboard Products also stressed the 4-cycle's tremendous oil savings, another big sales point made by Cross.

One readily discernable external difference between the two related motors was the gas tank. The Detroiter's tank was somewhat more rounded than that of the Cross Sea Gull 29.

Detroit Outboard Products really tried to entice potential dealers by offering to protect them "fully." The company swore that no direct factory-to-owner sales would ever take place "without paying full commission to the dealer controlling the territory." In addition the firm pledged to increase the product line by quickly following its 18-horse model with 5- and 10-hp versions, which were allegedly completely designed and ready for production. Furthermore, said the new company, with a Detroiter rig "the old bang-bang days are gone from outboarding." Boaters, they promised, would wait in line to buy its products.

By the next year, however, customer acceptance was still about as imaginary as mermaids, which were depicted swimming around the Detroiter's logo. The company's limited outboard production concluded with America's entry into World War II.

Dragonfly

Like its direct competitors in the air-prop outboard avenue, the air-cooled, single-cylinder Dragonfly was most attractive to swamp and shallow-water boaters. Aptly named by Robertson, Hedges, Inc., of Kansas City, Missouri, these mechanical dragonflies enjoyed a 10-year manufacturing run beginning in 1954.

The Dragonfly came in two sizes: 4.7 and 8.0 cubic inches. Over the years they generated power in the 2-to-5-hp range and sported model names like Troller and Cruiser.

Durkee

A 1930 motor, the Durkee was marketed by Durkee Manufacturing Company, which was based in Grassmere, New York.

Eclipse

See the listing for Bendix.

Elgin

Every old-outboard nut knows the feeling. Someone professes to have a real vintage boat motor for sale—maybe, if the offer is right.

> "Been in the family for yeeeaars! And it ran the last time we tried it, too."
> As you walk toward the guy's old shed, you inquire what color the engine is.
> "Uh, kinda medium green."
> Yes, there under a torn tarp is an *Elgin*!

Although most Elgins are not at all rare, the marque's survivors serve as a tribute to its reliable design and construction.

Elgin outboards first hit Sears stores and catalogs in 1946. They were eagerly supplied by the West Bend Aluminum Company (Hartford, Wisconsin), which led the premier with a 2-cycle, single-cylinder, air-cooled, 1¼-hp job. This rope-start, green Elgin with a yellow-gold decal was widely accepted and set the stage for subsequent, water-cooled one- and two-cylinder versions in 2½-to-7½-horse denominations.

A sturdy 16-hp twin (with shift) was added in 1949. The 16 had many innovative features, including a fiberglass hood and rewind starter knob at the base of the cowling. Such placement provided a lower center of gravity and prevented the outboard from kicking up when the cord was yanked.

In the mid-Fifties some other Elgins were equipped with gearshifts and electric starters (1956), and sported attractive

One of the first outboards to wear a fiberglass hood was the 1953, 16-hp Elgin, produced by West Bend and sold by Sears.

colors ranging from light green with gold accents, to coral and copper. Power on the top-of-the-line motors was faithfully increased.

Beginning in 1959 the Elgin line was a mix of West Bend– and McCulloch-produced outboards. McCulloch's involvement lasted through the time the Elgin name was switched to "Sears." The final West Bend Elgins were produced in the early Sixties.

For most boaters with a memory, the Elgin essence is embodied in a beat-up 5 ½ twin—the one wearing that little *Sears* script on its bare aluminum rope sheave—the one you could even start with a piece of clothesline and with a few pine needles floating in the gas tank. Until the last aluminum rowboat disappears from some little lake somewhere, there will always be Elgins. (See also West Bend, McCulloch, Waterwitch.)

Elto

Elto's ad agency probably purchased the "catch" pictured in this 1925 catalog photo at a local fish market. The motor is an Elto Ruddertwin with battery ignition (note the wires wrapped around the clamp bracket/carrying handle assembly). The aluminum flywheel "knuckle buster" starting knob was spring-loaded; it retracted when it wasn't being cranked. (Outboard Marine Corp.)

Ole Evinrude's wife Bess became ill around 1913. Because nothing meant more to Mr. Evinrude than his spouse, he decided to sell his portion of the famed outboard company (bearing the Evinrude name) in order to devote all his time to Bess's recuperation. After six years of leisurely auto and yacht travel, Mrs. Evinrude was restored. Ole's thoughts returned to motors.

By 1919 the outboard pioneer had come up with a 2 ½ to 3-hp kicker composed largely of war-proved aluminum. This opposed-twin-cylinder rig weighed in at just 47 pounds, representing greater portability than the old rowboat motors. Excited by the new project, Mr. Evinrude offered it to his old partner, who now owned all of the Evinrude Outboard Motor company. Surprisingly, the plan was quickly rejected, leaving Ole nearly heartbroken.

Bess encouraged her husband to reenter the outboard business himself. After all, his 1913, five-year noncompete clause with the Evinrude firm had expired.

"But, Bess," he reminded her, "the commercial use of our name was sold with the old company."

"Well, then, let me come up with something catchy," Bess suggested. "Maybe a clever, easy to remember name like Kodak."

So, identifying Ole's new motor as *Evinrude's Light Twin Outboard*, the creative woman coined the acronym ELTO, and a major outboard label was born.

The Elto motors were an instant hit, making Ole and Bess's new company profitable by its second year (1922). Elto's first offering was dubbed "Ruddertwin" (although its shiny aluminum exterior caused Ole to call it "Silvery") because it steered with a rather large rudder. After a few years of a thin, solid rudder, this model said good-bye to its traditional water pump and got a hollow, water-scooping rudder in 1924. Ignition was generated via battery and Atwater-Kent timer. The flywheel-knob-start Ruddertwin was upgraded to 4 hp in 1926.

Amidst billboards touting Atwater-Kent radio sets, Yellow Cabs, and men's drawers, a 1925-era 4-hp Super Elto Light Twin (Ruddertwin) is loaded onto a Model T Ford delivery truck. The "Propello" sign on the lower right of the store refers to Elto's cooling water intake system. Words on the top right of the store identify Elto as "Ole Evinrude's fastest motor!" At that time, the rival Evinrude company was not owned by the Evinrude family. (Outboard Marine Corp.)

By the late 1920s Ole and Bess's college-age son, Ralph, urged his folks to enter outboarding's new high-performance avenue. This plea was met in late 1927 with the two-cylinder, 7-hp Speedster, and the four-cylinder, dual-carbed Quad. Speedsters could plane a boat over 20 mph, while a good Quad would put a light hull on speaking terms with 40! Both products helped revolutionize the outboard industry by taking it out of the "putt-putt" realm. Eltos of this era wore Atwater-Kent timer-fired battery ignition and could be "started with a quarter turn" of the "knuckle buster" flywheel knob.

The Quad got updated in 1929 with more cubic inches and fancy cylinder covers. It and the '29 Speedster were available in standard and high-speed (with auxiliary air intakes, aluminum pistons, etc.) versions.

When Elto merged with Evinrude, and then with Lockwood in late 1929, Ole found himself in charge of three major outboard firms. The new corporate umbrella was named Outboard Motors Corporation (OMC), and Mr. Evinrude, his family, and associates opted to simplify advertising by highlighting the merger. A late-Thirties issue of *Fortune* provides some Monday-morning quarter-backing on the topic:

> The [new] company set out to impress upon the public that here was the ultimate fount of all outboarding wisdom. In a great institutional advertising campaign the grandeur of Outboard [Motors Corp.] as a merged entity was stressed, rather than the existence of its products [Elto, Evinrude, and Lockwood], and this was a mistake since it tended to wash out the name value of the separate lines. It also caused intense dismay among the several thousand Elto and Evinrude dealers who for years had been in competition.[15]

Actually, since the merger idea developed quite rapidly (in 1929), Elto had already planned a 1930 line of its own. This model year featured seven Eltos, from 2¾ to 35 hp. The two small Elto motors, the 2¾-hp Foldlite (which was actually an Outboard Motors Corporation engine) and 3½-hp lightweight, were twin-cylinder rigs which folded for portability and storage.

Top: Tilted 1929 Elto Speedster showing its very rare underwater exhaust tube. Bottom: An outboarder prepares to start his 1929 Elto Quad.

The well-tried standard (or Service) Speedster, touted as Elto's 7-hp "fast rugged utility model," could be ordered with rudder steering and optional underwater exhaust silencer. A new member of the 1930 Elto line checked in at 14 hp wearing the Senior Speedster decal. This beauty had standard underwater exhaust and optional electric starting.

Topping the Elto lineup was a 35-hp Quad. Like the Senior Speedster, it could be purchased with an electric starter, but was manually cranked by a cord instead of the Senior Speedster's flywheel knob.

For 1931 OMC began advertising Elto's trademark by touting "ELTO—BATTERY IGNITION OUTBOARD MOTORS." That year the popular Service Speedster was given 1 hp more (making 8 hp) and sold for $165. With an additional five-dollar bill, one could get the new 12-horse Special Speedster. This motor was somewhat of an amalgamation of OMC parts stock. Although it looked good, the Special Speedster's performance was no better.

Also introduced in 1931 was Elto's Junior Quad 18-hp motor, as well as an Evinrude Speeditwin takeoff called the Super C 25-hp model. "Tucked away in its crankcase [was] a new-type rotary valve that works marvels in performance and economy." The 35-horse Quad of 1930 was boosted to 40 hp for 1931. Electric starting was available for it, the Super C, Junior Quad, and Senior Speedster.

The year 1932 was a pretty tough one economically, but the Elto division of OMC came up with a new Super A 11-horse twin and a 4-hp Fisherman twin with a weedless prop.

Most folks could hardly pay the rent, let alone purchase a new outboard. As a result, ads shouted, "Here's ELTO quality at the lowest prices in ELTO history!" The retail price of some models (such as the Special Speedster) was actually reduced from the previous model year.

Eltos of 1933 still sported battery ignition, but switched to a new way of measuring horsepower. Sample Eltos were taken to the Pittsburgh (PA) Testing Lab, where they got rated for horsepower certified by the National Outboard Association. This new method provided an accurate standard but dropped the advertised output of most models. (OMC then affixed a little gold "certified NOA HP" medallion to its products.) The Senior Quad got bumped back from 40 to 31.2 hp; the Super C went from 25 hp to 21.1; while the Junior Quad, previously 18 hp, dropped to 16.2. Also affected by the new measurements was the Super A, going from 11 to 8.5 horses. By the way, this rather small (by today's standards) twin could be upgraded via an optional electric starter. New to the 1933 line was a nonfolding Lightweight 5.1-hp twin and Super Single, a 2.2-horse rig sporting front-mounted fuel tank.

Ole's wife Bess had passed away in 1933, and Ole was often clouded in a fog of loneliness. There were times, however, when he'd put the final touches on a new concept in outboard styling. A couple of shrouded, or Hooded Power, outboards were introduced for 1934. They gained positive attention and were the major focus of OMC's desired modernization direction.

Ole died during the summer of Elto's 1934 model run, signaling a de-emphasis on the Elto line. Around this time, Elto and Evinrude motors began being sold in the same dealer showroom. Advertising often linked the pair, urging boaters to move up to a new Evinrude-Elto. Magazine ads running at about the time of Ole's passing simply featured this theme and even included a little coupon you could fill out concerning your present (old clunker of an outboard) motor. After receiving such particulars (make, model year) and noting an *X* next to "Good _____, Fair _____, or Poor _____" condition, OMC would mail you back an appraisal along with a new Evinrude-Elto catalog.

By 1940 Elto had clearly taken a backseat to Evinrude as its economy line, and separate Elto-only advertising was not common. Eltos of this era had (with a few exceptions) been upgraded with flywheel magneto ignition, but usually lacked the fancy shrouding of Evinrudes.

A good example of this rested with the tiny ½-hp Elto Cub. The 8½-pound baby Elto differed from the similarly endowed Evinrude Mate in that the Cub had no powerhead covers. Believe it or not, when "ELTO put a new price tag on the world's handiest motor" in 1940, you could pick up a new Cub for $26.50!

OMC had been renamed (Outboard Marine and Manufacturing in 1936) when Johnson was acquired by Evinrude. Consequently, the Elto ID plate now said Evinrude Motors instead of Outboard Motors Corporation. (This change indicated the close, literal family relationship between the Elto and Evinrude divisions,

Half-hp Elto Cubs being tested prior to shipment to dealers. Motors number 3, 4, and 9 have conked out. Notice the starter cords in the upper left. (Shipyard Museum)

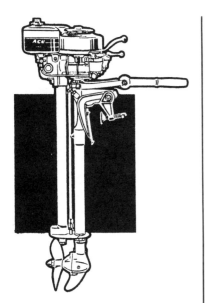

A 1936 Elto Ace.

as well as flagged the Evinrude division as a strong influence on, perhaps even the seat of, engineering and marketing forces within OMC.) Late-Thirties and early-Forties advertising for Evinrude's bargain stable plainly stated, "Every motor in the complete Elto Line is designed by Evinrude engineers and built to Evinrude standards of dependability, starting ease, and smooth, quiet operation." That standard 1940 Elto offering included the Cub; the 1.1-hp Pal single; the one-lung, 1.8-horse Ace; the 3-hp Handitwin; the Lightwin 5 hp; and the 8.5-horse Fleetwin (which had always been an Evinrude name).

As it became clear America would be embroiled in World War II, Evinrude officials placed Elto on the back burner. Elto ad literature coasted to a stop after about 1940.

Evinrude management opted not to return Elto to the immediate postwar lineup. In 1949, however, the Elto name made a very brief American reintroduction. These Eltos were based on a standard pair of economy kickers out of OMC's Gale Products plant. Labeled Sportster was a 5-horse, twin two-cylinder Elto, while a 12-hp twin got tagged with the famous Speedster model designation. This small family of Elto motors was mostly offered through Evinrude dealerships as the economy line. Elto disappeared from U.S. outboard catalogs the next year. Perhaps with OMC's 1950 introduction of the Gale-built Buccaneer, there was no need to have two budget brands.

The Elto line was produced and marketed in Canada for some time after World War II. Evinrude's Ontario factory turned out badge-engineered Eltos identical (except for decal and trim) to Gale's Buccaneer, Sea King, Brooklure, and others. In 1956, for example, Canadian-built Eltos (a rare sight in the States) ranged from a 3-hp single to an electric-start, 25-hp, 35.7-cubic-inch twin.

By the late 1960s, although no longer on the market, Elto began to enjoy another round of success. I wonder if Ole ever imagined his Silvery Ruddertwins, Speedsters, and Quads becoming some of the best-loved (and most desirable) kickers in today's antique outboarding scene.

Emmons

This outboard originated at the Emmons Specialty Company of Detroit. Similar to many of its World War I–era counterparts, the Emmons rowboat motor was sold from 1913 to 1916.

Ensign

Even though other makers unveiled numerous 1933 kickers, Van Blerck Marine of Newark, New Jersey, advertised that it had "the only MODERN outboard." The 4-cycle, four-cylinder (arranged like those of a Volkswagen Bug engine) Ensign power plant put out 30 hp and employed a "tractor" lower unit. This drive mechanism placed the propeller in front, instead of at the rear, of the gear case.

Ads said you could troll with the huge electric-starting outboard, but invited purchasers to open the Ensign's throttle, too. Obviously, any outboarder interested in this "car engine perched on a sleek lower unit" was more apt to buy such a rig for the latter suggestion. Not very many customers showed up, though, so the big Ensign did not return in 1934.

Ask a six-year-old kid to draw a picture of an outboard motor, and you'll most likely be presented with a good representation of an Eska. These single-cylinder kickers were perhaps more generic than any other and offered would-be yachtsmen an opportunity to forgo oars.

The first (1960) Eska motors were simply relabeled stock purchased from Clinton. Within a few years the Eska Company of Dubuque, Iowa, duplicated some of Clinton's tooling and began manufacturing its own lower units. On top of these, Eska put 2-cycle, air-cooled powerheads secured from the Tecumseh small engine people.

Eska initialed an agreement whereby it would pay Clinton (which backed off some of its outboard production) a royalty for every Eska sold.

Because a merchant needed only to commit to a couple of these "bargain-basement" motors per year, it was not uncommon to see little Eska franchises in country hardware and sporting goods stores.

In addition to marketing outboards under its own name, Eska supplied private-brand motors for the likes of Sears and Montgomery Ward. Over the years Eska called its various models names such as Golden Jet and Pathfinder.

Faced with foreign competition, a drop in the low-priced, gas-powered outboard market, and the desire on the part of some of its officers to retire, Eska closed up shop in the mid-Eighties. Fortunately, the company stayed in business long enough to provide motors for a lot of kids and the young at heart.

The Evansville dates from 1933 to 1946. Not much is remembered about this outboard once offered by the Evansville (Indiana) Gas Engine Works.

See Chapter 2 for background and details for Evinrude outboards.

Anyone saying a Fageol outboard looked like a small car engine would be right! The unusual Fifties rig was, in fact, comprised of a 44-cubic inch Crosley auto power plant mounted vertically on a beefed-up Scott-Atwater lower unit. (Inboard versions were also available.)

Legendary inboard racer Lou Fageol flipped his competition boat at 120 mph in 1955 and was laid up in the hospital. While recuperating, Fageol got his outboard idea. The 4-cycle, in-line, four-cylinder, 35-hp, Crosley-powered Fageol went on the market the following year. This premier model was dubbed FAGEOL 44 and was purchased by boaters wanting 4-cycle power and fuel economy.

In 1957 the 44 was joined by a more powerful GOLD CUP 60 model. This 60-cubic-inch motor developed 55 hp.[16] While the 1956

HOMELITE
4-Cycle-55 hp Outboard

The 1963 Homelite 55 evolved from a Crosley car engine and the Fageol outboard.

Fageols had a rounded top with a wraparound, Mercury-like ribbed center cowl, the 1957s wore a fiberglass top (with Merc-style ribs), covering only three-quarters of the twin-carb powerhead. Consequently, many complete Fageols looked as if important parts were missing. By 1957 Fageol's deluxe single-lever remote-control had been introduced. Dubbed the "One-Arm Bandit," this unit actually sported two levers (one for starting) but used a single stick for speed and shift.

The 1958 Fageol line included 35- and 40-horse versions. During this production run, however, Mr. Fageol passed away suddenly, and the project (which had been plagued by a weak lower unit design) lost its impetus.

By 1959 the Kent, Ohio, based Fageol Products Company (a division of Twin Coach Co.) was sold to the Crofton Manufacturing Company in Los Angeles. This firm had been marketing auto-related Crosley engine products, so the connection was natural. Even so, Crofton let its acquisition go after only two years of offering a handful of Crofton-labeled Fageols. This sale opened the way for the best remembered incarnation of a Crosley powerhead outboard when Textron's Homelite Division used its purchase as the base of the 1962 to 1966 Homelite 55-horse, four-cylinder, 4-cycle kicker. Rights to the Homelite motor were sold to Fisher Pierce Company, Inc., of Rockland, Massachusetts (maker of Boston Whaler boats), in 1966. Fisher Pierce called their product "Bearcat 55." Using engines from the English, Coventry Climax auto, they soon raised their offering to an 85-hp model. Ironically, some Crosley enthusiasts are now buying the Bearcat and Homelite 55s and converting them to automobile use. These outboards generate more power than a standard Crosley engine.

I once found an old FAGEOL 44 in a remote upstate New York marina. The huge thing showed very little use, as the instruction tags were still affixed to the battery cable. True to form, the rig's lower unit was missing.

"A guy on vacation paddled in with this years ago," the marina operator recalled. "Wanted a replacement lower unit part or something. Asked him, 'Are you kiddin'? Parts for that weird thing way up here?' Sold him a new 40-horse Johnson, and he went on his way."

My castoff treasure was to cost me $10—or $25 if I required the marina man's services to help me get the 175-pound beauty into my trunk!

Federal

The U.S. capital was home to the Federal Motor and Manufacturing Company. During 1914 and 1915 this firm, through its Newark, New Jersey, factory, built an interesting twin-cylinder, 3-hp, knob-started outboard with a "tilt-up" transom bracket. This was one of the first motors to offer the convenient tilting feature. (Although some early Evinrude owners enjoyed the same effect by removing their motor angle adjustment bolt.)

Instead of the traditional tiller handle, a pair of cords maneuvered the Federal. Grips on the cords' ends held additional line for control toward the bow of the boat. You could get the Federal with battery or gear-driven Bosch ignition. An underwater exhaust tube was optional. The lower unit could be turned around for reverse operation. Spark plugs pointed to the front and were parallel with the water's surface.

A summer 1915 *Motor Boating* advertisement for the Federal emphasized the twin's smooth running characteristics (as compared to the era's one-lungers). The ad showed a guy holding up an operating Federal and indicated the feat was done while the engine was turning 1,700 rpm! Nevertheless, the company took a turn for the worse and was bankrupt by the end of that year. (Note: This classy looking rig may have been revitalized in 1916. See National.)

See the listing for Saber.

Fedway Saber

Ferro

"Don't go rowing, go FERROwing!" suggested advertisements for this 2½-hp (at 850 rpm), single-cylinder outboard produced by the Ferro Machine and Foundry Company. Ads for the Cleveland, Ohio, firm's rowboat motor also pictured a pair of small boats headed for shore during a thunderstorm. One was being rowed by a sweaty, exhausted fellow (with his necktie unceremoniously undone). The other was being quickly "Ferrowed" to safety with a well-dressed, attractive woman at the controls! (I enjoy old outboards but, in that situation, would prefer oars.)

Some Ferros were adapted to canoe use by installing them in a special "well" one could cut into the center of one's craft. The "carpenter's plans" were available free from Ferro.

While many of its counterparts had simple fuel-mixing valves, Ferro bragged about a "genuine float feed carburetor." This was a major reason why Ferro said its motor was so dependable even "a girl can run it!" To give ears of any gender some quiet (without sapping the engine's power), a "scientifically constructed," water-cooled muffler was standard. A rudder, attached to the torque tube, turned with the lower unit for "propeller and rudder steering."

Ferros were fitted with a pair of petcocks. One, labeled a "priming cup," was tapped into the cylinder. The other, situated in the bottom of the crankcase, served as a drain. Some of the antique-looking motors stood on a "skeleton" skeg (while others were solid).

Buyers could choose between battery ignition or Bosch gear-driven, high-tension magneto ignition. The flywheel-knob-started Ferro was on the market from 1914 to 1917.

Firestone

The first outboards from the Akron, Ohio, Firestone Tire and Rubber Company were actually Scott-Atwater-produced kickers wearing the Champion label. During this time (1939–1942) the Champion outfit was little more than a middleman marketing organization.

125 The Big List

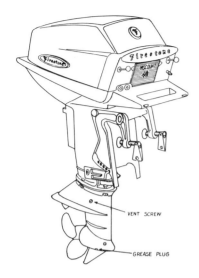

Above: West Bend-produced Firestone 40 Viscount.

Right: Early-1950s, 7.5-hp Firestone.

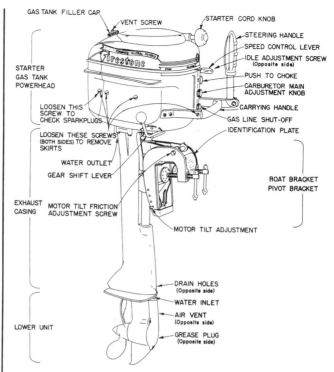

After World War II Champion decided to build its own motor factory. So Firestone turned directly to the Scott-Atwater people for a newly designed private-brand engine. The Firestone nameplate hit the water in 1946 and developed a respectable following among fishermen.

By the mid-Fifties the Scott-Atwater-built Firestones gained more horsepower and features. Most notable of the latter was the Knotometer on the 1956 5-, 10-, and 16-hp models. The Knotometer, a water speedometer, was built into the transom bracket assembly and dialed boat speed in knots as well as miles per hour. The handy device's pilot, or water pickup, was discreetly mounted in the leading edge of the lower unit. The Knotometer was exclusive to Firestone. It's strange that others haven't adopted such an accessory.

In the late Fifties the big tiremaker contracted with West Bend for its outboard supply. West Bend's successor, Chrysler, honored the remainder of the Firestone agreement.

By 1963, however, what had been a relatively complete line of motors was reduced to a few fishing engines when Firestone had Clinton take over the last two years of production of its outboard marque. These engines were identified as the Firestone Featherweight.

Flambeau

Here's an intriguing outboard you could "open up" two ways—by advancing the spark lever, or by placing the motor on its side, removing some screws, and literally opening the little kicker in half! The Flambeau's major components, from lower unit gears to top crankshaft bearing, fit into and were held together by two castings: a right and a left half.

This sandwich motor, made in Milwaukee by Metal Products Corporation, was introduced in 1946. Metal Products' president, George Kuehn, was an experienced outboarder, having been a class "C" amateur hydro-racing national champion in 1933. His company, however, never got into the production of fast motors.

Flambeaus were typically of the 2½-hp single-cylinder or 5-hp twin design. The 1950 models were rated at 3- and 6-hp, respectively, but dropped back to the lower figures the following year. The interesting little motors came standard with rope start, but rewind starters were available. Their unusual name may have come from Wisconsin's Lac du Flambeau Indian Reservation.[17] Native Americans in full regalia were sometimes pictured in company advertising. In addition to the trade name, Metal Products owned all of the Flambeau machining dies, but the casting, forging, and stamping were done by outside sources.[18]

The Flambeau ("the *TRULY* outboard"), which sat on the boat, had most of its powerhead mounted outboard. This resulted in very little fuel dripping inboard. (Of course, the waterway got an extra snootful.) On top of the gas tank (of some motors) was a knurled knob geared into a carb adjust mechanism.

From 1946 to 1949 the rig's exterior was unpainted aluminum with a yellow decal background. From 1950 Flambeaus wore a two-tone maroon and burgundy color configuration. Flambeaus of 1953 and later sported a lower-unit cavitation plate.

Metal Products got caught in the same bind as many other small outboard makers: It needed a larger power motor in order to compete in the growing Fifties watersport scene. The firm did work up a couple of 10-hp prototypes (looking just like an overgrown 5-horse model) for boat-show exhibition. Retooling costs probably prevented actual production.

In the early Fifties some 1,000 retail dealers handled Flambeau (mostly as a sideline). About 10 percent of total production was exported. In any event sales, which had never been remarkable, dropped further. This left little for Flambeau's promotional budget. Ads for the motors are virtually nonexistent past 1954, and Flambeau, "the Aristocrat of Outboard Motors," finally disappeared between 1956 and 1957.

An early-to-mid-Sixties private-brand marketed by J.C. Penney, the Foremost was produced by West Bend. These outboards were available in sizes such as 3½, 6, and 9.2 hp.

See the listing for Buccaneer.

The year 1920 saw the Gierholtt Gas Motor Corporation of Marine City, Michigan, introduce its "direct-drive" outboard. The single-cylinder motor could shed its gas tank and long drive shaft for

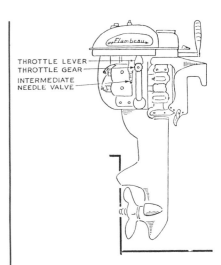

THROTTLE LEVER
THROTTLE GEAR
INTERMEDIATE
NEEDLE VALVE

Early-1950s Flambeau Twin.

The complete 1952 Flambeau line, single and twin. The motors were built in two parts, then "sandwiched" together.

Foremost

Gale

Gierholtt
(Hess)

Early-1920s Gierholtt diagram.

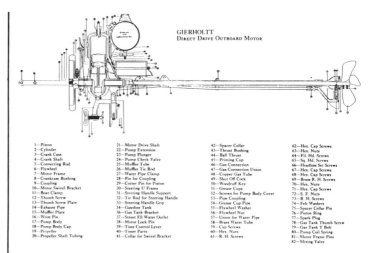

GIERHOLTT
DIRECT DRIVE OUTBOARD MOTOR

1—Piston	21—Motor Drive Shaft	42—Spacer Collar	62—Hex. Cap Screws
2—Cylinder	22—Pump Extension	43—Thrust Bushing	63—Hex. Nuts
3—Crank Case	23—Pump Plunger	44—Ball Thrust	64—Fil. Hd. Screws
4—Crank Shaft	24—Pump Check Valve	45—Priming Cup	65—Sq. Hd. Screws
5—Connecting Rod	25—Muffler Tube	46—Gas Connection	66—Headless Set Screws
6—Flywheel	26—Muffler Tie Rod	47—Gas Connection Union	67—Hex. Cap Screws
7—Motor Frame	27—Water Pipe Clamp	48—Copper Gas Tube	68—Hex. Cap Screws
8—Crankcase Bushing	28—Pin for Coupling	49—Shut Off Cock	69—Brass R. H. Screws
9—Coupling	29—Cotter Pin for Piston	50—Woodruff Key	70—Hex. Nuts
10—Motor Swivel Bracket	30—Steering U Frame	51—Grease Cups	71—Hex. Cap Screws
11—Boat Clamp	31—Steering Handle Support	52—Screws for Pump Body Cover	72—S. F. Nuts
12—Thumb Screw	32—Tie Rod for Steering Handle	53—Pipe Coupling	73—R. H. Screws
13—Thumb Screw Plate	33—Steering Handle Grip	54—Grease Cup Pipe	74—Felt Washers
14—Exhaust Pipe	34—Gasoline Tank	55—Flywheel Washer	75—Spacer Collar Pin
15—Muffler Plate	36—Gas Tank Bracket	56—Flywheel Nut	76—Piston Ring
16—Wrist Pin	37—Street Ell Water Outlet	57—Union for Water Pipe	77—Spark Plug
17—Pump Body	38—Motor Lock Pin	58—Brass Water Tube	78—Gas Tank Thumb Screw
18—Pump Body Cap	39—Time Control Lever	59—Cap Screws	79—Gas Tank T Bolt
19—Propeller	40—Timer Parts	60—Hex. Nuts	80—Motor Coil Spring
20—Propeller Shaft Tubing	41—Collar for Swivel Bracket	61—R. H. Screws	81—Motor Frame Pins
			82—Mixing Valve

Gierholtt's early-1920s "direct drive" kicker.

Gilmore

Gopher

Gray

easy carrying (via a snow-shovel-style handle) like "a handbag." Also, anyone realizing he really didn't want a Gierholtt outboard after all could convert his adaptable machine to inboard use.

The Gierholtt folks said their "outboard of no inconveniences" solved the starting, shallow water, and weed problems. Unfortunately, it wasn't able to do anything about the no-customers problem and went out of production two years later.

Gierholtt sold the outboard business to the Hess Motor Corporation from Algonac, Michigan. Hess gave its relabeled version of the Gierholtt a try from 1926 to 1928.

The Gilmore Marine Motor Corporation briefly entered the outboard business in 1920. By the following year the Marine City, Michigan, concern had left the field.

Designed by a mechanical engineering professor at the University of Minnesota, the Gopher outboards were actually produced (except for spark plugs and carbs) by college students. Two versions of the Gopher were built. The first version, from 1925, looked somewhat like a generic, forward-pointing, single-cylinder rowboat motor. More distinctive features included crank steering (similar to the Wright) and rounded gas tank.

By 1929 the professor simplified things and redesigned the Gopher as a direct-drive-style outboard (akin to the Palmer, Gierholtt, and Caille Liberty).

Over 100 "class project" Gophers were constructed. Some of the approximately 2½-hp outboards were sold to the public (for $75 to $80). Students with a spare twenty-dollar bill could take home their "assignment" for the cost of materials.[19]

In 1914 the Gray Motor Company of Detroit decided to try its luck in the fast-growing outboard motor market. Some 500 Gray Gearless outboards were produced between 1914 and 1917. This 52-pound, 3-hp (at 1,000 rpm) outboard was unique in that it used a flexible drive shaft to turn the prop on the end of a curved, "gearless" lower unit. Gray Gearless owners started their motors with a flywheel knob.

The Gray Motor Company also bought a few outboards from Caille, relabeled them, and sold the motors under the Gray nameplate. Gray's moniker has long been associated with the manufacture of 4-cycle inboard marine engines.

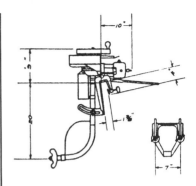

Gray Gearless outboards were produced from 1914 to 1917.

My guess is that this small 1960s outboard was a private-brand supplied by Clinton.

See the listing for Lancaster.

During the late Sixties, Birmingham (Ohio) Metal Products, Inc., manufactured a mean-looking pair of racing outboards. These Harrison class "A" (approximately 15-cubic-inch displacement) and "B" (approximately 20-cubic-inch) motors were designed for easy, quick disassembly and reassembly. Harrison lower units featured a "removable lower skeg and drain plug." Spark was available with "flywheel or battery ignition."

The Harrison racers' most prominent feature was a curved horn-of-plenty-type exhaust tube. This thing looked a bit like a saxophone and played its alcohol-burning tune just above the waterline. Birmingham shipped the Harrisons "completely tuned" for competition performance.

The manufacturer indicated one of its "B" models powered a hydro at over 88 mph. The firm also boasted of National Outboard Association straightaway records.

In the last years before the Great Depression, 311 interesting outboard motors found their way out of an old brick building in Hartford, Connecticut. These Hartford STURDY TWIN engines, just shy of 20-cubic-inch displacement, were touted as "exceptionally fast motors for class B racing enthusiasts."

The Hartford, offered by Gray and Prior Machine Company, was designed by partner George Prior. The first year for the Sturdy Twin was 1927. Production continued through much of 1929, with the bulk of the marque being constructed in 1928.

Although marketed for a scant three years, the outboard saw numerous changes. The muffler was modified a couple of times, finally ushering in an underwater exhaust tube in 1929.

Early gas tanks attractively stamped with the Hartford name were, by mid-1928, replaced by tanks bearing decals. A change of magneto called for a different size flywheel. Later Hartfords wore Tillotson (instead of Gray and Prior) carbs. An early water pump didn't work too well and was replaced by a water pickup scoop in

Gulf Queen

Guppy

Harrison

Hartford

back of the prop area. (The old-water-pump models could be returned to the shop for modification.)

Cast-iron cylinders and pistons gave way to a cast-iron-cylinder–aluminum-piston combo. This finally opened the route in 1929 for aluminum pistons and aluminum cylinders wearing steel sleeves (a real innovation at the time).

Not enough of these quality Hartfords were produced to compete seriously in the changing outboard industry. Consequently, near the end of 1929, when the nearby Indian Motorcycle Company of Springfield, Massachusetts, expressed interest in entering the boating field, Gray and Prior sold the cycle firm all of the Sturdy Twin patterns and tooling for some $15,000.

The first year of the new decade would see a transformed Hartford wearing the legendary Indian Silver Arrow nameplate.

Should you ever have the good fortune to scout out a Hartford, the serial number's last two digits will tell you its vintage.[20]

Henninger (H.A.)

One of a few early West Coast outboards, the Henninger was produced by the Henninger and Ayers Manufacturing Company of Portland, Oregon. Mr. Ayers got his initials mentioned in some Henninger ads when the motor was referred to as the H.A. No matter the motor had two names, as it was sold only a single year, 1918.

Hiawatha (1)

Montgomery Ward and Company's first private-brand outboard was the rudder-steered Hiawatha. This forward-pointing, single-cylinder rowboat motor developed 1 ¼ hp. The 2-cycle, flywheel-knob-start rig could be purchased from "Monkey Wards" with either battery ignition ($38.95) or flywheel magneto ($52.90).

According to the mail-order house's 1916 catalog, this kicker would be shipped to you "from a factory in Southern Michigan." Only Ward's officials were supposed to know it was the Caille outboard motor factory.

Hiawatha (2)

Gamble-Skogmo, Inc., a large Minneapolis-based retailer, first ordered a line of private-brand outboards in 1941. These Hiawatha motors were secured from OMC's Gale Products Division.

By 1956 Hiawathas were being built by the Scott-Atwater (subsequently McCulloch) people. This 1956 series, from 3.6 to 30 hp, was finished in an eye-catching aquamarine color. The larger motors featured a Scott-Atwater-introduced automatic boat bailer (working in conjunction with the water pump) called Bail Master.

Gambles, "the friendly store," ran beautiful multicolor ads in fishing magazines (very unusual for a private brand) and offered "big trade-in allowances" for those moving up to a Hiawatha motor.

The marque moved out of the outboard picture at the end of the 1961 boating season.

Hi-Speed

The Hi-Speed Motor Company of Chicago began offering an Evinrude rowboat-motor-type clone in 1914. By today's standards the Hi-Speed was anything but! Production, however, did come to a fast halt two years later.

Homelite

See the listing for Fageol.

Hubbell

A 1961 Hubbell KR racer on a Mercury Quicksilver drive shaft housing. The lower gearcase is missing. Tuned exhaust motor burns alcohol fuel.

When Evinrude and Johnson resumed outboard production following World War II, neither firm decided to reenter the racing scene. This move made it difficult for racers with prewar high-speed rigs to obtain new parts. As a result, OMC's chief marques were happy to sell Randolph Hubbell the rights to cook up factory-spec replacement racing-motor components.

Within five years Mr. Hubbell was making so many parts that (with the exception of items such as carbs and mags) he had enough stuff in his South El Monte, California, shop to build complete, new/old-stock style racing motors. Pretty soon, fast outboards, looking a lot like old Johnsons but bearing the Hubbell name, were showing up in competition. Most famous was his class "C" (Johnson PR) C-52 model.

Hubbell was obsessed with keeping the old class "A" Johnson KR racer competitive. Through the early Sixties he offered alcohol-burning versions of the "Hubbell KR" mounted on a sleek Mercury Quicksilver lower unit. The "Hubbell SR" class "B" opposed twin was similarly marketed. Hubbell also made outboards called Mercury "Wildcats." Using stock, gas-powered KG4H, KG7H, and Mark 20H Mercs, the Hubbell shop converted them to full-race, alcohol-burning, modified Mercury powerheads (on Quicksilver lower units). Wide, clear plastic fuel line, and a Hubbell cat (wearing a sailor hat) logo distinguished (externally) these super-high revving rigs from regular "H" model Mercurys. Anyone owning a Hubbell has a good example of a quality, limited-production racer.

Husky

A low-priced, mid-1960s outboard, the Husky was marketed by Ward International, Inc., of Studio City, California. (See Milburn)

Indian

Seeing the success of Elto and Johnson, the Springfield, Massachusetts, based Indian Motorcycle Company thought it might like to branch into the outboard business. Its opportunity came when the nearby Gray and Prior people decided to part with their inventory of Sturdy Twin outboard stock and related tooling and patterns.

This was in economically troubled late 1929, but Indian went ahead with a few Sturdy Twin modifications, turning the old predominantly aluminum Hartford into a shiny new 1930 Indian Silver Arrow. Most striking was the large, beautifully cast muffler assembly. It sported the famed Indian logo and was tastefully ribbed almost down to the water line. The Silver Arrow's throttle twist grip was borrowed from the firm's motorcycle parts bin.

Today the few remaining Indians certainly gain visual attention at vintage outboard meets, but most don't seem to run too well. Probably due to the fact the Indian was rushed into production and marketed only briefly, the little bugs never really got worked out of its design.

The failing early-Thirties economy, along with Indian's logical commitment to concentrate on cycles, caused the firm to bow out of outboarding in 1931. Similar to the premature passing of a pop personality, the Indian Silver Arrow's short life and royal lineage quickly made it a minor legend.

See Chapter 3.

Johnson

Joymotor

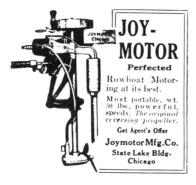

Joymotor ad, 1919.

The 1923 Joymotor model 7 was not as ornate as earlier models.

From 1915 to 1923 people at the Joy Engineering Company (later called Joymotor Manufacturing Company) of Chicago produced a run of interesting single-cylinder rowboat motors. Only a very few are still known to exist.

One Joymotor was found in the late 1960s by an Antique Outboard Motor Club member. He reports "the flywheel rim, muffler, magneto, water lines, and the entire lower unit were nickel plated. The exhaust manifold and crankcase (with removable bronze bearings) were excellent aluminum castings and were highly polished. Original colors were red tank and flywheel, blue cylinder, and black transom bracket. Ignition (on this model) was by an American-made Dixie magneto which sits on top of the squared cylinder and is geared directly to the crankshaft. Also mounted on the cylinder was a plunger-type water pump."[21]

Joymotors were available with battery, or, previously noted, magneto. Canoe owners could get an optional mounting bracket or a special Joy Low-Down canoe model. This adaptation, designed for nautical safety, featured a Joymotor with a very short torque tube. A hole was drilled through the bottom of the canoe, and "a board flange on the bottom of the tube pressed up against the bottom of the canoe, through the ⅞[-inch] board and then through the base of the bracket which supported the motor. A large nut came down around this tube and tightly clamped canoe, board and bracket in one solid piece. A rubber gasket prevented leakage."[22] This placed the Joymotor inside the canoe with its flywheel just above the gunwale, making for a more stable craft.

Joymotor ads often detailed a reversing feature. When the tiller handle was swung to the extreme left or right, the lower unit would rotate 180 degrees, allowing the prop to push the boat backwards. Dialing the tiller grip a half turn would lock the drive-shaft housing in any desired position. By the way, this housing, or torque tube, could "telescope" to fit transom heights from 17 inches to 21 inches deep.

The original water pump, situated at the powerhead, and the Joy Exhaust Silencer muffler (running directly under the fuel tank), were apparently redesigned in the late teens. A 1921 brochure pictured the silhouette of a model 7 Joymotor. This rig had a muffler pointing toward the water, as well as a hose to carry water up from the lower-unit–based pump. If ever there was an old outboard suitable for window display in an antique shop, the early Joymotor would get my vote.

A 4-cycle job out of a long-defunct firm called Jules Motor Corporation of Syracuse, the Jules was shipped from its central New York State port of entry from 1932 to 1933.

Jules

A Chicago firm, Karboat Manufacturing Company, produced this rare outboard in 1926.

Karboater

See listing for Air-Drive.

Kemp

A very obscure outboard from the 1930s, the Kingfisher was produced by the Loos Machine Shop of Colby, Wisconsin, for a now-forgotten Minneapolis retailer.

Kingfisher

It is estimated that 500 of these air-cooled, $5/8$-hp motors were built, but a fire at the shop claimed all detailed specs.

The Kingfisher was meant to be a rock-bottom low-priced outboard, and its designers were penny-wise in providing no opening for the addition of gear grease to the cast-aluminum lower unit. This economy also offered the Kingfisher owner no way to drain off any water that might have entered via the prop shaft. Consequently, many Kingfishers stored in freezing weather burst their lower units. It is also noted that the magneto spark lever could not be completely advanced unless the gas tank cap had its air vent screwed closed.[23] This is akin to a hiccup cure which requires a patient to hold his breath indefinitely.

What's in a name? Well, in the case of Koban, America's first successful two-cylinder outboard, portions of its creators' names constituted the logo. Milwaukee residents Arthur *Ko*ch and Walter *Ban*non designed their heavy-set rowboat motor in late 1913. This 1914 model featured detachable finned cylinder heads and battery ignition.

Koban

The next year's model, available with battery or magneto ignition, was minus a starting knob on its "steering wheel-like" rimmed flywheel. The firm said the thing was so easy to get going, who needed a cumbersome knob? By 1918, however, the starting knob (and it was a good-sized one) was back, sitting on top of a 14-pound flywheel! A flywheel-mounted magneto was offered.

On some Kobans the cylinders and crankcase were cast *en bloc*, or in one piece. With the exception of the earliest model, Koban cylinder heads were smooth, lightly rounded, detachable components bearing the brand name. The rounded fuel tanks on these motors look too small for the rest of the engine. Not too small, though, was the bulk of this twin.

By 1920, after some six years of production, Koban actually increased the iron content of its hefty cylinders. That made a 3-horse (at 900 rpm) portable rowboat motor weigh in at 85 pounds. Contributing to the bulk were bronze rudder steering mechanisms and optional underwater exhaust tubes. Cooling water was pumped to the cylinders by means of a couple of ball bearings acting as a check valve. The H_2O was coaxed into the valve via an exposed lower unit gear, which "twirled-in" its chilly prey. (Sounds great for weedy, sandy, or saltwater applications!)

As you can imagine, except for a few conservative diehards wanting a motor husky enough to survive getting run over by a bus, not many people were enchanted by Koban's weight. When the aluminum Eltos and Johnsons hit the early Twenties boating scene, the Koban became much less marketable. Koch and Bannon had already bailed out, selling the Koban Outboard Motor Company to Messrs. Schellin and Hoth.

In 1926 Koban, which was figuratively on its last heavy bronze lower-unit "legs," was sold by these partners to the Evinrude people. For a while Evinrude offered Koban parts and service, but opted not to continue Koban outboard production. It is possible the price of the Koban firm was low enough to warrant buying the company in order to rid the marketplace of another (albeit weak) rowboat-motor maker.

Recently discovered Evinrude documents list a model "100; Koban outboard motor assembly." It appears that, following Evinrude's 1926 purchase of the Koban firm, a few "leftovers" and/or Kobans made from parts obtained in the transaction, were offered for sale (on an informal basis) from 1927 to 1929. There doesn't seem to be any evidence that the Koban line was officially continued after 1926. Consequently post-1926 Kobans may have been peddled at the Evinrude factory store or at some of its more enterprising dealers.

If you find a Koban, the first digit of the serial number will tell the last digit of its year (up to 1919). In the case of 1920 to 1926 models, the first two numbers should reveal the manufacturing date.[24]

Lancaster Guppy

Large companies are always seeking diversification. During the early 1960s, the Lancaster (Pennsylvania) Pump and Manufacturing Company decided to use its respected pump technology and venture into the low-power-outboard business. The firm designed a lower unit complete with a small jet water pump (that propelled the boat via water pressure) and attached it to a Tecumseh lawn-mower-type powerhead. The result was called a Guppy model 30.

The novel motor steered with a U-shaped tiller rail, not unlike the top section of an aluminum lawn-mower handle. A change in the crank-to-driveshaft connection caused subsequent Guppy models to be classified as the 30A. The small jet outboard was finally taken off the market after 1967.

Some years ago, curiosity about the obsolete little Guppy led me to contact its former maker. The folks in Lancaster quickly indicated they retained no records covering their outboard products.

"Furthermore," someone there said, "just about all of the 500 or so Guppies had been sold to a supplier in Singapore." The mental picture of the tiny Guppy pushing a Chinese junk only strengthened my resolve to locate a Lancaster. (Perhaps such is the lure of the old-motor hobby.)

So far, a couple of these cute, one-cylinder, 2-cycle rigs have surfaced in the New York–New England region.

Lauson

The five Danish Lauson brothers set up shop in Wisconsin and by the close of the 1800s began experimenting with engine building. Light, high-speed farm tractors were but one of the product types developed by the Lauson Company. After making small, air-cooled, 4-cycle power plants for pumps, garden equipment, and motor scooters, the firm began considering other outlets for its technology.

In 1940 Lauson introduced a 2½-hp, 4-cycle, air-cooled, single-cylinder outboard dubbed the Sport King. While understandably not keeping pace with the sales of major brands, the little Lausons did gain a following. Saltwater boaters enjoyed an air-cooled product devoid of corrosion-prone water pumps and cylinder jackets. Because 4-cycle engines seem to idle well, anglers liked the way the Lausons could troll.

The year 1941 saw the introduction of a pair of Lauson outboards consisting of an air-cooled, 4-cycle, lawn-mower-style powerhead mated (under a circular collar) to either a standard or a long-length lower unit. Checking in at 2¼ and 4 hp, these particular Lausons, wearing small cylindrical gas tanks, were offered only one year.

After World War II the 2½-hp single was reintroduced. It was replaced in 1948 by an upgraded, 3-horse, rewind-start model and

Lauson Company's Sport King.

MODEL "S-300"
4-Cycle Air Cooled
Single Cylinder Sport King 3 H. P. Outboard

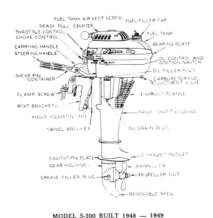

FUEL TANK AIR VENT SCREW — FUEL FILLER CAP
READY PULL STARTER
THROTTLE CONTROL
CHOKE CONTROL — FUEL TANK
CARRYING HANDLE — BEARING PLATE
STEERING HANDLE
OIL CONTROL AND IGNITION SWITCH
OIL FILLER PLUG
SHEAR PIN CONTAINER — CARBURETOR FUEL ADJUSTMENT VALVE
CLAMP SCREW — EXHAUST FLANGE
BOAT BRACKET
ANGLE ADJUSTING — DRIVE SHAFT HOUSING
SWIVEL BRACKET — OIL DRAIN PLUG
CAVITATION PLATE — EXHAUST OUTLET
GEAR HOUSING — PROPELLER
GREASE FILLER PLUG — PROPELLER NUT
REMOVABLE SKEG

MODEL S-300 BUILT 1948 — 1949

135   The Big List

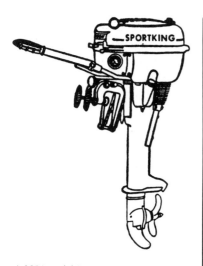
A 1956 model Sport King.

joined by a new opposed twin (also with rewind) generating 6 hp. In the early Fifties the bigger Lauson was offered with an optional F-N-R shifter. Unlike most other outboard shift mechanisms, Lauson placed its unit between drive shaft and powerhead (instead of making it integral with the lower gears). The shift Lauson didn't work too well. Consequently, a 6-horse twin was introduced, having forward and neutral via a clutch. This rig, as well as the standard, forward-only Lauson, were better performers.

My father recalls seeing, at a late-Forties New York boat show, Lauson's air-cooled, 25-hp prototype. He remembers it being painted brown and said the need for a flywheel cooling fan made the 4-cycle thing a real giant. No one else I've met ever mentioned viewing the big Lauson. A few lines of small print near the bottom of a 1940s (possibly 1941) Lauson outboard ad, however, promised "Coming! New Lauson 3-cylinder, 4-cycle Radial model outboard. Watch for details!" Perhaps this was the rig displayed at the show.

The company evidently realized that its largest market consisted of fishermen and opted not to enter the big-motor arena.

My grandfather was a bona fide Lauson enthusiast, finally trading in his trusty old 2½-hp Sport King for a bright blue 1950 6-horse model. He loved it, and as a Yale Ph.D. in chemistry, had numerous convincing arguments for Lauson ownership. That new motor ran great—until his passing, after which the chubby Lauson never worked right again. Really, you could pull and pull, drifting for miles, getting a couple of pops now and again. Experienced outboarders would borrow the Lauson for vacation and return it in the midst of bad words I'd never heard before. No cause for the motor's behavior was ever discovered. Perhaps it just missed its true owner.

Coincidentally, it was about 1956, right around the time my grandfather died, that Lauson's parent company (Hart-Carter of New Holstein, Wisconsin) decided to sell out to the Tecumseh small engine people. Tecumseh never reactivated Lauson's outboard motor division.

Lockwood (Lockwood-Ash)

Published a few short months before the merger with Evinrude and Elto, a 1929 Lockwood catalog proudly boasted of the status connected with being the "oldest marine engine manufacturer in the outboard motor business." Lockwood had built up its plant and held a good supply of "working capital." The firm's factory and equipment were "situated on a tract of land sufficient for any future expansion." Less than a year later, however, the Lockwood facility was closed.

At the turn of the century four Lockwood brothers formed a Jackson, Michigan, company. This outfit was engaged in everything from electrical wiring jobs and spark plug manufacturing to fixing and selling bicycles. Within a few years the Lockwoods had acquired an Oldsmobile car dealership franchise. In between selling and servicing autos and their other activities, they began building 2-cycle, single-cylinder inboard marine engines. By 1914 a Mr. Ash had entered the fray, and the busy little company went into the outboard motor business.

Lockwood-Ash's first outboard effort was a forward-pointing, single-cylinder rowboat motor. In addition to "customer-direct" sales, the 1914 battery ignition, rudder-steered Lockwood-Ash kicker was wholesaled to Sears-Roebuck and offered under the Motorgo label. A couple of years later flywheel magnetos were available on the little motors. At the close of World War I, Lockwood-Ash began backing off inboard production and introduced outboards with an optional rope-start flywheel sheave.

In the early Twenties Mr. Ash passed away, and his heirs eventually sold out to the Lockwoods. By 1924 a new Lockwood two-cylinder (model T) outboard motor was unveiled, and the inboards, along with other business interests, were dropped in favor of the outboard division.

The 1926 (model 62T) and 1927 (model 72T) twins attracted a good deal of attention, as the little 4-to-5-hp units could put a light boat on speaking terms with 20 mph. Although it seems elementary today, Lockwood pioneered copilot steering (you could let go of the tiller and the motor would stay on course) under the trademark Lockwood-Pilot.

With such innovation taken into consideration, a young neighbor of the Lockwoods was shocked to see one of the firm's founders buying a Sears outboard! The lad's disgust was calmed only after he learned that Lockwood was still supplying Sears with motors, and the purchase had been made for test purposes.

An extremely talented young engineer named Finn T. Irgens joined the growing outboard company in 1925 and played an important role in the development of the stirring 1928 Lockwood Ace (class "A" model 82A) and Chief (class "B" model 82B). These were fast engines and became instant hits. The 50-pound Ace made over 27 mph in time trials, while a Chief-powered speedboat traveled faster than 35 mph. One unusual Ace and Chief feature was the skegless lower unit. (A skeg could be installed as an option.) Propellers for these motors had a small cavity in each blade through which cooling water exited.

The 1929 (model 92A) Ace didn't get much modification over the previous year's offering, but its big sister (model 92B) received an underwater exhaust, making her the Silent Chief. A transparent Bakelite gas gauge graced the front of the gas tank. Carb and steering handle updates were also evident on the new Chief.

Although the original Chief's speed records were set with a service (or pleasure use) motor, Lockwood saw fit to augment its 1929 line with a model 92BR Racing Chief. This rig developed 30 percent more horsepower than the regular Silent Chief, and test runs pushed boats near the 40-mph mark. The Racing Chief was produced (in limited numbers) with "an entirely new type of [red] gasoline tank of pleasing but unusual appearance to add distinction and prevent confusion as to the exact type of motor." This beauty also wore dual carbs and a Lunkehheimer glass sight oiler

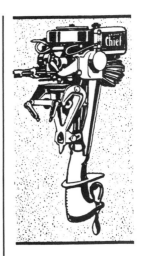

The 1929 Lockwood Silent Chief featured underwater "quiet" exhaust.

automatic lubricating system "so that fresh, undiluted oil is fed from a duplex drip cup directly to the main and connecting rod bearings." (Note: Some 92BR models had a pair of oilers—one over each cylinder.) Its smaller flywheel and magneto came from the Ace.

While the 1929 line was being introduced, Lockwood engineers were busy working on a class "D" (approximately 40-cubic-inch) racer to be called the Flying-Four. The big rig's 4-cycle, flat, opposed, four-cylinder powerhead (like the old VW auto engine) sat atop a modified Chief lower unit. By the time the Flying-Four was to be released, Lockwood was seriously considering a merger with Elto and Evinrude. Additionally, company technocrats realized their unconventional outboard would be too cumbersome to compete with similarly rated 2-cycle motors. Some prototypes were worked up, but the model never saw production.

The 92BR racer became a one-year offering and didn't get much of a chance to show off, either. By the fall of 1929 Lockwood had merged with Elto and Evinrude, creating a new organization known as Outboard Motors Corporation. The Jackson, Michigan, factory was locked up, and its employees given the option of moving to Milwaukee.

A 1930 Lockwood catalog, featuring a Silent Electric Starting Chief, was released by the new firm. In the grips of the unfolding economic depression, however, the marque was quietly discontinued.

Interestingly, some spec sheets list a 1931 Lockwood "4-60" racer. If, in fact, ever marketed, this rare item differed from the famed Elto 4-60 (four-cylinder, 60 cubic inches) high-speed outboard in decal and model number only. Also, according to a few vintage references, a handful of "B" Lockwoods may have made it to the 1932 model year. Otherwise, a small stock of lonely Chiefs was reclassified as Montgomery Ward's Sea Kings. These final Lockwood products, some fitted with strange crank-up, spring-loaded "inertia starters," were stripped of their true identity and sold through Ward's mail-order catalogs—a humble end for a once proud marque. Reportedly, though, as late as the 1950s people were contacting the Evinrude office requesting Lockwood "literature, parts, and dealer franchises."[25]

Majestic

Badge-engineered Champions wearing the Majestic label premiered in 1950 (although some early Majestics might be considered as 1949s). Outboard Motor Brands, Inc., headquartered at a post office box in Minneapolis, marketed this marque, referred to as "King of the Outboard Motors."

Because of common ownership, Majestic simply disappeared with Champion at the close of 1958.

Mann's Troller

This interesting, albeit generic, private-brand outboard was marketed, not by some national chain store retailer, but from a sporting goods shop in Pinckneyville, Illinois. Ad sheets out of Mann's Sporting Goods targeted resort owners, commercial fishermen, and sportsmen to consider its 5-hp "quiet-strong" outboard motor called the Mann's Troller M5T.

At 29 pounds, this 2-cycle, air-cooled outboard featured a remote 3-gallon "handy stowaway gas tank" and 360-degree "swivel" steering. Its single-cylinder powerhead carried a 90-day warranty, while the lower unit was guaranteed a full year. This time difference was due to the fact that these two major parts came from separate manufacturers.

Meant to be a very inexpensive way to get a small motor on your fishing boat, the Mann's Troller differed from a number of its private-brand sisters (such as Mono) in name sticker only.

Mariner

Although sharing a name with the more modern Mercury-marketed motor, this 1950s Mariner was sold through the Mariner Outboard Motor Company in Minneapolis. It was produced by Scott-Atwater, and finally by Champion.

Martin

"Slow down a little," my wife said, "this might be it."

"Let's see," I answered, glancing at directions scribbled hastily on the back of a new Johnson motor catalog. "Looks like we should turn in here."

Seconds after our car bumped down a dirt driveway, a bathrobe-clad senior citizen appeared at the screen door.

An hour earlier we'd stopped for ice cream at an Adirondack, New York, restaurant. I spotted a Johnson outboard dealership next door and walked over in search of old treasures.

"No, there's no vintage motors around here," the owner sternly noted. "But if you want some Martins, I will tell you where to find an old dealer. After Martin went under, this place just seemed to stop in time . . . still has some stuff for sale. You head down Route 8"—he pointed—"and take the first drive after the lake becomes visible through the pine trees."

I explained all this to the gentleman in the bathrobe. He smiled and led me toward an unpainted shed. When the small structure's weathered doors swung open, it became evident this excursion had been no wild-goose chase.

There, disguised as a rickety garage, was a full-fledged, albeit modest, Martin dealership—frozen in time for nearly 35 years. On the wall, near a window wearing a crinkled green shade, hung dozens of Martin gaskets, each on a marked display board. A workbench, horseshoed around the building's back portion, contained tools appropriate for Martin repair. New/old-stock Martin and Evinrude parts were stacked in small boxes. Overflow from this cache filled seven or eight worn bushel baskets.

A handy rack of outboard oil and grease leaned against the side wall. And next to the big workbench vise rested a pair of official Martin motor stands. A tired-looking single-cylinder Martin 20 had a customer tag affixed to the spark lever. The brittle paper

1947 Martin ad targets fishermen.

The 7.2-hp Martin 60.

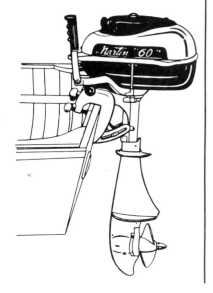

indicated its owner was some 25 years overdue. A red, combo life jacket–motor cover (complete with yellow Martin logo) topped the other engine.

My host slowly raised the motor covering the way a proud chef reveals his most tasty dish. There she was, a beautiful 1954 Martin 100.

"It's a 10-horse," he said, beaming. "We got it in here shortly before the home office called it quits. Used it a bit as a demo, but I'll bet there's no more than five or six hours on the old gal."

It was so exciting to be able to walk out of a bona fide Martin dealership over three decades after the motors had last been produced, with an almost-new Martin! It was so noteworthy, in fact, that we'd hardly turned onto the main road before I began to tell my wife the whole story of the Martin outboards.

That model 100 was one of about 300,000 Martins built between 1946 and 1954. The inspiration for these outboards came to engineer and former professional outboard racer George W. Martin. In the late 1930s Mr. Martin began planning a revolutionary new outboard using mechanically controlled intake poppet valves. "Mechanical timing of these valves meant equal fuel distribution making possible uninterrupted acceleration, ranging from the slowest, sputter-free trolling speed to full throttle in a matter of only a few seconds."[26] Having secured a U.S. patent on these valves, George Martin interested National Pressure Cooker Company of Eau Claire, Wisconsin, in financing an outboard-motor manufacturing project. An agreement was composed in 1943 providing the inventor with a royalty for every poppet valve engine sold.

After World War II the first couple hundred Martins (serial numbers began with C-5000) were "practically hand built" in an erstwhile printing plant.[27] The line's premier model was the Martin 60, so labeled because its designers figured the 11-cubic-inch powerhead would generate 6.0 hp. Prototypes, however, put out some 7.2 horses, and the smooth-running Martin started gaining a good reputation. Some of the early 60s did have a problem or two. I've encountered a number of these vintage rigs with cracked or broken transom clamp brackets, or other supporting cast pieces. This type of thing caused concern, and clearing up such weaknesses became a top priority.

Soon Martin manufacturing facilities were moved to a bigger site, and the line was expanded in 1947 with the two-cylinder, 4½-horse Martin 40. A 2½-hp Martin 20 single was added in late 1948.

The Martin 20 was a perfect little fishing motor. Robert Grubb, veteran outboard retailer and Test Editor of the Antique Outboard Motor Club, tried a tiny (1949) Martin 20 in 1984 and reported:

> This is the slowest trolling motor I have yet tested. It went so slow that on one attempt to make time runs, the current in the river was going faster than the motor. Noise level at idle is also very

impressive. It gets down to a very low level, more like the sound of a 4-cycle Lauson than any other 2-cycle I know of.[28]

By 1950 Martin entered the larger (for that time) motor province via introducing the 10-hp Martin 100. (Early versions were called Commando.) Like all of its sisters (except the subsequent 200), this rig had 360-degree steering. It also featured a third thumbscrew (between the two transom clamp knobs), which facilitated motor angle adjustment while under way. Many Martin models were fitted with a clever transom bracket that allowed the motor to be tilted up and swung inboard for lower-unit or propeller repair.

Unique to certain 100s was a neutral clutch and an "Aquamatic" button on the end of the tiller handle, which, when pressed, would instantly slow the motor. After the wave, approaching boat, or other obstacle passed, the button could be released, returning the engine to higher speeds. The 100 and 200 motors had a gas gauge on the front of the fuel tank.

During this era Martin had half a dozen salesmen on the road contacting and helping dealers and potential franchises. "Two servicemen worked in the field, holding service schools both at [regional] distribution points, and at the home plant."[29]

The year 1950 also saw the introduction of the Martin Hi-Speed 60. This tiny powerhouse (more than just a fishing engine hooked to a racing lower unit), beefed up with special steel rods and needle bearings, enlarged ports, and a steel high-compression cylinder head, was a real thoroughbred. George Martin's pet project pulled 16 hp on the factory dynamometer at 6,000-plus rpm.[30] The Hi-Speed 60's sleek lower unit was made for Martin by the Mayberry-Edwards Company in Florida and helped the racer achieve 5 to 7 mph more than a similar motor simply equipped with the standard fishing lower unit.

At 11 cubic inches, however, the Hi-Speed 60 didn't really fit well into any American Power Boating Association stock outboard racing class, and the busy little rig (sometimes fueled on alcohol) never really got the attention it deserved. Following the release of this limited production engine, Mr. Martin parted company with the National Pressure Cooker people.

By 1951 the firm was advertising heavily in publications ranging from *National Geographic* and *The Saturday Evening Post* to *Boys' Life*. Dealers were offered cooperative promotional funds in order to place local ads. Martin officials announced their desire to develop a full-line outboard offering. To start this trend, a big, 17-horse Martin 200 motor was unveiled to the press in 1951. When it became apparent these engines would not be ready for production, Martin PR men quietly indicated the Korean War had caused aluminum shortages that postponed the project.

Meanwhile, a Martin 60 derivative, the 66, spent 1950 in the catalog. The roster of 1951 included a 7½-horse updated version of the Martin 60 and 66 called the 75. Like some of the 100s, a number of these wore the Twistshift logo and could be popped

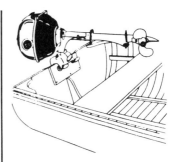

MOTOR IN SWIVEL POSITION

Martin's swivel feature.

1   The Aquamatic Control button operates only when the speed indicator lever is in the upper half of the speed range.

2   By pressing this button, speed is reduced to ⅓ full speed.

3   Upon releasing the Aquamatic Control button, the motor speed returns to that point at which the speed indicator lever is set in the high speed or upper range.

4   This device permits you to face forward and steer while you have complete control of your motor speed, and is an added safety feature.

5   The Aquamatic Control is non-operative when the speed indicator lever is in the lower half of the speed range.

Martin Aquamatic.

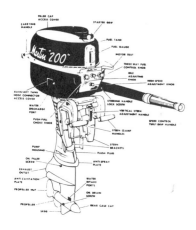

The exhaust section of the Martin 200 could be replaced with a piece 3 inches shorter for racing.

into neutral. (Reverse was accomplished by swinging the motor around 180 degrees.)

The lineup in 1952 included the trio of Martin 45 (a revised 40), 75, and 100. On the surface the 1953 model year seemed to hold lots of promise for Martin, as the firm had begun hyping its finally ready Martin 200 in the fall of '52. This Silver Streak 200, unlike the proposed 17-horse '51 edition, was rated at a full 20 hp. Its nonshift Torpedo lower unit rivaled Mercury's Quicksilver racing gear foot. By late 1953 or early 1954, a more pointy, streamlined gear-case cap and a 3-inch-shorter exhaust section could be ordered from the factory. These accessories made the regular Martin 200 (which was a pretty quick motor) into a real weekend racer.

The 1954 Martin family, much like the previous year, had the 20, the 45, the 75, the 100, and the 200. Press releases promised a gear-shift version of the 200, dubbed "Silver Liner." Although a demo motor or two were built, apparently none ever got into circulation.

The 200 series had actually been National Pressure Cooker's last-ditch attempt to transform its outboard division into a full-horsepower-range line, offering the boating public everything from fishing to waterskiing.

Around 1952 workers and management within the firm began squabbling about ways best to produce the rather complex poppet-valved Martins at a price appropriate to its ranking under Johnson, Evinrude, and Mercury. National Pressure Cooker started wondering if it was worth all the trouble. Once-strict factory standards began to slide. "Inspections became less rigid, and some bad motors got by, hurting sales."[31]

By mid-summer 1954, rumors of Martin's demise were confirmed and most of the workers got sent home. A few top Martin plant staffers were put in charge of supplying replacement parts for the thousands of motors still in use. Reportedly, though, a whole freight train full of Martin carbs, gas tanks, and powerhead shrouds was simply sent to the scrap yard.

During this period a dealers' used-motor trade-in publication warned that

> there were many closeouts on Martin Motors after the factory announced [it] would discontinue manufacturing outboard motors. This makes our survey on Martin not in accord with usual estimated prices.[32]

In the mid-Sixties National Pressure Cooker finally sold the remains of its Martin parts to a fellow in Rice Lake, Wisconsin. The remnants of that extensive stock passed into the hands of a small Nebraska firm, which reports doing a brisk mail-order business. It is evident that lots of George Martin's little poppet-valve motors, with a new part here and there, have no desire to slow down.

The Los Angeles–based McCulloch Corporation was already well known for its 2-cycle chain saws and kart engines when it went looking for ways to diversify. In 1956 McCulloch acquired Minneapolis outboard producer Scott-Atwater and jumped right into the boat motor business.

In 1964 Scott-Atwater's name (which had unofficially been shortened to Scott) was dropped entirely to make way for the McCulloch label. Around this time Sears-Roebuck also renamed its Elgin line. McCulloch produced outboards using the Sears label.

While most of the newly tagged McCullochs actually received their start as Scott-Atwaters, some, like the larger horsepower, three-cylinder models and the *OX* gas and diesel heavy-duty work motors, were designed by McCulloch engineers. Most memorable of the mid-Sixties McCulloch outboards were an air-cooled (although water quenched the hot motor leg exhaust section), 4-hp fishing motor and a series of low profile, 7½- and 9-horse fishing motors advertised as being "shorter than a striper, or shirt-sleeve." Some of these compact rigs even sported electric starting, making them about the smallest electric-start outboards in the industry's history.

McCulloch also marketed a couple of limited edition racing outboard motors (most notably a class "F" 60-cubic-inch model). The three-cylinder, triple-carbed, coverless hot rods had bright red powerheads sitting atop white, streamlined lower units. Despite such efforts, McCulloch began drawing away from the outboard picture, offering just a few fishing motors prior to closing its marine operation in the late 1960s.

McCULLOCH 590 AND 630   McCULLOCH 75

See Chapter 4.

Michigan Wheel Company, the well-known, Grand Rapids–based propeller maker, took a brief spin in the early rowboat motor market. Its Michigan outboard was current in 1916.

McCulloch

A pair of 3-cylinder, 1964 McCulloch outboards. The one on the left is a racing version.

Mercury
Michigan

Mid-Jet

The 1960s Mid-Jet, a water-jet thrust outboard.

A Mr. W.H. Schnacke of Rural Route #4, Evansville, Indiana, formed a little company to build "the newest in outboard motor design, versatility, safety, and economy." Schnacke Manufacturing Corporation called its Midwestern jet outboard product the Mid-Jet.

Like many of its competitors, the Mid-Jet used an air-cooled, 2-cycle Tecumseh Power Products powerhead especially designed for outboard-motor application. The lower unit, as described in a Mid-Jet service manual, was an aluminum casting.

> The one-piece drive shaft rides in a sealed ball bearing at the lower end and the 3-blade, 5-inch propeller screws directly on the end of the drive shaft. The propulsion unit is simple in construction and completely enclosed. A small amount of water entering the water housing is diverted through a water tube to cool the lower unit housing and exhaust gases. The remainder of the water is ejected at high speed through the discharge opening to propel the boat.[33]

The 27-pound, single-cylinder Mid-Jet came in models ranging from 2.4 to 5 hp. The larger power promised the shallow-water boater 65 pounds of thrust at 4,200 rpm.

Mid-Jets were available between 1961 and 1965. A June, 1969 letter in my files from the company founder indicates that although his firm had gone out of business, he still at that time had a few lower-unit parts on hand for Mid-Jet owners.

Mighty-Mite

See the listing for Neptune.

Milburn Cub (Continental, Commando, Husky)

Back in the late 1940s, somewhere in southern California, a guy ("experienced in nautical and aviation engineering") sat in front of a small drawing board and designed a pint-size outboard. Little did the fellow know that the history of his straightforward motor would one day be a source of confusion for old-outboard collectors.

First advertised in December 1948 as a potential Christmas present for lucky sportsmen, the subject motor began its life as the Milburn Cub. The H.B. Milburn Company of Los Angeles (with a New York City office tucked away in a Rockefeller Plaza room) tried to entice folks with the promise of a 30-day guarantee, and 1-to-6-mph performance from its 2½-hp (at 3,750 rpm) rope-start motor. Additionally, the manufacturers promised their air-cooled outboard would "never conk out because of water pump troubles." The Milburn Cub was identified solely by a small nameplate screwed to the front of its 2½-quart, cast-aluminum fuel tank. The skinny tiller handle seemed to be mounted to the wrong (left) side of the cute 2-cycle powerhead.

Conspicuously absent was a choke for the Milburn Cub's cast-aluminum carb. Because most operators had thumbs they could stick over the air intake while starting a cold motor, company officials didn't view the lack of a real choke mechanism as a problem. A copper tube from the tank to the carburetor might have been cut too long and consequently had a loop in it. The lawn-chair-gauge underwater exhaust tube, giving clearance for about 180-degree steering, was standard. For an extra three bucks you could get a model with exhaust piped through the torque tube, allowing 360-degree turning.

Early Milburn Cub ads included a tiny coupon (like those on the side of a breakfast cereal box offering Superman sweatshirts for $3.97) which read: "Enclosed is $ _____ for which please ship _____ Cub motors" at $69.50 each.

Just how many coupons were sent in is unknown, but sometime in the mid-Fifties it was evident that the Milburn was being handled by an L.K. Products of Culver City, California. This company apparently sold the outboard business to an outfit called Continental Manufacturing Corporation, also in Culver City. Continental put out a new 2½-hp motor called the Continental Commando, which weighed in at about 20 pounds and looked exactly like the deluxe (exhaust through the torque tube) Milburn. (Note: Some references call this motor the Sport.) New was a rewind-start model for $99.95, a 10-spot over the cost of the standard rope-start edition.

By early 1957 Continental ventured into an interesting marketing avenue by offering the little outboard in kit form, which saved the boater 25 percent of a finished motor's price. Instructions claimed "The Kit" outboard could be assembled on a fence or back of a chair, and you'd need only an adjustable wrench along with a couple of household-grade screwdrivers to do the job. Folks getting started on the Continental kit read:

> You have just purchased the finest light outboard motor in its field. [Of course, it was the *only* one in the kit genre.] All parts have been designed to aircraft specifications by aircraft engineers and manufactured to precision standards. Each part you have received has been meticulously inspected and if proper assembly instructions are followed will fit with its mating part. No forcing is necessary and care should be taken not to strip the threads.

In the early Sixties somebody told me about a "real cheap" outboard you could make yourself. As a kid seeking a very fast way to convince my dad to buy me a boat motor, "real cheap" were operative words. I borrowed a faded picture of a Continental ripped out of a boating magazine and wrote to the firm identified in the caption. Sometime in April 1964 a letter from Comanco, Inc., of Culver City, California, came my way heralding the 1963 air-cooled, rewind-start Commando VII outboard motor. The lower unit was identical to the Milburn and other Commandos (models V and VI), but the Tecumseh powerhead's shroud was sheet metal (like that of a power motor), and a cylindrical gas tank was hooked to the front of the thing. This time, the tiller handle was on the right side. Its funny-looking throttle lever was described as "pistol grip." The rig weighed about the same as its predecessors but developed 4 hp at 5,400 rpm. The typed brochure suggested that

> there's no need to let the Commando VII sit idle after the fishing and duck hunting season. Put it to work as a stationary engine to run pumps, saws, generators, even lawn mowers or go-karts.

Wow! I imagined, *outboards, saws, and go-karts, and all for just $99.95!*

Still, my parents took one look at the bargain-basement Commando and immediately decided to buy me a new Mercury—for which I've always credited the Comanco people.

The late Sixties saw me sentimentally inquire about my favorite little engine. A promotional letter finally came back from McMar, Commando Motor Division, Newport Beach, California. Pictured was that distinctive Milburn Cub–type lower unit under a Tecumseh single-cylinder, air-cooled, 2-cycle, "loop scavenged" powerhead. Both a Commando 500 (at 5 hp) and 750 (at 7½ hp) were offered. Each sipped fuel from a remote tank. A solid-state ignition could be ordered for the larger motor. Buyers were given their choice of three shaft lengths: 9, 18, or 24 inches.

I lost track of the little motors after that, but am reminded that none of the ads for any of the Milburn Cub–based products ever actually pictured the kicker in motion. One flyer, however, showed a kid *carrying* the thing, but it was not stated where he was taking it.

Adding a bit of intrigue to the Milburn/Comanco lineage was Ward International, Inc. This Studio City, California, firm was listed as producing a small outboard during the mid-Sixties called the Husky. A few Comanco parts lists mention the Husky (with that classic Milburn Cub lower unit) as a sister motor to the Commando. According to my notes, the Husky was marketed in 1963, 1966, and 1967. Perhaps Comanco provided the motors (with Tecumseh powerheads) to Ward International.

Miller (1)

A bit longer-lived than many competitors, the Miller Gas and Vacuum Engine Company of Chicago marketed rowboat motors from 1914 to 1923. Miller outboards were available with battery or gear-driven Bosch magneto ignition. An adjustable propeller was optional. Millers looked similar to Evinrude rowboat motors.

Miller (2)

Auto racing legend Harry A. Miller was said to have built a workable outboard in the late 1890s. By 1932 his Miller Motor Company of Los Angeles entered the realm of portable boat motor production with an intriguing four-cylinder (horizontal), in-line rig.

Like the previously marketed Submerged and subsequent Clarke, this product's powerhead rode completely underwater. Reportedly, problems with the complex castings let lubrication out and water in. This limited issue Miller was a one-year motor.

Miller (3)

Getting its early 1960s start at the Miller Engineering Company, in Shawnee, Oklahoma, this Miller was one of those air-prop fan outboards. From 1964 the Miller was offered by the Arrow Propeller Company of Memphis.

Mini

One of the most fact-filled leaflets in 1960s outboard advertising indicated this tiny motor was ideal for senior citizens. Weighing less than 9 pounds, the Mini outboard motor came as a "result of many years of testing and designing a multitude of combinations to achieve the smallest, lightest, most economical, least expensive, yet practical outboard motor attainable." Knight Distributing Company of Springfield, Massachusetts, was proud to acknowledge its air-cooled product as 100-percent manufactured and assembled in the USA.

Because Americans relate to empirical data, the model 10-S Mini outboard motor's "unbelievable propelling power" was verified in an "actual speed test." The pint-size kicker was "clocked at 4.2 mph with three men in a twelve-foot aluminum boat." For some long-forgotten reason, however, the photo captioned with these statistics showed a man and a woman in a sailing dinghy named the *Two-Teds*. The craft was inching along under power from an engine with no rewind starter or plastic powerhead cover (unlike the one prominently featured on the front of the informative brochure).

The single-cylinder, 2-cycle Mini outboard motor featured an adjustable shaft length and a 14-millimeter "shorty" spark plug. Its polycarbonate, semi-weedless propeller had a lifetime guarantee against breakage. Exhaust exited the cylinder through a piece of flexible gooseneck pipe before traveling to the water via a little rigid tube.

Customers purchasing the small motor had a little time to try it, and if not completely satisfied, return it within seven days. "Any damage or misuse of the product by the customer would be deducted from the purchase price." At $99.95 the 1-hp (at 6,300 rpm) outboard cost about the same as the garden weed whackers that its powerhead resembled.

Monarch

A sister motor to very early Champion outboards, the Monarch was the tiny Champ firm's low-priced offering.

Sig Konrad, who founded the Champion marque in 1926, built the first Monarch a short time later. The little motor's stately brand name was cast in large letters into the top of its fuel tank. SAINT PAUL, MINN. graced the rope sheave plate. About 600 of the water-cooled, $39.50, 2-hp Monarchs were produced. It is believed some 100 air-cooled versions were also marketed.

While some of the production wore a pair of piston rings, a few single-ringed rigs went through the company's door. Rather than mate the flywheel to the crankshaft with a keyway, the two were aligned with a simple timing mark (on each piece). This reduced the risk of powerhead damage due to running into rocks.[34]

The Monarch name disappeared after Mr. Konrad sold his Champion company rights in 1935.

Mono

Look for a powerhead diagram on a Mono outboard parts list, and you won't find it. That's because the Mono Manufacturing Company, based in Springfield, Missouri, got the 2-cycle engines for its outboards from the Tecumseh people.

Mono began marketing these single-cylinder, 360-degree-steering, low-priced fishing motors around 1963. Early Monos had exposed power plants with front-mounted cylindrical gas tanks. Later models wore plastic shrouds. Some came with a neutral clutch and a remote fuel tank resembling a 2½-gallon lawn mower gas can. Generally occupying the 3-to-7½-hp range, many Monos, although primarily air cooled, had a small tube protruding from the lower unit which supplied water to cool the muffler.

The Mono was essentially a private-brand–style outboard rivaling the Eska, the My-te, and the obscure Mann's Troller. Because the power plant came from Tecumseh, a firm with thousands of authorized repair shops, the Mono could be serviced in a wider range of locations than most major outboard products.

Motorgo

Probably the first serious private-brand outboard, the 1914 Motorgo, built by Lockwood, was sold by Sears-Roebuck. Although the Lockwood-made Motorgos were offered until about 1928, other well-known makers, such as Caille and Muncie, produced Motorgo-labeled outboards for the giant Chicago-based retailer.

It was not unusual for the Caille Motorgo rigs to lack identification except for a difficult-to-spot serial number stamped onto the block or transom clamp assembly. Some of these designations begin with *M*. If you come across a Caille with no name on the flywheel rope-sheave plate, you most likely have a Motorgo. Sears retitled most of its outboards Waterwitch by late 1933.

Early-30s, 10-hp Sears Motorgo, made by Caille. Note the priming cup on the front of the cylinder. The steering arm only turned the lower section.

Motorow

Although on occasion Uncle Sam has spent good money on items that don't work, the Motorow Engine Company of Chicago proudly advertised that the U.S. government purchased some 1915 Motorow outboards for "coast work."

Built from 1915 to 1918 by a "trained force of men," the single-cylinder, tin-can-mufflered Motorow featured "a pinion at the top of the drive shaft housing meshing into a segment gear at the end of the tiller handle, enabling one to steer perfectly and reverse instantly."

The company claimed ownership of the basic patents on this "positive mechanical reversing device." It also touted "velvety" smooth running because of a secret, exclusive (and unexplained) "vibration absorber."

The skegless Motorow was indeed an interesting World War I–era engine. Its claim, however, as "the *only* rowboat motor that reverses instantly . . ." should be more like: "the only one that reverses and is spelled with a capital *M*." Finally, while no old-outboard enthusiast has come up with an exact count, the Motorow people were fond of saying their product had "fewer parts than any other motor on the market."

Motor Troller

The Motor Troller Company of Westport, Connecticut, offered a post–World War II fishing outboard in 1947.

Muncie

See the listing for Neptune.

Munco

Circa 1933 the Munco Sales Company of Muncie, Indiana, tried to interest impecunious boaters by offering a $44.50, 2-horsepower, single-cylinder outboard motor kit.

"All you have to do," said Munco's tiny ads, "is assemble this tested outboard. No machining—a 12-year-old boy can put it together with a screwdriver and wrench."

The Munco kit outboard looked exactly like a 2-hp Neptune-brand kicker of similar vintage. It would seem likely that the Munco Sales Company was simply a small marketing arm of Neptune's parent, Muncie Gear Works. A little coupon on the bottom of Munco's advertising asked folks to send for "complete details concerning the assembly of the MUNCO OUTBOARD MOTOR."

Because no mention was made of Neptune or Muncie Gear Works lineage (except to say Munco's design was "tested"), it is possible this very obscure kit motor came with MUNCO cast into the rope sheave plate. Consequently, the Munco may be considered an autonomous marque.

My-te

City Engineering Company, Inc., an Indianapolis firm specializing in electric winches, hoists, and 6- to 12-volt trolling motors, marketed a 4-hp, 2-cycle, air-cooled outboard called the My-te IV. This early-Sixties, 29-pound rig was a good example of a simple, 2-cycle lawn mower engine mated to a generic lower unit.

The My-te IV was meant to compete with the majors' fishing models on price, as it sold for just under $100. This rig looked a lot like a Mono.

National

The National outboard, built from 1916 to 1918, had more cylinders than most contemporaries. The National Marine Motor Company of Newark came up with an ornate, opposed twin featuring an adjustable (forward-neutral-reverse pitch) propeller and a gas tank resembling the front of an old cash register drawer. Topping off this very antique-looking rig was a large fluted flywheel that would remind you of a church collection plate.

Neptune (1) (Caille)

Neptune (2) (Muncie)

Muncie Gear Works' Neptune logo.

Note: Because the similar twin-cylinder Federal was actually built in a Newark factory during 1914 and 1915, one could speculate a connection between the Federal and the National. Even the names had a similar "solid" (at least back in those days) ring.

From 1917 to 1925 the Caille outboard people marketed a bargain-price line dubbed Neptune. This offering was similar to Evinrude's lower-cost Buccaneer lineup of the Fifties. Single-cylinder Neptune rowboat motors came in 2- and 3½-hp sizes and sported such exotic model names as Czar, Czarina, Prince, King, Queen, and Empress. Both battery and magneto-ignition styles were available.

Additionally, Caille-built Neptunes (2 hp only) could be purchased in regular or canoe (mounted through a hole in the bottom of the craft) versions. According to sales literature, one of these rigs pushed the canoe *Hiawatha* 16 mph! This figure is akin to Johnson's famed 1925 publicity about its 6-hp Big Twin. The Neptune claim seems rather questionable.

The Muncie (Indiana) Gear Works was established in 1907. During its various evolutionary reorganizations it became well known in the young auto industry for the manufacture of gears and transmissions. Muncie entered the outboard business in 1930 via its own Neptune line. In addition the firm private-branded thinly disguised Neptunes to Sears-Roebuck (some relabeled Water Witch, others with a Motorgo tag), as well as to small sales organizations under the Portage and Sea-Gull nameplates.

A typical pre–World War II Neptune lineup included the Master Twin, a 16-hp opposed twin wearing the look of a poor man's Caille. This big rig with detachable cylinder heads had a tiller that turned only the lower unit and was built with "the liberal use of ball and roller bearings." Also available were alternate-firing 9½- and 6-horse twins, a 4-hp opposed twin with removable cylinder heads, the 2-hp Neptune single, and a Junior single producing 1.2 hp. This tiny, 17-pound putt-putt was the great-grandfather of the famed Neptune Mighty-Mite. Muncie's advertising stressed "outstanding quality, superior design, and skilled workmanship." In fact Neptunes, especially the early alternate-firing models, were rather well designed and should not be lumped into the outboard picture as just also-rans. In the area of weaknesses, however, Neptunes, like many of their contemporaries, quickly succumbed to the ravages of salt water.

Following World War II, Muncie jumped back into the outboard field through its ads featuring an old fisherman (cartoon character) named Neptune Ned. The firm promoted a 1945–46 line ranging from 1½ to 9½ hp. The stable of 1947 offered only 1½-, 2-, and 3½-horse products.

But the following year Muncie unveiled its newly designed/styled, shrouded, alternate-firing twins, such as the 10-hp model AA10. (There was also a shrouded single.) These metallic-green (occasionally maroon) motors with red tiller grips looked somewhat like Western Auto's Wizard outboards and the more expensive Johnson fishing motors of the day.

The new Neptunes would offer a boat shop unable to secure a major-label outboard franchise a good alternative line. Then for some reason, in 1949, the manufacturer "tried to sell these motors by mail order. This practice cost dealer support, and Muncie was not able to secure adequate dealer outlets in 1950–51 to warrant continuing in the outboard field."[35]

By 1951 the company's outboard motor promotion largely consisted of a small exhibit at the New York Boat Show.[36] Of course, this era also saw the Korean War, and Muncie's production facilities were tapped by the U.S. government to make jet engines. So there were no Neptunes in 1952 or 1953.

After completion of Defense Department work, Muncie decided to attempt a comeback into the kicker picture by filling a niche in the low-priced, micro-power outboard slot. It reintroduced the tiny (now 1.7 hp) single in 1954. Three years later the firm moved to Cordele, Georgia, and dubbed its little motor the Mighty-Mite. Although available as a sideline through a few marine and sporting goods stores, most Mighty-Mite purchases were transacted through factory-direct orders. Muncie's promotion was now the province of tiny folders touting the portability (especially for children and women) of the under-$100 putt-putt. For years this outboard was the best known (albeit outdated, with separate drive shaft and exhaust tubes) of all "basic eggbeaters." It was even offered as a top prize for junior super salespeople peddling the most novelties, seed packets, or *Grit* newspaper subscriptions.

The Georgia-based Muncie company was sold in 1969, and in time the outboard operation moved to Florida (where senior citizens assembled some of the motors). Following a few more transfers, it ended up in Connecticut. In the 1980s a 2-horse updated derivative (in complete or kit form with rewind starter and 360-degree steering) of the 1930s Junior single and the more recent Mighty-Mite was still being offered.

Because of such lineage, the new Mighty-Mite firm can be called the second oldest American maker (after OMC, with Evinrude and Johnson) of gasoline-powered outboard motors!

The famed 17-pound, 1.7-hp Neptune Mighty-Mite. Over the years this rig became America's most famous putt-putt.

A 1948-49, 10-hp Neptune. As most of these rigs were sold through the mail, few were purchased. This design was suspiciously close to popular small Johnsons of the day.

By cracky th' feller that ketches fish is th' one that keeps fishin' stead of rowin' and wishin'! Brother, buy a NEPTUNE!

NEPTUNE
OUTBOARD MOTORS

Circa-1946 "Neptune Ned" logo.

Niagara

Buffalo, New York, was home to Niagara Motors Corporation, producer of the Niagara rowboat motor. Introduced in 1918, the Niagara fell off the market by the end of that year.

Nichoalds

Little is remembered about this 1916 Detroit-produced rowboat motor. The 2-hp putt-putt wore a round gas tank.

No-Ro

In 1913 the No-Ro Motorworks of Boston (West Roxbury), Massachusetts, set out to save its potential customers from purchasing a single-cylinder rowboat motor "blunder," with those "disastrous vibratory effects." Keeping this in mind, the company came up with a 4-cycle, 3-to-4-hp opposed twin called the No-Ro Presto Motor.

In an effort to protect further its future clientele and its machinery "from dirt," the power plant (except the protruding cylinders) was enclosed. This arrangement gave the No-Ro some of the round Spinaway look and made the unusual kicker appear as if some important parts were missing. Alas, most early outboarders made the "mistake" of purchasing a single-cylinder, causing No-Ro to fold after 1916.

Northwestern

From 1912 to 1918 the Northwestern Motor Company (Eau Claire, Wisconsin) produced a 62-pound, 2-hp rowboat motor. The Northwestern was available with battery or gear-driven Bosch magneto ignition. A buyer could also choose between tin-can mufflering or underwater exhaust.

Northwesterns came with a bronze rudder-style lower unit and were handsomely painted in dark maroon and given a "piano finish." It appears the crankshaft extended a few inches above the knob-start flywheel. This may have allowed the introduction of upper main bearing grease in a way similar to that of the Wilcox-McKim motor.

Although elementary by modern standards, the Northwestern placed a rubber cover over the boat end of the spark plug. Anyone who has accidentally bumped into a bare-plug wire connection can appreciate such protective innovation.

Like many early outboard firms, the Northwestern folks sold their motor on a 30-day free-trial basis. Noting the average vacation was only about two weeks, this might have proved a risky business practice.

Notre Dame

Like the student-built "Gopher" outboards, Notre Dame kickers were projects of an engineering class, bearing the name of the university where they were designed and built (circa 1935). It is estimated less than 100 of the one-lung outboards were produced at the famed South Bend, Indiana institution. "Fighting Irish" engineering scholars also turned out a few single-cylinder inboard engines of similar vintage.

Nymph

The Nymph Motor Company offered an outboard motor from 1914 to 1916. Not much else is known about this Cleveland-based firm or its engine. The Nymph may have been copied from the Ferro, which was also built in Cleveland.

The well-accepted Chris-Craft outboards had been in production for only a few years before the famed boat maker closed its kicker division in late 1953.

A year later press releases from the executive offices of the Oliver Corporation announced the firm's purchase of the silent outboard factory, along with the rights to "two basic motors which are currently tooled and known to the public as Chris-Craft."

Attached to the typed statement was a publicity photo of what had been a Chris-Craft 5½-horse Challenger motor. Someone in the PR department retouched the picture so the Oliver name appeared on both sides of its gas tank. If any of these badge-engineered Chris-Craft/Olivers were marketed, it probably wasn't many.

Actually, Oliver promised to completely modernize these engines before releasing them to sales outlets.[37]

The old line farm machinery manufacturer began making good on its pledge by learning which updated features outboarders might appreciate. Survey results prompted Oliver to provide its new models with a full gear shift (an F-N-R prototype Oliver lower unit got tested under an old Chris-Craft 10 powerhead), twist speed-control tiller handle, and a Tenda-Matic remote fuel tank. The 1955-premier Olivers wore the old Chris-Craft model names. The new outboard division's 5½-hp motor was designated ("J") Challenger, and the bigger one, upgraded from 10 to 15 horses, sported the ("K") Commander tag.

The rigs were painted in rich blues, yellows, and reds; ads for them made the motors seem larger than life. In fact the actual outboards, with nicely accented fiberglass covers, were as attractive as any motor of the era.

For 1956, model names were dropped and an electric-start version of the 15-horse made the catalog.

When Oliver first contemplated getting into the boat-motor business, it knew additional models would be added to round out the line. It had hoped to release 25- and 30-hp motors by late '55. All research pointed toward the need for bigger engines. As a result, the 35-hp, electric-start Olympus was introduced in 1957. Also tuning up the roster was the announcement that the old 5½ and 15 would gain ½ horse and 1 hp, respectively.

Oliver brochures of 1958 again offered 6-, 16-, and 35-hp models. New that year, however, was an electric-start option on the 16.

For 1959 the Mohawk model name was assigned to the 6-horse motor. Oliver's 16 became the Lancer (with optional electric start and long shaft), with the 35 (long shaft available) remaining Olympus. In an effort to compete with the major brands' big motors (the 50-hp OMC and the Mercury 70), Oliver offered twin 35s with factory-matched, counter-rotating propellers (like Champion's dual 16½ Tandem 33) generating a combined 70 horses of boat thrust.

Oliver

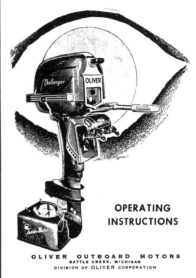

OPERATING
INSTRUCTIONS

OLIVER OUTBOARD MOTORS
BATTLE CREEK, MICHIGAN
DIVISION OF OLIVER CORPORATION

A 5½-hp, 1955 Oliver Challenger.

Oliver began searching for ways to make its outboard production more cost-effective. By 1960 the Oliver line was being manufactured in Great Britain. Advertisements of this period pictured an Oliver-powered cruiser rippling the coastal waters of a sleepy English village. The slogan "American designed—British built," had a nice ring to it, but did little to jingle the front doors of Oliver outboard dealerships.

In 1961 New York City designer Richard Arbib worked up some futuristic Oliver motor sketches. Although a few of the cosmetically engineered Olivers got into circulation, the venerable tractor firm decided to pull out of the water and closed its outboard division around the time President Eisenhower left office.

A.E. Olmstead & Sons

An old issue of the *National Sportsman* listed this mysterious manufacturer as having produced outboards from 1918 to 1926. Nine model years of motors should have added up to more information than a single, dusty magazine listing. No one ever came up with any other documentation, or even a brand name for the Olmstead outboard, and that made me suspicious. In any event, the original citation identified the phantom kicker as having been built in Pulaski, New York. As that locale was near my home, some detective work was in order.

A phone call to A.E. Olmstead's daughter revealed that, to the best of her knowledge, the small firm made an inboard, but not an outboard motor.

What makes this hobby interesting, however, is that now someone will probably send me a picture of four of them!

Outboard Jet

Like many of its water jet-propelled sisters, the Outboard Jet used an air-cooled Tecumseh powerhead. Outboard Jet, Inc., of Indianapolis, Indiana, should get credit, however, for placing the generic engine under a contoured shroud.

While most jet outboards shot thrust underwater, this one's push exited above the water line, thus "producing more efficient thrust, a more level ride, and greater fuel economy." The Outboard Jet could deliver 100 pounds of thrust, and all this without any portion of the lower unit extending below the boat's bottom. The "instant reversing," single-cylinder, 2-cycle Outboard Jet was supplied with a 3-gallon remote fuel tank. Options included a weed sweeper for passing through heavily vegetated waters, as well as a water hose attachment used in conjunction with the Outboard Jet's pump. This feature allowed lawn sprinkling, car washing, or fire fighting.

A model designated J-55 was introduced in 1963. An updated J-55B was manufactured from 1964 to 1966. Unfortunately, even though this product was advertised as "more fun than any 5 ½-hp motor you've ever tried!" not many folks gave the Outboard Jet a try.

Undaunted, the manufacturer was convinced it was on the right track and introduced an ambitious update by 1967. The new offering came in the form of a more sophisticated (compared to the previous engine) water-cooled, 2-cycle twin, labeled Outboard Jet OJ200. One owner of the 9½-hp unit reported its performance barely matched a conventional 6-hp prop-driven rig. Weeds (often a feature of shallow water, where one would tend to need a jet outboard) got caught on the water intake screen and caused problems. The stream of cooling water diverted from the jet pump diminished at low rpms and allowed the powerhead to get too hot.

Most outboard shoppers were still cool to the idea of water jet propulsion and continued to ignore this product.

In 1929 three major outboard firms merged. Combining Evinrude, Elto, and Lockwood, this merger probably saved the first two firms (the Lockwood name was quietly dropped by 1931) from the ravages of the Great Depression.

Motors wearing the OMC, or Outboard Motors Corporation, name were produced predominantly in Milwaukee and bore a strong likeness to various models in the Evinrude and Elto lines.

One of the most notable Outboard Motors Corporation models was the 1930 Foldlite. This 29-pound, 2¾-hp fishing motor had a hinge in the middle of the drive shaft housing that allowed the very portable motor to fold up when not in use. Also atypical of most of its contemporaries was the front-mounted Foldlite fuel tank.

The Outboard Motors Corporation ID was also well represented in the OMC 4-60, a four-cylinder, 60-cubic-inch racer. Ads assured the few fortunate Depression-era outboarders who could come up with $450 that the OMC 4-60 was readily available at "Elto, Evinrude, and Lockwood dealers throughout the world."

One of only a few New England–built outboards was the 1921 to 1922 Direct-Drive model from the Palmer Brothers Engine Company of Cos Cob, Connecticut. The single-cylinder, air-cooled Palmer featured an unusual transom bracket with a thumbscrew clamp on the outside of the boat. The Palmer outboard was a very limited production item.

The Palmer outboard.

Polar Motors, Inc., of La Crosse, Wisconsin, tried to warm up potential outboard customers with its 1964 ice boat outboard motor. The project was given the deep freeze by the following year.

Outboard Motors Corporation

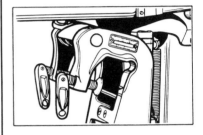

Many OMC post-war engines had ID plates on the clamp assembly.

Palmer

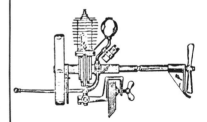

Polar

Portage

An obscure 1930s outboard, the Portage single, was identified as a product of Outboard Motor Sales and Service of Indianapolis, Indiana. In addition to a pair of tubes holding the drive shaft and exhaust, a third tube, running from powerhead to lower unit, housed the motor's waterlines. My guess is the 2-hp (at 2,800 rpm) Portage was simply a private-brand built for its seller by the Muncie (Neptune) Gear Works.

Power-Pak

After World War II boaters could consider the purchase of the new Power-Pak outboard from Propulsion Engine Corporation of Kansas City, Kansas. Power-Paks were available in 1945 and 1946 before leaving the changing postwar marketplace.

Production Foundries

The Production Foundries Company, Ann Arbor, Michigan, sold its motor minus a catchy brand name. This firm's outboard division was operational in 1923.

Quincy Looper

Quincy (Illinois) Welding Works began making aftermarket high-speed accessories for Mercury outboards in the late Forties. Small items such as open exhaust stacks and throttle/spark stop pieces gave way to larger Merc-oriented components.

Because it cast many of its own parts, Quincy was eventually able to come up with a complete Mercury derivative racer that scavenged fuel via the "loop charged" instead of the deflector method. These Quincy Loopers were made in small supply for exacting late Fifties and early Sixties outboard racing enthusiasts.

The alcohol-burning motors came in a variety of sizes such as class "A" (at 15 cubic inches), "B" (at 20 cubic inches), "C" (at 30 cubic inches), and "F" (at 60 cubic inches).

Racine

In the 1960s a lucky member of the Antique Outboard Motor Club discovered a rusty Racine tucked away in a New Jersey barn. That forward-pointing, single-cylinder engine built by the Racine Motor Oars Company of Racine, Wisconsin, features rudder steering and its name ornately emblazoned on its cast-iron knob-starting flywheel.

Racine rowboat motors were produced from 1913 to 1918 and boasted 2 hp at 800 rpm.

Red Top
(A/C—Auto City)

Daily output at Mercury or Evinrude easily outdistanced the 250 or so total outboard production from the tiny Auto City Outboard Association, Inc., of Detroit. Actually, the small firm made its single-cylinder Red Top motors in a modest, cement-block factory near Pontiac, Michigan.

The Red Top outboard, which generated about 4 to 5 hp, came with a rewind starter on top of its red gas tank and featured a unique steering system. A small tiller handle extended a few inches from the bottom of the powerhead and was connected at a 45-degree angle with another short handle sporting the plastic tiller grip. To turn the lower unit (the Red Top powerhead remained stationary), the up-pointing tiller grip was moved in an arch fashion down to the right or left.

It is believed the Auto City Outboard Association firm consisted of former staffers of the Packard car company. While the years have faded the facts surrounding the Red Top, a Caille-like appearance of some of its castings, as well as the red gas tank (many 1930s Caille outboards wore a red fuel tank and were dubbed Red Heads), leads one to speculate about a Caille connection. Caille, also a Detroit company, stopped outboard production in 1935. Perhaps some of the old Caille parts and castings were acquired by the Auto City Outboard Association people for use in their Red Top project.

A surviving member of the group guessed he had about two dozen coworkers in the tiny outboard firm.

The Red Top was said to outrun the Johnson fishing motors of the day. It was produced sometime during the close of World War II.[38]

Reveley

An early 1960s jet pump propulsion outboard, the Reveley came from the Meadville, Pennsylvania, Reveley Corporation.

Riley

During the mid-1950s, outboard cabin cruisers became quite the rage. For much less than the price of a stuffy yacht, one could get a nice 20-foot outboard cruiser, motor, and trailer. But craft such as these liked large motors—the bigger the better.

Johnson and Evinrude's top-of-the-line models were in the 25- to 35-hp range. Merc was up to 40 horses in 1954. Imagine a cruiser owner's surprise when he heard that some California outfit was selling an outboard actually capable of 75 hp!

The giant motor was from the George Riley Company of Los Angeles, and cooked up that power in a 4-cycle, five-cylinder, radial, flat-head engine. Tipping up the monster's fiberglass top revealed a British Lucas 12-volt electrical system. Pistons and bearings were said to be of Harley-Davidson motorcycle origin. An oil tank was mounted to the side of the cover. The face of the Riley looked at you through a pair of round gauges (oil pressure and amps), and the ignition key fit into an assembly between the two. A skipper could operate his 55-inch-tall giant outboard at the cruiser's steering console via a single-lever remote control.[39]

First marketed in 1954, the Riley's bulk couldn't compete with its competitors' better looks and established dealer/parts organization. Weaknesses with the lower unit also caused problems. This King Kong of the consumer outboard jungle disappeared after 1956.

Royal
(Atlas Royal)

Any happy motorist wanting to get on the water could ask his Esso gas station attendant for info about the Royal outboards.

First offered for the 1947–48 model year, the Gale Products–built Royal was distributed by Atlas Supply Company of Newark, New Jersey, to Esso (and Humble) related retailers

157   The Big List

Saber

Savage

Scott-Atwater

connected with Standard Oil of New Jersey, Kentucky, and Indiana. The 3-, 5-, 12-, and 25-hp 1956 line was Royal's last.

Outboards bearing the Saber name decal came from the Galesburg, Illinois, Gale Products Plant and were sold through various branches of the Minneapolis-headquartered Fedway Stores. These motors, also called Fedway Sabers, were available only in 1953. They came in denominations of 3, 5, and 12 hp.

See Chapter 1.

"The Adirondack resort had a whole fleet of wooden rowboats," explained my elderly friend, Sidney Tripp, "and each one of 'em wore a green and gold Scott-Atwater seven-and-a-half horse outboard. As camp manager, I had to help any guests who couldn't run the motors right. One particular outboard was a hard starter. Those Scotts had gearshifts, so we used to tow the rowboat behind our inboard runabout, get it goin' maybe twenty, twenty-five miles per hour, and throw the balky kicker in forward. She didn't like it much, but it got her goin' every time!

"One evening 'round nightfall," my friend continued despite the protest of rolling eyeballs, "we rescued a family stranded near the Four Brother Islands, 'bout three miles out from camp. I had them taken back in the inboard while I stayed to fix that very same Scott-Atwater. Knowing the finicky thing liked a hot spark, I advanced the mag, stood up, and really yanked.

"Well, sir, don't ya know, it roared to life on the second pull. Only thing was, the jack-rabbit start got the best of my footin' and I somersaulted into the lake!

"As mentioned earlier, it was gettin' pretty dark by then, but I was able to see the motor's direction as the renegade Scott sprayed me with her rooster tail and sped my boat away. Calculatin' the area of reentry," he smiled, "I swam to where the boat should eventually be comin' around. And nearly an hour later, I hear this distant HMMMMMMMMMMM, HMMMMMMMMMMM. It was the old Scott. She was bringing that boat back to me after all! Soon my opportunity came. So grabbin' onto the side of the speeding craft, I boosted myself on board, and pointed an accusin' finger at that Scott outboard. Could have sworn she kinda stuck her choke knob out at me. Anyhow, I decided to ignore it, and without saying a word let the old gal push me home."

Even as a kid, I was never quite sure about the authenticity of those Scott yarns. Actually, at the 1946 introduction of its own outboard motor line, Scott-Atwater faced somewhat of a credibility problem. Although few knew about it, the firm had been making motors since 1935, and in 1941 was considered the second largest (after Outboard Marine) U.S. outboard producer.

The Minneapolis company was started in 1932 (as a small tool-making and punch-press operation) by C.E. Scott and H.B. Atwater. The pair eventually obtained contracts from local establishments, such as Gold Medal Flour, for the production of promotional trinkets and advertising premiums. This worked well when the flour customers were attracted to the specials. Any marketing flop, however, would allow Scott-Atwater's employees to take a continual coffee break.

A Mr. DuMonte walked into the little factory in 1935 and asked if the firm could possibly help design and build a simple outboard motor for him to sell. Messrs. Scott and Atwater saw this request as a way to get steady work and soon presented DuMonte with a sample kicker. This putt-putt (offered at about half the price of its nearest competitor) was exhibited at the New York Boat Show, and "orders were placed for several hundred."

Right after the show Scott-Atwater turned most of its shop into an outboard factory. Some Champion decals were ordered and affixed to the little motors before Mr. DuMonte came by to pick them up for distribution. Still a bit apprehensive about the success of this venture, Scott-Atwater kept coming up with those little advertising items whenever Gold Medal Flour called.

But this nervousness was ended in 1939 when DuMonte secured a contract from Firestone Tire and Rubber Company. The agreement called for Firestone to distribute Champions in its

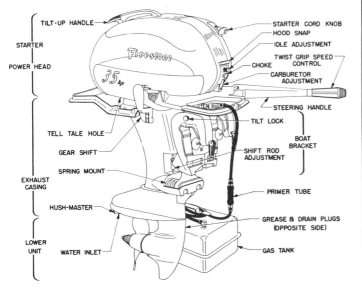

Firestone 35-hp Twin, built by Scott-Atwater.

TILT-UP HANDLE
STARTER CORD KNOB
HOOD SNAP
IDLE ADJUSTMENT
STARTER
TWIST GRIP SPEED CONTROL
POWER HEAD
CHOKE
CARBURETOR ADJUSTMENT
STEERING HANDLE
TILT LOCK
TELL TALE HOLE
BOAT BRACKET
GEAR SHIFT
SHIFT ROD ADJUSTMENT
SPRING MOUNT
EXHAUST CASING
PRIMER TUBE
HUSH-MASTER
GREASE & DRAIN PLUGS (OPPOSITE SIDE)
LOWER UNIT
WATER INLET
GAS TANK

159   The Big List

A 1949 advertisement for Scott-Atwater's new gearshift motors.

stores and franchise outlets (such as gas stations). Between 1939 and 1942, this marketing avenue sold all the Scott-Atwater–built Champions that the once-nervous little manufacturing concern could produce.

During World War II, Scott-Atwater was immersed in defense work, but frequently considered its postwar outboard options. Mr. DuMonte indicated he'd like to set up his own factory to build a new Champion line. Firestone wondered about its outboard motor status and went directly to Scott-Atwater with a request for kickers wearing its own Firestone label.

In 1946 both Scott-Atwater and Firestone motors hit the recreation-hungry marketplace. Larger facilities capable of handling the extra output were obtained.

Scott-Atwater didn't require its dealers to maintain an exclusive franchise. As a result marine shops with other makes were signed up. (This reasonable practice, which often placed Scott-Atwaters next to Mercurys on the showroom stands, allowed the line to expand its sales network quickly.)

Scott-Atwaters of 1946 were 3.6-horse, water-cooled singles (with optional rewind starter). In 1947 and again in '48, a 7½-hp twin was included in the lineup. Motors of this family received a rich, dark green paint job.

The company had been very busy working on an innovation it believed would set the firm apart from all competitors. The Scott-Atwater F-N-R gearshift was finally ready in 1949. Although Johnson had introduced a 10-horse shift model, Scott-Atwater offered a trio (4, 5, and 7½) with the shift feature. The line of 1950 contained all of these plus a new 16-hp shift rig. Scott-Atwater was also serious about its products' appearance and had the motors' external features done by New York industrial designer Francisco Cullura.

The 1951 lineup was unchanged except for the addition of a 10-hp model. Speed designations were serving as unofficial model names. For example, the big 16 was supposed to go 1 to 30 mph; hence, it became the 1-30. The basic 3.6 single (nonshift) could cover 1 to 12 mph and was labeled the 1-12, and so on.

The outboards started gaining positive attention, and Scott-Atwater, recalling its involvement with the flour company promotions, knew the importance of publicity. Besides actively participating in every major boat and sport show, as well as advertising nationally, the firm would pay up to 50 percent of the cost of local dealer ads.

Furthermore, Scott-Atwater not only provided dealerships with an "extensive mat service" (mats are newspaper/magazine ad sheets suitable for easy use in any publication), but also offered recorded (usually on big 16-inch transcription discs) radio commercials which could conveniently be tagged by a local station announcer with the dealer's address. This was an aggressive practice on the part of a relatively small, early Fifties company. Still more unusual in that radio and newspaper-oriented era was Scott-Atwater's offer to cover half the dealers' cost for air-

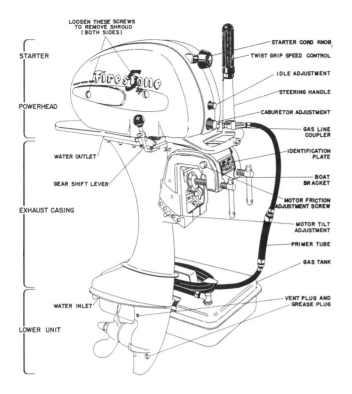

LOOSEN THESE SCREWS
TO REMOVE SHROUD
(BOTH SIDES)

STARTER CORD KNOB

TWIST GRIP SPEED CONTROL

IDLE ADJUSTMENT

STEERING HANDLE

CABURETOR ADJUSTMENT

GAS LINE
COUPLER

IDENTIFICATION
PLATE

BOAT
BRACKET

MOTOR FRICTION
ADJUSTMENT SCREW

MOTOR TILT
ADJUSTMENT

PRIMER TUBE

GAS TANK

VENT PLUG AND
GREASE PLUG

STARTER

POWERHEAD

WATER OUTLET

GEAR SHIFT LEVER

EXHAUST CASING

WATER INLET

LOWER UNIT

The 1956, 5-hp Firestone motor, built by
Scott-Atwater, had a thin, Gold Pennant
profile.

ing video versions of outboard ads on local TV stations. A 1951 survey found Scott-Atwater to be the only such organization to have prepared 60-second TV commercials "for dealer distribution."[40]

Ads in 1952 dropped the 4-hp rig, as the line included motors in 3.6-, 5-, 7½-, 10-, and 16-horse denominations. In 1953 two very unusual-looking Scott-Atwaters, dubbed Gold Pennant motors, were unveiled. These green-and-gold 7½- and 10-horse kickers had remote gas tanks and wore little chrome accent ears on each side of the two-piece cover shell. Because the Gold Pennant's profile was remarkably thin, you could get the idea the poor thing had been squished. Although well promoted, Gold Pennant motors (which some folks called pumpkin seeds) did not return the following year. The skinny styling was revised on Scott-Atwater's private-brand Corsair and Firestone outboards.

Scott-Atwater had tooled up for a new series of green (bottom shroud) and gold (top cover section) motors aimed at giving boaters the most useful nautical feature in marine history— a mechanical bailer. Unfortunately, this strong sales point eventually caused some folks to shake their heads in disgust.

All of the 1954s (except the 3.6 hp) had a little hose attached to a small rectangular aluminum assembly. The other end of the hose went to the motor. The green aluminum gizmo got placed in the bottom of the boat, and as a trademark (Bail-A-Matic) proudly emblazoned on the motor cover presumed, would automatically rid your craft of water.

Numerous problems with early Bail-A-Matic water pumps (also assigned to cool the cylinders) caused many a salty word to echo over worldwide waterways. As luck would have it, these parts were not easy to access and fix, either. In addition many Scott-Atwater repairs required special tools and a working knowledge of outboard innards, a pair of prerequisites seldom held by motor owners.

Bail-A-Matic, which was a darn good idea anyway, got heavily promoted through 1956. Although it remained on some subsequent models (even on Scott-Atwater's mid-Sixties successor, McCulloch), the system was de-emphasized from its original "top-feature" status.

The Scott-Atwater people had always planned on joining the full-line outboard producers and finally did so in 1955 with a 30-hp unit. This rig was upped to 33 horses in 1956.

Meantime, Messrs. Scott and Atwater were approached by McCulloch Corporation about the possibility of selling the outboard company. A deal was closed in 1956.

McCulloch discontinued the private-brand Corsair line (the old firm had been producing this badge-engineered product since 1948) and began referring to its outboard division as Scott. Even though the full Scott-Atwater name remained for a time on engine hoods, the shortened Scott title came as a relief to many who could never remember the second part anyway (kind of like *Sears* and Roebuck).

The new management enlarged the 1957 line by souping up the old 33 for a nice round 40 hp. It was offered in manual or electric start and could be equipped with a long shaft for large runabouts and cruisers. The 16-horse motor had an optional electrical start. Some of the Scott line's fiberglass hoods were available in a choice of eight colors.

Some McCulloch brass felt publicity generated via outboard racing was a good way to promote Scott. A 14-foot utility boat with twin Scott 40s won the 120-mile Malibu Beach open marathon during early 1957. In another California event the executive vice-president of McCulloch used a pair of 40-horse Scotts to push his 16-foot runabout to victory. These gains caused McCulloch to institute a "competition development" department. There was even hope Scott would produce a line of racing motors suitable for National Outboard Association and American Power Boat Association stock outboard classes. (At that time only Mercury and Champion offered a few such kickers.)

Rather than introduce a utilitarian 20-cubic-inch class "B" stocker, however, Scott decided to shoot for the world's outboard speed record of just over 100 mph. The company came up with a special gear box linking two of its soon-to-be-unveiled three-cylinder Flying Scott 60-hp powerheads. This rig, mounted on an unconventional Italian-built di Priolo lower unit, was dubbed the Scott-Atwater Square Six. Its torque tube protruded back of the motor at about a 30-degree angle and had triple anticavitation plates and an overdrive gear requiring a gallon and a half of SAE

90 lubricant per run! The Square Six was supposed to provide Scott with a "braggin' rights" display at the 1958 New York Boat Show. While it easily zipped a custom designed hydro to 80 mph, the six-cylinder, six-carb power plant didn't quite hit the desired 101.12-mph mark. Still, industry observers hoped the motor would serve as a catalyst for more racing outboards from Scott.[41]

The year 1958 saw the McCulloch-designed three-cylinder, in-line, 60-hp Flying Scott officially introduced. Electric-starting models now came with a generator for more dependable battery use. Model names of the late-Fifties Scotts took on a psychographic tone with nomenclature like Thrifty, Fishing, Family, Special, Sports, Super, and Royal.

During the early Sixties, most Scotts received a clean white paint scheme. The McCulloch people also offered custom fiberglass boats matched to their various outboards. The 1961–62 line ranged from 2.6 to 75.2 hp.

Popular during this era was the low-profile Fishing Scott. This uniquely shaped motor (positioned predominantly outboard like the old Flambeau) weighed but 40 pounds and measured only 30 inches high.

Scott, never one to pass up a useful feature, debuted its Shallowater Drive as standard equipment on the Royal Scott Custom 40 and Flying Scott 75.2-hp models. This remote tilt mechanism, operable from the front of the boat, used engine thrust to tilt the motor. This item could be used at higher speeds and allowed effective and safe cruising in 6 inches of water.

Also belonging to the early 1960s were a few hardy Scotts known as *OX*. These strong rigs (most of which occupied the 14-hp range and wore red covers) could be ordered with either a standard or geared-down lower unit for houseboat pushing and/or industrial applications. Thermostat cooling was added to later models. Diesel power was also an option.

By 1964 Scott's owners decided to relabel their motors with the McCulloch name, and another well-known Forties and Fifties marque faded into outboard history.

Sea-Bee (1)

The fighting Seabee military men racked up many honors during World War II. So in 1946, when the Goodyear Tire and Rubber Company of Akron, Ohio, wanted a good name for its private-brand outboard line, Sea-Bee fought its way to the top of the suggestion list. Sea-Bee motors, made by Gale Products Division of Outboard Marine, were marketed through 1959.

Owner's manuals printed for auto and catalog stores retailing Gale-made private-brand outboards.

The Big List

Sea-Bee (2)

This 1960s marque had no connection with the earlier Goodyear Sea-Bee. A trio of small engines in 1½-, 3-, and 4-hp denominations made up the Sea-Bee outboard line marketed by Robert T. Boomer of Venice, California. The 2-cycle, single-cylinder motors wore such model names as "Minor" and "Super 3." Some were available in long-shaft versions for auxiliary-power sailboat use.

Sea-Flyer

Not to be outdone by its tire competitors at Goodyear and Firestone, the BF Goodrich Company of Akron, Ohio, purchased a 1952 (some were considered 1951) stock of private-brand motors from Gale Products Division. The following year Goodrich's sea-green color Sea-Flyer outboards were being built at the Champion factory. By 1955 the Sea-Flyer had flown the coop.

Sea Gull (1)

See listing under Cross, earlier in this chapter.

Sea Gull (2)

Muncie Gear Works was under contract from the 1930s through about 1941 to supply outboards to the National Outboard Motor Company of Marshall, Michigan. To fulfill this agreement, Muncie's complete "Neptune" line from 1.2 to 16 hp was simply relabeled with the Sea Gull nameplate. These Sea Gulls had no relationship with the better-known British motors bearing the same moniker.

Sea King

"Only the finest motors have Sea King features," boasted a late-Forties Montgomery Ward and Company catalog. Its claim was based on the fact that Ward's Sea King outboards were typically supplied by the industry's major players.

The big Chicago-based mail-order house's first rowboat motor came in the form of a Caille-built, World War I–era kicker called Hiawatha. Montgomery Ward changed its marine line's name to Sea King and purchased product from the Evinrude-controlled Outboard Motors Corporation. During the early Thirties, OMC had an odd stock of idle class "B" Chiefs from its discontinued

Lockwood line. The firm honored part of its Montgomery Ward contract by sticking Sea King decals on these interesting motors. Some of the 15-horse twins had electric starters. A very few were equipped with unusual Bendix Eclipse crank-up inertia starters. (Today, these make up the rarest Sea Kings.)

By the late Thirties, Montgomery Ward (which also bought some Muncie-built outboards) purchased a supply of catalog engines from the Cedarburg (Wisconsin) Manufacturing Company. These erstwhile Thors, relabeled with the Sea King name, didn't run very well and gave Montgomery Ward a black eye. Meanwhile, Carl Kiekhaefer bought the Thor factory, fixed up some rejected Sea Kings, and earned a new contract with the large retailer. As a result, the early 1940s Sea King line comprised a mix of smaller Kiekhaefer motors and outboards produced by Evinrude's Gale Products Division.

Years ago I spotted an old Spring–Summer 1947 Montgomery Ward catalog peeking out from under a wicker rocker on the screened-in porch of a vintage lakeside cottage. The publication's Sea King section pictured a 1-horse "midget single," a 2.9-hp "large single," standard and deluxe (full-pivot reverse and rewind-start) 3.3-horse opposed twins, 5-hp standard and deluxe alternate-firing twins, a "super" 8½-hp, and "giant" 15.2-horse opposed twins. The 2.9-hp rig came from Kiekhaefer, with the remainder originating at Gale.

While the smaller motors could be mailed through the post office, large models were shipped by freight or express from Montgomery Ward's warehouses in Baltimore or Albany, New York. Sea Kings were sent with "full instructions and complete parts list." Spare parts were "carried in stock at your nearest Ward mail order house and at the motor factories."

By the early Fifties, Gale supplied the Sea King line via its standard stable of private-brand outboards: a 3-hp single, a 5-horse with neutral clutch, and a 12-hp gearshift-equipped alternate-firing twin. In 1955 the top Sea King had 22 hp, a remote Bo'sun fuel tank system, and optional electric starter. The next year the 22 was upped to 25. In addition a neat 12-hp electric-start outboard was introduced into the '56 Sea King lineup. Two years later, this smaller power-start model was gone, and a 35-horse twin was added to the roster. Early Sixties Montgomery Ward catalogs showed a few changes in power range. For example, a 15-hp twin and 60-hp quad were introduced.

Montgomery Ward made a bigger switch for the 1964–65 Sea King line by contracting with West Bend to supply its watersport section. Typically occupying the 3½-, 5½-, 6-, 8-, 9-, 20-, and up to 80-hp brackets, these mid-Sixties engines made up the final Sea Kings in our area of interest.

If you ever wonder why someone would buy an outboard from a catalog, convenience constitutes most of the answer. Prior to the 1960s not every locale was served by a marine store. Montgomery Ward catalogs brought the marina to rural customers. More importantly, huge retailers like Montgomery

"Just my size!" A youngster proudly displays his Montgomery Ward Sea King Midget Single egg beater, which sold for $27.95 in 1947.

Ward allowed items to be purchased on credit. That previously mentioned 1947 "midget single" was available through the mail to anyone willing to commit "$4 a month (or about 13 cents per day) on terms" for a Sea King sporting features found in "only the finest outboard motors."

Sea Pacer

Introduced in 1962 the Sea Pacer offered small boaters a 4-cycle powerhead. The air-cooled outboard in the 3-hp range featured a front and rear carrying handle assembly and Clinton-style lower units.

Sears

About 1964 America's largest retailer dropped the Elgin marque from its outboard line. The predominantly McCulloch-produced motors of this vintage simply bore the Sears name.

Skipper

Skipper was a rather rare private-brand built in the late 1940s and early 1950s by Muncie Gear Works (the Neptune people). It appears the company marketing Skipper outboards also contracted for some kickers from Outboard Marine's Gale Products Division. Regardless of their various origins, Skippers were constructed in 1½-, 3-, 5-, and 12-hp denominations.

Spartan

Metalex Ltd. of Richmond, in Vancouver, British Columbia, Canada, began marketing its Spartan V outboard in 1959. Presumably, this obscure motor was of the low-horsepower, fishing variety.

A letter in my files dated July, 1969 says "We have not been in the business of manufacturing this equipment for more than seven years and are unable to supply you with anything [information] in this regard."

Spinaway (Speedaway)

We sell "the motor that puts the *TING* in boating!" claimed a Spinaway advertisement. With ad copy like that, it is doubtful its author lasted to the 1924 end of the Spinaway production run.

Officially, the earliest Spinaways (1911) were called Speedaways, originating from the Speedaway Boat Motor Company, Freeport, Illinois. Three years later, the Hoefer Manufacturing Company owned the young rowboat motor firm and renamed it Spinaway Boat Motor Company.

Hoefer reminded small-boat owners that Roman soldiers once chained slaves to galley oars and suggested the modern equivalent of such harsh activity could best be avoided by purchasing a Spinaway.

One of the forward-pointing single's most prominent features was its round gas tank (of about equal size to the flywheel). Owners found a funnel was needed to fuel-up via the tank's small, side-mounted spout. Ignition was available from a battery or gear-driven Bosch mag. By the later Teens Spinaways could be ordered with a flywheel-enclosed magneto. In fact some wore an Evinrude flywheel and mag. (This could cause a Spinaway to be mistaken for an old Evinrude.) The rudder-steered Spinaway was finished in a moss green color, accented by various bronze and polished-aluminum parts.

Many examples came through the factory with nice identification detailing on the exhaust assembly. Early models had an underwater exhaust tube. Later ones simply used a rear-pointing muffler (in which case, the brand was put on the gas tank). Some Spinaways had starting knobs that recessed in a small flywheel cavity when the motor was either idle or spinning away.

During the final two years of production (1923 and 1924), a number of Spinaway opposed twins were produced. The '23 metered fuel with a generic mixing valve, while the '24 sported a Zenith carb. As was the case with some of the last singles, mag ignition was often from Evinrude. And then after that "all of the fun, pleasure, and wholesome diversion" from Spinaway came to a close.

A 1923 Spinaway outboard and logo.

Starling Jet

"From Propulsion Research, Inc. in Minneapolis, heart of the outboard country, came America's first production line jet propelled outboard." So stated the 1965 introductory brochure for the model P-500 Starling Jet "complete fishing motor."

Actually, other U.S. companies (such as Lancaster Pump) had similar products predating the Starling Jet, but this firm's Marine Jet Division was probably aiming at wider distribution. The 5-hp, air-cooled, single-cylinder powerhead was built by Clinton Engines Corporation of Maquoketa, Iowa, and looked identical to Clinton's own outboard power plant. The jet lower unit was of Propulsion Research's design and drew water through a grill into a small turbine. This internal turbine created "super hydro thrust" and pushed a jet stream through slots where a propeller would be on a regular outboard. The 29-pound, 2-cycle rig was marketed to fishermen wanting to maneuver in weedy, shallow waters. Safety-minded swimmers and skin divers were also targeted in ads stressing "prop-less" action.

At 6,800 rpm (a lot of revs for the lawn-mower-style powerhead), the Starling Jet gave 82 pounds of push. The company, however, suggested an operating range of 3,900 to 5,000 rpm.

This novel little motor came with a 3-gallon remote fuel tank and was available in "Jet White" for fishermen or "Olive Drab" for duck hunters. Neither group really responded to the thrust of Propulsion Research's message, and the Starling Jet was grounded a few years later.

St. Lawrence

Added to the list of circa World War I forward-pointing, single-cylinder rowboat motors was the St. Lawrence. Its manufacturer, the St. Lawrence Engine Company, equipped the (1916) motor with a knob-starting flywheel and rudder steering.

167   The Big List

Strelinger

Sometimes called the Strelmotor, this 1914–16 Detroit-built outboard's most striking feature was its long, direct-drive lower unit. The powerhead could be separated from the drive shaft assembly for easier carrying. The Strelinger Marine Company's offering generated 2 hp at 800 rpm.

The Strelinger people claimed their product would run six hours on a gallon of gas. They also guaranteed the motor for five years, but were out of business before that amount of time elapsed.

Submerged

See Chapter 1.

Swanson

See listing under Champion.

Sweet

Sweet motors were almost identical to Watermans. Both companies were located in Detroit.

Rather than a firm with a full-fledged outboard factory, the Sweet Manufacturing Company might actually have been an early private-brand motor distributor. From 1914 to 1916 the Detroit concern marketed a 4-hp (at 1,000 rpm) single that was virtually indistinguishable from a forward-pointing, horizontal-cylinder Waterman Porto.

It would be nearly impossible to tell a Sweet, minus its ID plate, from a nameless Waterman of similar vintage. Because Sweet and Waterman both hailed from what would become the "Motor City," it's unlikely Sweet simply copied Waterman's design without prior approval. My guess is that Sweets were built by Waterman, then sent to Sweet for labeling and distribution. Or, perhaps Sweet purchased pieces from Waterman and built up the motors in its shop. Whatever the case, there had to be some connection.

By the way, Sweet also offered a 2-hp (at 700 rpm) single that was a dead ringer for an Evinrude rowboat motor.

Ted Williams

The famous Red Sox hitter lent his name to a McCulloch-produced 1960s fishing motor sold by Sears. The Eska company may have also made some of these private-brand outboards,

Terry Troller

Meant to be a fishing motor, the 4-cycle Terry Troller from Terry Troller Manufacturing, Inc. (West Frankfort, Illinois) was on the market from 1960 to 1963. One of its most interesting features was a lawn-mower-style "wind-up and release" crank starter.

Thor

Thor Hansen often said, "Go ahead, drop any Thor outboard on cement! You will not harm it." Mr. Hansen, president of Cedarburg (Wisconsin) Manufacturing Company, even invited Thor owners to stick "a pencil into the carburetor air intake hole [breaking away any oily film] to assure quick starting."

Thor outboards, introduced in 1935, had a very "basic" appearance. The motors incorporated pressed-steel, cadmium-plated stampings for crankcase, gear housing, main stem, clamping bracket, and steering handle. This stuff was supposed to be "rustproof," but was in fact vulnerable to the elements—particularly salt water. The 1935, 2.4-hp single was advertised as "sturdy, simple, and quick starting!" While the first two claims were indeed true, the latter could, at best, be euphemized as a wish. Hansen's nearly featureless mixing valve/carb was usually the culprit.

In 1936 it was claimed that Thor outboards would "again astound the outboard world" with a 4.8-hp, two-cylinder version. At $42.50 for the single and $62.50 for the opposed twin, these motors were priced within the "range of every fisherman and sportsman."

By 1938 the angled lower-unit skeg, fashioned from steel stampings, was given a rounded look. Hansen had a little bit of luck selling a few of his motors. Then Montgomery Ward's catalog stores gave him a chance to use the "same engineering genius that upset all former standards of outboard value" and make up some motors to be sold under the Sea King label. Having purchased Sea Kings to push a boat, as opposed to pound cement, however, Montgomery Ward customers registered numerous complaints. That dissatisfaction, coupled with sagging Thor sales, caused Hansen to go out of business.

The closed-up Cedarburg Manufacturing Company was soon purchased by E.C. Kiekhaefer, who decided to rename it Kiekhaefer Corporation. The new firm was supposed to make electromagnetic auto components, but a lack of capital caused Kiekhaefer to rebuild the remaining stock of faulty Thor–Sea Kings. Montgomery Ward was so pleased with the results that Kiekhaefer figured he'd temporarily remain in the outboard business.

Under Kiekhaefer management the 1939 Thor line included a 2.4-hp Streamliner. Complete with new carb, this remnant of the old Thor single wore a streamlined, teardrop fuel tank. It is a rare and highly desired motor today. Also offered were alternate-firing, in-line two- and three-cylinder outboards. At 6.2 hp, the Pyramid 3 was the first of its configuration.

By 1940 Kiekhaefer opted to stay with the outboard industry, but dropped the Thor name in favor of his new Mercury marque.

A rowboat motor from Saginaw, Michigan, the Valley dates back to 1914.

While not an antique, wayward examples of this rig could throw an outboard enthusiast for a loop. Consequently, the Versatool is listed herein. Noting the proliferation of chainsaws, Versatool, Inc., of Sun Valley, California, developed a wide range of accessories that could be mated to a chainsaw engine.

Among the firm's hedgetrimmers, pumps, generators, and drills was the Versatool VT600 Aqua-Sport Outboard Attachment. Early 1980s Versatool brochures indicated you could remove your saw's chain, mount the outboard converter (steer with the saw handgrip), and "in seconds be ready to take your chainsaw

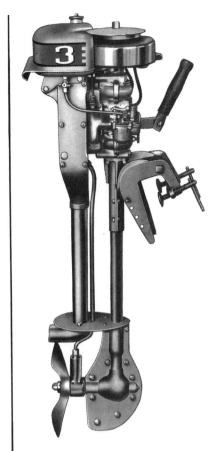

Steel stampings comprised portions of this 1938–39 Thor Pyramid-3, in-line outboard. Alternate fire on this 3-cylinder, 2-cycle, 6.2-hp model was touted as being as smooth as a 6-cylinder auto engine. A few of these rigs were fitted with cast lower gearcases. (Mercury Marine)

Valley

Versatool
(Aqua-Sport
Outboard
Attachment)

fishing." A 6-gallon (OMC) remote fuel tank could be fitted to the saw's carb for greater range.

At just under $100, this clever product represented an economical way for chainsaw owners to go outboarding. Because the outboard unit could be matched to an array of chainsaw brands, including those sharing outboard motor names (such as Western Auto-Wizard, Homelite, and McCulloch), one needs to be aware the resulting kicker is a conversion.

Viking

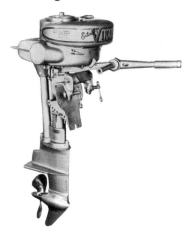

Like Sears, its American counterpart, the T. Eaton Company of Toronto, Ontario, offered a line of private-brand outboards. Over the years (from the 1930s to the 1960s) Eaton's Viking motors were supplied by manufacturers such as Muncie, Evinrude, Gale, and West Bend.[42]

The 8.5-hp 1940 Viking Twin was built by Evinrude for Canada's Eaton department stores. (Shipyard Museum)

Voyager

Relabeled 1950 Champions made up the first Voyager line. The thinly disguised Champs, like their sister Majestic outboards, were sold through Champion's subsidiary, Outboard Motor Brands, Inc., of Minneapolis, Minnesota. When Champion faded from sight in 1959, Voyager disappeared too.

Walnut

See the listing for Burtray.

Waterman

See the listing for Arrow (1).

Water Sprite

See the listing for Burtray.

Waterwitch

Sears-Roebuck got into the retail outboard business about 1913 or 1914. Its Motorgo kickers were produced by a number of firms. Around 1934 Sears switched its outboard name to Waterwitch. Muncie made some, and interestingly, even Johnson built a very few Waterwitches that were based on its 8.1-hp OK series motors.

When its 1930–36 outboard supply agreement with Muncie Gear Works was expiring, the big retailer turned to Kissel Industry Company of Hartford, Wisconsin, for help. This Kissel organization had been salvaged around 1930 from the remnants of the bankrupt Kissel Automobile Company. These folks were more than happy to contract with Sears, and from 1936 to 1942 came up with a rather wide selection of Waterwitch outboards.

Understandably, to the uninterested all Kissel Waterwitches look the same. Actually, however, these rigs ranged from a ¾-hp, air-cooled putt-putt, to a rare (about 600 built) 1941, 10-horse, alternate-firing twin. Its deluxe 5.75-hp model came with a rewind starter and a receptacle on the front of the gas tank into which a small light (or other accessory) could be plugged. Some of the most exotic Waterwitches, with their "twin-pod" fuel tanks, were styled by designer Raymond Loewy. Futuristic looks or not, many of these classics ran poorly, and Sears, ever mindful of customer satisfaction, recoiled under complaints.

Near the close of World War II the West Bend Aluminum Company purchased the Kissel plant, and Sears asked West Bend to come up with a new Elgin outboard by 1946. Even though the last Waterwitches officially rolled off the assembly line in 1942, it appears West Bend put together a few thousand from remaining parts stock in 1945. Actually, during the war, the government ordered a small run of 3½-hp Waterwitches for essential use by various domestic authorities. Note: The first Waterwitch motors were of Muncie manufacture and date from late 1933 to early 1937. They came in denominations from 2 to 16 hp.

Also a point of Waterwitch interest: The story line for Robert McCloskey's famous children's book, *One Morning in Maine*, included one of the famous Sears motors. The darn thing wouldn't start in the book, either.

Many people had been depending on the West Bend Aluminum Company's outboards for some 10 years before realizing the firm was ever in the boat-motor business. The story starts in 1944, when the famous kitchen utensil concern bought the (Hartford, Wisconsin) Kissel plant. That factory came with a Sears contract to produce outboard motors.

Although West Bend built a few Sears Waterwitch motors from existing stock, its engineers were asked to develop a completely new outboard for debut after World War II. They did, and the famous Elgin line sold like hotcakes from 1946 until ties with Sears were loosened in the early 1960s.

Meanwhile, West Bend's contract with the big retailer allowed for the relabeling of some Elgin motors. These green, badge-engineered rigs got to wear the West Bend name and were considered exports.

In 1955 the firm used a paint scheme different from the Elgins and offered West Bend outboards to the domestic market. The public demand for higher-horsepower motors caused West Bend wisely to offer a full line. This stable, which began at 2 hp, went to 25 hp, and soon 40 horses, culminated (in 1961) with an over-5-foot-tall, four-cylinder, in-line Tiger-Shark powerhouse rated at 80 hp. This piece was also offered in a modified form as the Shark-O-Matic inboard/outboard. West Bend assigned "fishy" names to many of its motors. Various models were labeled Shrimp, Pike, Muskie, Shark, and Barracuda.

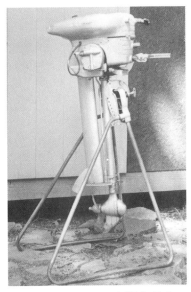

The 1942 Sears Waterwitch 5¾-hp Twin had rewind start and a tiny generator and receptacle plug for attaching a fishing light. Looks like it could come up the cellar stairs at night and attack somebody!

West Bend

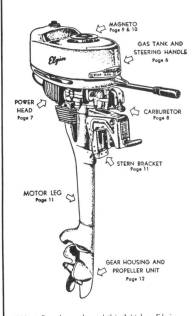

West Bend produced this 1¼-hp, Elgin air-cooled outboard for Sears in 1946.

The Big List

Late-1950s West Bend logo.

This boat is fitted with an 80-hp, 1964 West Bend motor.

Western Flyer

Whirlpool

Wilco

Wilcox

During this era, West Bend really began concentrating in the home appliance avenue, shifting some executive interest away from the outboard division.

By late 1964, after the unchanged 1965 models were announced, West Bend accepted a purchase order from Chrysler. Consequently, the 1965s were called WEST BEND—by CHRYSLER.

In retrospect West Bend always seemed to be lumped in with the also-rans of the day. This labeling was very unfair, however, as its outboards showed considerable reliability and innovation. West Bend–produced motors were the first to have a vacuum fuel system, a three-phase super-alternator generator, a low-level reduction gear starter, cushion mounting, V reed intake valves, an acoustical leg chamber, and a fiberglass motor cover.[43] All these features were available at pricing often lower than Mercury, Johnson, or Evinrude.

Perhaps if West Bend had enjoyed a stronger dealership network, its undue second-stringer image would have disappeared. In fact Chrysler's desire to buy West Bend's outboard division was heightened from evidence suggesting the product was, indeed, a quality marque suffering from being undersold.[44]

In 1941 and 1942 Outboard Marine's Gale Products Division of Galesburg, Illinois, produced this 2½- and 5-hp fishing-motor line for the Kansas City–based Western Auto Supply Company. World War II stopped Western Flyer production. Following that conflict, the famous auto parts and hardware chain came out with the Wizard outboard.

Not exactly the kind of old motor you'd expect to spot at a garage sale, the 4-cycle Whirlpool outboard was an experimental, three-cylinder, radial model. Built by the famous Whirlpool home appliance people in Los Angeles, this rig could be thrown into neutral by raising the tiller handle. The approximately 30-cubic-inch–displacement Whirlpool outboard motor was probably constructed in late 1927 and received rave reviews from folks who watched it race in California. Kudos aside, company execs decided to stick with machines capable of handling America's laundry, and hung any further plans for the Whirlpool outboard's production out to dry.

A Chicago firm marketed an Evinrude rowboat motor look-alike called the Wilco. Not to be confused with the Wilcox-McKim, the Wilco was available only in 1914.

Saginaw, Michigan, was home to the Wilcox-McKim Company, makers of the Wilcox (some were labeled Wilcox-McKim) outboard from 1914 to 1916. The 2½-hp, 70-pound engine was sparked by a gear-driven Dixie magneto. The flywheel starting knob rested in a cavity when not in use.

Interestingly, the very top of the crankshaft was hollow and extended an inch or so above the flywheel. Wilcox owners packed the crank top with grease to satisfy the upper main bearing.

The Wilcox steered with a rudder and had an underwater exhaust tube identical to the early Spinaway single.

Wisconsin

In a large field of quickly exhausted also-rans, the Wisconsin Machinery and Manufacturing Company made a relatively long-lived series of one-cylinder rowboat motors. The famous farm and industrial engine builder reminded potential customers that "the primary fact to observe in buying any mechanical device is the experience and reputation of its maker."

On patents issued late in the summer of 1913, Wisconsin began offering its 2-stroke, water-cooled outboards the following model year. Most Wisconsins were variations on two basic themes: a 2-hp Junior kicker (sometimes called model J, K, L, or M) and a 3½-horse rig (model N) especially adaptable for commercial use on fishing and livery boats, as well as tenders.

The smaller Wisconsin could be ordered with a battery ignition or a gear-driven Elkhart magneto (said to produce a good spark at 50 rpm). Owners of the 2-hp had the option of rudder or conventional propeller steering. The latter method's tiller could be twisted one-quarter turn, allowing the operator to lock in a specific direction.

Typically, the 3½-hp version came with a magneto and rudder steering. Wisconsin described its products as "simple, compact, capable of delivering wonderful power."

By the mid-1920s these rowboat motors were hopelessly outdated. (Note: Evinrude offered diehards a basic rowboat motor through 1928.) Even so, Wisconsin remained in the outboard business to 1930, possibly offering the few patrons of that era motors from new/old stock. Since the Milwaukee-based firm continued manufacturing its other product lines, parts and service for the Wisconsin outboards were available for a good number of years thereafter.

Before World War II, the fledgling Kiekhaefer Corporation entered the outboard business via supplying Montgomery Ward with some Sea King motors. After the war its recollections of that profitable relationship caused the manufacturer of Mercury outboards to get back into private-branding.

In 1946 Western Auto Supply Company of Kansas City, Missouri, contracted Kiekhaefer to relabel some basic 3.2- and 6-horse Mercs with Wizard decals.

By 1949 Western Auto catalogs listed a more deluxe 6-hp Super Twin. The following year Wizards took on a light green color and were offered in 6- and 10-hp sizes. A shift version of the 10 was added for 1952. This top-of-the-line Wizard rig was upgraded to 12 hp in 1954 and joined the standard 6 and 10 in the expanding line.

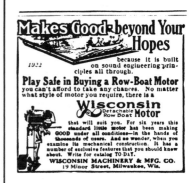

A 1922 Wisconsin rowboat motor ad.

Wizard

The 1953 Western Auto Wizard had definite Mercury traits.

For 1955 the old 6 was replaced with a Super 5. The following year Kiekhaefer supplied Western Auto with a slightly tuned-down version of its four-cylinder Mercury Mark 30. This Wizard Super Power 25 was also available with electric start.

For some reason an Oliver-built model, dubbed Powermatic 15, showed up in Wizard's '57 line. The 1958 series (5½, 15, and 35 hp) were all from Oliver.

For 1959 the catalog store went with Scott (McCulloch) and offered a stable of these products wearing the Wizard name, 3.6 to 40 hp.

Finally, the last of the full-line Wizards were Chrysler outboard products ordered from mid-1960s Western Auto catalogs.

The 1956/57 Wizard 25.

Wright

Where other rowboat motors had tiller handles, the Wright had a crank, which the operator turned for steering, or complete reversing. This 2-hp (at 675 rpm) forward-pointing single had a knob-start flywheel but no lower-unit skeg.

The Wright could be ordered with battery or flywheel magneto ignition and sported an aluminum crankcase, torque tube, and transom bracket.

A product of the C.T. Wright Engine Company of Greenville, Michigan, the Wright "attachable" (as compared with everyone else's "detachable") rowboat motor was marketed between 1914 and 1917.

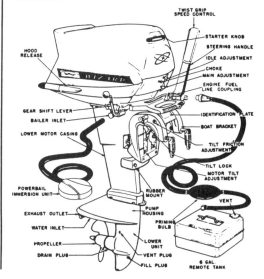

Early-1960s Wizard logo and 1961, 14.1-hp Wizard by Scott.

Notes

1. Phil Kranz, "The Aerothrust," *Antique Outboarder* (July 1971), pp. 22–24.
2. W.J. Webb, "Of Historical Interest, Amphion History," *Antique Outboarder* (October 1972), pp. 9–10.
3. Harold Polk, "A Waterman Story—My First Outboard," *Antique Outboarder* (January 1980), p. 27.
4. Sam Vance, "An Interesting Prototype," *Antique Outboarder* (April 1973), p. 13.
5. "It's News," *Boat Sport* (September 1954), p. 27.
6. *Motor Boating* (September 1925), p. 134.
7. Edwin R. Hodge, Jr., "A Study of the Outboard Motor Industry," (Ph.D. diss., Indiana University, 1951),
8. Ibid.
9. *Antique Outboarder* (January 1985), p. 21.
10. Glen Ollila, "The Champ," *Antique Outboarder* (October 1970), pp. 27–31.
11. Hodge, op. cit., p.
12. Don Peterson, "The Chrysler Story," *Antique Outboarder* (April 1976), pp. 39–43.
13. Phil Kranz, "Mini Outboard," *Antique Outboarder* (April 1975), p. 38.
14. Dave Batchelder, "Davis Experimental Radial Outboard," *Antique Outboarder* (July 1980), pp. 19–24.
15. "The Put-Put," *Fortune* (August 1938), p. 112.
16. Donald Peterson, "The Fageol Story," *Antique Outboarder* (October 1973), pp. 25–26.
17. Richard A. Hawie, "Notes from the Curator," *Antique Outboarder* (October 1985), pp. 12–15.
18. Hodge, op. cit., p.
19. LeRoi Russel, "The Minnesota Gopher," *Antique Outboarder* (October 1981), pp. 76–77.
20. Bill Andrulitis with Bob Zipps, "Hartford Sturdy Twin," *Antique Outboarder* (April 1975), pp. 32–37.
21. Pal Strot, "The Joymotor," *Antique Outboarder* (July 1976), pp. 38–40.
22. "Special Feature Articles—Joymotor Canoe Model Low Down—Safety First," *Antique Outboarder* (April 1988), p. 26.
23. Wayne Schoepke, "The Kingfisher," *Antique Outboarder* (October 1979), p. 41.
24. J.L. Smith, "The Koban Twin: 1914–1926," *Antique Outboarder* (October 1975), pp. 30–33.
25. Hodge, op. cit., p.
26. Ibid.
27. Chuck Sundby, "The Martin Motor," *Antique Outboarder* (January 1984), pp. 25–28.
28. Bob Grubb, "Test Editor Tests the 1949 Martin 20," *Antique Outboarder* (January 1984), pp. 22–24.
29. Hodge, op. cit., p.
30. Sundby, op. cit.
31. Ibid.
32. *1956 Outboarder Dealer Trade-In Guide* (Mishawaka, IN: Abos Publishing Co., 1956),

33. *Outboard Motor Service Manual*, 4th ed., Vol. 1 (Mishawaka, IN: Abos Marine Div. Technical Publications, 1967), p. 131.

34. T. Kilcoyne, "A Minnesota Milestone," *Antique Outboarder* (July 1983), pp. 5–8.

35. Hodge, op. cit., p.

36. Ibid.

37. "It's News—Oliver Outboard Motors," *Boat Sport* (February 1955), p. 3.

38. Bob Lomerson, "Mystery Outboard Somewhat Less of a Mystery," *Antique Outboarder* (April 1988), pp. 24–26.

39. Don Peterson, "Collector's Gallery, Riley," *Antique Outboarder* (January 1974), pp. 14–15.

40. Hodge, op. cit.

41. Hank Wieand Bowman, "Will it Top 101.12 Miles an Hour?" *Aqua Sport* (June/July 1958), pp. 21–36.

42. Art Doling, "Viking Outboard Numbers," Antique Outboarder (January 1989), pp. 70–71.

43. James L. Smith, "Tiger Shark, West Bend's Big Iron," *Antique Outboarder* (April 1979), pp. 8–10.

44. Peterson, "Chrysler Story," *Antique Outboarder* (April 1976), pp. 39–43.

Appendix A
Model/Year Guide

Evinrude, Elto, and Some Lockwood, Sea King, and Viking.

By the early 1960s, most Evinrude dealerships had their share of customers seeking parts or information about obsolete outboard motors. Because it was not uncommon for owner and dealer alike to have little more than a guess about the old kickers' true model name, year of manufacture, horsepower, etc., tracking down parts or pertinent details was a chore. In 1965, Evinrude released a Model/Year Guide, compiled from dusty factory paperwork, to assist dealers in locating other reference material about replacement parts. The Evinrude people indicate "all available records were researched to keep multiple-year listings at a minimum. In some instances, this could not be avoided. Should the model's years be given as 1927–31, for example, no closer identification could be provided." Some obscure Evinrude models were omitted from the 1965 guide. Most were extremely limited-production, early 1930s racing motors that only differed from some other rare racer in that one had an underwater exhaust or a similar long forgotten nuance. Also missing were a few "bombs," like the 1922, all-aluminum, Model K rowboat motor.

Very few Evinrude rowboat motors were actually produced in 1909. In fact, 1910 was probably the first year of real commercial production. As of 1990, the oldest known Evinrude wears the serial number 780. It came out of Vermont and has no skeg and no Evinrude logo lettering on its exhaust manifold. It is most likely a 1910 or 1911 motor.

By 1915, Evinrude had enough variations of its 2- and 3½-hp motors that rowboat motor sub-categories "A" through "H" were tacked onto the standard model designations. In most cases, these differences were slight, and records of the secondary classifications got overshadowed by time and subsequent model nomenclature. Therefore, there probably are Evinrudes (and other brands) which do not correspond with any list.

A curious lack of engineering data on some early Evinrude/Elto models and model changes leads me to believe many designs, developments, and modifications were informally drawn up by Ole Evinrude and implemented by factory staffers at the earliest convenience.

Notes: An "X" stamped after the serial number of an Evinrude/Elto usually signifies a factory-rebuilt motor.

Some Evinrudes, such as 4006, had an identical model number, but were different vintage motors. Numbers 2001-plus follow the 1959 listing.

Year	Model	HP
1909–12	---- / Single, #1 to 9,999	1.5
1913	---- / Single, #10,000 to 19,000	2.0
1914	---- / Single, #20,000 to 49,999	2.0
1921	---- / Twin, Elto, #1,000 to 1,920	3.0
1922	---- / Twin, Elto, #1,921 to A6,519	3.0
1915	A / Single, #3,000 to 3,999	3.5
1916	A / Single, #4,014 to 4,660	3.5
1917	A / Single, #4,661 to 4,950	3.5
1918	A / Single, #4,951 to 5,480	3.5
1919	A / Single, #5,481 to 6,050	3.5
1920	A / Single, #6,051 to 6,700	3.5
1921	A / Single, #6,701 to 6,908	3.5
1922	A / Single, #7,000 to 7,200	3.5
1915	A / Single, #50,000 to 54,999	2.0
1916	A / Single, #90,000 to 92,499	2.0
1917	A / Single, #95,000 to 96,998	2.0
1918	A / Single, #97,000 to 101,899	2.0
1919	A / Single, #101,900 to 103,799	2.0
1920	A / Single, #103,800 to 111,199	2.0
1921	A / Single, #111,200 to 116,980	2.0
1922	A / Single, #117,000 to 121,999	2.0
1923	A / Single, #122,000 to 123,999	2.0
1924	A / Single, #124,000 to 124,999	2.0
1925	A / Single, #125,000 to 126,349	2.0
1926	A / Single, #126,350 to 127,299	2.0
1927	A / Single, #127,300 to 127,959	2.0
1928	A / Single, #127,960 and up	2.0
1923	A / Twin, Elto, #6,520 to 12,000	3.0
1916	AA / Twin, (4-cycle) #53,420 to 54,415	4.0
1917	AA / Twin, (4-cycle) #54,416 to 54,819	4.0
1915	B / Single, #5,000 to 5,199	3.5
1916	B / Single, #5,200 to 5,374	3.5
1917	B / Single, #5,375 to 5,430	3.5
1918	B / Single, #5,431 to 5,580	3.5
1919	B / Single, #5,581 to 5,749	3.5
1920	B / Single, #5,750 to 5,850	3.5
1921	B / Single, #6,701 to 6,908	3.5
1922	B / Single, #7,000 to 7,200	3.5
1915	B / Single, #55,000 to 55,999	2.0

Year	Model	HP
1916	B / Single, #56,000 to 56,644	2.0
1917	B / Single, #56,645 to 57,299	2.0
1918	B / Single, #57,300 to 57,799	2.0
1919	B / Single, #57,800 to 58,699	2.0
1920	B / Single, #58,700 to 59,249	2.0
1921	B / Single, #59,250 to 59,499	2.0
1922	B / Single, #59,500 to 59,649	2.0
1923	B / Single, #59,650 to 65,000	2.0
1924	B / Single, #124,000 to 124,999	2.0
1925	B / Single, #125,000 to 126,349	2.0
1926	B / Single, #126,350 to 127,299	2.0
1927	B / Single, #127,300 to 127,959	2.0
1928	B / Single, #127,960 and up	2.0
1923	B / Twin, Elto, #6,520 to 12,000	3.0
1916	C / Single, #61,000 to 61,465	2.0
1924	C / Twin, Elto, #12,001 to 20,000	3.0
1925	C / Twin, Elto, #20,001 to 20,999	3.0
1916-24	CC / Single Cyl. Inboard	2.0
1923-26	CCV / Single Cyl. Pressure Pump	2.0
1916	D / Single, #66,000 to 66,799	2.0
1924	D / Twin, Elto, #12,001 to 20,000	3.0
1925	D / Twin, Elto, #20,001 to 20,999	3.0
1916-27	DD / Twin Cyl. Inboard	4.5
1916-27	DDR / Twin Cyl. Inboard (reverse)	4.5
1923-29	DDV / Twin Cyl. Pump	4.5
1915	E / Single-Canoe, #10,000 to 10,128	3.5
1916	EE / Twin (4-cycle), #59,000 to 59,056	4.0
1928	F / Fleetwin, #F1001 to F4000	6.0
1929	F / Fleetwin, #1F001 to 4F300	7.0
1928	FV / Twin Cyl. Pump	6.0
1926	G / Twin, Elto, #30,000 to 44,900	4.0
1928	H / Fastwin, #H1001 to H2500	12.0
1929	H / Fastwin, #1H001 to 13H250	14.0
1913	H / Single (bat) #1 to 299	3.5
1914	H / Single (mag) #300 to 2,999	3.5
1926	H / Twin, Elto, #30,000 to 44,900	4.0
1927	J / Twin, Elto, #45,000 to 54,799	4.0
1928	J / Twin, Elto, #54,800 to 56,859	4.0
1929	J / Twin, Elto, #56,860 to 59,999	4.0
1927	K / Twin, Elto, #45,000 to 54,799	4.0
1928	K / Twin, Elto, #54,800 to 56,859	4.0
1929	K / Twin, Elto, #56,860 to 59,999	4.0
1923-26	L / Big Twin	4.0
1923-26	LA / Big Twin	4.0
1923-26	LAT / Big Twin	4.0
1923	N / Sportwin, #N1,500 to N3,499	2.5
1924	N / Sportwin, #N3,500 to N8,499	2.5
1925	N / Sportwin, #N8,500 to N10,499	2.5
1926	N / Sportwin, #N10,500 to N13,499	2.5
1927	N / Sportwin, #N13,500 to N14,499	2.5
1928	N / Sportwin, #N14,500 to N14,750	2.5
1929	NF / Sportwin-Folding, #1N001 to 2N001	2.5
1923	NS / Sportwin, #NS1,500 to NS3,499	2.5
1924	NS / Sportwin, #NS3,500 to NS8,499	2.5
1925	NS / Sportwin, #NS8,500 to NS9,999	2.5
1926	NS / Sportwin, #NS10,000 to NS10,999	2.5
1927	NS / Sportwin, #NS11,000 to NS11,999	2.5
1919-29	P / Centrifugal Pump	2.0
1927	R / Fastwin	4.0
1927	RS / Fastwin	4.0
1927	RV / Twin Cylinder Pump	4.0
1927	T / Speeditwin	8.0
1927	TS / Speeditwin	8.0
1928	U / Speeditwin, #U1001 to U5200	16.0
1929	U / Speeditwin, #1U001 to 15U000	20.0
1925	52T / Lockwood Twin	7.0
1926	62T / Lockwood Twin	7.0
1927	72T / Lockwood Twin	7.0
1928	82A / Lockwood Ace	7.0
1928	82B / Lockwood Chief	11.0
1929	92A / Lockwood Ace	7.0
1929	92B / Lockwood Chief	14.0
1929	92BR / Lockwood Racing Chief	14.0
1929	142 / Centrifugal Pump	6.0
1929-32	143 / Speeditwin	20.0
1929-33	145 / Fastwin	14.0
1930-34	156 / Speeditwin	22.0
1930-34	157 / Speeditwin—6" Longer	22.0
1930	160 / Lockwood Chief	11.0
1930	161 / Lockwood Ace	7.0
1930	162 / OMC Foldlight	2.75
1930	163 / Lockwood Chief-Electric	11.0
1930	167 / Speeditwin-Electric	22.0
1930	168 / Speeditwin-Electric—6" Longer	22.0
1930	176 / OMC Speedibee Racer	20.0
1930	177 / Speeditwin Racer	----
1930	178 / OMC Four-Sixty Racer	----
1930	179 / Speeditwin Racer	----
1931	183 / Sportwin	2.5
1929	300 / Elto Service Speedster, #80,000 to 89,999S	7.0
1929	301 / Elto Service Speedster, 5" Longer, #80,000 to 89,999S	7.0
1929	302 / Elto Hi Speed Speedster, #80,000 to 89,999H	11.0
1929	303 / Elto Hi Speed Speedster, 5" Longer, #80,000 to 89,999H	11.0
1929	305 / Elto Service Quad, #75,000 to 79,999S	25.0
1929	306 / Elto Hi Speed Quad, #75,000 to 79,999H	25.0
1928	307 / Elto Service Quad, #70,000 to 74,999S	18.0
1928	308 / Elto Hi Speed Quad, #70,000 to 74,999H	18.0
1929	309 / Elto Lightweight, #90,000 to 99,999	3.5
1930	310 / Elto Senior Speedster	14.0
1930	311 / Elto Senior Speedster-Electric	14.0
1930	312 / Elto Sr. Speedster—5" Longer	14.0
1930	313 / Elto Sr. Speedster-Elec.—5" Longer	14.0
1930	314 / Elto Quad	30.0
1930	315 / Elto Quad-Electric	30.0
1930	335 / Elto Hi Speed Quad (50 cu.in.)	35.0
1930	336 / Elto Hi Speed Quad (60 cu.in.)	40.0
1929	340 / Elto Special Speedster	9.0
1930	344 / Elto Hi Speed Quad (50 cu.in.)	40.0
1930	348 / Elto Hi Speed Service Speedster	7.0
1928	355 / Elto Service Speedster, #60,000 to 69,999	7.0

1931	358 / Service Twin	4.0
1931	359 / Service Twin 5" Longer	4.0
1931	360 / Special Lightweight	3.5
1933	361 / Senior Speedster	13.7
1933	362 / Senior Speedster 5" Longer	13.7
1933	363 / Senior Speedster	13.7
1933	364 / Senior Speedster 5" Longer	13.7
1934	365 / Senior Speedster	13.7
1934	366 / Senior Speedster 5" Longer	13.7
1940–41	367 / Sea King #8813	1.8
1940–41	368 / Sea King #8814	3.0
1940–41	369 / Sea King #8815 Deluxe	3.0
1940–41	371 / Sea King #8816	5.0
1940–41	373 / Sea King #8817 Deluxe	5.0
1940–42	375 / Sea King #8818	15.2
1941	377 / Sea King #8822	1.0
1941–42	378 / Sea King #8823	3.3
1941–42	379 / Sea King #8824 Deluxe	3.3
1946–47	379 / Sea King #9008 Deluxe	3.3
1946–47	381 / Sea King #9002	1.0
1931–35	400 / Sea King #9186	4.0
1931	401 / Lightweight	4.0
1931	402 / Lightwin	4.0
1931	403 / Foldlight	2.75
1931	404 / Foldlight	2.75
1931	405 / Lightweight 5" Longer	4.0
1931	406 / Lightwin 5" Longer	4.0
1932	407 / Lightwin	4.0
1932	408 / Lightwin 5" Longer	4.0
1932	409 / Sportwin	4.0
1932	410 / Sportwin 5" Longer	4.0
1932	411 / Lightweight	4.0
1932	412 / Lightweight 5" Longer	4.0
1932–33	413 / Fisherman	4.0
1932–33	414 / Fisherman 5" Longer	4.0
1932–34	415 / Sea King-Folding #9200	3.0
1932–35	416 / Sea King #9186	4.0
1932–34	417 / Sea King #9194	8.0
1932	418 / Fleetwin	11.0
1932	419 / Fleetwin 5" Longer	11.0
1932–33	420 / Sturditwin	5.8
1932–33	421 / Sturditwin 5" Longer	5.8
1932	422 / Super 'A'	11.0
1932	423 / Super 'A' 5" Longer	11.0
1932–33	424 / Service 'A'	5.8
1932–33	425 / Service 'A' 5" Longer	5.8
1932	426 / Lightwin	4.0
1932	427 / Lightwin 5" Longer	4.0
1932	428 / Lightweight	4.0
1932	429 / Lightweight 5" Longer	4.0
1932	430 / Service 'A'	5.8
1932	431 / Service 'A' 5" Longer	5.8
1933	432 / Sport Single	2.2
1933	433 / Sport Single 5" Longer	2.2
1933	434 / Sport Single Full Reverse	2.2
1933	436 / Super Single	2.2
1933	437 / Super Single 5" Longer	2.2
1933	438 / Super Single Full Reverse	2.2
1933	440 / Sea King #8300	3.0
1933	441 / Viking	4.0
1933	442 / Lightwin	5.1
1933	443 / Lightwin 5" Longer	5.1
1933	444 / Lightweight	5.1
1933	445 / Lightweight 5" Longer	5.1
1933	446 / Lightwin — Full Reverse	5.1
1938	447 / Sea King #8763	1.8
1933	448 / Lightweight Full Reverse	5.1
1938	449 / Sea King #8764	2.8
1939	449 / Sea King #8766	3.0
1933	450 / Fleetwin	8.5
1933	451 / Fleetwin 5" Longer	8.5
1933	452 / Fleetwin Electric	8.5
1933	453 / Fleetwin Electric 5" Longer	8.5
1933	454 / OMC Midget Racer	----
1933	456 / Super 'A'	8.5
1933	457 / Super 'A' 5" Longer	8.5
1933	458 / Super 'A' Electric	8.5
1933	459 / Super 'A' Electric 5" Longer	8.5
1933	460 / Lightwin	5.1
1933	461 / Lightwin 5" Longer	5.1
1933	462 / Lightweight	5.1
1940	463 / Viking	1.8
1933	464 / Sport Single	2.2
1939	465 / Viking	1.8
1939	466 / Viking	5.0
1939	467 / Viking	8.5
1933	468 / Lightwin Full Reverse	5.1
1939	469 / Sea King #8809	1.0
1940	469 / Sea King #8812	1.0
1933	470 / Lightweight Full Reverse	5.1
1939–41	471 / Sea King #8811	8.5
1933	472 / Sport Single Full Reverse	2.2
1933	474 / Super Single Full Reverse	2.2
1940	475 / Viking	5.0
1933	476 / Sportwin	4.0
1939	477 / Sea King #8765	1.8
1933	478 / Fisherman	4.0
1933	479 / Fisherman 5" Longer	4.0
1933	481 / Electric Troller	----
1933	483 / Sportwin	4.0
1933	484 / Fisherman	4.0
1934	489 / Sea King #8390	2.2
1935	490 / Sea King #8800	2.2
1935	491 / Sea King #8801	4.0
1935–36	492 / Sea King #8802	8.5
1937–38	492 / Sea King #8808	8.5
1936	494 / Sea King #8803	4.0
1936–37	495 / Viking	4.0
1936–37	496 / Viking	8.5
1936	497 / Sea King #8802 5" Longer	8.5
1937	498 / Sea King #8806	2.5
1937–38	499 / Sea King #8807	4.2
1939	499 / Sea King #8810	5.0
1934–35	500 / Sea King #8394	11.0
1931–33	500 / Sea King #9188	15.0
1931	600 / Sea King #9190	21.0
1931–33	601 / Speeditwin	25.0
1931–33	602 / Speeditwin 5" Longer	25.0
1931–33	603 / Speeditwin Electric	25.0
1931–33	604 / Speeditwin Electric 5" Longer	25.0
1931–33	605 / Super 'C'	25.0
1931–33	606 / Super 'C' 5" Longer	25.0
1931–33	607 / Super 'C' Electric	25.0
1931–33	608 / Super 'C' Electric 5" Longer	25.0

Year	Model / Name	HP		Year	Model / Name	HP
1931	609 / Speeditwin Racer	----		1931	806 / Big Quad Electric	40.0
1931	610 / Super 'C' Racer	----		1931	807 / Big Quad Electric, 5" Longer	40.0
1931–32	615 / Sea King #9190	21.0		1931	808 / Big Four Electric	40.0
1931–32	616 / Sea King #9150	21.0		1931	809 / Big Four Electric, 5" Longer	40.0
1931–32	617 / Sea King #9196	21.0		1931	810 / Big Quad, Eclipse Starter	40.0
1932	618 / Speeditwin	25.0		1931	811 / Big Quad, Eclipse, 5" Longer	40.0
1932	619 / Speeditwin 5" Longer	25.0		1931	812 / Big Four, Eclipse Starter	40.0
1932	620 / Speeditwin Electric	25.0		1931	813 / Big Four, Eclipse, 5" Longer	40.0
1932	621 / Speeditwin Electric 5" Longer	25.0		1932	814 / Big Four	40.0
1932	624 / Super 'C'	25.0		1932	815 / Big Four, 5" Longer	40.0
1932	625 / Super 'C' 5" Longer	25.0		1932	816 / Big Four Electric	40.0
1932	626 / Super 'C' Electric	25.0		1932	817 / Big Four Electric, 5" Longer	40.0
1932	627 / Super 'C' Electric 5" Longer	25.0		1932	818 / Big Four, Eclipse Starter	40.0
1932	630 / Speeditwin Racer	----		1932	819 / Big Four, Eclipse, 5" Longer	40.0
1932	631 / Super 'C' Racer	----		1932	820 / Big Quad	40.0
1933	634 / Speeditwin	21.1		1932	821 / Big Quad, 5" Longer	40.0
1933	635 / Speeditwin 5" Longer	21.1		1932	822 / Big Quad Electric	40.0
1933	636 / Speeditwin Electric	21.1		1932	823 / Big Quad Electric, 5" Longer	40.0
1933	637 / Speeditwin Electric 5" Longer	21.1		1932	824 / Big Quad, Eclipse Starter	40.0
1933	638 / Super 'C'	21.1		1932	825 / Big Quad, Eclipse, 5" Longer	40.0
1933	639 / Super 'C' 5" Longer	21.1		1932	826 / Four-Sixty Racer	----
1933	640 / Super 'C' Electric	21.1		1932	827 / Four-Sixty, Dual Ign.	----
1933	641 / Super 'C' Electric 5" Longer	21.1		1933	828 / Four-Sixty Racer	----
1933	642 / Super 'C' Racer	----		1933	829 / Four-Sixty, Dual Ign.	----
1933	643 / Speeditwin Racer	----		1931	900 / Junior Quad	18.0
1931	700 / Senior Quad	35.0		1931	901 / Junior Quad, 5" Longer	18.0
1931	701 / Senior Quad 5" Longer	35.0		1931	902 / Sportfour	18.0
1931	702 / Senior Quad Electric	35.0		1931	903 / Sportfour, 5" Longer	18.0
1931	703 / Senior Quad Electric 5" Longer	35.0		1933–36	904 / Centrifugal Pump, 2 ½"	8.5
1931	704 / Speedifour	35.0		1931–33	905 / Special Speedster	12.0
1931	705 / Speedifour 5" Longer	35.0		1931–33	906 / Special Speedster, 5" Longer	12.0
1931	706 / Speedifour Electric	35.0		1931–33	907 / Special Speedster, 10" Longer	12.0
1931	707 / Speedifour Electric 5" Longer	35.0		1933	909 / Hi Pressure Pump, 1 ½"	12.0
1931	708 / Senior Quad. Eclipse Starter	35.0		1931	910 / Hi Pressure Pump, 1 ½"	12.0
1931	709 / Senior Quad. Eclipse, 5" Longer	35.0		1933	911 / Hi Pressure Pump, 2"	12.0
1931	710 / Speedifour, Eclipse Starter	35.0		1932	912 / Sportfour	18.0
1931	711 / Speedifour, Eclipse, 5" Longer	35.0		1932	913 / Sportfour, 5" Longer	18.0
1932	715 / Speedifour	36.0		1932	914 / Junior Quad	18.0
1932	716 / Speedifour, 5" Longer	36.0		1932	915 / Junior Quad 5" Longer	18.0
1932	717 / Speedifour Electric	36.0		1932–36	916 / Speedibike	0.75
1932	718 / Speedifour Electric 5" Longer	36.0		1934	917 / Road King	0.5
1932	719 / Speedifour, Eclipse Starter	36.0		1932	918 / Lawn Boy Power Mower	0.75
1932	720 / Speedifour, Eclipse, 5" Longer	36.0		1933	920 / Sportfour	18.0
1932	721 / Senior Quad	36.0		1933	921 / Sportfour, 5" Longer	18.0
1932	722 / Senior Quad, 5" Longer	36.0		1933	922 / Sportfour Electric	18.0
1932	723 / Senior Quad Electric	36.0		1933	923 / Sportfour Electric, 5" Longer	18.0
1932	724 / Senior Quad Electric, 5" Longer	36.0		1933	924 / Junior Quad	18.0
1932	725 / Senior Quad, Eclipse Starter	36.0		1933	925 / Junior Quad, 5" Longer	18.0
1932	726 / Senior Quad, Eclipse, 5" Longer	36.0		1933	926 / Junior Quad Electric	18.0
1933	728 / Speedifour	31.2		1933	927 / Junior Quad Electric 5" Longer	18.0
1933	729 / Speedifour, 5" Longer	31.2		1933–35	928 / Lawn Boy Power Mower	0.75
1933	730 / Speedifour Electric	31.2		1934	929 / Lawn Boy Power Mower	0.75
1933	731 / Speedifour Electric, 5" Longer	31.2		1933–36	930 / Shop King	----
1933	732 / Senior Quad	31.2		1935–36	932 / Centrifugal H.P. Pump, 1 ½"	9.2
1933	733 / Senior Quad, 5" Longer	31.2		1935	933 / Centrifugal H.P. Pump, 1 ½"	9.2
1933	734 / Senior Quad Electric	31.2		1937–38	936 / Streamflow Bicycle, Standard	----
1933	735 / Senior Quad Electric, 5" Longer	31.2		1937–38	937 / Streamflow Bicycle, Imperial	----
1931	800 / Big Quad	40.0		1936	938 / Lawn Boy Power Mower	0.75
1931	801 / Big Quad, 5" Longer	40.0		1936	939 / Lawn Boy Power Mower	0.75
1931	802 / Big Four	40.0		1937–38	941 / Streamflow Bicycle, Standard	----
1931	803 / Big Four, 5" Longer	40.0		1937–38	942 / Streamflow Bicycle, Imperial	----
1931	804 / Four-Sixty Racer	----		1937–38	948 / Lawn Boy Power Mower	0.75

1939–41	952 / Lawn Boy Power Mower	0.75
1938–42	958 / Lawn Boy Power Mower	0.75
1934	4000 / Single	2.2
1934	4001 / Single, 5" Longer	2.2
1934	4002 / Single	2.2
1934	4003 / Single, 5" Longer	2.2
1934	4004 / Single	2.2
1934	4005 / Single, 5" Longer	2.2
1934	4006 / Single	2.2
1934	4007 / Single, 5" Longer	2.2
1934	4008 / Single	2.2
1934	4009 / Single, 5" Longer	2.2
1934	4010 / Single	2.2
1934	4011 / Single, 5" Longer	2.2
1934	4012 / Single	2.2
1934	4013 / Single, 5" Longer	2.2
1934	4014 / Single	2.2
1934	4015 / Single, 5" Longer	2.2
1934	4016 / Fisherman	4.0
1934	4017 / Fisherman, 5" Longer	4.0
1934	4018 / Fisherman	4.0
1934	4019 / Fisherman, 5" Longer	4.0
1934	4020 / Lightwin	5.1
1934	4021 / Lightwin, 5" Longer	5.1
1934	4022 / Lightwin	5.1
1934	4023 / Lightwin, 5" Longer	5.1
1934	4024 / Lightwin	5.1
1934	4025 / Lightwin, 5" Longer	5.1
1934	4026 / Lightwin	5.1
1934	4027 / Lightwin, 5" Longer	5.1
1934	4028 / Midget Racer	----
1934–36	4029 / All Electric	----
1934	4030 / Lightwin Imperial	5.5
1934	4031 / Lightwin Imperial, 5" Longer	5.5
1934	4032 / Lightwin Imperial	5.5
1934	4033 / Lightwin Imperial, 5" Longer	5.5
1934	4034 / Fleetwin	8.5
1934	4035 / Fleetwin, 5" Longer	8.5
1934	4036 / Fleetwin Electric	8.5
1934	4037 / Fleetwin Electric, 5" Longer	8.5
1934	4038 / Fleetwin	8.5
1934	4039 / Fleetwin, 5" Longer	8.5
1934	4040 / Fleetwin Electric	8.5
1934	4041 / Fleetwin Electric, 5" Longer	8.5
1934–35	4042 / Lightfour Imperial	9.2
1934–35	4043 / Lightfour Imperial, 5" Longer	9.2
1934–35	4044 / Lightfour Imperial	9.2
1934–35	4045 / Lightfour Imperial, 5" Longer	9.2
1934–35	4046 / Lightfour Imperial	9.2
1934–35	4047 / Lightfour Imperial, 5" Longer	9.2
1934–35	4048 / Lightfour Imperial	9.2
1934–35	4049 / Lightfour Imperial, 5" Longer	9.2
1934	4050 / Lightwin Imperial	5.5
1934	4051 / Lightwin Imperial, 5" Longer	5.5
1934	4052 / Lightwin Imperial	5.5
1934	4053 / Lightwin Imperial, 5" Longer	5.5
1934	4054 / Lightwin Imperial	5.5
1934	4055 / Lightwin Imperial, 5" Longer	5.5
1934	4056 / Lightwin Imperial	5.5
1934	4057 / Lightwin Imperial, 5" Longer	5.5
1934	4058 / Single	2.2
1934	4059 / Single, 5" Longer	2.2

1934	4060 / Single	2.2
1934	4061 / Single, 5" Longer	2.2
1934	4062 / Single	2.2
1934	4063 / Single, 5" Longer	2.2
1934	4064 / Single	2.2
1934	4065 / Single, 5" Longer	2.2
1934	4066 / Fisherman	4.0
1934	4067 / Fisherman, 5" Longer	4.0
1934	4068 / Fisherman	4.0
1934	4069 / Fisherman 5" Longer	4.0
1934	4070 / Lightwin Imperial	5.5
1934	4071 / Lightwin Imperial, 5" Longer	5.5
1934	4072 / Lightwin Imperial	5.5
1934	4073 / Lightwin Imperial, 5" Longer	5.5
1934	4074 / Lightwin Imperial, 15" Longer	5.5
1934	4075 / Lightwin Imperial, 15" Longer	5.5
1934	4076 / Lightfour Imperial, 15" Longer	9.2
1934	4077 / Lightfour Imperial, 15" Longer	9.2
1934	4078 / Single	2.2
1934	4079 / Single, 5" Longer	2.2
1934	4080 / Single	2.2
1934	4081 / Single, 5" Longer	2.2
1934	4082 / Fisherman	4.0
1934	4083 / Fisherman, 5" Longer	4.0
1934	4084 / Fisherman	4.0
1934	4085 / Fisherman, 5" Longer	4.0
1934	4086 / Lightwin Imperial, 15" Longer	5.5
1934	4087 / Lightwin Imperial, 15" Longer	5.5
1934	4088 / Lightfour Imperial, 15" Longer	9.2
1934	4089 / Lightfour Imperial, 15" Longer	9.2
1935	4091 / Sportsman	1.5
1935	4092 / Fisherman, Weedless	4.0
1935	4093 / Fisherman	4.0
1935	4094 / Fisherman, 5" Longer	4.0
1935	4095 / Fisherman	4.0
1935	4096 / Fisherman, 5" Longer	4.0
1935	4097 / Lightwin	4.6
1935	4098 / Lightwin, 5" Longer	4.6
1935	4099 / Lightwin	4.6
1935	4101 / Lightwin, 5" Longer	4.6
1935	4102 / Lightwin Imperial	5.0
1935	4103 / Lightwin Imperial, 5" Longer	5.0
1935	4104 / Lightwin Imperial	5.0
1935	4105 / Lightwin Imperial, 5" Longer	5.0
1935	4106 / Lightwin Imperial	5.0
1935	4107 / Lightwin Imperial, 5" Longer	5.0
1935	4108 / Lightwin Imperial	5.0
1935	4109 / Lightwin Imperial, 5" Longer	5.0
1935	4111 / Lightfour Imperial	9.2
1935	4112 / Lightfour Imperial, 5" Longer	9.2
1935	4113 / Lightfour Imperial	9.2
1935	4114 / Lightfour Imperial, 5" Longer	9.2
1935	4115 / Lightfour Imperial	9.2
1935	4116 / Lightfour Imperial, 5" Longer	9.2
1935	4117 / Lightfour Imperial	9.2
1935	4118 / Lightfour Imperial, 5" Longer	9.2
1935	4119 / Midget Racer	----
1935	4121 / Weedless Fisherman	4.0
1935	4122 / Fisherman	4.0
1935	4123 / Fisherman	4.0
1935	4124 / Fisherman, 5" Longer	4.0
1935	4125 / Fisherman	4.0

Year	Model	HP
1935	4126 / Fisherman, 5" Longer	4.0
1935	4127 / Lightwin, 15" Longer	4.6
1935	4128 / Lightwin, 15" Longer	4.6
1935	4129 / Lightwin Imperial, 15" Longer	5.0
1935	4131 / Lightwin Imperial, 15" Longer	5.0
1935	4132 / Lightwin Imperial, 15" Longer	5.0
1935	4133 / Lightwin Imperial, 15" Longer	5.0
1935	4134 / Lightfour Imperial, 15" Longer	9.2
1935	4135 / Lightfour Imperial, 15" Longer	9.2
1935	4136 / Lightfour Imperial, 15" Longer	9.2
1935	4137 / Lightfour Imperial, 15" Longer	9.2
1935	4138 / Fisherman	4.0
1935	4139 / Sportsman, 5" Longer	1.5
1935	4142 / Lightwin	4.6
1935	4143 / Fisherman	4.0
1935	4144 / Yacht Fisherman	4.0
1936	4144 / Yacht Service Twin	4.3
1936–37	4145 / Ace	1.4
1936	4146 / Sportsman	1.5
1936	4147 / Sportsman, 5" Longer	1.5
1936	4148 / Fisherman	4.4
1936	4149 / Fisherman, 5" Longer	4.4
1936	4151 / Service Twin	4.3
1936	4152 / Weedless Fisherman	4.4
1936	4153 / Lightwin	4.7
1936	4154 / Lightwin, 5" Longer	4.7
1936	4155 / Lightwin, 15" Longer	4.7
1936	4156 / Sportwin	2.5
1936	4157 / Sportwin, 5" Longer	2.5
1936	4158 / Handitwin	2.5
1936	4159 / Handitwin 5" Longer	2.5
1936	4161 / Service Twin	4.3
1936	4162 / Service Twin, 5" Longer	4.3
1936	4163 / Service Twin	4.3
1936	4164 / Service Twin, 5" Longer	4.3
1936	4165 / Lightwin Imperial	5.0
1936	4166 / Lightwin Imperial, 5" Longer	5.0
1936	4167 / Lightwin Imperial, 15" Longer	5.0
1936	4168 / Lightwin Imperial	5.0
1936	4169 / Lightwin Imperial, 5" Longer	5.0
1936	4171 / Lightwin Imperial, 15" Longer	5.0
1936	4172 / Lightwin Imperial	5.0
1936	4173 / Lightwin Imperial, 5" Longer	5.0
1936	4174 / Lightwin Imperial, 15" Longer	5.0
1936	4175 / Lightwin Imperial	5.0
1936	4176 / Lightwin Imperial, 5" Longer	5.0
1936	4177 / Lightwin Imperial, 15" Longer	5.0
1936	4178 / Lightfour Imperial	9.2
1936	4179 / Lightfour Imperial, 5" Longer	9.2
1936	4180 / Lightfour Imperial, 15" Longer	9.2
1936	4181 / Lightfour Imperial	9.2
1936	4182 / Lightfour Imperial, 5" Longer	9.2
1936	4183 / Lightfour Imperial, 15" Longer	9.2
1936	4184 / Midget Racer	----
1936	4185 / Lightfour Imperial	9.2
1936	4186 / Lightfour Imperial, 5" Longer	9.2
1936	4187 / Lightfour Imperial, 15" Longer	9.2
1936	4188 / Lightfour Imperial	9.2
1936	4189 / Lightfour Imperial, 5" Longer	9.2
1936	4190 / Lightfour Imperial, Heavy Duty	9.2
1936	4191 / Lightfour Imperial, 15" Longer	9.2
1936–38	4192 / Yacht Fisherman	4.4
1936	4193 / Service Twin	4.3
1936	4194 / Fisherman	4.4
1936	4195 / Ace, 5" Longer	1.4
1936	4196 / Lightwin Heavy Duty	4.7
1936	4197 / Lightwin H.D., 15" Longer	4.7
1936	4198 / Lightwin H.D., 5" Longer	4.7
1936	4199 / Lightfour H.D., 15" Longer	9.2
1936	4200 / Lightfour H.D., 5" Longer	9.2
1937	4201 / Scout	0.9
1937	4203 / Pal	0.9
1937	4205 / Ace	1.4
1937	4206 / Ace, 5" Longer	1.4
1937	4207 / Sportsman	1.6
1937	4208 / Sportsman, 5" Longer	1.6
1937	4209 / Sportwin	2.5
1937	4211 / Sportwin, 5" Longer	2.5
1937	4212 / Handitwin	2.5
1937	4213 / Handitwin, 5" Longer	2.5
1937	4214 / Service Twin	4.3
1937	4215 / Service Twin, 5" Longer	4.3
1937	4216 / Service Twin	4.3
1937	4217 / Service Twin, 5" Longer	4.3
1937	4218 / Service Twin	4.3
1937	4219 / Handifour	9.2
1937	4221 / Lightwin	4.7
1937	4222 / Lightwin, 5" Longer	4.7
1937	4223 / Lightwin, 15" Longer	4.7
1937	4224 / Lightwin Heavy Duty	4.7
1937	4225 / Lightwin H.D., 5" Longer	4.7
1937	4226 / Lightwin H.D., 15" Longer	4.7
1937	4227 / Fisherman	4.4
1937	4228 / Fisherman, 5" Longer	4.4
1937	4229 / Weedless Service Twin	4.3
1937	4231 / Lightfour	9.2
1937	4232 / Lightfour, 5" Longer	9.2
1937	4233 / Lightfour, 15" Longer	9.2
1937	4234 / Lightfour Heavy Duty	9.2
1937	4235 / Lightfour H.D., 5" Longer	9.2
1937	4236 / Lightfour H.D., 15" Longer	9.2
1937	4237 / Lightfour	9.2
1937	4238 / Lightfour, 5" Longer	9.2
1937	4239 / Lightfour, 15" Longer	9.2
1937	4241 / Lightfour Heavy Duty	9.2
1937	4242 / Lightfour H.D., 5" Longer	9.2
1937	4243 / Lightfour H.D., 15" Longer	9.2
1937	4244 / Midget Racer	----
1937	4245 / Handifour, 5" Longer	9.2
1937	4246 / Handifour, 15" Longer	9.2
1937	4247 / Handifour Heavy Duty	9.2
1937	4248 / Handifour H.D., 5" Longer	9.2
1937	4249 / Handifour H.D., 15" Longer	9.2
1937	4251 / Weedless Fisherman	4.4
1938	4252 / Ranger	1.1
1938	4253 / Pal	1.1
1938	4254 / Sportsman	2.0
1938	4255 / Sportsman, 5" Longer	2.0
1938	4256 / Ace	1.8
1938	4257 / Ace, 5" Longer	1.8
1938	4258 / Sportwin	3.0
1938	4259 / Sportwin, 5" Longer	3.0
1938	4261 / Handitwin	2.8
1938	4262 / Handitwin, 5" Longer	2.8

Year	Model	HP
1939–41	4263 / Mate	0.5
1939–41	4264 / Cub	0.5
1939	4265 / Ranger — to S/N 04000	1.1
1940	S/N 04001 to 05500	1.1
1941	S/N 05501 and up	1.1
1938	4266 / Pal — to S/N 02000	1.1
1939	S/N 02001 to 07000	1.1
1940	S/N 07001 to 12000	1.1
1941	S/N 12000 and up	1.1
1938	4267 / Fisherman	4.7
1938	4268 / Fisherman, 5" Longer	4.7
1938	4269 / Weedless Fisherman	4.7
1938	4271 / Lightfour	9.2
1938	4272 / Lightfour, 5" Longer	9.2
1938	4273 / Lightfour, 15" Longer	9.2
1938	4274 / Lightfour Heavy Duty	9.2
1938	4275 / Lightfour H.D., 5" Longer	9.2
1938	4276 / Lightfour H.D., 15" Longer	9.2
1938	4277 / Lightfour	9.2
1938	4278 / Lightfour, 5" Longer	9.2
1938	4279 / Lightfour, 15" Longer	9.2
1938	4281 / Lightfour Heavy Duty	9.2
1938	4282 / Lightfour H.D., 5" Longer	9.2
1938	4283 / Lightfour H.D., 15" Longer	9.2
1938	4284 / Midget Racer	----
1938	4285 / Sportsman	2.0
1938	4286 / Sportsman, 5" Longer	2.0
1938	4287 / Sportwin	3.0
1938	4288 / Sportwin, 5" Longer	3.0
1938	4289 / Lightwin	4.7
1938	4291 / Lightwin, 5" Longer	4.7
1938	4292 / Lightwin, 5" Longer	4.7
1938	4293 / Lightwin Heavy Duty	4.7
1938	4294 / Lightwin H.D., 5" Longer	4.7
1938	4295 / Lightwin H.D., 15" Longer	4.7
1939	4296 / Sportsman	2.0
1939	4297 / Sportsman, 5" Longer	2.0
1939	4298 / Sportsman	2.0
1939	4299 / Sportsman, 5" Longer	2.0
1939	4301 / Ace	1.8
1939	4302 / Ace, 5" Longer	1.8
1939	4303 / Sportwin	3.3
1939	4304 / Sportwin, 5" Longer	3.3
1939	4305 / Sportwin	3.3
1939	4306 / Sportwin, 5" Longer	3.3
1939	4307 / Handitwin	3.0
1939	4308 / Handitwin, 5" Longer	3.0
1939	4309 / Fisherman	5.4
1939	4311 / Fisherman, 5" Longer	5.4
1939	4312 / Weedless Fisherman	5.4
1939	4313 / Lightwin – to S/N 03000	5.0
1940	S/N 03001 to 04000	5.0
1941	S/N 04001 and up	5.0
	4314 / Lightwin, 5" Longer (S/N, year & HP same as model 4313)	
1939	4315 / Lightfour – to S/N 03000	9.7
1940	S/N 03001 to 04000	9.7
1941	S/N 04001 to 05000	9.7
1945	S/N 05001 to 90000	9.7
1941	S/N 90001 to 91000	9.7
1942	S/N 91001 and up	9.7
	4316 / Lightfour, 5" Longer (S/N, year & HP same as model 4315)	
	4317 / Lightfour, 15" Longer (S/N, year & HP same as model 4315)	
	4318 / Lightfour Heavy Duty (S/N, year & HP same as model 4315)	
	4319 / Lightfour H.D. 5" Longer (S/N, year & HP same as model 4315)	
	4321 / Lightfour H.D., 15" Longer (S/N, year & HP same as model 4315)	
1939	4322 / Lightfour – to S/N 03000	9.7
1940	S/N 03001 to 04000	9.7
1941	S/N 04001 to 05000	9.7
1945	S/N 05001 to 90000	9.7
1941	S/N 90001 to 91000	9.7
1942	S/N 91001 and up	9.7
	4323 / Lightfour, 5" Longer (S/N, year & HP same as model 4322)	
	4324 / Lightfour, 15" Longer (S/N, year & HP same as model 4322)	
	4325 / Lightfour Heavy Duty (S/N, year & HP same as model 4322)	
	4326 / Lightfour H.D., 5" Longer (S/N, year & HP same as model 4322)	
	4327 / Lightfour H.D., 15" Longer (S/N, year & HP same as model 4322)	
1939–41	4328 / Midget Racer	----
1939	4329 / Ace	1.8
1939	4331 / Ace, 5" Longer	1.8
1939	4332 / Handitwin	3.0
1939	4333 / Handitwin, 5" Longer	3.0
1939	4334 / Ranger – to S/N 04000	1.1
1940	S/N 04001 to 07000	1.1
1941	S/N 07001 and up	1.1
1939–41	4335 / Fleetwin	8.5
1939–41	4336 / Fleetwin, 5" Longer	8.5
	4337 / Lightwin Heavy Duty (S/N, year & HP same as model 4313)	
	4338 / Lightwin H.D., 5" Longer (S/N, year & HP same as model 4313)	
	4339 / Lightwin H.D., 15" Longer (S/N, year & HP same as model 4313)	
1940–41	4341 / Weedless Lightwin	5.0
1940	4346 / Sportsman	2.0
1940	4347 / Sportsman, 5" Longer	2.0
1940	4348 / Sportsman	2.0
1940	4349 / Sportsman, 5" Longer	2.0
1940	4351 / Ace – to S/N 03500	1.8

1941	S/N 03501 and up	1.8
	4352 / Ace, 5" Longer	
	(S/N, year & HP same as model 4351)	
1940	4353 / Sportwin	3.3
1940	4354 / Sportwin, 5" Longer	3.3
1940	4355 / Sportwin	3.3
1940	4356 / Sportwin, 5" Longer	3.3
1940	4357 / Handitwin – to S/N 04000	3.0
1940	S/N 04001 and up	3.0
	4358 / Handitwin, 5" Longer	
	(S/N, year & HP same as model 4357)	
1940–41	4359 / Zephyr	5.4
1940–41	4361 / Zephyr, 5" Longer	5.4
1940–41	4362 / Zephyr	5.4
1940–41	4363 / Zephyr, 5" Longer	5.4
1941	4364 / Sportsman – to S/N 10000	2.0
1942	S/N 10001 and up	2.0
	4365 / Sportsman, 5" Longer	
	(S/N, year & HP same as model 4364)	
	4366 / Sportsman	
	(S/N, year & HP same as model 4364)	
	4367 / Sportsman, 5" Longer	
	(S/N, year & HP same as model 4364)	
1941	4368 / Sportwin – to S/N 18000	3.3
1946	S/N 18001 and up	3.3
	4369 / Sportwin, 5" Longer	
	(S/N, year & HP same as model 4368)	
1941	4371 / Sportwin – to S/N 10000	3.3
1946	S/N 10001 to 30000	3.3
1947	S/N 30001 and up	3.3
	4372 / Sportwin, 5" Longer	
	(S/N, year & HP same as model 4371)	
1942	4373 / Lightfour Heavy Duty	9.7
1942	4374 / Lightfour H.D., 15" Longer	9.7
1943	4375 / Lightfour H.D., 15" Longer	9.7
1943	4376 / Lightfour H.D., 15" Longer	9.7
1943	4377 / Lightfour H.D., 15" Longer	9.7
1945–46	4378 / Zephyr	5.4
1945–46	4379 / Zephyr, 5" Longer	5.4
1945–46	4381 / Zephyr	5.4
1945–46	4382 / Zephyr, 5" Longer	5.4
1945	4383 / Lightfour – to S/N 04000	9.7
1946	S/N 04001 to 16000	9.7
1947	S/N 16001 to 25000	9.7
1948	S/N 25001 to 33000	9.7
1949	S/N 33001 and up	9.7
	4384 / Lightfour, 5" Longer	
	(S/N, year & HP same as model 4383)	
	4385 / Lightfour, 15" Longer	
	(S/N, year & HP same as model 4383)	
	4386 / Lightfour Heavy Duty	
	(S/N, year & HP same as model 4383)	
	4387 / Lightfour H.D., 5" Longer	
	(S/N, year & HP same as model 4383)	
	4388 / Lightfour H.D., 15" Longer	
	S/N, year & HP same as model 4383)	
	4389 / Lightfour	
	(S/N, year & HP same as model 4383)	
	4391 / Lightfour, 5" Longer	
	(S/N, year & HP same as model 4383)	
	4392 / Lightfour, 15" Longer	
	(S/N, year & HP same as model 4383)	
	4393 / Lightfour Heavy Duty	
	(S/N, year & HP same as model 4383)	
	4394 / Lightfour H.D., 5" Longer	
	(S/N, year & HP same as model 4383)	
	4395 / Lightfour H.D., 15" Longer	
	(S/N, year & HP same as model 4383)	
1945	4398 / Lightfour Heavy Duty, 5" Longer	9.7
1946	4402 / Zephyr – to S/N 25000	5.4
1947	S/N 25001 to 40000	5.4
1948	S/N 40001 and up	5.4
	4403 / Zephyr, 5" Longer	
	(S/N, year & HP same as model 4402)	
	4404 / Zephyr	
	(S/N, year & HP same as model 4402)	
	4405 / Zephyr, 5" Longer	
	(S/N, year & HP same as model 4402)	
1946–47	4406 / Ranger	1.1
1946–47	4407 / Ranger	1.1
1946	4409 / Sportsman	2.0
1946	4411 / Sportsman, 5" Longer	2.0
1946	4412 / Sportsman	2.0
1946	4413 / Sportsman, 5" Longer	2.0
1947	4414 / Sportsman	2.0
1947	4415 / Sportsman, 5" Longer	2.0
1947	4416 / Sportsman	2.0
1947	4417 / Sportsman, 5" Longer	2.0
1947	4418 / Sportwin	3.3
1947	4419 / Sportwin, 5" Longer	3.3
1947	4421 / Sportwin	3.3
1947	4422 / Sportwin, 5" Longer	3.3
1948	4423 / Sportwin – to S/N 43000	3.3
1949	S/N 43001 to 80000	3.3
1951	S/N 80001 to 99999	3.3
1950–51	S/N with six digits	3.3
	4424 / Sportwin, 5" Longer	
	(S/N, year & HP same as model 4423)	
1948	4425 / Sportsman – to S/N 13000	1.5
1949	S/N 13001 and up	1.5
1950–51	S/N suffixed by 'C'	1.5
1949	4429 / Zephyr	5.4
1949	4431 / Zephyr, 5" Longer	5.4
1949	4432 / Sportster	5.0
1950	4434 / Fleetwin	7.5
1950	4435 / Fleetwin, 5" Longer	7.5
1950	4438 / Fastwin	14.0
1950	4439 / Fastwin, 5" Longer	14.0
1951	4441 / Fastwin – to S/N 20620	14.0
1952	S/N 20621 and up	14.0
	4442 / Fastwin, 5" Longer	
	(S/N, year & HP same as model 4441)	

<table>
<tr><td>1951</td><td>4443 / Fleetwin – to S/N 43599</td><td>7.5</td></tr>
<tr><td>1952</td><td>S/N 43600 and up</td><td>7.5</td></tr>
<tr><td></td><td>4444 / Fleetwin, 5" Longer
(S/N, year & HP same as model 4443)</td><td></td></tr>
<tr><td>1952</td><td>4447 / Fleetwin</td><td>7.5</td></tr>
<tr><td>1952</td><td>4448 / Fleetwin, 5" Longer</td><td>7.5</td></tr>
<tr><td>1949</td><td>5101 / Speedster</td><td>12.0</td></tr>
<tr><td>1949</td><td>5102 / Speedster, 5" Longer</td><td>12.0</td></tr>
<tr><td>1956</td><td>5512 / Fisherman</td><td>5.5</td></tr>
<tr><td>1956</td><td>5513 / Fisherman, 5" Longer</td><td>5.5</td></tr>
<tr><td>1957</td><td>5514 / Fisherman</td><td>5.5</td></tr>
<tr><td>1957</td><td>5515 / Fisherman, 5" Longer</td><td>5.5</td></tr>
<tr><td>1958</td><td>5516 / Fisherman</td><td>5.5</td></tr>
<tr><td>1958</td><td>5517 / Fisherman, 5" Longer</td><td>5.5</td></tr>
<tr><td>1959</td><td>5518 / Fisherman</td><td>5.5</td></tr>
<tr><td>1959</td><td>5519 / Fisherman, 5" Longer</td><td>5.5</td></tr>
<tr><td>1934</td><td>6000 / Speeditwin</td><td>21.1</td></tr>
<tr><td>1934</td><td>6001 / Speeditwin, 5" Longer</td><td>21.1</td></tr>
<tr><td>1934</td><td>6002 / Speeditwin Electric</td><td>21.1</td></tr>
<tr><td>1934</td><td>6003 / Speeditwin Electric, 5" Longer</td><td>21.1</td></tr>
<tr><td>1934</td><td>6004 Speeditwin</td><td>21.1</td></tr>
<tr><td>1934</td><td>6005 / Speeditwin, 5" Longer</td><td>21.1</td></tr>
<tr><td>1934</td><td>6006 / Speeditwin Electric</td><td>21.1</td></tr>
<tr><td>1934</td><td>6007 / Speeditwin Electric, 5" Longer</td><td>21.1</td></tr>
<tr><td>1934</td><td>6008 / Speeditwin Racer</td><td>----</td></tr>
<tr><td>1935</td><td>6011 / Speeditwin</td><td>21.1</td></tr>
<tr><td>1935</td><td>6012 / Speeditwin, 5" Longer</td><td>21.1</td></tr>
<tr><td>1935</td><td>6013 / Speeditwin Electric</td><td>21.1</td></tr>
<tr><td>1935</td><td>6014 / Speeditwin Electric, 5" Longer</td><td>21.1</td></tr>
<tr><td>1935</td><td>6015 / Speeditwin</td><td>21.1</td></tr>
<tr><td>1935</td><td>6016 / Speeditwin, 5" Longer</td><td>21.1</td></tr>
<tr><td>1935</td><td>6017 / Speeditwin Racer</td><td>----</td></tr>
<tr><td>1936</td><td>6018 / Speeditwin</td><td>21.1</td></tr>
<tr><td>1936</td><td>6019 / Speeditwin, 5" Longer</td><td>21.1</td></tr>
<tr><td>1936</td><td>6021 / Speeditwin Electric</td><td>21.1</td></tr>
<tr><td>1936</td><td>6022 / Speeditwin Electric, 5" Longer</td><td>21.1</td></tr>
<tr><td>1936</td><td>6023 / Speeditwin</td><td>21.1</td></tr>
<tr><td>1936</td><td>6024 / Speeditwin, 5" Longer</td><td>21.1</td></tr>
<tr><td>1936</td><td>6025 / Speeditwin Racer</td><td>----</td></tr>
<tr><td>1937</td><td>6026 / Speeditwin</td><td>22.5</td></tr>
<tr><td>1937</td><td>6027 / Speeditwin, 5" Longer</td><td>22.5</td></tr>
<tr><td>1937</td><td>6028 / Speeditwin Electric</td><td>22.5</td></tr>
<tr><td>1937</td><td>6029 / Speeditwin Electric, 5" Longer</td><td>22.5</td></tr>
<tr><td>1937</td><td>6031 / Speeditwin</td><td>22.5</td></tr>
<tr><td>1937</td><td>6032 / Speeditwin, 5" Longer</td><td>22.5</td></tr>
<tr><td>1937</td><td>6033 / Speeditwin Racer</td><td>----</td></tr>
<tr><td>1938</td><td>6034 / Speeditwin</td><td>22.5</td></tr>
<tr><td>1938</td><td>6035 / Speeditwin, 5" Longer</td><td>22.5</td></tr>
<tr><td>1938</td><td>6036 / Speeditwin Electric</td><td>22.5</td></tr>
<tr><td>1938</td><td>6037 / Speeditwin Electric, 5" Longer</td><td>22.5</td></tr>
<tr><td>1938</td><td>6038 / Speeditwin Racer</td><td>----</td></tr>
<tr><td>1939</td><td>6039 / Speeditwin – to S/N 01000</td><td>22.5</td></tr>
<tr><td>1940</td><td>S/N 01001 to 02200</td><td>22.5</td></tr>
<tr><td>1941</td><td>S/N 02201 to 05000</td><td>22.5</td></tr>
<tr><td>1946</td><td>S/N 05001 to 10000</td><td>22.5</td></tr>
<tr><td>1947</td><td>S/N 10001 to 11000</td><td>22.5</td></tr>
<tr><td>1948</td><td>S/N 11001 to 23100</td><td>22.5</td></tr>
<tr><td>1949</td><td>S/N 23101 to 26184</td><td>22.5</td></tr>
<tr><td>1950</td><td>S/N 26185 and up</td><td>22.5</td></tr>
<tr><td></td><td>6041 / Speeditwin, 5" Longer
(S/N, year & HP same as model 6039)</td><td></td></tr>
<tr><td>1939-40</td><td>6042 / Speeditwin Racer</td><td>----</td></tr>
<tr><td>1941</td><td>6043 / Speeditwin Racer</td><td>----</td></tr>
<tr><td>1934</td><td>7000 / Speediquad</td><td>31.2</td></tr>
<tr><td>1934</td><td>7001 / Speediquad, 5" Longer</td><td>31.2</td></tr>
<tr><td>1934</td><td>7002 / Speediquad Electric</td><td>31.2</td></tr>
<tr><td>1934</td><td>7003 / Speediquad Electric, 5" Longer</td><td>31.2</td></tr>
<tr><td>1934</td><td>7004 / Speediquad</td><td>31.2</td></tr>
<tr><td>1934</td><td>7005 / Speediquad, 5" Longer</td><td>31.2</td></tr>
<tr><td>1934</td><td>7006 / Speediquad Electric</td><td>31.2</td></tr>
<tr><td>1934</td><td>7007 / Speediquad Electric, 5" Longer</td><td>31.2</td></tr>
<tr><td>1935</td><td>7008 / Speediquad</td><td>31.2</td></tr>
<tr><td>1935</td><td>7009 / Speediquad, 5" Longer</td><td>31.2</td></tr>
<tr><td>1935</td><td>7011 / Speediquad Electric</td><td>31.2</td></tr>
<tr><td>1935</td><td>7012 / Speediquad Electric, 5" Longer</td><td>31.2</td></tr>
<tr><td>1935</td><td>7013 / Speediquad</td><td>31.2</td></tr>
<tr><td>1935</td><td>7014 / Speediquad, 5" Longer</td><td>31.2</td></tr>
<tr><td>1936</td><td>7015 / Speediquad</td><td>31.2</td></tr>
<tr><td>1936</td><td>7016 / Speediquad, 5" Longer</td><td>31.2</td></tr>
<tr><td>1936</td><td>7017 / Speediquad Electric</td><td>31.2</td></tr>
<tr><td>1936</td><td>7018 / Speediquad Electric, 5" Longer</td><td>31.2</td></tr>
<tr><td>1936</td><td>7019 / Speediquad</td><td>31.2</td></tr>
<tr><td>1936</td><td>7021 / Speediquad, 5" Longer</td><td>31.2</td></tr>
<tr><td>1937</td><td>7022 / Speedifour</td><td>33.4</td></tr>
<tr><td>1937</td><td>7023 / Speedifour, 5" Longer</td><td>33.4</td></tr>
<tr><td>1937</td><td>7024 / Speedifour Electric</td><td>33.4</td></tr>
<tr><td>1937</td><td>7025 / Speedifour Electric, 5" Longer</td><td>33.4</td></tr>
<tr><td>1938</td><td>7026 / Speedifour</td><td>33.4</td></tr>
<tr><td>1938</td><td>7027 / Speedifour, 5" Longer</td><td>33.4</td></tr>
<tr><td>1938</td><td>7028 / Speedifour Electric</td><td>33.4</td></tr>
<tr><td>1938</td><td>7029 / Speedifour Electric, 5" Longer</td><td>33.4</td></tr>
<tr><td>1939</td><td>7031 / Speedifour – to S/N 01000</td><td>33.4</td></tr>
<tr><td>1940</td><td>S/N 01001 to 02000</td><td>33.4</td></tr>
<tr><td>1941</td><td>S/N 02001 to 03000</td><td>33.4</td></tr>
<tr><td>1946</td><td>S/N 03001 to 04000</td><td>33.4</td></tr>
<tr><td>1947</td><td>S/N 04001 to 07000</td><td>33.4</td></tr>
<tr><td>1948</td><td>S/N 07001 to 10000</td><td>33.4</td></tr>
<tr><td>1949</td><td>S/N 10001 to 12000</td><td>33.4</td></tr>
<tr><td>1950</td><td>S/N 12001 and up</td><td>33.4</td></tr>
<tr><td></td><td>7032 / Speedifour, 5" Longer
(S/N, year & HP same as model 7031)</td><td></td></tr>
<tr><td>1939</td><td>7033 / Speedifour Electric – to S/N 01000</td><td>33.4</td></tr>
<tr><td>1940</td><td>S/N 01001 to 02000</td><td>33.4</td></tr>
<tr><td>1941</td><td>S/N 02001 and up</td><td>33.4</td></tr>
<tr><td></td><td>7034 / Speedifour Electric, 5" Longer
(S/N, year & HP same as model 7033)</td><td></td></tr>
<tr><td>1942</td><td>7035 / Speedifour, 5" Longer</td><td>33.4</td></tr>
<tr><td>1953</td><td>7512 / Fleetwin</td><td>7.5</td></tr>
<tr><td>1953</td><td>7513 / Fleetwin, 5" Longer</td><td>7.5</td></tr>
<tr><td>1954</td><td>7514 / Fleetwin</td><td>7.5</td></tr>
<tr><td>1954</td><td>7515 / Fleetwin, 5" Longer</td><td>7.5</td></tr>
</table>

Year	Model / Name	HP		Year	Model / Name	HP
1954	7516 / Fleetwin	7.5		1956	10012 / Sportwin	10.0
1954	7517 / Fleetwin, 5" Longer	7.5		1956	10013 / Sportwin, 5" Longer	10.0
1955	7518 / Fleetwin	7.5		1957	10014 / Sportwin	10.0
1955	7519 / Fleetwin, 5" Longer	7.5		1957	10015 / Sportwin, 5" Longer	10.0
1956	7520 / Fleetwin	7.5		1958	10016 / Sportwin	10.0
1956	7521 / Fleetwin, 5" Longer	7.5		1958	10017 / Sportwin, 5" Longer	10.0
1957	7522 / Fleetwin	7.5		1959	10018 / Sportwin	10.0
1957	7523 / Fleetwin, 5" Longer	7.5		1959	10019 / Sportwin, 5" Longer	10.0
1958	7524 / Fleetwin	7.5		1953	15012 / Fastwin – to S/N 19000	15.0
1958	7525 / Fleetwin, 5" Longer	7.5		1954	S/N 19001	15.0
1934	8000 / Four-Sixty Racer	----			and up	
1934	8001 / Class 'X' Racer	----			15013 / Fastwin, 5" Longer	
1935	8002 / Four-Sixty Racer	----			(S/N, year & HP same as model 15012)	
1936	8003 / Four-Sixty Racer	----		1955	15014 / Fastwin	15.0
1937	8004 / Four-Sixty Racer	----		1955	15015 / Fastwin, 5" Longer	15.0
1938	8005 / Four-Sixty Racer	----		1956	15016 / Fastwin	15.0
1939–41	8006 / Four-Sixty Racer	----		1956	15017 / Fastwin, 5" Longer	15.0
1943	8008 / Storm Boat Motor	50.0		1957	15020 / Fastwin	18.0
1946	8014 / Big Four	50.0		1957	15021 / Fastwin, 5" Longer	18.0
1949	8015 / Big Four	50.0		1958	15024 / Fastwin	18.0
1934	9000 / Sportfour	16.2		1958	15025 / Fastwin, 5" Longer	18.0
1934	9001 / Sportfour, 5" Longer	16.2		1959	15028 / Fastwin	18.0
1934	9002 / Sportfour Electric	16.2		1959	15029 / Fastwin, 5" Longer	18.0
1934	9003 / Sportfour Electric, 5" Longer	16.2		1956	15918 / Fastwin Electric	15.0
1934	9004 / Sportfour	16.2		1956	15919 / Fastwin Electric, 5" Longer	15.0
1934	9005 / Sportfour, 5" Longer	16.2		1957	15922 / Fastwin Electric	18.0
1934	9006 / Sportfour Electric	16.2		1957	15923 / Fastwin Electric, 5" Longer	18.0
1934	9007 / Sportfour Electric, 5" Longer	16.2		1958	15926 / Fastwin Electric	18.0
1935	9008 / Sportfour	16.2		1958	15927 / Fastwin Electric, 5" Longer	18.0
1935	9009 / Sportfour, 5" Longer	16.2		1953	25012 / Big Twin – to S/N 70000	25.0
1935	9011 / Sportfour Electric	16.2		1954	S/N 70001	25.0
1935	9012 / Sportfour Electric, 5" Longer	16.2			and up	
1935	9013 / Sportfour	16.2			25013 / Big Twin, 5" Longer	
1935	9014 / Sportfour, 5" Longer	16.2			(S/N, year & HP same as model 25012)	
1936	9015 / Sportfour	16.2		1954	25014 / Big Twin	25.0
1936	9016 / Sportfour, 5" Longer	16.2		1954	25015 / Big Twin, 5" Longer	25.0
1936	9017 / Sportfour Electric	16.2		1955	25018 / Big Twin	25.0
1936	9018 / Sportfour Electric, 5" Longer	16.2		1955	25019 / Big Twin, 5" Longer	25.0
1936	9019 / Sportfour	16.2		1956	25022 / Big Twin	30.0
1936	9021 / Sportfour, 5" Longer	16.2		1956	25023 / Big Twin, 5" Longer	30.0
1937	9022 / Sportfour	16.2		1957	25028 / Big Twin	35.0
1937	9023 / Sportfour, 5" Longer	16.2		1957	25029 / Big Twin, 5" Longer	35.0
1937	9024 / Sportfour Electric	16.2		1958	25034 / Big Twin	35.0
1937	9025 / Sportfour Electric, 5" Longer	16.2		1958	25035 / Big Twin, 5" Longer	35.0
1938	9026 / Sportfour	16.2		1956	25526 / Lark	30.0
1938	9027 / Sportfour, 5" Longer	16.2		1956	25527 / Lark, 5" Longer	30.0
1938	9028 / Sportfour Electric	16.2		1957	25532 / Lark	35.0
1938	9029 / Sportfour Electric, 5" Longer	16.2		1957	25533 / Lark, 5" Longer	35.0
1939	9031 / Sportfour	16.2		1954	25916 / Big Twin Electric	25.0
1939	9032 / Sportfour, 5" Longer	16.2		1954	25917 / Big Twin Electric, 5" Longer	25.0
1939	9033 / Sportfour Electric	16.2		1955	25920 / Big Twin Electric	25.0
1939	9034 / Sportfour Electric, 5" Longer	16.2		1955	25921 / Big Twin Electric, 5" Longer	25.0
1940	9035 / Sportfour to S/N 01000	17.6		1956	25924 / Big Twin Electric	30.0
1941	S/N 01001 and up	17.6		1956	25925 / Big Twin Electric, 5" Longer	30.0
	9036 / Sportfour, 5" Longer			1957	25930 / Big Twin Electric	35.0
	(S/N, year & HP same as model 9035)			1957	25931 / Big Twin Electric, 5" Longer	35.0
	9037 / Sportfour			1958	25936 / Big Twin Electric	35.0
	(S/N, year & HP same as model 9035)			1958	25937 / Big Twin Electric, 5" Longer	35.0
	9038 / Sportfour, 5" Longer			1959	35012 / Big Twin	35.0
	(S/N, year & HP same as model 9035)			1959	35013 / Big Twin, 5" Longer	35.0
1941	9039 / Heavy Duty Twin	15.0		1958	35514 / Lark	35.0
1941	9041 / Sportfour	17.6		1958	35515 / Lark, 5" Longer	35.0

1959	35516 / Lark	35.0
1959	35517 / Lark, 5" Longer	35.0
1958	50012 / Four-Fifty	50.0
1958	50013 / Four-Fifty, 5" Longer	50.0
1959	50016 / Four-Fifty	50.0
1959	50017 / Four-Fifty, 5" Longer	50.0
1958	50514 / Starflite	50.0
1958	50515 / Starflite, 5" Longer	50.0
1959	50518 / Starflite	50.0
1959	50519 / Starflite, 5" Longer	50.0
1959	50816 / Four-Fifty Electric	50.0
1959	50817 / Four-Fifty Electric, 5" Longer	50.0
1951	2001 / Big Twin – to S/N 11000	25.0
1952	S/N 11001 and up	25.0
	2002 / Big Twin, 5" Longer	
	(S/N, year & HP same as model 2001)	
1952	2003 / Big Twin	25.0
1952	2004 / Big Twin, 5" Longer	25.0
1952	3012 / Lightwin – to S/N 09000	3.0
1953	S/N 09001 to 34000	3.0
1954	S/N 34001 and up	3.0
	3013 / Lightwin, 5" Longer	
	(S/N, year & HP same as model 3012)	
1955	3014 / Lightwin	3.0
1955	3015 / Lightwin, 5" Longer	3.0
1955	3016 / Ducktwin	3.0
1956	3018 / Lightwin	3.0
1956	3019 / Lightwin, 5" Longer	3.0
1956	3020 / Ducktwin	3.0
1957	3022 / Lightwin	3.0
1957	3023 / Lightwin, 5" Longer	3.0
1957	3024 / Ducktwin	3.0
1958	3026 / Lightwin	3.0
1958	3027 / Lightwin, 5" Longer	3.0
1958	3028 / Ducktwin	3.0
1959	3030 / Lightwin	3.0
1959	3031 / Lightwin, 5" Longer	3.0
1959	3032 / Ducktwin	3.0
1960	3034 / Lightwin	3.0
1960	3035 / Lightwin 5" Longer	3.0
1960	3036 / Ducktwin	3.0
1961	3038 / Lightwin	3.0
1961	3039 / Lightwin 5" Longer	3.0
1961	3040 / Ducktwin	3.0
1962	3042 / Lightwin	3.0
1962	3043 / Lightwin 5" Longer	3.0
1962	3044 / Ducktwin	3.0
1963	3302 / Lightwin	3.0
1963	3303 / Lightwin 5" Longer	3.0
1963	3312 / Ducktwin	3.0
1964	3402 / Lightwin	3.0
1964	3403 / Lightwin 5" Longer	3.0
1964	3412 / Ducktwin	3.0
1964	3432 / Yachtwin	3.0
1964	3433 / Yachtwin 5" Longer	3.0
1965	3502 / Lightwin	3.0
1965	3503 / Lightwin 5" Longer	3.0
1965	3512 / Ducktwin	3.0
1965	3532 / Yachtwin	3.0
1965	3533 / Yachtwin 5" Longer	3.0
1966	3602 / Lightwin (Folding)	3.0
1966	3603 / Lightwin 5" Longer (Folding)	3.0
1966–67	3612 / Ducktwin (Folding)	3.0
1966	3632 / Yachtwin (Folding)	3.0
1966	3633 / Yachtwin 5" Longer (Folding)	3.0
1967	3702 / Lightwin (Folding)	3.0
1967	3703 / Lightwin 5" Longer (Folding)	3.0
1967	3706 / Lightwin (Rigid)	3.0
1967	3707 / Lightwin 5" Longer (Rigid)	3.0
1967	3712 / Ducktwin (Folding)	3.0
1967	3716 / Ducktwin (Rigid)	3.0
1967	3732 / Yachtwin (Folding)	3.0
1967	3733 / Yachtwin 5" Longer (Folding)	3.0
1967	3736 / Yachtwin (Rigid)	3.0
1967	3737 / Yachtwin 5" Longer (Rigid)	3.0
1968	3802 / Lightwin (Folding)	3.0
1968	3803 / Lightwin 5" Longer (Folding)	3.0
1968	3806 / Lightwin (Rigid)	3.0
1968	3807 / Lightwin 5" Longer (Rigid)	3.0
1968	3832 / Yachtwin (Folding)	3.0
1968	3833 / Yachtwin 5" Longer (Folding)	3.0
1968	3836 / Yachtwin (Rigid)	3.0
1968	3837 / Yachtwin 5" Longer (Rigid)	3.0
1970	4006 / Lightwin (Rigid)	4.0
1970	4036 / Yachtwin (Rigid)	4.0
1969	4902 / Lightwin (Folding)	4.0
1969	4906 / Lightwin (Rigid)	4.0
1969	4936 / Yachtwin (Rigid)	4.0
1963	5302 / Fisherman	5.5
1963	5303 / Fisherman 5" Longer	5.5
1964	5402 / Fisherman	5.5
1964	5403 / Fisherman 5" Longer	5.5
1965	5502 / Angler	5.0
1965	5503 / Angler 5" Longer	5.0
1960	5520 / Fisherman	5.5
1960	5521 / Fisherman 5" Longer	5.5
1961	5522 / Fisherman	5.5
1961	5523 / Fisherman 5" Longer	5.5
1962	5524 / Fisherman	5.5
1962	5525 / Fisherman 5" Longer	5.5
1966	5602 / Angler	5.0
1966	5603 / Angler 5" Longer	5.0
1967	5702 / Angler	5.0
1967	5703 / Angler 5" Longer	5.0
1968	5802 / Angler	5.0
1968	5803 / Angler 5" Longer	5.0
1970	6002 / Fisherman	6.0
1970	6003 / Fisherman 5" Longer	6.0
1965	6502 / Fisherman	6.0
1965	6503 / Fisherman 5" Longer	6.0
1966	6602 / Fisherman	6.0
1966	6603 / Fisherman 5" Longer	6.0
1967	6702 / Fisherman	6.0
1967	6703 / Fisherman 5" Longer	6.0
1968	6802 / Fisherman	6.0
1968	6803 / Fisherman 5" Longer	6.0
1969	6902 / Fisherman	6.0
1969	6903 / Fisherman 5" Longer	6.0
1970	9022 / Sportwin	9.5
1970	9023 / Sportwin 5" Longer	9.5
1964	9422 / Sportwin	9.5
1964	9423 / Sportwin 5" Longer	9.5
1965	9522 / Sportwin	9.5

Year	Model	HP
1965	9523 / Sportwin 5" Longer	9.5
1966	9622 / Sportwin	9.5
1966	9623 / Sportwin 5" Longer	9.5
1967	9722 / Sportwin	9.5
1967	9723 / Sportwin 5" Longer	9.5
1968	9822 / Sportwin	9.5
1968	9823 / Sportwin 5" Longer	9.5
1969	9922 / Sportwin	9.5
1969	9923 / Sportwin 5" Longer	9.5
1960	10020 / Sportwin	10.0
1960	10021 / Sportwin 5" Longer	10.0
1961	10022 / Sportwin	10.0
1961	10023 / Sportwin 5" Longer	10.0
1962	10024 / Sportwin	10.0
1962	10025 / Sportwin 5" Longer	10.0
1963	10302 / Sportwin	10.0
1963	10303 / Sportwin 5" Longer	10.0
1960	15032 / Fastwin	18.0
1960	15033 / Fastwin 5" Longer	18.0
1961	15034 / Fastwin	18.0
1961	15035 / Fastwin 5" Longer	18.0
1962	15036 / Fastwin	18.0
1962	15037 / Fastwin 5" Longer	18.0
1970	18002 / Fastwin	18.0
1970	18003 / Fastwin 5" Longer	18.0
1963	18302 / Fastwin	18.0
1963	18303 / Fastwin 5" Longer	18.0
1964	18402 / Fastwin	18.0
1964	18403 / Fastwin 5" Longer	18.0
1965	18502 / Fastwin	18.0
1965	18503 / Fastwin 5" Longer	18.0
1966	18602 / Fastwin	18.0
1966	18603 / Fastwin 5" Longer	18.0
1967	18702 / Fastwin	18.0
1967	18703 / Fastwin 5" Longer	18.0
1968	18802 / Fastwin	18.0
1968	18803 / Fastwin 5" Longer	18.0
1969	18902 / Fastwin	18.0
1969	18903 / Fastwin 5" Longer	18.0
1970	25002 / Sportster	25.0
1970	25003 / Sportster 5" Longer	25.0
1969	25902 / Sportster	25.0
1969	25903 / Sportster 5" Longer	25.0
1970	27010 / Sportsman 16' I/O	155.0
1962	28202 / Speeditwin	28.0
1962	28203 / Speeditwin 5" Longer	28.0
1963	28302 / Speeditwin	28.0
1963	28303 / Speeditwin 5" Longer	28.0
1964	28402 / Speeditwin	28.0
1964	28403 / Speeditwin 5" Longer	28.0
1970	33002 / Ski Twin	33.0
1970	33003 / Ski Twin 5" Longer	33.0
1970	33052 / Ski Twin Elec.	33.0
1970	33053 / Ski Twin Elec. 5" Longer	33.0
1965	33502 / Ski Twin	33.0
1965	33503 / Ski Twin 5" Longer	33.0
1965	33552 / Ski Twin Elec.	33.0
1965	33553 / Ski Twin Elec. 5" Longer	33.0
1966	33602 / Ski Twin	33.0
1966	33603 / Ski Twin 5" Longer	33.0
1966	33652 / Ski Twin Elec.	33.0
1966	33653 / Ski Twin Elec. 5" Longer	33.0
1967	33702 / Ski Twin	33.0
1967	33703 / Ski Twin 5" Longer	33.0
1967	33752 / Ski Twin Elec.	33.0
1967	33753 / Ski Twin Elec. 5" Longer	33.0
1968	33802 / Ski Twin	33.0
1968	33803 / Ski Twin 5" Longer	33.0
1968	33852 / Ski Twin Elec.	33.0
1968	33853 / Ski Twin Elec. 5" Longer	33.0
1969	33902 / Ski Twin	33.0
1969	33903 / Ski Twin 5" Longer	33.0
1969	33952 / Ski Twin Elec.	33.0
1969	33953 / Ski Twin Elec. 5" Longer	33.0
1960	35018 / Big Twin	40.0
1960	35019 / Big Twin 5" Longer	40.0
1961	35022 / Big Twin	40.0
1961	35023 / Big Twin 5" Longer	40.0
1962	35028 / Big Twin	40.0
1962	35029 / Big Twin 5" Longer	40.0
1960	35520 / Lark	40.0
1960	35521 / Lark 5" Longer	40.0
1961	35524 / Lark	40.0
1961	35525 / Lark 5" Longer	40.0
1962	35530 / Lark	40.0
1962	35531 / Lark 5" Longer	40.0
1962	35932 / Lark Sel.	40.0
1962	35933 / Lark Sel. 5" Longer	40.0
1970	37010 / Explorer 16' I/O	155.0
1970	40002 / Big Twin	40.0
1970	40003 / Big Twin 5" Longer	40.0
1970	40052 / Big Twin Elec.	40.0
1970	40053 / Big Twin Elec. 5" Longer	40.0
1970	40072 / Lark Sel.	40.0
1970	40073 / Lark Sel. 5" Longer	40.0
1963	40302 / Big Twin	40.0
1963	40303 / Big Twin 5" Longer	40.0
1963	40352 / Big Twin Elec.	40.0
1963	40353 / Big Twin Elec. 5" Longer	40.0
1963	40362 / Lark Sel. (Bl.)	40.0
1963	40363 / Lark Sel. (Bl.) 5" Longer	40.0
1963	40372 / Lark Sel. (Gr.)	40.0
1963	40373 / Lark Sel. (Gr.) 5" Longer	40.0
1964	40402 / Big Twin	40.0
1964	40403 / Big Twin 5" Longer	40.0
1964	40452 / Big Twin Elec.	40.0
1964	40453 / Big Twin Elec. 5" Longer	40.0
1964	40462 / Lark Sel. (Bl.)	40.0
1964	40463 / Lark Sel. (Bl.) 5" Longer	40.0
1964	40472 / Lark Sel. (Gr.)	40.0
1964	40473 / Lark Sel. (Gr.) 5" Longer	40.0
1965	40502 / Big Twin	40.0
1965	40503 / Big Twin 5" Longer	40.0
1965	40552 / Big Twin Elec.	40.0
1965	40553 / Big Twin Elec. 5" Longer	40.0
1965	40562 / Lark Sel. (Bl.)	40.0
1965	40563 / Lark Sel. (Bl.) 5" Longer	40.0
1965	40572 / Lark Sel. (Gr.)	40.0
1965	40573 / Lark Sel. (Gr.) 5" Longer	40.0
1966	40602 / Big Twin	40.0
1966	40603 / Big Twin 5" Longer	40.0
1966	40652 / Big Twin Elec.	40.0
1966	40653 / Big Twin Elec. 5" Longer	40.0
1966	40662 / Lark Sel. (Bl.)	40.0

Year	Model	HP
1966	40663 / Lark Sel. (Bl.) 5" Longer	40.0
1966	40672 / Lark Sel. (Gr.)	40.0
1966	40673 / Lark Sel. (Gr.) 5" Longer	40.0
1967	40702 / Big Twin	40.0
1967	40703 / Big Twin 5" Longer	40.0
1967	40752 / Big Twin Elec.	40.0
1967	40753 / Big Twin Elec. 5" Longer	40.0
1967	40772 / Lark Sel.	40.0
1967	40773 / Lark Sel. 5" Longer	40.0
1968	40802 / Big Twin	40.0
1968	40803 / Big Twin 5" Longer	40.0
1968	40852 / Big Twin Elec.	40.0
1968	40853 / Big Twin Elec. 5" Longer	40.0
1968	40872 / Lark Sel.	40.0
1968	40873 / Lark Sel. 5" Longer	40.0
1969	40902 / Big Twin	40.0
1969	40903 / Big Twin 5" Longer	40.0
1969	40952 / Big Twin Elec.	40.0
1969	40953 / Big Twin Elec. 5" Longer	40.0
1969	40972 / Lark Sel.	40.0
1969	40973 / Lark Sel. 5" Longer	40.0
1970	47010 / Sport Fisherman 19' I/O	120.0
1960	50522 / Starflite	75.0
1960	50523 / Starflite 5" Longer	75.0
1961	50524 / Starflite	75.0
1961	50525 / Starflite 5" Longer	75.0
1962	50528 / Starflite	75.0
1962	50529 / Starflite 5" Longer	75.0
1961	50926 / Starflite U.C.	75.0
1961	50927 / Starflite U.C. 5" Longer	75.0
1962	50930 / Starflite Sel.	75.0
1962	50931 / Starflite Sel. 5" Longer	75.0
1968	55872 / Triumph	55.0
1968	55873 / Triumph 5" Longer	55.0
1969	55972 / Triumph	55.0
1969	55973 / Triumph 5" Longer	55.0
1970	57010 / Dolphin 19' I/O	210.0
1970	60072 / Triumph	60.0
1970	60073 / Triumph 5" Longer	60.0
1964	60432 / Sportfour H.D.	60.0
1964	60433 / Sportfour H.D. 5" Longer	60.0
1964	60452 / Sportfour	60.0
1964	60453 / Sportfour 5" Longer	60.0
1965	60532 / Sportfour H.D.	60.0
1965	60533 / Sportfour H.D. 5" Longer	60.0
1965	60552 / Sportfour	60.0
1965	60553 / Sportfour 5" Longer	60.0
1966	60632 / Sportfour H.D.	60.0
1966	60633 / Sportfour H.D. 5" Longer	60.0
1966	60652 / Sportfour	60.0
1966	60653 / Sportfour 5" Longer	60.0
1967	60732 / Sportfour H.D.	60.0
1967	60733 / Sportfour H.D. 5" Longer	60.0
1967	60752 / Sportfour	60.0
1967	60753 / Sportfour 5" Longer	60.0
1968	65832 / Sportfour H.D.	65.0
1968	65833 / Sportfour H.D. 5" Longer	65.0
1968	65852 / Sportfour	65.0
1968	65853 / Sportfour 5" Longer	65.0
1970	67010 / Rogue II 19' I/O	210.0
1963	75352 / Speedifour	75.0
1963	75353 / Speedifour 5" Longer	75.0
1963	75382 / Starflite (Bl.)	75.0
1963	75383 / Starflite (Bl.) 5" Longer	75.0
1963	75392 / Starflite (Gr.)	75.0
1963	75393 / Starflite (Gr.) 5" Longer	75.0
1964	75432 / Speedifour H.D.	75.0
1964	75433 / Speedifour H.D. 5" Longer	75.0
1964	75452 / Speedifour	75.0
1964	75453 / Speedifour 5" Longer	75.0
1964	75482 / Starflite (Bl.)	75.0
1964	75483 / Starflite (Bl.) 5" Longer	75.0
1964	75492 / Starflite (Gr.)	75.0
1964	75493 / Starflite (Gr.) 5" Longer	75.0
1965	75532 / Speedifour H.D.	75.0
1965	75533 / Speedifour H.D. 5" Longer	75.0
1965	75552 / Speedifour	75.0
1965	75553 / Speedifour 5" Longer	75.0
1965	75582 / Starflite (Bl.)	75.0
1965	75583 / Starflite (Bl.) 5" Longer	75.0
1965	75592 / Starflite (Gr.)	75.0
1965	75593 / Starflite (Gr.) 5" Longer	75.0
1966	80652 / Speedifour	80.0
1966	80653 / Speedifour 5" Longer	80.0
1966	80682 / Starflite (Bl.)	80.0
1966	80683 / Starflite (Bl.) 5" Longer	80.0
1966	80692 / Starflite (Gr.)	80.0
1966	80693 / Starflite (Gr.) 5" Longer	80.0
1967	80752 / Speedifour	80.0
1967	80753 / Speedifour 5" Longer	80.0
1967	80792 / Starflite	80.0
1967	80793 / Starflite 5" Longer	80.0
1970	85093 / Starflite 5" Longer	85.0
1968	85852 / Speedifour	85.0
1968	85853 / Speedifour 5" Longer	85.0
1968	85892 / Starflite	85.0
1968	85893 / Starflite 5" Longer	85.0
1969	85993 / Starflite 5" Longer	85.0
1964	90482 / Starflite (Bl.)	90.0
1964	90483 / Starflite (Bl.) 5" Longer	90.0
1964	90492 / Starflite (Gr.)	90.0
1964	90493 / Starflite (Gr.) 5" Longer	90.0
1965	90582 / Starflite (Bl.)	90.0
1965	90583 / Starflite (Bl.) 5" Longer	90.0
1965	90592 / Starflite (Gr.)	90.0
1965	90593 / Starflite (Gr.) 5" Longer	90.0
1966	100683 / Starflite (Bl.) 5" Longer	100.0
1966	100693 / Starflite (Gr.) 5" Longer	100.0
1967	100782 / Starflite	100.0
1967	100783 / Starflite 5" Longer	100.0
1968	100882 / Starflite	100.0
1968	100883 / Starflite 5" Longer	100.0
1970	107010 / 16' Trailer W/O Brk.	----
1970	115083 / Starflite 5" Longer	115.0
1967-68	115742 / X-115 Racer	115.0
1969	115983 / Starflite 5" Longer	115.0

Johnson. Like the lengthy Evinrude list, the Johnson guide was compiled to help dealers better identify customers' vintage motors. Although much of this document has been in circulation since the 1950s, the factory never updated it to include certain "rare" models from the 1920s–30s. Most of the missing motors are variations of standard models identified on the Johnson chart. For example:

- Model C is an early-20s model A twin equipped with a canoe mounting bracket.
- Model B-35 is similar to K-35, except that its transom mount bolts to the boat's stern.
- PB motors have *bronze* lower units.
- "L" means *long* shaft.
- Electric-starting Johnsons from the early 30s built on the S and V model motors are called SE-50 and VE-50.
- Aquaflyer models from the early 1930s have electric starting but no integral fuel tank. These rigs were made specifically for custom Johnson boats and drink gas from onboard tanks. The Aquaflyer SA-50, PA-50, and VA-50s are among the rarest of Johnson outboard products.
- The 1931, limited-production, XR-55 racer doesn't show up on many Johnson lists. The idea of selling this 4-cylinder, high speed rig to depression-ravaged potential customers was a bit far-fetched.
- 1934, 70 series Johnsons are scarce; this was a year of very low production.

The Johnson list does not identify certain carryover years of racing models. For example, the firm did make a 1933 PR-65 and a 1936 KR-80, but so few were produced that they were omitted from the list. Due to leftovers and economic considerations, some models were offered multiple years.

Other rather obscure Johnson products include the model AZ (as in AZ-50 and AZ-80). These opposed twins from the 1930s have above-water exhaust and may have been water pump powerheads (rated at 4 hp). The OB-60 (about 1932) was an opposed twin from Johnson's Canadian factory. This 4-hp kicker, equipped with a bronze lower unit, was probably built for export from North America. The 5-hp TS-20, an immediate post-World War II motor, wore rope (non-rewind) starting. TS-20 was an alternate-firing twin akin to the rewind-start TD-20.

Johnson

Year	Model	HP
1922–23	A	2
1922–23	BN	2
1924	A	2
1924	BN	2
1925	A-25	2
1925	AB-25	2
1925	J-25	1.5
1926	A-25	2
1926	AB-25	2
1926	J-25	1.5
1926	P-30	6
1928	A-35	2½
1927	J-25	1.5
1927	P-35	8
1927	K-35	6
1928	A-35	2½

Year	Model	HP
1928	J-25	1.5
1928	K-40	7.15
1928	P-40	13.15
1928	TR-40	25.75
1929	A-45	3
1929	J-25	1.5
1929	K-45	7.15
1929	P-45	12
1929	S-45	13
1929	V-45	26
1929	SR-45	16
1929	VR-45	32
1929	TR-40	25.75
1930–32	J-25	1.5
1930–32	A-50	4
1930–32	K-50	8
1931–32	KR-55	12
1930–32	P-50	20
1930–32	PR-50	24
1931–32	PR-55	27
1930–32	PR-60	27
1930–32	S-45	13
1930–32	SR-50	16
1930–32	SR-55	18
1930–32	SR-60	
1930–32	V-45	26
1930–32	VR-50	32
1930–32	VR-55	36
1930–32	KR-55	12
1931–32	OA-55	3
1932	OA-60	3
1931–32	OK-55	8
1932	OK-60	7
1933	J-65*	*1.4
1933	OA-65	2.8
1933	A-65	4.1
1933	K-65	9.2
1933	S-65	13.3
1933	P-65	21.4
1933	V-65	26.1
1934	J-70	1.4
1934	F-70	3.3
1934	A-70	4.1
1934	K-70	9.2
1934	S-70	13.3
1934	P-70	21.4
1934	V-70	26.1
1935	J-75	1.4
1935	F-75	3.3
1935	300	3.7
1935	A-75	4.5
1935	K-75	9.3
1935	P-75	22
1935	OK-75	8.1
1936	A-80	4.5
1936	K-80	9.3
1936	J-80	1.7
1936	P-80	22
1936	100	1.7
1936	200	3.3
1936	300	3.7
1937	LS-37	2.1

1937	DS-37	2.1	1947	HD-25	2.5
1937	LT-37	4.2	1947	TD-20	5.0
1937	DT-37	4.2	1947	KD-15	9.8
1937	210	3.3	1947	SD-15	16.0
1937	110	1.7	1947	PO-15	22.0
1937	AA-37	4.5	1948	HD-25	2.5
1937	KA-37	9.3	1948	TD-20	5.0
1937	PO-37	22.0	1948	KD-15	9.8
1938	MS-38	1.1	1948	SD-15	16.0
1938	MD-38	1.1	1948	PO-15	22.0
1938	LS-38	2.1	1949	HD-25	2.5
1938	DS-38	2.1	1949	TD-20	5.0
1938	LT-38	4.2	1949	QD-10	10.0
1938	DT-38	4.2	1949	SD-20	16.0
1938	KA-38	9.3	1949	PO-15	22.0
1938	PO-38	22.0	1950	HD-25	2.5
1939	MS-39	1.1	1950	TN-25, 26	5.0
1939	MD-39	1.1	1950	QD-10, 11	10.0
1939	HS-39	2.5	1950	SD-20	16.0
1939	HA-39	2.5	1950	PO-15	22.0
1939	HD-39	2.5	1951	HD-26	2.5
1939	LT-39	5.0	1951	TN-27	5.0
1939	AT-39	5.0	1951	QD-12	10.0
1939	DT-39	5.0	1951	RD-10-11	25.0
1939	KA-39	9.8	1951	RD-12	25.0
1939	PO-39	22.0	1952	JW-10	3.0
1940	MS-15	1.5	1952	TN-28	5.0
1940	MD-15	1.5	1952	QD-13	10.0
1940	HS-10, 15	2.5	1952	RD-13	25.0
1940	HA-10, 15	2.5	1953	JW-10	3
1940	HD-10, 15	2.5	1953	TN-28	5
1940	LT-10	5.0	1953	QD-14	10
1940	AT-10	5.0	1953	QD-14A	10
1940	DT-10	5.0	1953	RD-14	25
1940	KA-10	9.8	1953	RD-15	25
1940	SD-10	16.0	1954	JW-10	3.0
1940	PO-10	22	1954	CD-10-11	5.5
1941	MS-20	1.5	1954	QD-15	10.0
1941	MD-20	1.5	1954	RD-16, 16A	25.0
1941	HS-20	2.5	1954	RDE-16, 16A	25.0
1941	HD-20	2.5	1955	JW-11	3.0
1941	TS-15	5.0	1955	CD-12	5.5
1941	TD-15	5.0	1955	QD-16	10.0
1941	KS-15	9.8	1955	RD-17	25.0
1941	KD-15	9.8	1955	RDE-17	25.0
1941	SD-10	16.0	1956	JW-12	3.0
1941	PO-15	22.0	1956	CD-13	5.5
1942	MS-20	1.5	1956	AD-10	7.5
1942	MD-20	1.5	1956	QD-17	10.0
1942	HS-20	2.5	1956	FD-10	15.0
1942	HD-20	2.5	1956	FDE-10	15.0
1942	TS-15	5.0	1956	RD-18	30.0
1942	TD-15	5.0	1956	RDE-18	30.0
1942	KS-15	9.8	1956	RJE-18	30.0
1942	KD-15	9.8	1957	JW-13	3.0
1942	SD-10	16.0	1957	CD-14	5.5
1942	PO-15	22.0	1957	AD-11	7.5
1946	HD-25	2.5	1957	QD-18	10.0
1946	TD-20	5.0	1957	FD-11	18.0
1946	KD-15	9.8	1957	FDE-11	18.0
1946	SD-15	16.0	1957	RD-19	35.0
1946	PO-15	22.0	1957	RDE-19	35.0

Year	Model	HP
1957	RJE-19	35.0
1958	JW-14	3.0
1958	CD-15	5.5
1958	AD-12	7.5
1958	QD-19	10.0
1958	FD-12	18.0
1958	FDE-12	18.0
1958	RD-19C	35.0
1958	RDE-19C	35.0
1958	RDS-20	35.0
1958	V4-10	50.0
1958	V4S-10	50.0
1959	JW-15	3
1959	CD-16	5.5
1959	QD-20	10
1959	FD-13	18
1959	RD-21	35
1959	RDS-21	35
1959	V4-11	50
1959	V4S-11	50
1960	JW-16	3
1960	CD-17	5.5
1960	QD-21	10
1960	FD-14	18
1960	RD-22	40
1960	RDS-22	40
1960	V4S-12	75
1961	JW-17	3
1961	CD-18	5.5
1961	QD-22	10
1961	FD-15	18
1961	RD-23	40
1961	RDS-23	40
1961	V4S-13	75
1961	V4A-13	75
1962	JW-17R	3
1962	CD-19	5.5
1962	QD-23	10
1962	FD-16	18
1962	RX-10C	28
1962	RD-24	40
1962	RDS-24	40
1962	RK-24	40
1962	V4S-14	75
1962	V4A-14	75
1963	JW-18	3
1963	CD-20	5.5
1963	QD-24	10
1963	FD-17	18
1963	RX-11	28
1963	RD-25	40
1963	RDS-25	40
1963	RK-25	40
1963	V4S-15	75
1963	V4A-15	75
1964	JW-19	3
1964	JH-19	3
1964	CD-21	5.5
1964	MQ-10	9.5
1964	FD-18	18
1964	RX-12	28
1964	RD-26	40
1964	RDS-26	40
1964	RK-26	40
1964	VX-10	60
1964	V4S-16	75
1964	V4A-16	75
1964	V4M-10	90

* J-65 1933 and all following motors are O.B.C. Certified Horsepower ratings.

Johnson Serial Numbers

PLEASE NOTE: Some of these serial numbers were actually stamped in motors produced very late in the year just previous to their true model year. For example, the 1953 Johnson, number 1,000,000, was built in November 1952.

Year	Numbers	
Very Late 1921	506 –	606
1922	606 –	3,930
1923	3,931 –	7,500
1924	7,501 –	20,000
1925	20,001 –	30,559
1926	30,560 –	44,977
1927	44,978 –	65,524
1928	65,525 –	96,408
1929	96,409 –	128,000
1930	128,001 –	152,777
1931	152,778 –	161,326
1932	161,327 –	167,430
1933	167,431 –	208,583
1934	208,584 –	219,371
1935	219,372 –	232,156
1936	232,157 –	252,675
1937	252,676 –	283,888
1938	283,889 –	315,166
1939	315,167 –	355,971
1940	355,972 –	397,900
1941	397,901 –	439,206
1942	439,207 –	460,782
1943–45*	460,783 –	491,736
1946	491,737 –	538,800
1947	538,801 –	614,514
1948	614,515 –	698,874
1949	698,875 –	787,023
1950	787,024 –	869,939 inclusive.
1951	869,940 –	920,479
1952	920,480 –	980,883
1953	980,884 – 1,079,711	
1954	1,079,712 – 1,194,192	
1955	1,194,193 – 1,328,372	
1956	1,328,373 – 1,493,185	
1957	1,493,186 – 1,660,474	
1958	1,660,475 – 1,743,080	
1959	1,743,081 – 1,995,465	
1960	1,995,611 – 2,105,657**	
1961	2,105,658 – 2,249,094	

* Most of this production figure was assigned to military use.
** It is not certain why there are 146 missing serial numbers between 1959-60.

Mercury. The KG9-1 motor was the first Merc 4 cylinder to wear a re-wind starter. Previous KG9 and KF9 models had an exposed, chrome flywheel. While no official verification exists, some KF9/KG9/KG9-1 Mercs might have red (instead of the usual cedar green) paint. I have seen some red rigs that appear to be factory original. (Some Merc accessory catalogs list "Mercury Red" paint.) A few advertisements picture shiny, chromed (or buffed aluminum) early 4-cylinder Mercury powerhead cowling.

Some sources identify Mercs with long, Quicksilver lower units as "QS" motors. The KG4H and similar Quicksilver models were probably available on a limited basis through the late 1950s.

Mercury 1940–55 motors typically take ⅜ pint of oil per gallon of gasoline; racing versions use ¾ pint. The 1956–62 Mercs get 6 ounces of oil per gallon of gas, while racers take 12 ounces. By 1963, Mercury went to a 50 to 1 oil/gas mix (12 ounces per 5 gallons of gasoline). Merc said 6 ounces of regular oil per gallon was OK in a pinch. Check with a Mercury dealer for the best mixture.

Most Mercs with breaker points accepted a .018" setting. Spark plug gap generally was .025 on pre-1960 rigs.

An asterisk (*) after an HP rating indicates "horsepower varies with engine revolutions per minute." Most early Merc literature, however, carried no RPM rating for the high speed motors.

About 1956, Merc replaced the standard Mark 20H short Quicksilver racing lower unit drive-shaft housing with a chubby, "howler" tuned exhaust piece, sometimes called the "toilet-bowl" lower unit. The original Mark 20H Carter carburetor was switched to a Tillotson model.

The Mark 58 Super Thunderbolt also was available as: 58S, with electric start; 58E, with electric start and generator; and 58EL, with electric start and generator and long shaft.

Mercury's 1959 motors may also be tagged with the following designations: L (longshaft), M (manual start), S (electric start), E (electric start and generator). Top of the line models with chrome top and bottom cowl strips and chrome front shield and handle were available. "Dynafloat" shock absorbers and a safety-tilt-up switch accessory were available on Mark 28A, 58A, and 78A.

Mercury

Year	Model	HP
1940	K1 / Special	2.5
1940	K2 / Standard	3
1940	K3 / Deluxe	3
1940	K4 / Alternate	6
1940	K5 / Alternate Deluxe	6
1941	KB1 / Comet	2.9
1941	KB1A / Comet Deluxe	3.1
1941	KB2 / Streamliner	3.2
1941–42	KB3 / Torpedo	3.2
1941–42	KB4 / Rocket	5.8
1941	KB-5 / Rocket Deluxe	6
1946	KB4-1 / Rocket	6
1946–47	KD3 / Comet	3.2
1946–47	KD4 / Rocket	6
1947	KD3S / Comet	3.2
1947	KD4S / Rocket	6
1947–48	KE3 / Comet Deluxe	3.6
1947–52	KE4 / Rocket Deluxe	7.5
1947	KE4A / Rocket Deluxe	6
1947–49	KE7 / Lightning Deluxe	10
1949–50	KF3 / Comet	3.5
1949–50	KF7 / Super 10	10
1949–50	KF7HD / Super 10 Heavy-Duty (racer)	10+
1949–50	KF7Q / Super 10 (w/long Quicksilver racing lower unit)	10+
1949–50	KF9 / Thunderbolt	25+*
1949–50	KF9Q / Thunderbolt (may also have been available in "HD" series)	25+*
1949–52	KF5 / Super 5	5
1950–52	KG4 / Rocket Hurricane	7.5+*
1950–52	KG4H / Rocket Hurricane (w/Quicksilver racing lower unit)	7.5+*
1950–52	KG7 / Super 10 Hurricane	10+*
1950–52	KG7H / Super 10 Hurricane (w/Quicksilver racing lower unit)	10+*
1950–52	KG7Q / Super 10 Hurricane (w/long Quicksilver racing lower unit)	10+*
1950–52	KG9 / Thunderbolt	25+*
1951	KG9-1 / Thunderbolt	25+*
1950–52	KG9Q / Thunderbolt (w/long Quicksilver racing lower unit) (Some sources call this motor the KG9QS.)	25+*
1952	KH7 / Cruiser (shift) (Also called Super 10 Hurricane Cruiser.)	10+*
1953–55	Mark 5 / (Also called Super 5.)	5
1953–55	Mark 7 / Rocket Deluxe	7.5
1953	Mark 15 / —	10
1953–55	Mark 20 / Hurricane	16
1953–54	Mark 40 / Thunderbolt	25+*
1953–55	Mark 40H / Thunderbolt (w/short Quicksilver racing lower unit)	25+*
1954–56	Mark 20H / Hurricane (w/short Quicksilver lower unit)	16+*
1954	Mark 50 / Thunderbolt	40
1954	Mark 50E / Thunderbolt MercElectric (electric start)	40
1955	Mark 6 / Comet (Silent Six)	5.9
1955	Mark 25 / Hurricane	18
1955	Mark 25E / Hurricane MercElectric (electric start)	18
1956–58	Mark 25 / Hurricane	20
1956–57	Mark 25E / Hurricane MercElectric	20
1955–58	Mark 55 / Thunderbolt	40
1955–58	Mark 55E / Thunderbolt MercElectric	40
1956–58	Mark 55H / Thunderbolt Hydro	40+*
1956–58	Mark 6 / Comet (Silent Six)	6
1956–58	Mark 30 / Turbo-Four	30
1956–58	Mark 30E / Turbo-Four MercElectric	30
1956–58	Mark 30H / Turbo-Four Hydro	30+*
1957–58	Mark 10 / Trol-Twin Rocket	10
1957–58	Mark 75 (E) / Marathon Six	60
1957–58	Mark 75H / Marathon Six Hydro	60+*
1958	Mark 28 / Super Hurricane	22
1958	Mark 58 / Super Thunderbolt	45

Year	Model	HP
1958	Mark 78E / Super Marathon Six (Also available w/longshaft and electric start as Mark 78EL)	70
1959	Mark 6A / Comet Silent Six	6
1959	Mark 10A / Trol-Twin Rocket	10
1959	Mark 15A / Rocket	15
1959	Mark 28A / Super Hurricane	22
1959	Mark 35A / Thunderbolt	35
1959	Mark 55A / Thunderbolt	40
1959	Mark 58A / Super Thunderbolt	45
1959	Mark 75A / Marathon Six	60
1959	Mark 78A / Super Marathon Six	70
1960	Merc 100 / (automatic transmission)	10
1960–61	Merc 150 / (automatic transmission)	15
1960–61	Merc 200 / (automatic transmission)	22
1960	Merc 300 / —	35
1960–61	Merc 400 / —	45
1960	Merc 600 / —	60
1960–61	Merc 700 / (direct-reverse)	70
1960–61	Merc 800 / (direct-reverse)	80
1961	Merc 800 / (gear shift)	80
1961–62	Merc 700 / (gear shift)	70
1961	Merc 500 / —	50
1961	Merc 350 / 4-Cylinder	40
1961–68	Merc 60 / —	6
1962–69	Merc 110 / —	9.8
1963–69	Merc 200 / (gear shift)	20
1962	Merc 250 / —	25
1963–65	Merc 350 / 2-Cylinder	35
1962	Merc 450 / —	45
1962–66	Merc 500 / "Jet-Prop"	50
1963–66	Merc 650 / —	65
1962	Merc 850 / (76 cubic inch version)	85
1963–64	Merc 850 / (90 cubic inch version)	85
1962–65	Merc 1000 / —	100
1964–68	Merc 39 / —	3.9
1968	Merc 60J / (w/small Quicksilver racing lower unit)	6
1965	Merc 900 / —	90
1966	Merc 950 / (also Merc 950SS in 66–67)	95
1966	Merc 1100 / (also Merc 1100SS in 1967)	110
1967	Merc 500S / (also 500M)	50
1967–69	Merc 500SS / —	50
1967	Merc 650S / —	65
1967–69	Merc 650SS / —	65
1968–69	Merc 1000SS / —	100
1666–69	Merc 350 / —	35
1968–69	Merc 1250SS / —	125
1968	Merc 1250BP / (w/racing lower unit equipped with shift)	125
1967–69	Merc 350 / —	35
1969	Merc 800 / (4-cylinder version)	80
1969	Merc 40 / —	4
1969	Merc 75 / —	7.5

Gale Products Private Brands.

Gale Products produced many motors that were marketed under more than one marque. Where two model numbers appear in the charts, the first is the customer's number; the second (after the slash mark) is Gale's own designation. Otherwise, only one model number applies.

Gale Products

Year	Model	HP
Western Auto "Western Flyer"		
1941–42	121W	2.5
1941–42	122W	2.5
1941–42	251W	5.0
1941–42	252W	5.0
Goodrich "Sea Flyer"		
1952	45-050 / 3D10	3
1951	64-180 / 5D10	5
1952	45-060 / 5D10	5
1952	45-070 / 12D10	12
Gamble Skogmo "Hiawatha"		
1948–49	840MI-25-7945A / 1H5	1.5
1941–42	25-S / 121	2.5
1941–42	25-DL / 122	2.5
1945–46	25-3258 / 131	3.0
1947	25-7955 / 1H1	3.0
1947	47-3S / 1H1	3.0
1947–48	25-7956 / 1H4	3.0
1948–49	840MI-25-7957A / 1H6	3.0
1949–50	050MI-25-7958A / 1H9	3.0
1941–42	50-S / 251	5.0
1941–42	50-DL / 252	5.0
1945–46	50-SA / 251A	5.0
1945–46	50-DLA / 252A	5.0
1947	47-5D / 2H2	5.0
1947	25-7970 / 2H2	5.0
1947–48	25-7971 / 2H3	5.0
1948	840MI-25-7972A / 2H7	5.0
1949–50	940MI-25-7972A / 2H7	5.0
1948	840MI-25-7980A / 2H8	12.0
1949–50	940MI-25-7980A / 2H8	12.0
1951	150MI-25-7959A / 3D10	3
1953	350MI-25-7959B / 3D10	3
1953	350MI-25-7959C / 3D11	3
1954	450MI-25-7959A / 3D11	3
1955	550MI-25-7959A / 3D11	3
1953	350MI-25-7972B / 5S10	5
1951	150MI-25-7973A / 5D10	5
1952	250MI-25-7973A / 5D10	5
1953	350MI-25-7973B / 5D10	5
1954	450MI-25-7973A / 5D10	5
1951	150MI-25-7981A / 12D10	12
1952	250MI-25-7981A / 12D10	12
1953	350MI-25-7981B / 12D10	12
1954	450MI-25-7982 / 12D11	12
1955	550MI-25-7982A / 12D11	12
Fedway "Saber"		
1953	3D10D / 3D10	3
1953	3D11D / 3D11	3
1953	5S10D / 5S10	5
1953	5D10D / 5D10	5
1953	12S10D / 12S10	12
1953	12D10D / 12D10	12
AMC "Saber"		
1955	3D12M / 3D12	3
1955	5S12M / 5S12	5
1955	5D11M / 5D11	5
1955	12D11M / 12D11	12

Year	Model	
1955	22D10M / 22D10	22
1955	22DE10M / 22DE10	22
1956	3D13M / 3D13	3
1956	5S12M / 5S12	5
1956	5D12M / 5D12	5
1956	5D13M / 5D13	5
1956	12D13M / 12D13	12
1956	22D11M / 22D11	25
1956	22D13M / 22D13	25
1956	22DE11M / 22DE11	25

Atlas "Royal"

Year	Model	
1948–49	1A5	1.5
1950	1A9	3.0
1947–48	2A3	5.0
1949–50	2A7	5.0
1948–50	2A8	12.0
1952–53	3D10A / 3D10	3
1953–55	3D11A / 3D11	3
1955	3D12A / 3D12	3
1953–54	5S10A / 5S10	5
1955	5S11A / 5S11	5
1951–54	5D10A / 5D10	5
1955	5D11A / 5D11	5
1953	12S10A / 12S10	12
1951–53	12D10A / 12D10	12
1954–55	12D11A / 12D11	12
1955	22D10A / 22D10	22
1955	22DE10A / 22DE10	22
1955	22D12A / 22D12	22
1955	22DE12A / 22DE12	22
1956	3D13A / 3D13	3
1956	5D12A / 5D12	5
1956	5D13A / 5D13	5
1956	12D13A / 12D13	12
1956	25D11A / 22D11	25
1956	25D13A / 22D13	25
1956	25DE11A / 22DE11	25
1956	25DE13A / 22DE13	25

Gale Products "Buccaneer"

Year	Model	
1950	1B10	1.5
1950	1B9	3.0
1950	2B7	5.0
1950	2B8	12.0
1951–53	3D10B / 3D10	3
1953–55	3D11B / 3D11	3
1955	3D12B / 3D12	3
1951–54	5S10B / 5S10	5
1955	5S11B / 5S11	5
1951–54	5D10B / 5D10	5
1955	5D11B / 5D11	5
1951–53	12S10B / 12S10	12
1951–53	12D10B / 12D10	12
1954–55	12D11B / 12D11	12
1955	22D10B / 22D10	22
1955	22DE10B / 22DE10	22
1955	22D12B / 22D12	22
1955	22DE12B / 22DE12	22
1956	3D13B / 3D13	3
1956	5S12B / 5S12	5
1956	5D12B / 5D12	5
1956	5D13B / 5D13	5
1956	12S12B / 12S12	12

Year	Model	
1956	12D13B / 12D13	12
1956	12D14B / 12D14	12
1956	12DE13B / 12DE13	12
1956	22D11B / 22D11	25
1956	22D13B / 22D13	25
1956	22DE11B / 22DE11	25
1956	22DE13B / 22DE13	25
1957	3D14B / 3D14	3
1957	5S13B / 5S13	5
1957	5D14B / 5D14	5
1957	12S13B / 12S13	12
1957	12D15B / 12D15	12
1957	12DE15B / 12DE15	12
1957	22D14B / 22D14	25
1957	22DE14B / 22DE14	25
1958	3D15B Deluxe	3
1958	5S14B Standard	5
1958	5D15B Deluxe	5
1958	12S15B Standard	12
1958	12D17B Deluxe	12
1958	22D15B Manual	25
1958	22DE15B Electric	25
1958	35DE10B Electric	35
1959	3D15B Deluxe	3
1959	5D16B Deluxe	5
1959	12D18B Deluxe	12
1959	22D16B Deluxe	25
1959	22DE16B Deluxe Electric	25
1959	35D11B Deluxe	35
1959	35D12B Deluxe	35
1959	35DE11B Deluxe Electric	35
1959	35DE12B Deluxe Electric	35
1960	3D16B Deluxe	3
1960	5D17B Deluxe	5
1960	15D10B Deluxe	15
1960	22D17B Deluxe	25
1960	22DE17B Deluxe Electric	25
1960	35D13B Deluxe	35
1960	35DE13B Deluxe Electric	35
1961	3D17B Deluxe	3
1961	5D18B, 5D19B, 5D21B Deluxe	5
1961	5DL18B, 5DL19B, 5DL21B	5
1961	15D11B, 15D12B Deluxe	15
1961	15DL11B, 15DL12B	15
1961	25D18B, 25D20B Deluxe	25
1961	25DL18B, 25DL20B	25
1961	25DE18B, 25DE20B Deluxe Electric	25
1961	25DEL18B, 25DEL20B	25
1961	40D14B Deluxe	40
1961	40DL14B	40
1961	40DE14B Deluxe Electric	40
1961	40DEL14B	40
1961	40DG14B	40
1961	40DGL14B	40
1962	3D18B Deluxe	3
1962	5D20B Deluxe	5
1962	5DL20B	5
1962	15D13B, 15D14B Deluxe	15
1962	15DL13B, 15DL14B	15
1962	25D19B Deluxe	25
1962	25DL19B	25
1962	25DE19B Deluxe Electric	25
1962	25DEL19B	25

1962	40D15B Deluxe	40
1962	40DL15B	40
1962	40DE15B Deluxe Electric	40
1962	40DEL15B	40
1962	40DG15B	40
1962	40DGL15B	40
1963	3D19B Deluxe	3
1963	5D22B Deluxe	5
1963	15D15B Deluxe	15
1963	15D15P	15
1963	15DL15B	15
1963	25D21B Deluxe	25
1963	25DL21B	25
1963	25DE21B Deluxe Electric	25
1963	25DEL21B	25
1963	40D17B Deluxe	40
1963	40DL17B	40
1963	40DE17B Deluxe Electric	40
1963	40DE17P	40
1963	40DEL17B	40
1963	40DG17B	40
1963	40DGL17B	40
1963	V-Sovereign	60

Spiegel "Brooklure"

1950	230-50-1 / 1S10	1.5
1950	230-50-3 / 1S9	3.0
1950	230-50-5 / 2S7	5.0
1950	230-50-12 / 2S8	12.0
1951–53	230-51-3D / 3D10	3
1953–55	230-51-3DA / 3D11	3
1955	230-51-3DB / 3D12	3
1951–54	230-51-5S / 5S10	5
1951–54	230-51-5D / 5D10	5
1955	230-55-5D / 5D11	5
1953	230-51-12S / 12S10	12
1951–53	230-51-12D / 12D10	12
1954	230-53-12D / 12D11	12
1955	230-55-22DS / 22D10	22
1955	230-55-22DE / 22DE10	22
1956	50T3341 / 3D13	3
1956	50T3342 / 5S12	5
1956	50T3343 / 5D12	5
1956	50T3343A / 5D13	5
1956	50T3344 / 12D13	12
1956	50T3345 / 22D11	25
1956	50T3346 / 22DE11	25
1957	50T3337 / 3D14	3
1957	50T3343B / 5D14	5
1957	50T3338 / 12D15	12
1957	50T3339 / 22D14	25
1957	50T3340 / 22DE14	25
1958	50Z3323 Deluxe	3
1958	50Z3324 Deluxe	5
1958	50Z3325 Deluxe	12
1958	50Z3326 Manual	25
1958	50Z3327 Electric	25

Goodyear "Sea Bee"

1948–49	025-3562 / 1G5	1.5
1949–50	025-3562A / 1G10	1.5
1945–46	025-3555 / 135A	3.0

1947	1G1	3.0
1947–48	1G4	3.0
1948–49	025-3563 / 1G6	3.0
1949–50	025-3566 / 1G9	3.0
1945–46	025-3550 / 256A	5.0
1947	2G2	5.0
1947–48	2G3	5.0
1948	025-3564 / 2G7	5.0
1949–50	025-3564A / 2G7	5.0
1948	025-3565 / 2G8	12.0
1949–50	025-3565A / 2G8	12.0
1951–53	025-3567 (3D10G) / 3D10	3
1953	025-3567 (3D11G) / 3D11	3
1954–55	025-3574 (3D11G) / 3D11	3
1955	25-3574 (3D12G) / 3D12	3
1951–54	025-3568 (5S10G) / 5S10	5
1955	025-3602 (5S11G) / 5S11	5
1951–53	025-3569 (5D10G) / 5D10	5
1954	025-3573 (5D10G) / 5D10	5
1955	025-3603 (5D11G) / 5D11	5
1951–53	025-3570 (12S10G) / 12S10	12
1951–53	025-3571 (12D10G) / 12D10	12
1954–55	25-3572 (12D11G) / 12D11	12
1955	25-3604 (22D10G) / 22D10	22
1955	25-3605 (22DE10G) / 22DE10	22
1955	25-3604 (22D12G) / 22D12	22
1955	25-3605 (22DE12G) / 22DE12	22
1956	225-3606 (3D13G) / 3D13	3
1956	225-3607 (5S12G) / 5S12	5
1956	225-3608 (5D12G) / 5D12	5
1956	225-3608 (5D13G) / 5D13	5
1956	225-3609 (12D13G) / 12D13	12
1956	225-3609 (12D14G) / 12D14	12
1956	225-3610 (22D11G) / 22D11	25
1956	225-3610 (22D13G) / 22D13	25
1956	225-3611 (22DE11G) / 22DE11	25
1956	225-3611 (22DE11G) / 22DE13	25
1957	225-3612 (3D14G) / 3D14	3
1957	225-3613 (5D13G) / 5S13	5
1957	225-3614 (5D14G) / 5D14	5
1957	225-3615 (12D15G) / 12D15	12
1957	225-3616 (22D14G) / 22D14	25
1957	225-3617 (22DE14G) / 22DE14	25
1958	3D15 G Code 225-3619 Deluxe	3
1958	5S14G Code 225-3620 Standard	5
1958	5D15G Code 225-3621 Deluxe	5
1958	12D17G Code 225-3622 Deluxe	12
1958	22D15G Code 225-3623 Manual	25
1958	22DE15G Code 225-3624 Electric	25
1958	35DE10G Code 225-3625 Electric	35
1959	3D15G Code 225-3619 Deluxe	3
1959	5D16G Code 225-3450 Deluxe	5
1959	12D18G Code 225-3451 Deluxe	12
1959	22D16G Code 225-3452 Deluxe	25
1959	22DE16G Code 225-3453 Deluxe Electric	25
1959	35D11G Code 225-3454 Deluxe	35
1959	35D12G Code 225-3454A Deluxe	35
1959	35DE11G Code 225-3455 Deluxe Electric	35
1959	35DE12G Code 225-3455A Deluxe Electric	35

	Montgomery Ward "Sea King"	
1948–49	84GG9003A / 1W5	1.5
1949–50	94GG9003B / 1W10	1.5
1941–42	24GG9351A / 125	2.5
1945–46	64GG9005 / 133	3.0
1947	74GG9005A / 1W1	3.0
1947–48	74GG9006 / 1W4	3.0
1948–49	84GG9007A / 1W6	3.0
1949–50	94GG9009A / 1W9	3.0
1941–42	14GG8826 / 253	5.0
1941–42	14GG8827 / 254	5.0
1945	54GG9010 / 253A	5.0
1945	54GG9011 / 254A	5.0
1946	64GG9010 / 253A	5.0
1946	64GG9011 / 254A	5.0
1947	74GG9011A / 2W2	5.0
1947–48	74GG9012 / 2W3	5.0
1948	84GG9014A / 2W7	5.0
1949–50	94GG9014A / 2W7	5.0
1948	84GG9017A / 2W8	12.0
1949–50	94GG9017A / 2W8	12.0
1951	15GG9004A / 3D10	3
1952	25GG9004A / 3D10	3
1953	35GG9004A / 3D10	3
1953	35GG9004B / 3D11	3
1954	45GG9004A / 3D11	3
1955	GG-9004A / 3D11	3
1955	GG-9004B / 3D12	3
1951	15GG9014A / 5S10	5
1953	35GG9014A / 5S10	5
1954	45GG9014A / 5S10	5
1955	GG-9001A / 5S11	5
1955	GG-9001B / 5S12	5
1951	15GG9015A / 5D10	5
1952	25GG9015A / 5D10	5
1953	35GG9015A / 5D10	5
1954	45GG9015A / 5D10	5
1955	GG-9013A / 5D11	5
1951	15GG9017A / 12S10	12
1953	35GG9017A / 12S10	12
1951	15GG9018A / 12D10	12
1952	25GG9018A / 12D10	12
1953	35GG9018A / 12D10	12
1954–55	GG-9016A / 12D11	12
1955	GG-9019A / 22D10	22
1955	GG-9020A / 22DE10	22
1955	GG-9019B / 22D12	22
1955	GG-9020B / 22DE12	22
1956	GG-9000A / 3D13	3
1956	GG-9001C / 5S12	5
1956	GG-9002A / 5D12	5
1956	GG-9002B / 5D13	5
1956	GG-9016B / 12S12	12
1956	GG-9021A / 12D13	12
1956	GG-9021B / 12D14	12
1956	GG-9024A / 12DE13	12
1956	GG-9022A / 22D11	25
1956	GG-9022B / 22D13	25
1956	GG-9023A / 22DE11	25
1956	GG-9023B / 22DE13	25
1957	GG-9006A / 3D14	3
1957	GG-9003A / 5S13	5

1957	GG-8960A / 5D14	5
1957	GG-9016C / 12S13	12
1957	GG-8971A / 12D15	12
1957	GG-9005A / 12DE15	12
1957	GG-9025A / 22D14	25
1957	GG-9026A / 22DE14	25
1958	GG-8962A Deluxe	3
1958	GG-8963A Standard	5
1958	GG-8977A Deluxe	5
1958	GG-8978A Standard	12
1958	GG-8981A Deluxe	12
1958	GG-8985A Manual	25
1958	GG-8992A Electric	25
1958	GG-8997A Electric	35
1959	GG8962B Deluxe	3
1959	GG8977B Deluxe	5
1959	GG8981B Deluxe	12
1959	GG8985B Deluxe	25
1959	GG8992B Deluxe Electric	25
1959	GG8942A Deluxe	35
1959	GG8942B Deluxe	35
1959	GG8997B Deluxe Electric	35
1959	GG8997C Deluxe Electric	35
1960	GG8804A Deluxe	3
1960	GG8822A Deluxe	5
1960	GG8823A Deluxe	15
1960	GG8834A Deluxe	25
1960	GG8835A Deluxe Electric	25
1960	GG8836A Deluxe	35
1960	GG8837A Deluxe Electric	35
1961	GG-18735A Deluxe	3
1961	GG-18736A, GG-18736B, GG-18736C Deluxe	5
1961	GG-18737A, GG-18737B Deluxe	15
1961	GG-18738A, GG-18738B Deluxe	25
1961	GG-18739A, GG-18739B	25
1961	GG-18740A, GG-18740B Deluxe Electric	25
1961	GG-18741A, GG-18741B	25
1961	GG-18742A Deluxe	40
1961	GG-18743A	40
1961	GG-18744A Deluxe Electric	40
1961	GG-18745A	40
1962	GG-18735B Deluxe	3
1962	GG-18736D Deluxe	5
1962	GG-18737C, GG-18737D Deluxe	15
1962	GG-18742B Deluxe	40
1962	GG-18743B	40
1962	GG-18744B Deluxe Electric	40
1962	GG-18745B	40
1963	GG-18800A Deluxe	3
1963	GG-18801A Deluxe	5
1963	GG-18802A Deluxe	15
1963	GG-18734C	15
1963	GG-18803A Deluxe	25
1963	GG-18804A Deluxe	40
1963	GG-18805A Deluxe Electric	40
1963	GG-18757P	40
1963	GG-18806A	40

Sears, Roebuck and Co. Pre-World War II Private Brands. Sears' oldest
outboards, the 1914–27 Motorgos, were one-lung

rowboat motors built by Lockwood-Ash. Early models had rudder steering. Some had flywheel magneto ignition, while less expensive styles fired via battery. All were about 2 hp. Late-30s Sears literature noted that "positive identification of these motors has been lost with the passing of years," so the ID numbers usually found on top of the cylinder assembly may not be of much use today.

In 1925, Sears catalogs carried standard-issue Johnson model A (catalog number 835), and model C (canoe mount, number 836) twins. No Sears ID appeared on these motors. Consequently, unless one has the original sales slip, identification of a 1925 Sears-Johnson is difficult. An April 1937 Sears information booklet describes these models as "outboard motors manufactured by Jacobsen Manufacturing Company, formerly Johnson Motors." The manual goes on to say that parts for such kickers should be ordered "from an authorized Johnson dealer, or direct from the Jacobsen Manufacturing Company of Racine, Wisconsin." Sears then states that parts lists for the Johnson models A and C are not available, and suggests that "sample parts be sent to Jacobsen to be duplicated." Since new/old stock Johnson A parts occasionally pop-up today, and were never impossible to find, such statements are puzzling. Furthermore, the claim that no Johnson parts lists existed in 1937 is very odd. And the Sears reference to a Johnson–Jacobsen Manufacturing Company relationship is one I cannot explain.

From 1928-32, Sears Motorgo outboards originated at the Caille Motor Company factory. (The 1931 Muncie Gear Works Motorgo was an exception.) Most Caille Motorgo models wore ID/serial numbers on the transom clamp bracket.

As a result of Caille's financial difficulties during the depression, Sears decided to purchase outboard products from Muncie Gear Works. The Sears Motorgo marque was continued until about 1934, when its kicker line was renamed "Waterwitch."

In 1936, Kissel Industries offered Sears outboard motors at prices they couldn't refuse. The giant retailer bought and sold gangs of these tiny eggbeaters, beginning with the 1936 Waterwitch model MB-10 single and MB-20 twin cylinder motors.

Year	Model / Sears Catalog Number	HP
	Caille Motorgo	
1928	Junior Twin / 5771-890	2¾
1929	Senior Twin / 5770	10
1930	Junior / 8206	6
1930	Senior / 8214	14
1930	Big Boy / 8220	20
1931–32	Junior / 7206	6
1931–32	Senior / 7214	14
1931–32	Big Boy / 7220	20
	Muncie Gear Works	
1931	Motorgo OB-2CD / Special	3
1931–32	Motorgo OB-3 / 7203	3
1933	Motorgo OB-4 / Special	4
1933	Motorgo OB-5 / 5805	5
1933–35	Motorgo Waterwitch OB-1 / 5802	2
1933–34	Motorgo Waterwitch OB-15 / 5816	15

1934	Waterwitch OB-31 / 5804	4
1935	Waterwitch OB-61 / 5805	6
1935	Waterwitch OB-32C / 5804	4
1935	Waterwitch OB-63 / 5806	6
1935–36	Waterwitch OB-16 / 5816	16
1936	Waterwitch OB-11 / Special	2
1936	Waterwitch OB-34 / Special	4
1936	Waterwitch OB-64 / Special	6
	Waterwitch (Kissel)	
1936–37	MB-10	2.5
1936	MB-20	4
1937	571.20	4
1938	571.21	4
1938	571.10	2.5
1938	571.30	¾
1938–40	550.75 (Johnson Waterwitch)	8.5
1939	571.31 (571.32)	¾
1939	571.11	2.5
1939	571.22	4.75
1940	571.33 (571.34 & 34A)	¾
1940	571.40	2.75
1940	571.12	3.5
1940	571.23	5.75
1941	571.35	1
1941	571.41 (571.42 & 43)	3
1941	571.13 (571.14)	3.5
1941	571.24	5.75
1941	571.50 (alternate firing twin)	10
1942	571.36	1
1942–45	571.44	3
1942	571.15	3.5
1942	571.26	5.75
1945	571.44W**	3

** Assembled by West Bend from new/old stock Kissel parts.

Caille.
Some true "gadgeteer's motors" sported this marque. Caille's background in slot machine manufacturing led them to produce outboards with interesting features like variable pitch propellers, dual carburetors/linkage, and tractor lower unit. (Because Caille props and related linkage were so complex, hitting a rock or other underwater obstruction could be costly.) Many Caille cylinders were fitted with "priming cups" for easier starting. One could pour a few drops of gas into the cup, open the spigot, and introduce fuel directly into the firing chamber. Multiflex (or Multi-Flex) was Caille's "multi-flexible control" handle, which facilitated steering, throttle setting, and propeller pitch adjustment.

The settings in a 5-Speed-model Caille were: reverse; neutral; trolling; low-speed forward; and high-speed forward.

Caille's "Red Head" trademark was made memorable by its logo: A pretty young woman's head, red hair streaming back, rising from a Caille-powered boat. Appropriately, these gas tanks were usually painted red.

A good Caille had a solid feel not present in many other brands. (Caille is pronounced "Kale.")

Caille

Year	Model	HP
1913	Rudder steered single without skeg	2
1914	Rudder steered single with skeg	2

Year	Model	HP
1915–25	Single cylinder 5-Speed (some had rewind start)	2
1916	Heavy single	3.5
1917–25	Neptune (Caille's bargain brand; regular & canoe versions)	2
1917–31	Liberty Single (direct drive prop shaft; slight variations during production run)	2
1924–28	Liberty Twin (direct drive prop shaft)	4
1925–27	Lightweight Twin 5-Speed (also called Pennant)	2¾
1927	Master Twin 5-Speed	4.5
1928	Junior Twin model 10 (also available in 5-Speed)	2¾
1928	Master Twin model 20	6
1928	Racer model 30	10
1929	5-Speed model 12	2¾
1929	5-Speed model 22 Master Twin	6
1929	Champion Racer model 34 (tractor lower unit)	14
1929	Commodore model 32	12
1929	Admiral model 42	18
1929	Flash Racer model 36 (tractor lower unit/dual carbs)	16.5
1929	Streak Racer model 46 (tractor lower unit/dual carbs)	22
1929	Monarch Racer model 44 (tractor lower unit)	20
1930	Master 14 Red Head (also "Companion" model 14*)	6
1930	Master Multiflex 15 (15A) Red Head	6
1930	Model 25 (Utility) Red Head	15
1930	Model 26 (Utility Multiflex) Red Head w/electric start	15
1930–32	Model 40 Racer (tractor lower unit/dual carbs)	17
1930	Model 45 (Utility) Red Head	21
1930	Model 47 (Utility Multiflex) Red Head w/electric start	21
1930–32	Model 50 Racer (tractor lower unit) Red Head	23
1930–35	Model 51 (Utility Multiflex) Red Head (also model 51A)	23
1931–35	Model 16 (Utility) Red Head	8
1931–35	Model 15 (Utility Multiflex) Red Head (1933 model 15A – 10HP)	8
1931–35	Model 27 (Utility) Red Head	15
1931–32	Model 28 (Utility) Red Head w/electric start	15
1931–35	Model 29 (Utility Multiflex) (also model 29A)	16
1931	Model 35 Racer (tractor lower unit/dual carbs)	12
1931–35	Model 48 (Utility) Red Head	21
1931–32	Model 49 (Utility) Red Head w/electric start	21
1932–35	Model 79 single ($79)	4
1934–35	Model 88 single	2¼
1934–35	Model 99 single	5½
1934–35	Model 109 single	2¼
1934–35	Model 119 single (also model 119A)	5½
1934–35	Model 129	10
1934–35	Model 144	10+
1934–35	Model 169 (also model 169A)	10+
1934–35	Model 197	16+
1934–35	Model 232 (also model 232A)	16+
1934–35	Model 249	23
1934–35	Model 296 (also model 296A)	23

* Companion Model 14 could be made more compact by removing two bolts on driveshaft housing, and separating lower unit from top of motor.

Champion. The point gap setting for Champion motors is generally .018". Most models use ½ pint of oil per gallon of gasoline. Hot Rod models take ¾ to 1 pint, depending on application. "Hydro-Drive" models featured a hydraulic fluid drive style lower unit transmission. Its "Magic-Wand" control lever could be positioned for propeller slippage, facilitating very accurate trolling speeds.

Champion

Year	Model	HP
1946–47	1J Standard Single	4.2
1946–47	2J Deluxe Single	4.2
1948	1K Standard Single	4.2
1948	2K Deluxe Single	4.2
1948	4K Twin	7.9
1949	1K	4.2
1949	2K	4.2
1949	4K	7.9
1949	4KS Special Racer	7.9
1950	1L	4.2
1950	2K	4.2
1950	2L-HD (Hydro-Drive)	4.2
1950	4K	7.9
1950	4L-HD (Hydro-Drive)	7.9
1950	4LS Special Racer	7.9
1951–52	1L	4.2
1951–52	2K	4.2
1951–52	2L-HD	4.2
1951	4K	7.9
1951–52	4L	8.5
1951–52	4L-HD	8.5
1951–52	4L-S Hot Rod	8.5
1953	2M	3.5
1953	3M-GS (Gear Shift)	5
1953	4M-GS	7.5
1953	4M-HD (Hydro-Drive)	7.5
1953	6M-GS	15
1953	6M-HD	15
1953	4M-HR Class "J" Hot Rod	7.5
1953	5M-HR Class "A" Hot Rod	----
1953	6M-HR Class "B" Hot Rod	15
1954	2MM	3.5
1954	3M-GS	5
1954	4M-GS	7.5
1954	4M-HD	7.5
1954	6M-GS	14
1954	6M-HD	15
1954	4M-HR Class "J" Hot Rod	----
1954	4M-HR "J" Hot Rod Midget w/extra small lower unit	----
1954	5M-HR	----
1954	6M-HR	----
1955	2MM	3.5
1955	3MM-GS Power Shift	5.5

Year	Model	HP
1955	4MM-GS Power Shift	7.5
1955	6MM-GS Power Shift	16.5
1955	6MS-GS (w/Mid-Ship controls)	16.5
1955	4MM-HR	----
1955	6MM-HR	----
1956	2N	4.2
1956	3N-S	6
1956	4N-D	7.8
1956	6N-D	16.5
1956	6N-MS (w/Mid-Ship controls)	16.5
1956	6N-HR Class "B" Hot Rod	----
1957–58	2N	4.2
1957–58	3N-S	6
1957–58	4N-D	7.8
1957–58	6N-D	16.5
1957–58	6N-MS	16.5
1957–58	T6N-MS Tandem 33 (this package consisted of twin 16.5-hp Champions)	33
1957–58	6N-HR Class "B" Hot Rod	----

Corsair.

Corsair outboards, built by Scott-Atwater, take ½ pint of oil per gallon of gasoline. Breaker point setting is .020".

Corsair

Year	Model	HP
1948	4820 (4821)	3.6
1948	4823	7.5
1949	4921	4
1949	4927	5
1949	4923	7.5
1950–51	5020 (5020-5120+ is 1951 version)	3.6
1950–51	5021 (5020-5121+ is 1951 version)	4
1950–52	5027 (5027-5127+ is 1951. 2725+ is 1952 motor)	5
1950–52	5023 (5023-5123+ is 1951. 2325+ is 1952 motor)	7.5
1950–52	5028 (5028-5128+ is 1951. 2825+ is 1952 motor)	10
1953	2735	5
1953	2335	7.5
1953	2835	10
1954	2745	5
1954	2345	7.5
1954	2845	10
1954	2945	16
1955	2755	5
1955	2355	7.5
1955	2855	10
1955	2955	16
1956	2765	5
1956	2365	7.5
1956	2965	16
1956	2665 (2665-3 if electric start)	30

Elgin (Sears, Roebuck and Co.).

The point gap setting for Elgin motors is .020". Most models use ½ pint of oil per gallon of gasoline; some pre-1952 models take ¾ pint.

Serial numbers are found immediately after the model numbers. A 1949–50 version of the 16-hp model was designated 571.5882. Elgin's "571" models were built by West Bend; "574s" came from McCulloch Corp.

Elgin

Year	Model	HP
1946	571.58301	1 ¼
1946	571.58401	2 ½
1946	571.58501	3 ½
1946	571.58601	5 ½
1947	571.58521	3 ½
1947	571.58611	5 ½
1947	571.58621	5 ½
1948	571.58521	3 ½
1948	571.58621	5 ½
1948	571.58721	6
1949	571.58541	5
1949	571.58731	7 ½
1950	571.58531	5
1950	571.58551	5
1950	571.58701	6
1950	571.58741	7 ½
1951	571.58561	5
1951	571.58641	6
1951	571.58751	7 ½
1951	571.58821	16
1951	571.58841	16
1952	571.58201	2
1952	571.58561	5
1952	571.58751	7 ½
1952	571.58822	16
1952	571.58842	16
1953	571.58202	2
1953	571.58562	5
1953	571.58642	6
1953	571.58761	7 ½
1953	571.58823	16
1953	571.58824	16
1953	571.58843	16
1953	571.58844	16
1954	571.58211	2
1954	571.58571	5
1954	571.58651	6
1954	571.58652	6
1954	571.58771	7 ½
1954	571.58772	7 ½
1954	571.58851	16
1955	571.58211	2
1955	571.58571	5
1955	571.58711	7 ½
1955	571.58772	7 ½
1955	571.58901	12
1955	571.59401	25
1956	571.58211	2
1956	571.5950	5 ½
1956	571.5970	7 ½
1956	571.5890	12
1956	571.5940	25
1956	571.5960 (electric start)	25
1957	571.58221	2
1957	571.58781	7 ½
1957	571.59521	5 ½

Year	Model	HP
1957	571.59721	7 ½
1957	571.58941	12
1957	571.58951 (longshaft)	12
1957	571.59421	30
1957	571.59431 (longshaft)	30
1957	571.59621 (electric start)	30
1957	571.59631 (electric start / longshaft)	30
1957	571.59801 (electric start / generator)	30
1957	571.59811 (electric start / generator / longshaft)	30
1958*	5823	2
1958	5953	5 ½
1958	5973	7 ½
1958	5978	7 ½
1958	5896	12
1958	5897 (longshaft)	12
1958	5893	12
1958	5944	35
1958	5945 (longshaft)	35
1958	5982 (electric start / 6 Amp generator)	35
1958	5983 (electric start / longshaft w/6 Amp generator)	35
1958	5990 (electric start w/20 Amp generator)	35
1958	5991 (electric start w/20 Amp generator and longshaft)	35
1959	571.5824	2
1959	571.5879 "Special Value Motor"	7 ½
1959	571.5954	5 ½
1959	571.5974	7 ½
1959	571.5898	12
1959	571.5899 (longshaft)	12
1959	571.5982 (electric start / generator)	35
1959	571.5983 (electric start / generator w/longshaft)	35
1959	571.5990 (electric start / generator)	35
1959	571.5991 (electric start / generator w/longshaft)	35
1959	574.6025	25
1959	574.6026 (longshaft)	25
1959	574.6027 (electric start / generator)	25
1959	574.6028 (longshaft)	25
1959	574.6040	40
1959	574.6041 (longshaft)	40
1959	574.6042 (electric start / generator)	40
1959	574.6043 (longshaft)	40
1959	574.6060 (electric start / generator)	60
1959	574.6061 (longshaft)	60

* 1958 model numbers may be preceded by "571."

Firestone.

Firestone's 1950s motors were made by Scott-Atwater. Some parts are interchangeable between the two marques.

All models generally use ½ pint oil per gallon of gasoline. Breaker point setting is .020".

Firestone

Year	Model	HP
1946	133-6-460 (also: -462, -463; -464 if rewind starter)	3.5
1947	133-7-476 (-477 if rewind starter)	3.5
1947	133-7-479	7.5
1948	133-8-486 (-487 if rewind starter)	3.5
1948	133-8-489	7.5
1949	10-A-1 (-2 if rewind starter)	3.6
1949	10-A-51	4
1949	10-A-52	5
1949	10-A-53	7.5
1950–55	10-A-71	3.6
1950	10-A-72	4
1950–53	10-A-73	5
1950–52	10-A-74	7.5
1950–52	10-A-75	10
1953–55	10-A-103	7.5
1953–55	10-A-104	10
1954–55	10-A-102	5
1954–55	10-A-105	16
1956–57	10-A-111	3.6
1956–57	10-A-112	5
1956–57	10-A-113	10
1956–57	10-A-114	16
1956	10-A-115 (-116 if electric start)	30
1957	10-A-117	35
1957	10-A-118 (w/electric start; -119 if longshaft)	35
1958	1085	3.6
1958	1785	5
1958	1885	10
1958	1985	16
1958	1685	38
1958	1316 (w/electric start; 1416 if longshaft)	38
1959	10-A-111	3.6
1959	10-A-112	5
1959	10-A-120	10
1959	10-A-114	16
1959	10-A-122 (w/electric start; -123 if longshaft)	39.1

Flambeau.

Flambeau's odd appearance set it apart from mainstream motors and made it, at best, a novelty. One used-outboard price guide estimated the 1955 trade-in value for a 1947–48 Flambeau at about five bucks! By 1958, the firm was defunct.

Flambeau rigs are difficult to date. They were a rare sight during their production run, and documentation is equally scarce. Furthermore, model numbers were not chronologically specific. I believe the seldom-changed numbers allowed "left-overs" to be sold for as long as it took to liquidate stock.

Some sources list a 3-hp Flambeau motor. A 10-horse prototype was developed in the early 1950s, but it never got into the showroom. Flambeaus produced from 1953 on usually are equipped with an anti-cavitation plate. Breaker point setting is .020". Oil/gas mix is ⅔ pint per gallon. Although spec sheets often indicate all 1950–56 models had rewind start, Flambeaus from that vintage have turned up without such a convenience. Rewind was an option (according to company literature) during 1946–49.

Flambeau

Year	Model	HP
1946–51	2.5-46-1 (not marketed in 1950)	2.5
1946–48	5-46-1	5

1949–56	174050	5
1949–54	174520	2.5
1955–56	125520	2.5

Hiawatha

Hiawatha. From 1946 to 1955, Hiawatha motors were built by Gale Products (see Gale Model/Year charts). By 1956, they were produced by Scott-Atwater.

Hiawathas have a .020" breaker point setting. The oil/gas mix is ½ pint per gallon.

Hiawatha

Year	Model	HP
1956	7960A / 4065+	3.6
1956	7970A / 4765+	5
1956	7985A / 4365+	7.5
1956	7995A / 4965+	16
1956	8005A / 4665+	30
1956	8006A / 4665-3+ (w/electric start)	30
1957	4075	3.6
1957	4775	5
1957	4375	7.5
1957	4975	16
1957	4675 (4675-3 if electric start)	35
1958	4085	3.6
1958	4785	5
1958	4385	7.5
1958	4885	10
1958	4985	16
1958	4685 (346+ if electric start)	38
1959	7960 / 140A+	3.6
1959	7987 / 4385+	7.5
1959	7992 / 4885+	10
1959	8001 / 145A+ (8002 / 345A+ if electric start)	25
1959	8015 / 4685+ (8016 / 346+ if electric start)	38
1959	8018 / 346A+	40

Lauson. Lausons have a 4-cycle powerhead; don't mix oil and gas. Breaker point gap is generally .020".

Lauson

Year	Model	HP
1947	OB-410	2.5
1948–49	S-300	3
1948–49	T-600	6
1950	S-350	3
1950	T-650	6
1951–52	T-651 (R if reverse)	6
1952	S-351	3
1953–56	S-353	3
1953–56	T-653	6
1953–55	T-653R (reverse gear)	6
1955–56	T653N (Neutral clutch)	6

Majestic and Voyager. These outboards were built by Champion. Some parts are interchangeable with those of the "parent" motors. Champion offered these kickers through a "blind," Minneapolis, Minnesota post office box, as well as wholesaling them to numerous sporting goods and chain store outlets. Consequently some owners may refer to their Majestic/Voyagers as products of a specific retailer.

Breaker point settings are .018". 1949–53 models (except 1953 M-3L-GS/V-3L-GS) use ¾ pint of oil per gallon of gasoline. All others take ½ pint. GS models featured a gear shift.

Majestic/Voyager

Year	Model	HP
1949–50	1MB / 1VB (1950–51)	4.2
1949–52	2MB (rewind start)	4.2
1949–52	4MB	7.9
1950–51	1MBB	4.2
1953	M-2L / V-2L	3.5
1953	M-4L-GS / V-4L-GS	8.5
1953–54	M-3L-GS / V-3L-GS	5.5
1954–55	M-2LL / V-2LL	3.5
1954–55	M-3LL-GS / V-3LL-GS	5.5
1954–55	M-4LL-GS / V-4LL-GS	7.5
1954–55	M-6LL-GS / V-6LL-GS	15
1956–58	M-2N / V-2N	4.2
1956–58	M-3N-GS / V-3N-GS	6
1956–58	M-4N-GS / V-4N-GS	7.8
1956–58	M-6N-GS / V-6N-GS	15

Martin. In 1951, Martin literature unveiled a 17-hp model 200. I do not know if any of these, aside from a pre-production motor, were put into circulation. Any reference to a 17-hp Martin is a "false start" notation.

EHA indicates motors with factory installed fuel pump and auxiliary Cruise-More tank; EHO indicates motors without fuel pump and tank. Some 200 models simply begin identification with the EH designation. There are also EHO engines with dealer or owner installed fuel pumps. Some read EHD or EHO3.

The 200 Silver Liner was to be a full shift version of the standard, forward-only 200. Although there is evidence of one being demonstrated, none have surfaced since then. The 1953 shift 200 is also questionable.

The 200-M differed from the standard motor in that a section of its underwater exhaust outlet was cut off, eliminating some exhaust restriction. It also had a streamlined, racing gearcase cap. A full race version called the 200-S had an underwater exhaust section which was 3 inches shorter. It was equipped with a fuel pump, fitted for a racing throttle cable, and wore a very pointy, streamlined gearcase nose cap.

Because items like fuel pump, racing exhaust, gearcase cap, and racing throttle linkage could be purchased as accessories, it is difficult to identify "factory-equipped" Martin racers.

Martins typically have a breaker point setting of .020". Specs for the 200 models, as well as most of the 60s and 75s, call for ¾ pint of oil per gallon of gasoline; others take ½ pint. Racers in the 200 series need 1¼ pints.

A few "leftover" Martin 60 Hi-Speed Racers were marketed in 1951.

Martin

Year	Model*	HP
1946	60 / 5,000	7.2
1947	40 / 5,000	4.5

1947	60 / 20,000	7.2
1948	20 / 5,000	2 1/3
1948	40 / 19,665	4.5
1948	60 / 69,083	7.2
1949	40 / 37,924	4.5
1949	60 / 93,374	7.2
1949	60 Hi-Speed	7.2+
1950	20 / 11,635	2 1/3
1950	40 / 44,987	4.5
1950	60 / C96,000	7.2
1950	60 Hi-Speed	7.2+
1950	66 / TC105,669	7.2
1950	100 / D5,000	10
1951	20 / 11,699	2 1/3
1951	45 / BB50,638	4.5
1951	75 / CB108,003	7.5
1951	100 / DA17,171	10
1951	200 Twist-Shift	17
1951	200 Hi-Speed, model P-T	17
1952	45 / BB58,635	4.5
1952	75 Twist-Shift / CC116,949	7.5
1952	100 Twist-Shift / DB18,901	10
1953	20 / A15,846	2 1/3
1953	45 / BB59,904	4.5
1953	75 Twist-Shift / CC152,469	7.5
1953	100 Twist-Shift / DB28,439	10
1953	200 Silver Streak / EHA-9,000	20
1953	200 Silver Streak / EHO-9,000	20
1953	200 (w/gear shift) (same as other 1953, 200)	20
1954	20	2 1/3
1954	45	4.5
1954	75	7.5
1954	100	10
1954	200 Standard Silver Streak	20
1954	200 Silver Liner	20
1954	200-M	20
1954	200-S	20

* Number after slash is serial number for first motor that year.

Muncie/Neptune.
The breaker point setting for these motors is .015" for pre-1947 models. Others had a .020" factory breaker point setting. Oil/gasoline mixtures are as follows: 9.5, 10, and 1949 10.5-horse motors take 1 pint per gallon. All other 1945–49 models use 2/3 pint. Model AA6 takes 3/4 pint, as does AA2. Remaining 1950–56 motors accept 2/3 pint per gallon. The Mighty-Mite kickers run well on 1/2 pint.

Muncie/Neptune

Year	Model	HP
1945–46	15A1 (Neptune) / 15B1 (Muncie)	1.5
1945–46	15B2	2
1945–46	15A3 (also 15AA3 in Deluxe style)	3.5
1945–46	15B4 (Muncie)	4
1945–46	15A6 (also 15AA6 in Deluxe version)	6
1945–46	15A9 (also 15AA9)	9.5
1947	17A1	1.5
1947	17A2	2
1947	17A3	3.5
1948–51	A1 (Available in 1948 as B1 without motor cowling)	1.7

1948–49	A2	3.3
1948–51	AA2	3.3
1948–51	AA4	5
1948–51	AA6	7
1948–51	AA10 (10 HP rating in 1948)	10.5
1952–53	(no motors produced)	
1954–56	AA1 (Some A1 "leftovers" sold)	1.7
1956–59	AA1-A (Mighty-Mite)	1.7

Oliver.
All models have a breaker point setting of .018" except the 1957s which have a .020" setting. All 1955–56 motors use 1/2 pint oil per gallon of gas; others use 3/8 pint, except models J3, J-4, J5, and J-5L, which take 1/2 pint.

The 5.5-, 6-, 15-, and 16-HP models have similarities to the Chris-Craft outboards they replaced.

Oliver

Year	Model	HP
1955	J (Some designated 55-J)	5.5
1955	K (Some designated 55-K)	15
1956	J2	5.5
1956	K2 (K2E if electric start)	15
1957	J3	6
1957	K3 (K3E if electric start)	16
1957	B	35
1958	J-4	6
1958	K-4 (K-4E if electric start)	16
1958	B-2	35
1959	J-5 (J-5L if longshaft)	6
1959	K-5 (K-5E if electric start; K-5L if longshaft)	16
1959	B-3 (B-3L if longshaft)	35
1959	B-3CR (Two 35-hp motors sold as package; B-3CRL if motors are longshaft)	70*

* Combined HP rating. Twins factory equipped with counter rotating props.

B.F. Goodrich Sea Flyer.
Sea Flyers from 1951–52 were built by OMC's Gale Products; 1953–54 models came from Champion Outboard Company. Gale Sea Flyers use 1/2 pint oil per gallon. Their breaker point setting should be .020". Champion-made Sea Flyers have a .018" breaker point setting. The 1953, 3.5- and 8.5-horse motors use 3/4 pint oil per gallon of gas; others take 1/2 pint.

B.F. Goodrich Sea Flyer

Year	Model	HP
1951–52	5D10	5
1952	3D10	3
1952	12D10	12
1953	G-2L	3.5
1953	G-3L-GS*	5.5
1953	G-4L-GS*	8.5
1954	G-3LL	5.5
1954	G-3LL-GS*	5.5
1954	G-4LL-GS*	7.5
1954	G-6LL-GS*	15

* Gear shift model.

Scott-Atwater.

On many Scott-Atwater motors, the serial number follows the model number.

Point setting is .020″. Fuel mixture is generally ½ pint oil per gallon of gasoline; 1959 models use ⅜ pint.

Scott-Atwater

Year	Model	HP
1946	461	3.6
1946	467	3.6
1947	470	3.6
1947	471	3.6
1947	473	7.5
1948	480	3.6
1948	481	3.6
1948	483	7.5
1949	480*	3.6
1949	481*	3.6
1949	483*	7.5
1949	491 Shift	4
1949	497 Shift	5
1949	493 Shift	7.5
1950	500	3.6
1950	501	4
1950	507	5
1950	503	7.5
1950	509	16
1951	510 (non-shift) "1-12"	3.6
1951	511 "1-14"	4
1951	517 "1-16"	5
1951	513 "1-20"	7.5
1951	518 "1-25"	10
1951	519 "1-30"	16
1952	3025 "1-12" (non-shift)	3.6
1952	3725 "1-16"	5
1952	3325 "1-20"	7.5
1952	3825 "1-25"	10
1952	3925 "1-30"	16
1953	3035 (non-shift)	3.6
1953	3735	5
1953	3335 Gold Pennant Motor	7.5
1953	3835 Gold Pennant Motor	10
1953	3935	16
1954	3045	3.6
1954	3745 Bail-A-Matic	5
1954	3345 Bail-A-Matic	7.5
1954	3845 Bail-A-Matic	10
1954	3945 Bail-A-Matic	16
1955	3055	3.6
1955	3755	5
1955	3355	7.5
1955	3855	10
1955	3955	16
1955	3655 (Also available w/electric start)	30
1956	3065 Sportster	3.6
1956	3765	5
1956	3365	7.5
1956	3865	10
1956	3965	16
1956	3965-3 (electric start)	16
1956	3665	33
1956	3665-3 (electric start)	33
1957	3075	3.6
1957	3775 ("-2" suffix if longshaft)	5
1957	3375 ("-2" suffix if longshaft)	7.5
1957	3875 ("-2" suffix if longshaft)	10
1957	3975 ("-2" suffix if longshaft)	16
1957	3975-3 (electric start; "-4" if longshaft)	16
1957	3675 ("-2" suffix if longshaft)	40
1957	3675-3 (electric start; "-4" if longshaft)	40
1957	3675-5 Royal Scott ("-6" if longshaft)	40
1958	3085 Scotty	3.6
1958	3785 (1237 if longshaft)	5
1958	3385 (1233 if longshaft)	7.5
1958	3855 (1238 if longshaft)	10
1958	3985 (1239 if longshaft)	16
1958	135 (235 if longshaft)	22
1958	335 (w/electric start / generator; 435 if longshaft)	22
1958	3685 (1236 if longshaft)	40
1958	1336 (w/electric start / generator; 1436 if longshaft)	40
1958	1536 (w/electric start / generator; 1636 if longshaft)	40
1958	332 (w/electric start / generator; 432 if longshaft)	60
1959	130A	3.6
1959	137A	5
1959	133A	7.5
1959	138A	10
1959	135A (235A if longshaft)	25
1959	335A (w/electric start / generator; 435A if longshaft)	25
1959	136A (236A if longshaft)	40
1959	336A (w/electric start / generator; 436A if longshaft)	40
1959	536A (w/electric start / generator; 636A if longshaft)	40
1959	332A (w/electric start / generator; 432A if longshaft)	60

*Leftover 1948 non-shift models.

West Bend.

Pre-1955 West Bend-labeled motors were built for the export market. The 2-hp model has an air-cooled powerhead. West Bend outboards typically use ½ pint oil per gallon of gasoline. Breaker point setting is .020″. Some West Bend components are interchangeable with Sears Elgin motors.

West Bend

Year	Model	HP
1955–56	160211	2
1955	160571	5
1955	160772	7.5
1956	160501	5.5
1956	160701	7.5
1956	160902	12
1956	1609403	25
1957	160221	2
1957	160521 (160531 if longshaft)	6
1957	160721 (160731 if longshaft)	8
1957	160941 (160951 if longshaft)	12

1957	160421 (160431 if longshaft)	30
1957	160621 (w/electric start; 160631 if longshaft)	30
1957	160801 (electric start w/generator; 160811 if longshaft)	30
1958	280	2
1958	680 (681 if longshaft)	6
1958	880 (881 if longshaft)	8
1958	1280 (1281 if longshaft)	12
1958	3580 (3581 if longshaft)	35
1958	3582 (w/electric start; 3583 if longshaft)	35
1958	3584 (w/electric start / standard generator; 3585 if longshaft)	35
1958	3586 (w/electric start and Super Alternator/Generator; 3587 if longshaft)	35
1959	290	2
1959	690 (691 if longshaft)	6
1959	890 (891 if longshaft)	8
1959	1290 (1291 if longshaft)	12
1959	1690 (1691 if longshaft)	16
1959	3594 (3595 if longshaft)	35
1959	3598 (w/electric start / generator; 3599 if longshaft)	35
1959	4090 (4091 if longshaft)	40
1959	4096 (w/electric start / generator; 4097 if longshaft)	40

Wizard.

During the summer of 1963, the Kiekhaefer Corp. released a chart linking various Mercury outboards with the Wizard motors it built for Western Auto. Many Mercury dealers were unhappy that the less expensive, private-brand Wizard line shared so many Mercury characteristics. Kiekhaefer claimed that "Wizard outboards do not incorporate all the features of Mercury Outboard Motors, nor are all the parts interchangeable"; but there were enough similarities to warrant compilation of the following table.

Wizard	Mercury
WA2	K1
WA3	K2
WA6	K4 – K5
WB2	KB1
WB3	K2 – KB2 – KB3
WB4	KB4
WB6	KB5
WD3	KD3
WD3S	KD3S
WD4	KD4
WD4S	KD4S
WF4 – WG4	KD4
WF7	KE7 – KF7
WG7 – WG7A	KG7
WH7	KH7
WH6 – WH6A	Mark 6
WK7	Mark 20* – Mark 20**
WJ7 – WM7	Mark 20* – KG7**
WM7A	Mark 25* – KG7**
WN7 – WN7A	Mark 25*
WA25 – WA25E	Mark 30 – Mark 30E

* Type Powerhead
** Type Lower Unit

Breaker point setting for Wizard motors is .018", except .010" for the 1956–57, 25-hp motor, and .020" for 1959 models. The 1959 line requires ½ pint oil per gallon of gasoline. The 1955–58s (except the 1958, 5.5-horse outboard) take ⅜ pint per gallon. Wizards from 1947–54 like ¾ pint, while the oldest, 1946 Wizards use ½ pint oil to each gallon of gasoline. Any Mercury-built Wizard on a Quicksilver racing lower unit should get greater lubricating consideration.

Because many Western Auto stores were owned and operated independent of the Western Auto parent organization, some leftover Wizards may have been locally marketed a few years after their actual model year.

Wizard

Year	Model	HP
1946	WD-3	3.2
1946	WD-4	6
1947–48	WD-3S	3.2
1947–48	WD-4S	6
1949–50	WF-4	6
1950	WF-7	10
1951–54	WG-4	6
1951–53	WG-7	10
1952–53	WH-7	10
1953	WG-7A	10
1954	WJ-7	10
1954	WK-7	12
1955–56	WH-6	5
1955	WM-7	10
1955	WN-7	12
1956–57	WM-7A	10
1956–57	WN-7A	12
1956–57	WA-25 (WA-25E if electric start)	25
1957	WH-6A	5
1957	Powermatic 15 (OC-1575)	15
1958	OC-585	5.5
1958	OC-1585	15
1958	OC-3585 (OC-3585E if electric start)	35
1959	MLM-6903A	3.6
1959	MLM-6907A	7.5
1959	MLM-6910A	10
1959	MLM-6925A	25
1959	MLM-6940A (MLM-6941A if electric start)	40

Appendix B

Outboard Motor Spark Plug Chart

The Champion Spark Plug Company has been catering to outboard motor applications for decades. The following lists identify such plugs, and which engines they fit. Listings from 1954 through 1970 are included herein. They cover most every model. Brands on the chart, not otherwise handled in this book (such as Boatimpeller, Anzani-Pilot, etc.) are typically of foreign manufacture.

Champion Outboard Spark Plugs by Heat Range

THREAD SIZE	HEAT RANGE	OUTBOARD TYPES	THREAD SIZE	HEAT RANGE	OUTBOARD TYPES
14mm ⅜″ Reach	HOT ⬆ ⬇ COLD	J-12J...... J-11J...... J-8J...... J-7J...... J-6J...... J-62R...... J-4J...... J-57R...... J-2J......	14mm ½″ Reach	HOT ◆ COLD	L-9J...... L-7J...... L-4J......
14mm Surface Gap ⅜″ Reach ½″ Reach ½″ Reach ¾″ Reach	....	J-19V...... L-20V...... L-19V...... N-19V......	14mm ¾″ Reach	HOT ⬆ ⬇ COLD	....
14mm ⅜″ Reach Bantam Type	HOT ⬆ ⬇ COLD	CJ-14...... CJ-11...... CJ-8...... CJ-6...... CJ-4......	18mm ½″ Reach **⅝″ Reach	HOT ⬆ ⬇ COLD	D-16J...... K-15J...... D-9J......
14mm ⅜″ Reach Special*	HOT ◆ COLD	....	⅞″-18	HOT ⬆ ⬇ COLD	....

OUTBOARD ENGINES

(1970)

MODEL	PLUG	GAP
AERO MARINE 4 h.p.	J-14Y	.035
5 h.p.	H-10J	.035
7½ h.p.	CJ-8	.035
AIRBOY (Air Propeller) Mdl. 20, 40	J-8J	.030
Model 50	J-6J	.030
ANZANI Pilot (British)	L-10	.020
APACHE J-5	TJ-8J	.030
J-9	J-12J	.030
BOATIMPELLER	D-9	.020
BRITISH SEAGULL All	D-21	.020
BROOKLURE All	J-6J	.030
BUCCANEER All mdls. thru '59	J-6J or J-4J	.030
For later models see Gale		
BUNDY 1961 models	J-6J	.025
All others	L-86	.025
CAILLE 35, 40, 45, 50	K-60R	.016
All other 18mm Heads	UD-16	.025
All ⅞" Heads	W-14	.025
CAL-JET Jetmaster	H-4	.030
Econojet, Ramjet	J-8J	.030
CHAMPION A, 1B, R1C, S1C, S1D	D-16	.025
2B, 3B, D1C, D1D, D3D, S2C, S2D	D-16	.025
D2C, D2D, D1E, S1E, 1J, 2J, 1K, 2K, 4K, 1L, 4L, 2M, 2L-HD, 4L-HD, B1F, D1F, D2F, S1F, S2F, 2G, M2G, 2H, 2MM, 2N	D-16	.030
3G, 1H, 3H, M1G, D1G, S1G	H-10J	.025
D4G, M4G, S4G	H-10J	.025
4KS, 4LS, 4LS-1X (Normal)	D-6	.030
(Racing)	K-60R	.020
4KS (Normal)	D-9	.030
(Racing)	K-60R	.020
3M-GS, 4M-GS, 3MM-GS, 4MM-GS, 3N-S, 4N-D	J-7J	.030
4M-HR, 6M-HR, 4MM-HR, 6MM-HR	J-62R	.020
6M-GS, 6MS-GS, 6MM-GS, 6M-D, 6N-MS	J-8J	.030
6N-HR	K-60R	.020
CHIEF J-5	TJ-8J	.030
J-9	J-12J	.030
CHRIS-CRAFT All	J-8J	.028
CHRYSLER All 3½ h.p.	H-8J	.030
1967 6 h.p.	H-10J	.030
1967 Models 9.2, 20, 35, 45, 50, 75, 100	J-4J	.030
1968-'70 Models 4.4, 5, 6.6, 7, 9.9, 20, 35, 45 h.p.	L-4J	.030
1968-'70 70, 75, 85, 105, 120, 135 h.p., w Magnapower Ign.	L-20V	—
55 h.p. w/Magnapower Ign	L-20V	—
All other 55 h.p. models	L-4J	.030
CLINTON J-7, J-8	H-10J	.030
J-9	J-12J	.030
J-5	TJ-8J	.030
BJ9, AJ9, J-200, J-350, J-500, J-700	CJ-8	.030
COMMANDO All models	J-11	.025
COMMODORE 2 h.p.	H-10J	.030
7½, 10 h.p.	H-8J	.030
18, 40 h.p.	J-4J	.030
CORSAIR All 3.6, 4, 5, 7½ h.p. mdls	H-10J	.035
1950-'52 10 h.p.	CJ-8	.035
1953-'56 10 h.p.	H-10J	.035
All 16 h.p. models	D-9J	.035
1956 (30 h.p.)	J-6J	.030
CROFTON	J-6J	.025
CROSS 563-S	D-9J	.020
582-R	K-57R	.015
Radial & All others	UD-16 or D-16	.025
ECLIPSE thru 1936	J-8J	.025
1937 thru 1942	H-10J	.025
ELGIN 58201, 58202 (2 h.p.), 58401 (2½ h.p.), 58561, 58562, 58571, 58651 (5 h.p.), 58641, 58642, 58652 (6 h.p.), 58851, 58821 thru 58824, 58841, 58843, 58844 (16 h.p.)	J-12J	.050
58231, 58250 (2 h.p.), 58501 thru 58551, 58601 thru 58621, 58701 thru 58731, 58741 (7½ h.p.), 58751, 58761, 58772 (7½ h.p.), 58211, 58771 (7½ h.p.), 58711, 58221, 5833 (2 h.p.), 58781 (7½ h.p.)	J-11J	.050

MODEL	PLUG	GAP
ELGIN—Continued		
58321, 58331, 58241 & 59241 (2 h.p.); 6001, 58563, 59501, 59521, 59541 (5.5 h.p.) 6002, 6003 (3½ h.p.); 6006 (6 h.p.); 6009, 6010 (7½ h.p.)	H-10J	.030
59701, 59721, 59731, 58741, 59741, 59751, 58791, 58341, 59791 (7.5 h.p.); 59011 (8 h.p.); 59891 (10 h.p.); 58902, 58912, 58941, 58961, 58971, 58951, 58801, 58891, 59561, 59881, 58991, (12 h.p.); 59601, 59861, 59871, (25 h.p.); 59421, 59431, 59621, 59631, 59801, 59811, (30 h.p.); 59402, 59403, 59412, 59413, 59441, 59451, 59831, 59821, 59901, 59911, (35 h.p.)	H-8J	.030
6012 (12 h.p.); 6025, 6028, 6032 (25 h.p.); 6040, 6043-6047 (40 h.p.); 6060-6063 (60 h.p.); 6013, 6014, 6015, 6069 (14 h.p.); 6033, 6035 (27.7 h.p.); 6034, 6036, 6037, 6038 (28 h.p.)	J-6J	.035
59661, 59671 (18 h.p.); 594001, 594011, 594021, 594031, 59461, 59471 (40 h.p.); 6070 (28 h.p.)	J-4J	.030
6005 (6 h.p.); 6008 (7½ h.p.); 6068 (6 h.p.); 6060, 6061 (7½ h.p.)	H-10J	.035
6052, 6053 (43.7 h.p.); 6072, 6073 (75.2 h.p.); 6054, 6055, 6056, 6057 (45 h.p.); 6074, 6075, 6076, 6077 (75 h.p.)	J-4J	.035
60900 (2 h.p.); 6092 (3½ h.p.)	TJ-8J*	.030
*Engs. without Spec. Connector use CJ-8		
6091 (3½ h.p.); 6066, 6067 (9 h.p.)	CJ-8	.030
6062, 6063 (45 h.p.); 6064, 6065 (75 h.p.)	UJ-17V	—
ELGIN (Canada) 6 h.p.	H-10J	.030
3½, 7½, 12, 30 h.p.	H-8J	.030
9.2, 20, 45, 50, 80 h.p.	J-4J	.030
ELTO Foldlight (2¾ h.p.)	K-15J	.025
Fisherman, Lightwin, Imperial Service "A", Super "A"	K-15J	.025
Fleetwin (8.5 h.p.), Senior Speedster (13.7 h.p.)	K-15J	.025
Single, Super Single (2.2 h.p.)	K-15J	.025
Big Quad, Speeditwin, Super "C", Senior & Junior Quad	D-9J	.025
Handifour, Lightfour, Imperial	D-9J	.025
Spec. Speedster (9 h.p.)	UD-16 or D-16	.025
Speedster 1949 (12 h.p.), Sportster (5 h.p.)	J-6J	.025
ELTO (Canada) after 1949 - Except C2E7 & C2E8	J-6J	.030
C2E7, C2E8	J-6J	.025
ESKA 300	J-11J	.030
400, 1703, 1713 (3.5 h.p.), 1183, 1185, 1187, 1193, 1195, 1197	J-8J	.030
1705, 1715 (5 h.p.)	J-6J	.030
1707, 1717 (7 h.p.)	UJ-10Y	.030
500, 600	CJ-8	.035
Models using Clinton J-5 Eng.	TJ-8J*	.030
*Engs. without Spec. Connector use CJ-8		
EVINRUDE Big Four 1946-'50 (50 h.p.)	K-60R	.020
Big Twin '51-'55 (25 h.p.), Fleetwin 1950-'58 (7½ h.p.), Fastwin '50-'52 (14 h.p.), '55-'57 (15 h.p.), Super Fastwin '53-'54, Lightwin '52 (5.2 h.p.), Sportsman '48-'51 (1½ h.p.) Sportwin '48-'51 (3.3 h.p.)	J-6J	.030
Big Twin '56-'70 (30-40 h.p.), 1969-'70 Sportster (25 h.p.), Speeditwin '62-'64 (28 h.p.), Lark '56-'70 (30-40 h.p.), Four-Fifty (50 h.p.), Starflite (75 h.p.), Speedifour '63-'67 (75 h.p.), Sportfour '64-'67 (60 h.p.), Ski Twin '66-'70 (33 h.p.)	J-4J	.030
Starflite '64-'65 (90 h.p.)	J-4J	.030
Starflite '66-'67 (80-100 h.p.)	J-4J	.030
Models w CD Ignition: Speedifour 85, Sportfour 65, Starflite 85, Starflite 100S, Starflite 115S, Triumph, X115 (55-115 h.p.)	L-19V	—
Speeditwin '50-'52 (22½ h.p.)	D-9J	.030
Fastwin '58-'70 (18 h.p.), Ducktwin (3 h.p.), Lightwin '53-'70 (3-4 h.p.), Fisherman '56-'70 (5½-6 h.p.), Sportwin '56-'70 (10 h.p.), Mate (1½ h.p.), Angler '65-'68 (5 h.p.), Yachtwin '64-'70 (3-4 h.p.)	J-6J or J-4J	.030

MODEL	PLUG	GAP
EVINRUDE—Continued		
Light Four (9.7 h.p.), Speedifour 18mm Head	D-9J	.025
Ranger (1.1 h.p.)	H-10J	.025
Zephyr (5.5 h.p.)	J-6J	.025
Acquanaut (Diving Unit)	CJ-14	.025
FAGEOL 44	J-6 or J-6J	.025
FIRESTONE All 3.6, 4, 5, 7½ h.p. mdls	H-10J	.035
1950-'52 10 h.p.	CJ-8	.035
1953-'56 10 h.p.	H-10J	.035
All 16 h.p. models	D-9J	.035
1956 30 h.p.	J-6J	.035
1960-'62 models (2 h.p.)	H-10J	.030
7½, 8, 12, 25, 30 h.p.	H-8J	.030
40 h.p.	J-4J	.030
1966 Featherweight 5	J-12J	.030
FISHER-PIERCE Bearcat 55	J-6	.025
FLAMBEAU Single (2.5 h.p.), Twin (5 h.p.)	J-8J	.025
FOREMOST 3½ h.p.	H-8J	.030
6 h.p.	H-10J	.030
9.2 h.p.	J-4J	.030
GALE Buccaneer 3, 5, 5.5, 12, 15, 25 h.p.	J-6J or J-4J	.030
Buccaneer 35, 40, 60 h.p., Sovereign 35, 40, 60 h.p.	J-4J	.030
GULF QUEEN	J-12J	.030
GUPPY	J-8J	.030
HARTFORD All models	UD-16 or D-16	.020
HIAWATHA thru 1949	J-7J	.030
1950 thru 1955	J-6J	.030
1956-'62 3, 3.6, 5, 6, 7½ h.p.	H-10J	.035
1956-'60 16 h.p.	D-9J	.035
1956 30 h.p., 1957 35 h.p.	J-6J	.030
1958-'62 12, 25 h.p.	J-6J	.035
1958-'62 38, 40 & 60 h.p.	J-4J	.035
HOMELITE (4-cycle)	J-6	.025
INDIAN All models	UD-16 or D-16	.025
JOHNSON 1969-'70 Models:		
115, 85, 60, 55 h.p.	L-19V	—
40, 33, 25 h.p.	J-4J	.030
20, 9½, 6, 4, 1½ h.p.	J-6J or J-4J	.030
A & AA Series (2-4½ h.p.); BN; F70, F75 (3.3 h.p.); J25 to J75 (1½ h.p.); OA55 to OA65 (3 h.p.); SD20 (16 h.p.); 200, 210 (3.3 h.p.); K50 to K70 (8-9 h.p.); K75, K80, KA37, KA38 (8-9 h.p.); KA10, KA39, KD15, KS15 (9-10 h.p.); SD10, SD15 (16 h.p.), P30 (6 h.p.)	D-9J	.030
AD Series (7½ h.p.); CD Series (5½-6 h.p.); FD, FDE, FDEL, FDL Series (15-20 h.p.); HD Series (2½ h.p.); JH & JW Series (3 h.p.); LD (5 h.p.); MD20, MS20 (1½ h.p.); MQ Series (9½ h.p.); QD, QDL Series (10 h.p.); SC (1½ h.p.); TD, TN, TS Series (5 h.p.)	J-6J or J-4J	.030
RD, RDE, RDEL, RDL, RDSL, RDS, RJ, RJE, RJEL, RK, RKL, RX Series (25-40 h.p.); V4, V4H, V4A, V4AL, V4S, VX, VXH, VXL Series (50-75 h.p.)	J-4J	.030
1964-'65 V4M (90 h.p.)	J-4J	.030
1966 V4ML Golden Meteor V-100	J-4J	.030
AT10 to AT39 (5 h.p.); DS37, DS38 (2 h.p.); DT10 to DT39 (5 h.p.); HA10 to HA39 (2½ h.p.); HD, HS Series (2½ h.p.); J-80 (1.7 h.p.); LS37, LS38 (2 h.p.); LT10 to LT39 (5 h.p.); MD, MS Series (1½ h.p.); 100, 110 (1.7 h.p.); 300 (3.7 h.p.)	J-8J	.030
K35 (6-7 h.p.); PO15 1949-'50 mdls. (22 h.p.); VE50 (26 h.p.)	K-60R	.020
K40, K45 (6-7 h.p.); OK55 to OK75, P35 (8 h.p.)	K-60R	.020
P40 (13 h.p.); P45 (12 h.p.); P50 (20 h.p.); P65, P70 (21.5 h.p.); P75, P80, PA50, PE50, PO10 to PO39 (22 h.p.); S45 to S70, SA50, SE50 (13 h.p.); TR40, V45 to V70, VA50	K-60R	.020

If desired, special spark plug types with Gold Palladium alloy electrodes may be substituted as follows:

UJ-11G ... J-7J, J-8J, J-11J   UJ-7G ... J-4J, J-6J

(1970)

MODEL	PLUG	GAP
JOHNSON—Continued		
Models w/CD Ignition:		
GT, TR, V4A, V4S, V4TL, VX, VXH (55-115 h.p.)	L-19V	—
Air-Buoy (Diving Unit)	CJ-14	.025
KONIG Racing	L-57R	.016
500 c.c. 75 h.p. model	L-54R	.016
LAUSON thru 1949	J-8 or J-8J	.025
After 1949	J-8 or J-8J	.030
MAJESTIC 1MB, ZMB, 4MB, 1MBB, M-2L, M-4L-GS, M-2LL, M-2N	UD-16 or D-16	.030
M-3L-GS, M-3N-GS, M-4N-GS, M-3LL-GS, M-4LL-GS	J-7J	.030
M-6LL-GS, M-6N-GS	J-8J	.030
MARINER (See Champion)		
MARTIN 20 (2⅓ h.p.), 100 (10 h.p.)	J-6J	.035
40 (4½ h.p.), 45 (4½ h.p.)	J-8J	.035
60 (7.2 h.p.), 66 (7.2 h.p.), 75 (7½ h.p.)	J-8J	.035
60 High Speed (7½ h.p.) (gasoline)	J-6J	.035
(alcohol mixture)	J-57R	.020
200 Silver Streak (17 h.p.)	J-62R	.023
McCULLOCH 1964-'69 Models		
3½, 7½ h.p., 4 h.p. w/Long shaft	H-10J	.035
4 h.p.	J-14Y	.035
9 h.p.	CJ-8	.035
9½ h.p.	J-7J	.035
14 h.p., OX140 (14 h.p.)	J-4J	.035
Manual: 28, 45 h.p., OX450 (45 h.p.)	J-4J	.035
Electric: 45 h.p., OX450 (45 h.p.)	UJ-17V	—
590/630	J-4J	.035
75 h.p.	UJ-17V	—
Diesel Engine	AG-10	—
MERCURY Mark 20H (16 h.p.); Mark 55H (40 h.p.)	J-62R or J-57R	.025
K1 (2.5 h.p.); K2, K3 (3 h.p.); K4, K5 (6 h.p.); KB1 (2.9 h.p.); KB1A (3.1 h.p.); KB2; KB3 (3.2 h.p.); KB4 (5.8 h.p.); KB5 (6 h.p.); KB4-1 (5.8 h.p.); KD3 (3.2 h.p.); KD3S (3.2 h.p.)	J-8J	.025
KD4, KD4S (6 h.p.); KE3 (3.6 h.p.); KE4 (7.5 h.p.); KE4A (6 h.p.); KE7 (10 h.p.); KF3 (3.5 h.p.); KF5 (5 h.p.); KF7 (10 h.p.); KF9 (25 h.p.); KG4 (7.5 h.p.); Mark Series 5 (5 h.p.); 6 (6 h.p.); 7 (7.5 h.p.); 10, 15 (10 h.p.); 15A (15 h.p.)	J-7J	.025
Merc 39 (3.9 h.p.) (Prior to 1967)	J-8J	.025
Merc 39 (3.9 h.p.) 1967-'68; Merc 40 (4 h.p.) 1969	L-9J	.030
Merc 60 (6 h.p.) 1967-'68; Merc 75 (7.5 h.p.) 1969	L-7J	.030
Merc Series 60 (6 h.p.); 100, 110 (10 h.p.); 150 (15 h.p.): (Prior to 1967)	J-7J	.025
Merc 110, 200, 500M, 500S 650S (65 h.p.) 1967-'68	L-4J	.030
Merc 110, 200	L-4J	.030
Merc 350 (35-40 h.p.)		
Thru 1965	J-6J	.025
1966	J-4J	.025
1967-'69	L-4J	.030
KG7, KH7, KG7H (10 h.p.); KG4H (7.5 h.p.); KG9, KG9H (25 h.p.)	J-6J	.025
Mark Series: 20 (16 h.p.); 25 (25 h.p.); 28 (22 h.p.); 58 (45 h.p.); 30, 30H (31 h.p.); 35A (35 h.p.); 50, 50H, 55 (40 h.p.); 75 (60 h.p.); 78 (70 h.p.)	J-6J	.025
Merc Series: 200 (20-22 h.p.); 250 (25 h.p.); 300 (35 h.p.); 400, 450 (45 h.p.); 600 (60 h.p.); 700 (70 h.p.)	J-6J	.025
500 (50 h.p.) '65-'66 models; 650 & 650S (65 h.p.); 850 (85 h.p.); 900 (90 h.p.); 1000 (100 h.p.)	J-4J	.025
Merc 800E (80 h.p.) Ser. No. 1403610 and below	J-2J	.025
Merc 800EL (80 h.p.) Ser. No. 1405606 and below	J-2J	.025
All other Merc 800E and 800EL mdls	J-4J	.025
Merc 950 (95 h.p.); 1100 (110 h.p.)	L-4J	.025
1966-'70 All models w/Thunderbolt (C.D.) Ignition	L-19V	—

MODEL	PLUG	GAP
MID-JET M-2, M-3	J-4J	.030
M-4	L-4J	.030
MILBURN Cub	J-11J	.018
MONARCH	J-11J	.032
MUNCIE 11B1, 15B1 (1½ h.p.)	J-11J	.025
11B4, 11B6, 11B10, 15B4, 17B1	J-6J	.025
11B2, 15B2 (2 h.p.); 11B16 (16 h.p.)	K-15J	.025
WC-1 (1.7 h.p.)	J-8J	.025
MY-TE-IV Power Products Engine	J-8J	.030
NEPTUNE OB1, 2, 2C, 3, 4, 5, 31, 32, 51, 63	UD-16 or D-16	.025
OB15, 16, 17 (16 h.p.)	K-57R	.015
OB11, 12, 34, 64, 65, 102, 112, 238, 239, 438, 439, 638, 639, 1016; 1638, 1639 (16 h.p.); 10A16, 11A16 (16 h.p.); 11A2 (2 h.p.); 16A39	K-15J	.025
101, 189, 139; 1A39, 10A1 (1½ h.p.)	J-8J	.025
111, 11A1, 15A1 (1½ h.p.)	J-11J	.025
104, 106, 113, 114, 116, 539, 938, 939, 1010, 1110, 4A39, 5A39, 9A39, 10A4, 10A6, 11A3, 11AA3, 11AA10; 10A10 (9½ h.p.); 11A6, 11AA6 (6 h.p.); 15A3, 15AA3 (3½ h.p.); 15A6, 15AA6 (6 h.p.); 15A9, 15AA9 (9½ h.p.); 17A1, 17A2, 17A3, A1, AA1, AA1A, A2, AA2, AA4, AA6, AA10 (10 h.p.)	J-6J	.025
OLIVER Challenger J, J-2 (5.5 h.p.); J-3, J-4, J-5, J-6 (6 h.p.)	J-8J	.030
Commander (15 h.p.); K, K-2 (15 h.p.); K-3, K-4, K-5, K-6 (16 h.p.)	H-8J	.030
B, B-2, B-3 (35 h.p.)	D-9J	.030
OUTBOARD JET		
J55, J55B (5.5 h.p.)	J-6J	.030
PEERLESS J-5	TJ-8J	.030
J-9	J-12J	.030
PERKINS		
1959-'61 6 h.p.	J-8J	.028
16 h.p.	H-8J	.028
40 h.p.	L-86*	.035
1959-'60 35 h.p. (18mm Hd.)	D-9J	.035
1961 35 h.p. (14mm Hd.)	L-86*	.035
1962-'65 4½ h.p., 6½ h.p.	J-8J	.028
18 h.p.	H-8J	.028
30 h.p., 40 h.p.	L-86*	.035
*Alternates—L-85 or H-8J		
RILEY 75 h.p. Four Cycle 5-Cyl. Radial	J-6	.025
ROYAL (Atlas) thru 1949	J-7J	.030
After 1949	J-6J	.030
SABER (Fedway) All models	J-6J	.030
SEA-DOO Jet-Powered Aqua Scooter w/Rotax Engine	K-9	.025
SCOTT (McCulloch)		
1959-'60 12, 25, 40 & 60 h.p.	J-6J	.035
3.6, 6, 7½ & 10 h.p.	H-10J	.035
1961 43.7, 75.2 h.p.	J-4J	.035
14.1, 27.7 h.p.	J-6J	.035
7.5 h.p.	H-10J	.035
1961 75.2 Custom	UJ-17V	—
1961-'62 Scotty (3.5 h.p.)	H-10J	.035
1962-'63 Flying Scott (75 h.p.)	UJ-17V	—
Royal Scott Elec. (45 h.p.)	UJ-17V	—
Royal Scott Manual (45 h.p.)	J-4J	.035
Sports Scott (28 h.p.)	J-6J	.035
Fleet Scott & Power Scott (14 h.p.)	J-6J	.035
Fishing Scott (7.5 h.p.)	H-10J	.035
Diesel Mdls. (glow plug)	AG-10	—
SCOTT-ATWATER All 3.6, 4, 5, 7½ h.p.		
1953-'58 10 h.p.	H-10J	.035
1950-'52 10 h.p.	CJ-8	.035
All 16 h.p.	D-9J	.035
1955 30 h.p.	J-6J	.030
1956 33 h.p.	J-6J	.030
1958 22-25 h.p.; 40 h.p.; 60 h.p.	J-6J	.035
SEA-BEE (Goodyear) 1946 thru 1949	J-7J	.025
1950-'59	J-6J	.030
1960 models	J-6J or J-4J	.030
SEA-FLYER (Goodrich)	J-6J	.030

MODEL	PLUG	GAP
SEA-KING (Ward's) 371, 373	K-15J	.025
712	K-57R	.018
Others thru 1949	J-7J	.025
1950-'63 All 1½-25 h.p. mdls.	J-6J or J-4J	.030
All 35-60 h.p. mdls.	J-4J	.030
1964-'70 3½, 5.8 h.p.	H-8J	.030
1964-'65 9 h.p.	H-8J	.030
1966-'69 9.2 h.p.	J-4J	.030
1964-'67 20-80 h.p.	J-4J	.030
1967-'70 6 h.p.	H-10J	.030
1968-'70 9.6, 20, 35, 45, 55 h.p.	L-4J	.030
SEARS 1964-'65 6003 (3½ h.p.); 6004 (6 h.p.); 6010, 6012 (7½ h.p.)	H-10J	.035
6015 (14 h.p.); 6037, 6038 (28 h.p.)	J-6J	.035
6056, 6057, 6058 (45 h.p.); 6076, 6077, 6078 (75 h.p.)	J-4J	.035
6091 (3½ h.p.)	TJ-8J	.030
5927 (12 h.p.)	H-8J	.030
5941 (35 h.p.)	J-4J	.030
1966 6091, 6094	CJ-8	.030
SPRITE J-5	TJ-8J	.030
STARLING JET 5 h.p.	J-12J	.025
SWANSON-CHAMP		
Hot Rod 5NHR	J-57R	—
6NHR	K-57R	—
TERRY TROLLER (4-cycle) Mdl. T4T	J-8J	.025
Mdl. T5T	H-10	.025
VIKING thru 1949	J-8J	.025
1950-1965	J-6J	.025
1965-'70 Models:		
3½, 15 h.p.; 9 h.p. (1965)	H-8J	.030
6 h.p.	H-10J	.030
9.2 ('66-'70), 20, 35, 50 h.p. (thru '67)	J-4J	.030
1968-'70 9.6, 20, 35, 55 h.p.	L-4J	.030
VOLVO-PENTA		
Acquamatic BB70	J-6 or J-6J	.028
Sustained Hi-Speed	J-4J	.028
Acquamatic 100	L-5	.028
VOYAGER 1VA, 2VA, 1VB, V-2L, V-4L-GS, V-2LL, V-2N	UD-16 or D-16	.030
V-3L-GS, V-3N-GS, V-4N-GS, V-3LL-GS, V-4LL-GS	J-7J	.030
V-6LL-GS, V-6N-GS	J-8J	.030
WESTERN FLYER (Western Auto)	J-7J	.025
WEST BEND		
1955 5 h.p.	J-12J	.050
1955 7½ h.p.	J-11J	.050
1956-1958 2 h.p.	J-11J	.050
1956 5½ h.p.	H-10J	.035
1956-1957 12 h.p.	H-8J	.025
1956-1963 7½, 25, 30 h.p.	H-8J	.030
1957-1959 6 h.p.	H-10J	.030
1957 8 h.p.	H-8J	.035
1958-1960 8, 16, 35, 40 h.p.	H-8J	.030
1958-1963 12 h.p.	H-8J	.030
1959-1961 2 h.p.	H-10J	.030
1960-1962 18 h.p.	J-4J	.030
1961 6 h.p.	H-8J	.030
1961-1962 40 h.p.	J-4J	.030
1961-1965 20, 45, 80 h.p.	J-4J	.030
1962-1965 3½, 9, 10 h.p.	H-8J	.030
1963-1965 6 h.p.	H-10J	.030
1964-1965 35, 50 h.p.	J-4J	.030
WIZARD WD3, WD3S (3.2 h.p.); WF4, WG4 (6 h.p.); WF7, WG7, WH7, WG7A, WJ7 (10 h.p.)	J-8J	.025
WD4, WD4S (6 h.p.); WH6, WH6-1 (5 h.p.); WK7, WM7, WM7A (10 h.p.)	J-7J	.025
WN7, WN7A (12 h.p.); WH6A (5 h.p.); WA25, WA25E (25 h.p.)	J-6J	.025
OC575, OC585 (5.5 h.p.)	J-8J	.030
OC1575, OC1585 (15 h.p.)	H-8J	.030
OC3585 (35 h.p.)	D-9J	.030
1959-'64 3½, 6, 7½, 10 h.p.	H-10J	.035
12, 14, 25 h.p.	J-6J	.035
40, 60 h.p.	J-4J	.035
1965 thru '70 3½ h.p.; 9 h.p. (1965)	H-8J	.030
6 h.p.	H-10J	.030
20 h.p. (thru '67); 9.2 h.p. ('66-'70)	J-4J	.030
20 h.p. ('68-'70)	L-4J	.030
YAMAHA All models	L-86	.025

If desired, special spark plug types with Gold Palladium alloy electrodes may be substituted as follows:

UJ-11G .... J-7J, J-8J, J-11J   UJ-7G J-4J, J-6J

OUTBOARD MOTORS

NOTE—Most manufacturers recommend use of non-detergent motor oils or special outboard oils. For breaking-in new or reconditioned motors it is generally advisable to use 50% more oil in the gasoline for the first 12 hours. Follow manufacturer's recommendations.

The following oil-fuel mixes are listed as a convenient reference only. Always check Operators' Manuals.

(1954)

MAKE AND MODEL	Spark Plug Type	Spark Plug Gap	Contact Point Gap	Oil Fuel Mix Per Gallon: Pints	Oil Fuel Mix Per Gallon: SAE Grade
ANZANI Pilot (British)	L-10	.020	.018	½	30
BENDIX (See "Eclipse")					
BOATIMPELLER ☆ .... **5 Com. or**	H-17-A*	.020	.020	⅜	40
BROOKLURE ☆ 1200	J-6J	.030	.020	1	30
All others	J-6J	.030	.020	½	30
BUCCANEER ☆ All models	J-6J	.030	.020	½	30
CAILLE 35, 40, 45, 50	R-1	.025	.020	½	30
All other 18mm Hds	7	.025	.020	½	30
All ⅞" Hds	1 Com.	.025	.020	½	30
CHAMPION ☆ A, 1B, R1C, S1C, S1D .... **9 or**	C-15*	.025	.018	½	30
2B, 3B, D1C, D1D, D3D, S2C, S2D .... **9 or**	C-15*	.025	.018	¾	30
D2C, D2D, D1E, S1E, 1J, 2J, 1K, 2K, 4K, 1L, 4L	7	.030	.018	¾	30
B1F, D1F, D2F, S1F, S2F, 2G, M2G, 2H	7	.030	.015	¾	30
1J, 2J, 1K, 2K, 2L-HD, 4L-HD	7	.030	.018	¾	30
3G, 1H, 3H, M1G, D1G, S1G	H-10	.025	.015	¾	30
D4G, M4G, S4G	H-9	.025	.015	¾	30
4KS, 4LS, 4LS-1X (Normal) .... **4 Com. or**	H-16-A*	.030	.018	2	30
(Racing)	R-7	.020	.018	2	30
4KS (Normal) .... **5 Com. or**	H-17-A*	.030	.018	2	30
(Racing)	R-7	.020	.018	2	30
3M-GS, 4M-GS, 4M-HD	J-7J	.035	.018	½	30
4M-HR, 6M-GS, 6M-HD, 6M-HR (Normal)	J-7J	.035	.018	¾	30
(Racing)	J-3	.025	.018	¾	30
CHRIS-CRAFT ☆ J (5.5 h.p.)	J-8J	.028	.018	½	30
Commander K (10 h.p.)	J-7J	.028	.018	½	30
CLARKE TROLLER ☆	V-1	.014	.018	½	30
CORSAIR ☆ 5028 (10 h.p.) thru '52	HT-10J	.035	.020	½	30
5020 (3.6 h.p.), 5021 (4 h.p.), 5023 (7.5 h.p.), 5027 (5 h.p.)	H-10J	.035	.020	½	30
1953 (10 h.p.)	H-10J	.035	.020	½	30
CROSS Radial	C-7	.025	.020	½	30
563-S	5MJ	.020	.020	½	30
582-R	R-1	.015	.020	½	30
All others	7	.025	.020	½	30
ECLIPSE thru 1936	J-8J	.025	.020	½	30
1937 thru 1940	H-10J	.025	.020	¾	30
ELGIN ☆ 58201, 58202 (2 h.p.)	J-12J	.050	.020	½	30
58301 (1¼ h.p.)	J-12J	.040	.020	¾	30
58401 (2½ h.p.)	J-12J	.050	.020	½	40
85501 thru 58551	J-11J	.050	.020	¾	30–40
58561, 58562 (5 h.p.)	J-12J	.050	.020	½	30–40
58561 (5 h.p.), 58562	J-12J	.050	.020	½	30–40
58601 thru 58621	J-11J	.050	.020	¾	30
58641 (6 h.p.)	J-12J	.050	.020	¾	30
58642 (6 h.p.)	J-12J	.050	.020	½	30
58701 thru 58731	J-11J	.050	.020	¾	40
58741 (7½ h.p.)	J-11J	.050	.020	¾	30–40
58751, 58761 (7½ h.p.)	J-11J	.050	.020	½	30–40
58761	J-12J	.050	.020	½	30–40
58821 (16 h.p.)	J-12J	.050	.020	¾	30
58822	J-12J	.050	.015	½	30–40
58823	J-12J	.050	.020	½	30–40
58843, 58824 (16 h.p.)	J-12J	.050	.020	½	30
58841 (16 h.p.)	J-12J	.050	.015	¾	30
ELTO ☆					
Ace, Handitwin—1936 .... **9 or**	C-15*	.025	.020	⅓	40
1937 thru 1941	C-7	.025	.020	⅓	40
Cub (½ h.p.) 1939	J-12J	.025	.020	⅓	40
1940 thru 1941	H-10J	.025	.020	⅓	40
Pal (1.1 h.p.) 1937 thru 1941	H-10J	.025	.020	⅓	40
Lightweight 1929-'30	7	.025	.020	⅓	40
1931 thru 1933	6M	.025	.020	⅓	40
Lightwin (5 h.p.) 1920-'27	7	.025	.020	⅓	40
1934 thru 1941 (4-5 h.p.)	6M	.025	.020	⅓	40
Service Twin 1928-'31 (3-4 h.p.)	7	.025	.020	½	40
1936 thru 1937 (4.3 h.p.)	6M	.025	.020	½	40
Quad 1928 thru 1929 (30 h.p.)	7	.025	.020	⅓	40
Fisherman, Lightwin, Imperial, Service "A" Super "A"	6M	.025	.020	½	40
Fleetwin (8.5 h.p.) Senior Speedster (13.7 h.p.)	6M	.025	.020	1	40
Foldlight (2¾ h.p.)	6M	.025	.020	¾	40
Single, Super Single (2.2 h.p.)	6M	.025	.020	⅔	40
Big Quad, Speeditwin Super "C", Senior Quad Junior Quad	5MJ	.025	.020	1½	40
Handifour, Lightfour, Imperial	5MJ	.025	.020	¾	40
Spec. Speedster (9 h.p.)	7	.025	.020	¾	40
Speedster 1928-'31 (7 h.p.)	7	.025	.020	¾	40
1949 (12 h.p.)	J-6J	.025	.020	1	40
Sportster (5 h.p.)	J-6J	.025	.020	½	40
ELTO RACING ☆					
Midget Racer	R-1	.015	.015	1½	60
Racing Speedtwin 1934	R-1	.015	.015	2	60
1935	R-11	.015	.015	2	60
Racing 460, 1933-'34	R-1	.015	.015	2	60
1935	R-11	.015	.015	2	60
Racing Super "C" 1930-'33	R-1	.015	.015	2	60
Model 460 1930-'32	R-1	.015	.015	2	60
EVINRUDE ☆ Big Four 1931-'32	5MJ	.025	.020	1½	40
1946 thru 1950 (50 h.p.)	R-7	.020	.020	¾	40
Big Twin 1931-'32 (4 h.p.)	0 Com.	.025	.020	½	40
1951-'54 (25 h.p.)	J-6J	.030	.020	½	*40
Single "A" (2 h.p.)	0 Com.	.025	.020	⅔	40
Fleetwin 1928-'29 (6-7 h.p.)	0 Com.	.025	.020	⅔	40
1930 thru 1934 (8-11 h.p.)	6M	.025	.020	1	40
1950 thru 1954 (7½ h.p.)	J-6J	.030	.020	½	30–40
Speeditwin 1927-'29 (16 h.p.)	0 Com.	.025	.020	2	40
1930 thru 1931 (22½ h.p.)	7	.025	.020	2	40
1950 thru 1952 (22½ h.p.)	5MJ	.030	.020	¾	40
Fastwin 1927-'29 (4-14 h.p.)	0 Com.	.025	.020	1½	40
1930 thru 1933 (14 h.p.)	6M	.025	.020	1½	40
1950 thru 1952 (14 h.p.)	J-6J	.030	.020	½	30–40
Super Fastwin '53-'54 (15 h.p.)	J-6J	.030	.020	½*	30–40
Lightwin 1931-'38 (4-5.6 h.p.)	6M	.025	.020	⅓	40
1952 (5.2 h.p.)	J-6J	.030	.020	½	30
1953-'54 (3 h.p.)	J-6J	.030	.020	½	30
Fisherman (5.4 h.p.)	6M	.025	.020	½	40
Sturditwin (8 h.p.)	6M	.025	.020	1	40
Foldlight (2¾ h.p.)	6M	.025	.020	¾	40
Sport Single (2.2 h.p.)	6M	.025	.020	⅔	40
Light Four (9.7 h.p.)	5MJ	.025	.020	¾	40
Speedifour, Speediquad, Speediquad Imperial	5MJ	.025	.020	1½	40
Sport Four, Sport Four Imperial	5MJ	.025	.020	1	40
Mate (½ h.p.), Ranger (1.1 h.p.)	H-10J	.025	.020	⅓	40
Scout	J-8J	.025	.020	⅓	40
Sportsman 1935-'38 (1½ h.p.) .... **9 or**	C-15*	.025	.020	⅓	40
1939 thru 1947 (2 h.p.)	H-10J	.025	.020	⅓	40
1948 thru 1951 (1½ h.p.)	J-6J	.003	.020	⅓	30–40
Sportwin '36-'38 (2½-3 h.p.) . **9 or**	C-15*	.025	.020	⅓	40
1939 thru 1947 (3 h.p.)	H-10J	.025	.020	⅓	40
1948 thru 1951 (3.3 h.p.)	J-6J	.030	.020	⅓	30–40
Zephyr (5½ h.p.)	J-6J	.025	.020	½	40
*1954 Models 1 qt. to 5 gallons					
EVINRUDE RACING ☆					
Racing Speeditwin 1931-'34	R-1	.015	.015	2	60
After 1934	R-11	.015	.015	2	60
Racing 460 1933-'34	R-1	.015	.015	2	60
After 1934	R-11	.015	.015	2	60
Model 460 1931	R-7	.015	.015	2	60
1932	R-1	.015	.015	2	60
FIRESTONE ☆ 10-A-75 (10 h.p.)	HT-10J	.035	.020	½	30
10 h.p. 1953, All others thru 1953	H-10J	.035	.020	½	30
FLAMBEAU Single (2.5 h.p.), Twin (5 h.p.)	J-7J	.025	.020	⅔	40
HARTFORD All models	8 Com.	.020	.018	½	30
HIAWATHA ☆ thru 1949	J-7J	.030	.020	½	30
1950 thru 1953	J-6J	.030	.020	½	30
INDIAN ☆ All models	7	.025	.020	½	30
JOHNSON ☆					
A; A25-A45 (2-3 h.p.); A50-A80; AA37 (4½ h.p.); BN; F70, F75 (3.3 h.p.); J25-J75 (1½ h.p.); J80 (1.7 h.p.); OA55, 60, 65 (3 h.p.); SD20 (16 h.p.); 200, 210	5MJ	.030	.020	½	40
AT10-AT39 (5 h.p.); DS37, DS38; DT10-DT39; HA10-HA39 (2½ h.p.); HD10-HD39; HS10, HS15, HS39 (2½ h.p.); LT10-LT39; LS37, LS38, MS & MD15, 38, 39; 100, 110, 300	J-8J	.030	.030	½	40
HS & HD 20, 25 (2½ h.p.), 26; MD & MS 20 (1½ h.p.); QD10-QD14 (10 h.p.); RD10, RD11; TN25-TN28; TS & TD15, 20 (5 h.p.)	J-6J	.030	.020	½	40
JW10 (3 h.p.); RD12-RD15 (25 h.p.)	J-6J	.030	.020	½	30
K35 (6-7 h.p.); PO15 1949 & 1950 models	R-7	.020	.020	½	40
K40, K45; OK55, OK60, OK75 (7.8 h.p.); P35	R-7	.020	.020	¾	40
K75, K80; KA10-KA39; KS15, KD15 (9.8 h.p.); SD10, SD15 (16 h.p.)	5MJ	.030	.020	1	40
K50, K65, K70; P30	5MJ	.030	.020	¾	40
P40-P80; PE & PA50; PO10-PO39 (22 h.p.); S45-S70 (13.3 h.p.); SE50, SA50; TR40; V45-V70 (26 h.p.); VE & VA50	R-7	.020	.020	1	40
LAUSON ☆ thru 1949	J-8	.025	.020	....	30†
1950 thru 1953	J-8	.030	.020	....	30†
†4-cycle engine. Crankcase oil only. Do not mix oil and gasoline.					
LOCKWOOD ☆	6M	.025	.020	½	30
MAJESTIC ☆ thru 1952, M-2-L, M-4-LGS	7	.030	.018	¾	30
M-3-LGS	J-7J	.035	.018	½	30
M-6-LGS	J-7J	.035	.018	¾	30

OUTBOARD MOTORS—Continued

NOTE—Most manufacturers recommend use of non-detergent motor oils or special outboard oils. For breaking-in new or reconditioned motors it is generally advisable to use 50% more oil in the gasoline for the first 12 hours. Follow manufacturer's recommendations. The following oil-fuel mixes are listed as a convenient reference only. Always check Operator's Manuals.

MAKE AND MODEL	Spark Plug Type	Spark Plug Gap	Contact Point Gap	Oil Fuel Mix Per Gallon	
				Pints	SAE Grade
MARINER ☆ M1G, M4G	H-10	.025	.020	½	30
M2G	7	.025	.020	½	30
MARTIN ☆ 20 (2⅓ h.p.), 100 (10 h.p.)	J-6J	.035	.020	½	40
40 (4½ h.p.), 45 (4½ h.p.)	J-8J	.035	.020	½	40
60 (7.2 h.p.), 66 (7.2 h.p.), 75 (7½ h.p.)	J-8J	.035	.020	¾	40
60 High Speed (7½ h.p.)					
(gasoline)	J-6J	.035	.020	1	40
(alcohol mixture)	J-2	.035	.020	1	40
200 Silver Streak (17 h.p.)	J-3	.025	.020	¾	40
MERCURY ☆ For Racing all mdls.	K-3	.025	.018	¾	30
K1 (2.5 h.p.); K2, K3 (3 h.p.); K4, K5 (6 h.p.); KB1 (2.9 h.p.); KB1A (3.1 h.p.); KB2; KB3 (3.2 h.p.); KB4 (5.8 h.p.); KB5 (6 h.p.); KE41 (5.8 h.p.); KD3 (3.2 h.p.); KD3S (3.2 h.p.)	J-8J	.025	.018	Mfr. recommends mixing: ½ pint Aeromarine 2-cycle oil or ½ pint premium 100% non additive SAE 30 oil with one gallon auto type gas min. 72 octane.	
KD4, KD4S (6 h.p.); KE3 (3.6 h.p.); KE7, KF7 (10 h.p.); Mark 7 (7.5 h.p.)	J-7J	.025	.018		
KE4 (7.5 h.p.); KF5 (5 h.p.)	J-7J	.030	.018		
KF3 (3.5 h.p.)					
Phelon Magneto	J-7J	.035	.018		
Scintilla Magneto	J-7J	.025	.018		
KG4 (7.5 h.p.); KG4H (7.5 h.p.)	J-7J	.035	.018		
KG7 (10 h.p.)					
Phelon Magneto	J-6J	.035	.018		
Scintilla Magneto	J-6J	.030	.018		
KH7 (10 h.p.); KG7Q (10 h.p.)	J-6J	.030	.018		
KG4Q (7.5 h.p.)	J-6J	.035	.018		
Mark 5 (5 h.p.)	J-7J	.030	.018		
Mark 15 (10 h.p.)	J-7J	.040	.018		
Mark 20 (16 h.p.); KG7H (10 h.p.)	J-6J	.030	.018		
KF9 (25 h.p.)	J-7J	.030	.016	¾	30
KG9 (25 h.p.)	J-6J	.030	.016	¾	30
KG9Q (25 h.p.)	J-6J	.025	.018	¾	30
Mark 40 (25 h.p.)	J-6J	.030	.012	¾	30
Mark 40H (25 h.p.)	J-6J	.025	.012	¾	30
MILBURN ☆ Cub	J-11	.018	.018	1	40
MONARCH ☆	J-11J	.032	.020	½	30
MUNCIE ☆ 11B1, 15B1 (1½ h.p.)	J-11J	.025	.015	⅔	30
11B4, 11B6, 11B10, 15B4, 17B1	J-6	.025	.020	⅔	40
11B2, 15B2 (2 h.p.)	6M	.025	.015	⅔	30
11B16 (16 h.p.)	6M	.025	.020	1	40
NEPTUNE ☆ OB1, 2, 2C, 3, 4, 5, 31, 32, 51, 63	7	.025	.020	⅔	30
OB15, 16, 17 (16 h.p.)	R-1	.015	.020	1	40
OB11, 12, 34, 64, 65, 102, 112, 238, 239, 438, 439, 638, 639, 1016	6M	.025	.020	⅔	30
1638, 1639 (16 h.p.)	6M	.025	.020	1	30
10A16, 11A16 (16 h.p.)	6M	.025	.020	1	40
11A2 (2 h.p.), 16A39	6M	.025	.015	⅔	30
101, 189, 139	J-8J	.025	.020	⅔	30
1A39, 10A1 (1½ h.p.)	J-8J	.025	.020	1	40
111, 11A1, 15A1 (1½ h.p.)	J-11J	.025	.015	⅔	30
104, 106, 113, 114, 116, 539, 938, 939, 1010, 1110, 4A39, 5A39, 9A39, 10A4, 10A6, 11A3, 11AA3, 11AA10	J-6J	.025	.020	⅔	30
10A10 (9½ h.p.)	J-6J	.025	.020	1	40
11A6, 11AA6 (6 h.p.)	J-6J	.025	.020	⅔	40
15A3, 15AA3 (3½ h.p.)	J-6J	.025	.015	⅔	30
15A6, 15AA6 (6 h.p.)	J-6J	.025	.015	⅔	40
15A9, 15AA9 (9½ h.p.)	J-6J	.025	.015	1	40
17A1, 17A2, 17A3, A1, A2, AA2, AA4, AA6	J-6J	.025	.020	⅔	30
AA10 (10 h.p.)	J-6J	.025	.020	1	40
ROYAL ☆ (Atlas) thru 1949	J-7J	.030	.020	½	30
1950 thru 1953	J-6J	.030	.020	½	30
SABER (Fedway) All models	J-6J	.030	.020	½	30
SCOTT-ATWATER ☆					
461 thru 497	H-10J	.032	.020	½	30
500 thru 507	H-10J	.035	.020	½	30
509, 1-30 (16 h.p.)	5MJ	.035	.020	½	30
1-12 (3.6 h.p.), 1-14 (4 h.p.), 1-16 (5 h.p.), 1-20 (7.5 h.p.)	H-10J	.035	.020	½	30
1-25 (10 h.p.) thru 1952	HT-10J	.035	.020	½	30
(10 h.p.) 1953	H-10J	.035	.020	½	30
SEA-BEE ☆ (Goodyear)					
1946 thru 1949	J-7J	.025	.020	½	30
1950 thru 1953	J-6J	.030	.020	½	30
SEA-FLYER ☆ (Goodrich)	J-6J	.030	.020	½	30
SEA-KING ☆ (Ward's) 371, 373	6M	.025	.020	½	30
712	R-1	.020	.020	½	30
Others thru 1949	J-7J	.025	.020	½	30
1950 thru 1953	J-6J	.030	.020	½	30
THOR ☆ 10mm Heads	Y-6	.025	.020	⅔	30
18mm Heads	6M	.020	.020	1	30
VIKING ☆ (Canada)	J-8	.025	.020	½	30
VOYAGER ☆ thru 1952, V-2-L, V-4-LGS	7	.030	.018	¾	30
V-3-LGS	J-7J	.035	.018	½	30
V-6-LGS	J-7J	.035	.018	¾	30
WATERWITCH ☆ (Sears)					
MB10, MB20, 10, 11, 20, 21, 22	C-7	.025	.020	¾	30
30, 40	J-11	.025	.020	¾	30
31 thru 34A, 41 thru 44W, 90	J-7	.030	.020	¾	30
35, 36, 50	H-10	.025	.020	¾	30
12 thru 15, 23, 24	C-7	.025	.020	¾	30
WESTERN FLYER ☆ (Western Auto)	J-7J	.025	.020	½	30
WEST BEND ☆ (Canada)					
15030 (1½ h.p.)	J-12J	.040	.020	¾	30
15040 (2½ h.p.)	J-12J	.050	.020	½	40
15050-15055, 15074 (7½ h.p.)	J-11J	.050	.020	¾	30-40
15056 (5 h.p.), 150202 (2 h.p.), 150823 (16 h.p.)	J-12J	.050	.020	½	30-40
15064 (6 h.p.), 15082 (16 h.p.), 15084 (16 h.p.)	J-12J	.050	.020	¾	30
15060-15062	J-11J	.050	.020	¾	30
15075 (7½ h.p.), 150761 (7½ h.p.)	J-11J	.050	.020	½	30-40
WIZARD ☆					
WD3 (3.2 h.p.)	J-8J	.025	.020	½	30
WD4 (6 h p.)	J-7J	.030	.020	½	30
WD4S (6 h.p.)	J-7J	.030	.020	¾	30
WD3S (3.2 h.p.)	J-8J	.025	.020	¾	30
WF4 (6 h.p.)	J-8J	.025	.020	¾	30
WF7 (10 h.p.)	J-8J	.025	.020	¾	30
WG4 (6 h.p.)	J-8J	.025	.020	¾	30
WG7 (10 h.p.)	J-8J	.025	.020	¾	30
WH7 (10 h.p.)	J-8J	.025	.020	¾	30
WG7A (10 h.p.)	J-8J	.025	.020	¾	30

Discontinued Spark Plug List

Discont'd Plug Type	Replaced Plug Type	Discont'd Plug Type	Replaced Plug Type	Discont'd Plug Type	Replaced Plug Type	Discont'd Plug Type	Replaced Plug Type	Discont'd Plug Type	Replaced Plug Type	Discont'd Plug Type	Replaced Plug Type
0-COM	W10	X5-COM	RD9	RP7	P7	L9J	L90C	XEH11	XEH8	UEJ14	XEJ12
C0	W14	XE5-COM	ED9	UK7	K7	N9Y	N9YC	XEJ11	XEJ12	UF14Y	RF14YC
E0-COM	EW90	XEJ5	RJ6C	XE7	XED16	OBL9Y	RV9YC	XF11Y	RF11YC	XD14	RD14
1	W14	XJ5	RJ6C	XEJ7	XEJ8	RBL9Y	RV9YC	XH11	RH10	XEJ14	XEJ12
C1	W18	XN5	RN5C	XEL7A	REL88B	RBN9Y	RS9YC	XJ11	RJ11	XF14Y	RF14YC
1-COM	W14	Y5	UY6	XJ7	RJ8C	RF9Y	RF9YC	XJ11Y	RJ12YC	XH14Y	H14Y
ORD-1	XMJ14	6	W18	XL7	RL82C	RF9Y5	RF9YC	12	D16	XJ14Y	RJ14YC
QN1	N1	6-COM	D14	Z7G	Z6	RN9Y	RN9YC	BN12Y	RS12YC	XN14Y	RN14YC
TAC-1	REL88B	6-COM-D	D14	8	D16	RN9Y	RN9YC	EJ12	XEJ12	15	D16
2	W18	6-COM-62	D14	8-COM	D16	UF9Y	F9YC	H12J	H12	15A	D16
2-COM	W18	6M	K15J	8-COM-C	D23	UN9Y	N9YC	J12	UJ12	15-SPEC	D16
2-COM-L	W18	6MJ	K15J	8-COM-D	D23	XD9	RD9	J12JM	J12J	A15	25
AG2	CH2	A6	A6YC	8-COM-K	D15Y	XE9	XED16	J12Y	J12YC	J15	K15J
J2	J57R	A6Y	A6YC	8-SPEC	D16	XED9-COM	XED16	L12Y	L87YC	L15Y	L95Y
J2J	UJ2J	AG6	CH6	A8	A8YC	XEH9	XEH8	N12Y	N12YC	RBL15Y	RV15YC
L2G	L55G	BN6Y	S6YC	A8Y	A8YC	XEK9	ED9	NA12	N57R	RBL15Y4	RV15YC4
N2	N2C	DJ6	DJ6J	BL8	RV8C	XF9Y	RF9YC	ON12Y	RN12YC	RBL15Y6	RV15YC8
N2G	N2C	E6-COM	XED14	D8	K97F	XH9	RH8	P12Y	P10	RBL15Y8	RV15YC8
ORD-2	XMJ17	EJ6	XEJ6	DJ8	DJ8J	XJ9Y	RJ12YC	RBL12	RV12C	UD15Y	D15Y
QN2	QN2C	EJ6J	XEJ6	DL8	K98F	XN9Y	RN9YC	RBL12-6	RV12C6	UL15Y	L95Y
QN2G	QN2C	J6	J6C	DL8C	K98F	10	D16	RBN12Y	RS12YC	XEC15	XED16
RN2	RN2C	J6J	J6C	E8-COM	XED16	10-COM	D23	RF12	RF10C	C16C	W16Y
RN2G	RN2C	J6JM	J6C	ED8	K97F	10-COM-64	D23	RF12-5	RF10C	D16M	D16
TAC-2	RML12	JT6	CJ6	EDL8	K98F	A10	A8YC	RJ12Y	RJ12YC	ED16	XED16
3	W16Y	KCJ6	CJ6	EH8	XEH8	C10S	XEJ6	RJ12Y6	RJ12YC6	H16	D6
3-COM	W18	L6G	L82C	EJ8	XEJ8	C10	D9	RL12Y	RL87YC	H16A	D6
AG3	CH3	N6	N5C	EJ8J	XEJ8	EC10	EW90	RN12GY	RN12YC	N16Y	N16YC
BL3	V4C	N6Y	N6YC	H8JM	H8J	EH10	XEH8	RN12Y	RN12YC	RN16Y	N16YC
L3G	L77JC	N6YCX	N6YC	J8	J8C	F10	F10C	RZN12Y	RS12YC	UED16	XED16
N3	N3C	N6GY	N6YC	J8J	J8C	H10JM	H10J	RZN12Y5	RS12YC6	UK16V	K7
N3G	N3C	P6	P7	J8JM	CJ8	HT10J	CJ8	UL12Y	L87YC	XD16	RD16
ON3	QN3C	R6	A6YC	JT8	CJ8	J10	J62R	UN12Y	N12YC	XD16J	RD16J
QN3	QN3C	R6G	A6YC	K8G	K8	J10-COM	J6C	XH12	RH10	XN16Y	RN16Y
RN3	RN3C	RA6	RA6YC	L8	L90	J10-COM-J	J6C	XJ12	RJ12	H17	D9
RN3G	RN3C	RA6Y	RA6YC	LB8	L90	J10Y	J12YC	XJ12Y	RJ12YC	H17A	D9
XN3	RN3C	RBN6Y	RS6YC	N8B	N8	L10	L90C	XL12Y	RL87YC	RBL17Y	RV17YC
4	W16Y	RCJ6	CJ6	NA8	N5C	L10S	L82C	XN12Y	RN12YC	RBL17Y6	RV17YC6
4-COM	D6	RD6	D6	N8Y	N9YC	N10PY	N11YC	13	D16	UDJ17V	CJ4
AG4	CH4	RJ6	RJ6C	P8G	P7	N10Y	N11YC	A13	30	UJ17V	UJ2J
BL4	V4C	RJ6J	RJ6C	R8	RA8YC	N10Y4	N11YC4	BL13Y	V12YC	UL17V	UL81C
C4	W16Y	RN6	RN5C	RA8	RA8YC	NA10	N3C	J13	30	18	K15J
C4X	W16Y	RN6GY	RN6YC	RA8Y	RA8YC	P10	P8Y	J13-0	30	J18Y	J18YC
J4	J4C	RN6Y	RN6YC	RBL8	RV8C	RF10	RF10C	J13Y	J12YC	N18	N16YC
J4J	J4C	UJ6	J6C	RBL8-6	RV8C6	RJ10Y	RJ12YC	N13L	RN13LYC	RJ18Y	RJ18YC
J4JM	J4C	UJ6M	J6C	RJ8	RJ8C	RN10GY	N89GY	N13Y	N12YC	RJ18Y6	RJ18YC6
L4G	L77JC	X6-COM	RD14	RJ8J	RJ8C	RN10Y	N12YC	RBL13Y	RV12C6	RJ18Y8	RJ18YC8
L4J	L82C	XD6	D6	TJ8J	CJ8	RN10Y4	RN11YC4	RBL13Y6	RV12YC6	UJ18Y	J18YC
N4	N4C	XE6-COM	XED14	UCJ8G	CJ8	RU10Y	J12YC	RBN13Y	RS12YC	XEN18	XEN14
N4G	N4C	XEJ6J	XEJ6	UJ8	J8C	UJ8	J8C	RJ13Y	RJ12YC	XH18Y	RH18Y
RJ4	J4C	XJ6	RJ6C	X8-COM	RD16	XEF10	EF10	UBL13Y	V12YC	XJ18Y	RJ18YC
RJ4J	J4C	XJ6J	RJ6C	XE8-COM	XED16	XEH10	XEH8	XJ13Y	RJ12YC	J19V	UJ2J
RL4J	RL82C	XN6	RN5C	XEH8J	XEH8	XF10	RF10C	14	D16	L19V	L20V
RN4	RN4C	Y6	UY6	XEJ8J	XEJ8	XH10	RH10	A14	30	UL19V	UL81C
RN4G	RN4C	XY6	UY6	XH8	RH8	XH10J	RH10	A14-0	30	XMJ19	XMJ20
TAC-4	XML12	7	D16	XH8J	RH8	XJ13Y	RJ12YC	C14	30	20	W20
UCJ4G	CJ4	7-COM	D16	XJ8	RJ8C	11	D16	D14M	D14	21	W10
UJ4J	UJ81C	BL7Y	V9YC	XJ8J	RJ8C	BL11Y	V12YC	EC14	EW90	XED21	XED16
UL4J	UL81C	BN7Y	S7YC	XN8	RN8	CJ11	CJ8	EF14	EF10	22	W20
X4-COM	D6	C7	D16	XN8B	RN8	EH11	XEH8	F14Y	RF14YC	F22	F11YC
XJ4J	J4C	E7	XED16	XNA8	RN5C	EJ11	XEJ12	HO14S	REB37E	J23	25
XN4	RN4C	F7Y	F7YC	Y8	UY6	F11Y	F11YC	J14	UJ12	24	25
Y4	UY6	J7	J8C	Z8	RZ8	H11	H10	J14C1	J99	G24	34
Y4A	UY6	J7J	J8C	9	D21	H11J	H10	J14-64CL	J99	A25	25
5	3X	J7JM	J8C	9-COM	D23	J11JM	J11J	J14J	CJ14	A26	D16
5-COM	D9	L7	L82C	AG9	CH9	J11Y	J12YC	J14Y	J14YC	C26	M41E
5M	D9J	L7J	L82C	BL9Y	V9YC	K11	UK10	L14	L90C	AG27	CH27
5MJ	D9J	N7GY	N7YC	BN9Y	S9YC	L11S	L82C	MJ14	XMJ14	C27	M41E
AG5	CH3	N7Y	N7YC	D9JM	D9J	N11Y	N11YC	NA14	N54R	AG28	CH28
BL5	V4C	P7Y	P8Y	EH9	XEH8	OJ11Y	RJ12YC	N14Y	RN14YC	29	30
C5	W14	QL7J	RL82C	EK9	ED9	ON11Y	RN11YC	RBN14Y	RS14YC	31	25
E5-COM	ED9	QL7J5	RL82C	F9Y	F9YC	RBL11Y	RV12YC	RBN14Y4	RS14YC	AG32	CH32
J5	J6C	R7B	D6	H9	H8	RBL11Y6	RV12YC6	RF14Y	RF14YC	A34	32
J5-COM	RJ81B	RBL7Y	RV9YC	H9-COM	H8	RF11Y	RF11YC	RF14Y4	RF14YC	35-COM	W18
J5J	J6C	RBN7Y	RS7YC	H9J	H8J	RJ11Y	RJ12YC	RJ14Y	RJ14YC	36	C97B
L5	L82C	RJ7	RJ8C	J9-LONG	H10	RN11Y	RN11YC	RN14Y	RN14YC	C36	B86N
L5J	L82C	RL7J	RL82C	J9	J6C	UF11Y	F11YC	RN14Y6	RN12YC6	AG39	CH39
N5	N5C	RN7GY	RN7YC	J9J	J6C	UJ11P	UJ11G			40	K98F
N5M	N5C	RN7Y	RN7YC	J9Y	J12YC						
N5G	N5C	UCJ7G	CJ8	K9	K8						
RN5	RN5C	UJ7G	UJ11G	L9G	L82C						

Index

For an alphabetical listing of manufacturers, see also Chapter 11, The Big List.